THE KINGDOM OF THE OF THE BEAST

AND THE END OF THE WORLD

The Truth About the End of This World According to Matthew 24, The Book of Revelation, Daniel and Other End Times Prophecies

J. C. ALEXANDER

PRESS

ACW Press
Ozark, AL 36360

Italics in Scripture verses are the author's emphases.

Scripture quotations are taken from the King James Version of the Bible.

This book is the definitive work on eschatology. It is the "Prayer of Jabez" of prophecy. It is the "Purpose Driven Life" of end-times understanding. It is written and designed for personal or classroom study. Nearly all of the scriptures that are referenced are contained in the book to help facilitate and simplify study. The King James Version of the Bible is considered the most accurate interpretation of the Bible available. As such, it was used in this study. Other versions have experienced minor interpretations that change the entire meaning of certain passages.

The Kingdom of the Beast and the End of the World
Copyright ©2005 J.C. Alexander
All rights reserved

Cover Design by Alpha Advertising
Interior Design by Pine Hill Graphics

Packaged by ACW Press
1200 HWY 231 South #273
Ozark, AL 36360
www.acwpress.com
The views expressed or implied in this work do not necessarily reflect those of ACW Press. Ultimate design, content, and editorial accuracy of this work is the responsibility of the author(s).

Library of Congress Cataloging-in-Publication Data
(Provided by Cassidy Cataloguing Services, Inc.)

Alexander, J. C.

    The kingdom of the beast and the end of the world : the truth about the
end of this world according to Matthew 24, the book of Revelation,
Daniel and other end times prophecies / J. C. Alexander. -- 1st ed. --
Ozark, AL : ACW Press, 2005.

    p. ; cm.
    ISBN: 1-932124-53-5

    1. Bible--Prophecies--End of the world. 2. End of the world--
Biblical teaching. I. Title.

BS649.E63 A44 2005
236/.9--dc22   0505

Printed in the United States of America.

TABLE OF CONTENTS

INTRODUCTION

I grew up in the ever-expanding suburbs of Washington DC, a middle-class neighborhood with small Cape Cod houses that went on forever. My family was at the lower end of the middle class. To be honest, I'd have to say that we were right at the bottom. We always had just enough to get by with very little left over. The street I lived on ran up the north side of a large hill and back down on the other side. Our house was halfway up the hill on the northern side. That street and the hill it traversed were my life for many years.

The neighborhood kids could always find ways to entertain themselves. Throwing quinces and crab apples at the Gillespie's roof. Sneaking into the Hartman's pool, when we were supposed to be having a nice quite uneventful backyard sleep out. At the bottom of the hill, in the intersection, we would play baseball, football, Frisbee, kick the can. We would do bike tricks, run races and anything else we could think of, including just sitting around powwow style and shooting the breeze.

Across the street in the Tompson's driveway, we would play four man wiffleball. A challenge with the house right on the left side of the sloping driveway and a cut hill on the right with a fence at the top of it, and only two persons on each team. We had to settle for just a home plate and second base and they had to be stretched out further than usual to give the fielding team a little defensive advantage. The field was severely narrowed and foul balls were plentiful because of the house on the left and the hill on the right, but we still had some great games.

When the cold air of winter settled in, we began to look forward to those snowy days when the hill became our winter playground. Snowball fights, snow forts, snow ice cream and, best of all, sledding. Owning a Flexible Flyer sled was a must if you lived on our hill. We would form trains by lining up the sleds and latching onto the feet of the person ahead. We had races, built ramps to fly over, dared anyone to be the first down the hill and wrecked anyone we could catch up to. At evening time, as the sun was going down, the snow started to ice over. We would then sit one person on the front of the sled and a second would stand on the back. Down the hill we would fly trying to round the corner onto the next street. More often than not, we would slide hard to the left and go into, or straight through, the hedges on the side of the road. Poor hedges, and poor Mr. Jones. Aside from our occasional thoughtless and dunderheaded behaviors, it was all great clean fun.

But life wasn't all fun and games on the hill. Every Wednesday night and Sunday morning my brothers and I would have to climb to the top of that hill and descend the opposite side to the bottom where the Baptist church sat, which I attended during my early years. This wasn't any old Baptist church though. It was a large four story building that seemed so modern back then. It had everything: a large sanctuary with padded pews, a fellowship hall with industrial kitchen for hosting all kinds of events, classrooms galore, storage rooms, boiler rooms and even a church library. What it didn't have was a whole lot of life.

Don't get me wrong. The people were great and everyone seemed to have a sincerity about their Christian lifestyle, but something was lacking. The pastor's messages were always a little flat. He would start with a Scripture verse, then go off on a tangent. And there seemed to be a division between the members. Not the kind of divisiveness that splits a church, it's just that while some members seemed to accept the Word of God at face value and cherish it, others always had a way of explaining away its promises and pronouncements. They would say, "Oh, I know it says that, but what it means is this. It's a spiritual thing you see, and we must decipher and interpret it." I don't know if they realized it or not, but they were stripping the very life and meaning out of the Word of God, rendering it useless.

Whenever they would read a verse, it would go straight into my heart, almost entirely bypassing my head. The Word was alive; it was living in me, but then they would put a knife into the heart of hope with their negative statements of unbelief. They could kill off hope and stifle the understanding, but they could not quite quench the flame ignited by hearing God's Word. Maybe they felt it too. Maybe that's why they were there in the first place. Maybe they just didn't know how to understand or how to accept the truth of God's Word.

One Sunday my older brother went forward during the service for salvation. I didn't quite understand what it was all about, and oddly enough, I didn't ask him about it either. It didn't seem to take effect in him anyway. He went on to become somewhat of a tyrant and slightly bitter towards religion. As for myself, I was at that age of about twelve or thirteen years old when most young boys start to look at the world around them and wonder who they really are and what life is all about. One Sunday I went to the front foyer of the church where racks of gospel pamphlets were kept. I took The Four Spiritual Laws and some other pamphlets home, read them in my bedroom with no one else around and prayed to receive Jesus into my heart and life.

It's amazing how awful I felt inside at such a young age. I didn't have any problem admitting that I was a sinner and that I needed a savior. I knew it was what I needed. For one whole 24-hour period nothing happened. I was a little dejected but it didn't even occur to me to give up. I went back to my room the next day, picked up those pamphlets again and just laid it out to God. I said, "God, I believe that this is your word. I did what it says to do and I still feel rotten inside. But, I don't care. I'm not going to try to change myself. I can't do it. I can't make your word work, that's your job. But as far as I'm concerned, as of this time yesterday when I prayed, I am born again."

I put the pamphlets down and began to walk away when suddenly a sweet refreshing swept through the midst of my being. I felt like my inner being had been flushed and now everything was fresh and clean. I was born again! My heart had been renewed. I had approached God as a little boy with an attitude that bordered on disrespect, but God saw it otherwise. He saw a steadfast determination in believing His word. He saw faith in action. Little did I know, but at that early age I was learning to trust God by trusting His word.

I really don't remember how my quest to understanding the end-time prophecies began. Somewhere along the line I heard or read something that stuck with me, and I have been thinking about the end of the world according to the Scriptures ever since. It's just a part of who I am. I have always had the sense that it is so close that I will probably see it come myself. Through my salvation experience, God had just begun to teach me the lessons of faith and understanding His Word that would help me finally come to a place where I can say that I do understand the prophecies, and they are a lot easier to understand than most people would think. The problem has been that too many people of good intentions are teaching everything but the truth about the end-times, and once you have learned some of those things it becomes very difficult to see past them. However, that is what we are going to do in this book.

PREPARATIONS

To prepare ourselves to understand the end-times, we have to start thinking of the Tribulation and the Wrath of God as two separate and distinct time periods divided by the Rapture of the Church. When you say the words "Great Tribulation," most people subconsciously, and sometimes consciously, think of a time when the Antichrist is causing great troubles for left behind Christians, even as God is pouring out His wrath on a disobedient world. A lot of people believe this starts only after the Rapture has occurred. These beliefs are based on many years of traditional thinking and ideas that have not always been the mainstream of Christian thinking.

Controversy and misunderstanding has always surrounded the end-times prophecies, even during the time of the early Church. Most early Christian leaders were looking for the Rapture at the end of the Tribulation, just prior to the Wrath of God, and yet, Paul had to write to many early believers in 2 Thessalonians 2 who thought the Rapture was imminent, and those in 2 Timothy 2:18 who thought the Rapture had already come and gone. Most churches today just pass on their old traditional teachings of the end-times without ever stopping to ask questions. At the same time, the bookstores are littered with prophecy books written by people who have recognized the cracks, chinks and major fault lines that are so evident and prevalent in all the prevailing end-times doctrines. These authors and theologians have tried to unravel the mysteries of the end-times anew but with little success. More often than not they fill in a chink or repair a crack only to have a new one develop. The problem goes straight down into the foundation they are building on. If you start out with the wrong foundation, you end up having to patch a whole lot of cracks where things don't come together properly. The time has come to question the foundational ideas that have been taught for far too long and get back to what Paul, Peter and yes, even Jesus believed.

Part of the foundational problem is in the ordering of events. If you get the order of the major events wrong, then the fault lines are going to appear soon after. The doctrine that is built on an improper ordering of events will start showing chinks and cracks almost immediately. Those who hold to the improper foundation begin to chip away at the Scriptures, trying to make them fit properly on the same faulty foundation only to create their own little fissures. This is done by endless word studies that are meant to search out a different meaning for every word that doesn't properly fit on the foundation without redefining it. Other methods include pulling scriptures out of context and attaching them to other scriptures to create a whole new context that is designed to cover up the fault lines, or going outside of the Scriptures to find support from nonbiblical sources. And, of course, there are those who receive brand spanking new revelations every time they climb out of bed that have nothing to do with what the Bible says.

By the time you have read through this book, you will have seen the same theme and sequence of events (foundation) laid out over and over again many times. That sequence appears in Matthew 24 and is repeated several times in Revelation, and it is always the same. The Antichrist comes on the scene and causes great tribulation through wars, famines and persecution of the Church and Israel. After the Tribulation, the Body of Christ is raptured, and God begins to pour out His wrath on sinners. As stated, we will see this theme and sequence first in Matthew 24, and then it is repeated in Revelation 6–11. After that, chapter 12 begins the same theme and sequence over again. Revelation 12 through the end of the book gives us a full historical view of the plan of salvation from the beginning of God's redemptive work to the time when He completes His work and creates a new heaven and new earth in which we can live "happily ever after." The only thing out of place in the second half of the Book of Revelation is chapter 14, verses 6-20 where God, in just fifteen verses, gives us the end-times sequence of events once again. Those fifteen verses are strategically placed for a reason. We will discuss that reason when we get to that chapter.

Daniel's writings concentrate primarily on the Tribulation, but the same sequence is present.

In all of these books there is a lot of talk about persecution. The more you read the Scriptures, the more you realize that most of the activity described in the end-times prophecies is taking place around the Middle East and Israel where the Antichrist and his ten-nation empire will be located. That does not mean it won't be spilling over into many other nations or even the whole earth. In fact, if nothing else major happens between now and then, the world could be referring to the Tribulation as World War III or the Final Middle East Conflict, as opposed to calling it a one-world government or the Great Tribulation. Hopefully, there will be many nations where things are not quite so bad and where righteousness is actually practiced and allowed to flourish. From the Scriptures, we actually see much resistance to the Antichrist, and those "righteous" nations may even attempt to assist Israel in their struggle against the Antichrist—but only time will tell for sure. There will be nations, whether they are righteous or not, that will resist the beast and make war against him. However, the idea that Christians are just whisked away before anything bad could possibly happen to them is not supported by the Scriptures. We do not go through the Wrath of God, but the Bible never says that we will not see tribulation or persecution. Having said that, it must be understood that most of the bad things we read in Revelation pertain to the Wrath of God and not the Tribulation. There will be no stinging locust, scorching sun or 200,000,000 horsemen during the Tribulation. That is all a part of God's wrath.

It's important that we not get too technical when interpreting Scripture; otherwise, we end up getting lost. For instance, if we read about the four beasts in Daniel 7—the first being the ancient Babylonian Empire and the last being the beast empire of the Antichrist—and the four beasts in Revelation 4 that are gathered before the throne of God praising Him, and then try to make some kind of correlation between them, we will be hopelessly confused. The only real correlation between them is the use of the word "beast," and that is because it is just the right word to describe each of them but for different reasons. By the same token, if we spend all of our time trying to make every little word have some deep hidden meaning, we are going to be among those who are forever learning (the prophecies) but never able to come to the knowledge of the truth. (2 Timothy 3:7) The purpose of this book is to understand what God is saying to us in the simplest form possible.

You are encouraged to open your own Bible frequently to double-check the Scriptures to make sure you are not being led astray. The King James Version of the Bible was used for this book because it cannot be beat as far as the purity of the translation. Some of the newer versions have been rewritten with a certain amount of interpretation thrown in as opposed to simply translating verbatim from the original Greek and Hebrew. Having different versions is great when you're reading about concepts and ideas. To read something from a different perspective with a different wording can sometimes be just what is needed to open our understanding. However, things need to be technically accurate in what they are saying or you lose the message God was communicating in the first place. This is especially true with prophecy. If you use a different version of the Bible, the same message we get from the King James Version should have carried through into the more modern vernacular. If your version is radically different, you should consider purchasing a different Bible.

A few topics need to be clearly understood before we get started on the rest of this book. Because Daniel's seventieth week from Daniel 9 and the battle of Gog of Magog from Ezekiel 38 and 39 are mentioned quite often throughout the book, they will be explained from the outset to eliminate any misunderstanding. We want to look at how the Bible uses phrases that refer to the end-times also, such as the end, the final end, the latter days and so forth. If we don't discuss how these phrases are used it could result in much confusion as we go along. After that, we will look at the Day of the Lord and then determine what the "last day" is that Jesus referred to repeatedly in John 6. Also, we want to clear up some confusion about the second coming of Christ. And finally, we are going to establish working definitions for the words "tribulation" and "wrath" as they are used in regards to the end-times, and make note of the clear difference between the two. Dealing with all of these now will make for better comprehension throughout the rest of the book. First, let's look at Daniel's seventy weeks.

DANIEL'S SEVENTY WEEKS

[24]*Seventy weeks are determined upon thy people and upon thy holy city,* to finish the transgression, and to make an end of sins, and to make reconciliation for iniquity, and to bring in everlasting righteousness, and to seal up the vision and prophecy, and to anoint the most Holy. [25]Know, therefore, and understand, that from the going forth of the commandment to restore and to build Jerusalem unto the Messiah, the Prince, shall be seven weeks, and threescore and two weeks: the street shall be built again, and the wall, even in troublous times. [26]And after threescore and two weeks shall Messiah be cut off, but not for himself: and the people of the prince that shall come shall destroy the city and the sanctuary; and the end of it shall be with a flood, and unto the end of the war desolations are determined. [27]*And he shall confirm the covenant with many for one week:* and in the midst of the week he shall cause the sacrifice and the oblation to cease, and for the overspreading of abominations he shall make it desolate, even until the consummation, and that determined shall be poured upon the desolate.

Daniel 9:24-27

The seventy weeks are actually seventy groups of seven years, which equals four hundred and ninety years. The first sixty-nine weeks have already been accomplished historically from the time Artaxerxes I, the king of Persia, gave a command to rebuild the walls of Jerusalem to the time that Jesus was crucified on the cross. That is a total of four hundred and eighty-three years, which is the seven weeks and sixty-two weeks of verse 25 combined, leaving just one week of seven years that have yet to be fulfilled. That seven-year period is separated from the rest of the four-hundred-and-ninety-year total as God allows the Gospel Age to be completed. When the gospel has finally been preached in all the world, a final separating between sinners and saints will begin and last for the entire seven years of Daniel's seventieth week.

Daniel's seventieth week is actually the last seven years of world history before the Wrath of God begins. Contrary to what some believe, it is the final seven years of grace, but that grace will occur right alongside Satan's final seven years of fury as he puts the gospel to a final test. The final proclamation of the gospel will only mark the beginning of the end. After the gospel has been thoroughly preached throughout the entire world to the point where God is satisfied that all people have heard enough to make an informed decision between accepting Jesus Christ as Lord and Savior or facing His wrath, then the Antichrist will come on the scene. He will turn many people away from God out of fear and hatred or towards God in love or, in some cases, desperation. Verse 27 above tells us that the Antichrist will make a covenant of peace with Israel that is supposed to last for seven years, but that he will intentionally break it in the middle of the seven years. The treaty is never meant to bring real peace to Israel, but rather, it is a means of setting Israel up for their own slaughter. When the Antichrist breaks the covenant of peace and puts a stop to the daily sacrifice at the halfway point, the Great Tribulation will begin.

Daniel's seventieth week is the same as Jacob's trouble. Jeremiah 30:7 tells us "that day is great, so that none is like it: it is even the time of Jacob's trouble; but he shall be saved out of it." This statement is referring more to the second half of the final seven years when the Great Tribulation will unfold. The first half of the week will seem like a time of celebration for those in Israel who have rejected God's covenant of peace through Christ Jesus because they will finally have an agreement with their Arab neighbors that assures them their security. However, as things become steadily worse for Israel, many will turn to Jesus for their salvation. Those who continue to reject the drawing of the Holy Spirit will be crying, "Peace! Peace!" until their destruction comes suddenly upon them. The final salvation for the nation of Israel comes only after the Tribulation and the Wrath of God have run their full course. Jerusalem will be established forever as the City of God, and the Israelis will be special servants to God. The Jews who receive Jesus, which includes the 144,000, will inhabit Israel forever along with the rest of the saints.

GOG

The next thing we want to look at comes from Ezekiel 38 and 39. To eliminate any confusion that might otherwise arise, we need a thorough understanding of Gog of Magog and his place in history during the latter days. Those two chapters are a prophecy concerning a future event in which many nations will join together in an attempt to destroy Israel. As you read through chapter 38, notice in verses 8 and 16 that God is declaring to us that this is an event that will unfold in the latter days. Also notice in the first six verses God is actually naming nations that will join together under the protective covering of Gog to launch this attack against Israel, both for the looting of her wealth and the destruction of her people and national identity. At several places in these two chapters God declares to us that He will use this event to sanctify Himself in the eyes of both Israel and the heathen nations that surround her. He does this by putting confusion on the armies that will surround Israel and by using the forces of nature to overwhelm and eliminate most of the enemy soldiers.

> [1]And the Word of the Lord came unto me, saying, [2]Son of man, set thy face against *Gog, the land of Magog, the chief prince of Meshech and Tubal*, and prophesy against him, [3]And say, Thus saith the Lord God; Behold, I am against thee, O Gog, the chief prince of Meshech and Tubal: [4]And I will turn thee back, and put hooks into thy jaws, and I will bring thee forth, and all thine army, horses and horsemen, all of them clothed with all sorts of armor, even a great company with bucklers and shields, all of them handling swords: [5]*Persia, Ethiopia, and Libya with them*; all of them with shield and helmet: [6]*Gomer, and all his bands; the house of Togarmah of the north quarters, and all his bands: and many people with thee.* [7]Be thou prepared, and prepare for thyself, thou, and all thy company that are assembled unto thee, and *be thou a guard unto them.* [8]After many days thou shalt be visited: *in the latter years thou shalt come into the land that is brought back from the sword*, and is gathered out of many people, *against the mountains of Israel*, which have been always waste: but it is brought forth out

of the nations, and they shall dwell safely, all of them. *⁹Thou shalt ascend and come like a storm, thou shalt be like a cloud to cover the land, thou, and all thy bands, and many people with thee.* ¹⁰Thus saith the Lord God; It shall also come to pass, that at the same time shall things come into thy mind, and thou shalt think an evil thought: *¹¹And thou shalt say, I will go up to the land of unwalled villages; I will go to them that are at rest, that dwell safely, all of them dwelling without walls, and having neither bars nor gates, ¹²To take a spoil, and to take a prey; to turn thine hand upon the desolate places that are now inhabited, and upon the people that are gathered out of the nations, which have gotten cattle and goods, that dwell in the midst of the land.* ¹³Sheba, and Dedan, and the merchants of Tarshish, with all the young lions thereof, shall say unto thee, Art thou come to take a spoil? hast thou gathered thy company to take a prey? to carry away silver and gold, to take away cattle and goods, to take a great spoil? ¹⁴Therefore, son of man, prophesy and say unto Gog, Thus saith the Lord God; In that day when my people of Israel dwelleth safely, shalt thou not know it? *¹⁵And thou shalt come from thy place out of the north parts, thou, and many people with thee, all of them riding upon horses, a great company, and a mighty army: ¹⁶And thou shalt come up against my people of Israel,* as a cloud to cover the land; *it shall be in the latter days,* and I will bring thee against my land, that the heathen may know me, when I shall be sanctified in thee, O Gog, before their eyes. ¹⁷Thus saith the Lord God; Art thou he of whom I have spoken in old time by my servants the prophets of Israel, which prophesied in those days many years that I would bring thee against them? *¹⁸And it shall come to pass at the same time when Gog shall come against the land of Israel, saith the Lord God,* that my fury shall come up in my face. *¹⁹For in* my jealousy and in the fire of my wrath have I spoken, Surely in that day there shall be a great shaking in the land of Israel; ²⁰So that the fishes of the sea, and the fowls of the heaven, and the beasts of the field, and all creeping things that creep upon the earth, and all the men that are upon the face of the earth, shall shake at my presence, and the mountains shall be thrown down, and the steep places shall fall, and every wall shall fall to the ground. [21]*And I will call for a sword against him throughout all* my mountains, saith the Lord God: every man's sword shall be against his brother. [22]*And I will plead against him with pestilence and with blood; and I will rain upon him, and upon his bands, and upon the many people that are with him, an overflowing rain, and great hailstones, fire, and brimstone.* [23]Thus will I magnify myself, and sanctify myself; and I will be known in the eyes of many nations, and they shall know that I am the Lord.

Ezekiel 38:1-23

When God speaks of the spiritual rulers of cities and nations in the Bible, He refers to them in the masculine gender. When He refers to the cities and nations themselves, He refers to them in the feminine gender. This is because the cities and nations are joined to and submitted unto the rulers just like in a marriage relationship. The name Gog is probably the name of the spiritual prince that rules the land of Magog. Magog is hard to find on even ancient maps, but the consensus is that it is either Turkey or Russia or a combination of the two. In verses 2 and 3 above, Gog is referred to as the chief prince of Meshach and Tubal. Gomer and Togarmah are both mentioned in verse 6. In Genesis 10, we learn that the sons of Japheth (who is the son of Noah) are Gomer, Magog, Madai, Javan, Tubal, Meshech and Tiras. Of these seven, Magog, Meshech, Tubal and Gomer are the ones who settled Turkey, and they would be the ones who eventually continued to migrate due north into the Soviet Union. Togarmah is a son of Gomer who also settled a part of Turkey. If Magog is not the Soviet Union, it is certainly Turkey since God calls Gog the chief prince of the different provinces of Turkey.

Those families which were driven out of Babel and began settling Europe and Asia are not mentioned in Ezekiel 38. However, the Middle East and North Africa are a different story. Persia does not exist as a nation today, but the land mass that it used to occupy is currently occupied by Iran, Iraq, Syria, Jordan, Lebanon, parts of Saudi Arabia, Egypt, Turkey, Pakistan, Afghanistan, Turkmenistan and Uzbekistan. Iran is the one nation that is a direct descendant from Persia. Ethiopia and Libya both represented a greater portion of the African continent in the past; therefore, the naming of them in Ezekiel could mean that there will be other African nations who join with Gog to attack Israel, but not necessarily. What is interesting about the list of countries is that it includes all the areas first settled by the three sons of Noah and their children. Their descendants who remained in these ancient lands should be the ones who hold on to the remembrance of God's great flood judgment better than any of those who moved out into the furthest reaches of the planet, but instead, they appear in a lineup of rogue nations who, more than any other nations on earth, hate the Jews and the God of heaven.

The very mention of these nations brings a flood of thoughts of war, terrorism and an undying hatred of Israel. In recent history, Moscow has certainly had its share of influence over each of the nations that are named, mostly by supplying them with arms and military expertise. This was more prevalent before the downfall of the Soviet Union as a superpower. Part of the reason for the wars Israel has embarked upon in the past is that Russia had stored large caches of arms in surrounding countries in preparation for a blitzkrieg type war against Israel. They were never successful in pulling it off because of US and Israeli intelligence and Israel's superior warfare. When Gog launches the future attack mentioned in Ezekiel, it will also meet with failure, but this time it will be because of *divine* intelligence and warfare. It will be nearly impossible for other nations to aid Israel because to defeat the enemy would surely destroy Israel in the process.

For a long time Turkey has maintained a secular government with ties to the U.S. and Europe, but forces are at work right now to turn it towards a more Islamic state, which would enhance its ties to the Arab world and weaken its ties to the others. Turkey is a very interesting country, both historically and geographically. From the early 1300s until World War I, the Ottomans ruled Turkey. The Ottoman Empire at its high point ruled most of the territory described by Ezekiel above. They controlled the land of Israel but at a time when the land was not occupied by the nation or people of Israel. The capital was in Constantinople (modern Istanbul) from which Constantine also ruled the Roman Empire. Constantine built Constantinople in a.d. 313 upon a high plateau overlooking the Sea of Marmara. The unique location of Turkey makes it a sort of a land bridge or crossroads joining the Middle East to Russia in the north and Europe to the northeast. Turkey is considered to be a part of both Europe and the Mid East at the same time. Russian ships in the Black Sea must pass through the strait of Bosporus of Turkey to get to the Mediterranean Sea. Turkey is also where the seven churches of Asia, mentioned in Revelation 2 and 3, were located.

All of the nations named above, excluding Russia, if not Islamic governments, have large majorities of Muslims living in them—some of them with numbers exceeding 95 percent. The reason this is important is because Islam is an Antichrist and anti-Jewish religion at its very core. From the very pages of the Koran, we see verses that warn Muslims about Christians and Jews. They are both called infidels and losers that will see the flames of hell if they do not convert to Islam. Christians are called perverters of "The Book." The New Testament is considered a perversion of the truth.

Muslims are told to live at peace with all people even as they are given the right to own slaves, given the responsibility of ruling over and putting under tribute all non-Muslims who live in their communities and directed to fight a jihad against anyone who provokes or stands against them. A Jihad is any struggle a Muslim must go through in the practice of Islam. An armed, holy war is considered a lesser jihad, but the Koran describes it as a means of dealing with any opposition they encounter. Jews and Christians are singled out as primary targets of jihad, which makes sense from a religious point of view since they practice an anti-Islamic religion and serve a different God.

Islam and the Arab national identity are two major reasons the battle of Gog of Magog will be fought. Israelis are considered to be illegal occupants on Arab land. The whole Arab world and much of the Muslim world are opposed to Israel remaining a nation to the point that they are willing to lay down their own lives and the lives of their children to remove the Jews from what they consider to be their own land. The Palestinian issue adds fuel to the fire. Many so-called Palestinians are from other Arab countries, but because of the blinding hatred Arabs and many Muslims have for Israel, they are willing to believe the lies that swirl around the whole issue. The Palestinians control a part of the temple mount where the Jewish temple will be built again in the future. The Dome of the Rock, where Muslims believe that Mohammed ascended into heaven to pray with Jesus, Moses and Elijah, is located on the temple mount, and the Arabs want it all for themselves. They want the Jews out—no matter what the cost.

God instructs Gog in verse 38:7 to be a guard unto these nations. Russia currently is the only nation that has a close working relationship with this group of nations and that has the military strength to provide a shield of interference for them against NATO, the U.S. or any other allies of Israel who might want to prevent this attack. Russia will have an economic incentive for attacking Israel. Verse 12 above explains that they will come to take all of the goods and resources God has blessed Israel with since bringing them back into their own land. In verse 2 below, we see that Gog comes from the north. North of Israel is Turkey and beyond that is Russia. In fact, Moscow is directly due north of Jerusalem which is one of several reasons why many believe Russia will lead this group of armies once again as they attempted to do in 1967 during the six-day war.

> [1]Therefore, thou son of man, prophesy against Gog, and say, Thus saith the Lord God; Behold, I am against thee, O Gog, the chief prince of Meshech and Tubal: [2]And I will turn thee back, and *leave but the sixth part of thee*, and *will cause thee to come up from the north parts, and will bring thee upon the mountains of Israel:* [3]*And I will smite thy bow out of thy left hand, and will cause thine arrows to fall out of thy right hand.* [4]*Thou shalt fall upon the mountains of Israel, thou, and all thy bands, and the people that is with thee: I will give thee unto the ravenous birds of every sort, and to the beasts of the field to be devoured.* [5]*Thou shalt fall upon the open field: for I have spoken it, saith the Lord* God. [6]And I will send a fire on Magog, and among them that dwell carelessly in the isles: and they shall know that I am the Lord. [7]So will I make my holy name known in the midst of my people Israel; and I will not let them pollute my holy name any more: and the heathen shall know that I am the Lord, the Holy One in Israel. [8]Behold, it is come, and it is done, saith the Lord God; this is the day whereof I have spoken.
>
> *Ezekiel 39:1-29*

In the following verses we notice that it will take Israel seven years to consume the spoils of war which are left behind by the defeated armies of Gog. That means the Antichrist cannot be the leader of the pack for this attack because he does not attack until halfway through his seven-year time of turmoil, which would leave only three-and-one-half years for Israel to gather their plunder. On the contrary, when the Antichrist does attack, it will begin the final three-and-one-half years of world history which is the Great Tribulation, immediately followed by the Wrath of God. When he attacks, the Bible informs us that many saints, unsaved Jews, and the city of Jerusalem will be given over into his hand. He will overrun Jerusalem, slaughter or enslave the Jews who remain in the city and single out Christians for destruction. That is not what is happening here. This is God's last intervention on a broad scale to protect all of Israel and to maintain peace on the earth. To the contrary, during the Great Tribulation, God will protect his 144,000 elect Israelites from the Antichrist and will deliver many of His saints even as others fall to persecution, but He will not prevent the Antichrist from overthrowing Jerusalem. The Tribulation is something God has predetermined that He will allow to take place. He will allow Satan one last chance to tread down Israel and to try the saints. Those saints who want to keep their souls will either have to trust God for deliverance or give up their lives in exchange for their souls.

The Antichrist will rise up to rule the nations of Gog soon after they have been defeated by God. The seven-year peace accord that the Antichrist makes with Israel will overlap the seven years in which the Jews are consuming the spoils with which the armies of Gog littered the nation of Israel. In the middle of the seven years the Antichrist breaks the peace accord, and the Tribulation begins. That is one of the ways God provides for His 144,000 chosen Jews in the wilderness.

> [9]And *they that dwell in the cities of Israel shall go forth, and shall set on fire and burn the weapons, both the shields and the bucklers, the bows and the arrows, and the handstaves, and the spears,* and *they shall burn them with fire seven years:* [10]So that *they shall take no wood out of the field, neither cut down any out of the forests; for they shall burn the weapons with fire: and they shall spoil those that spoiled*

them, and rob those that robbed them, saith the Lord God.
[11]And it shall come to pass in that day, that I will give unto Gog a place there of graves in Israel, the valley of the passengers on the east of the sea: and it shall stop the noses of the passengers: and there shall they bury Gog and all his multitude: and they shall call it the Valley of Hamon-gog. [12]And seven months shall the house of Israel be burying of them, that they may cleanse the land. [13]Yea, all the people of the land shall bury them; and it shall be to their a renown on the day that I shall be glorified, saith the Lord God. [14]And they shall sever out men of continual employment, passing through the land to bury with the passengers those that remain upon the face of the earth, to cleanse it: after the end of seven months shall they search. [15]And the passengers that pass through the land, when any seeth a man's bone, then shall he set up a sign by it, till the buriers have buried it in the Valley of Hamon-gog. [16]And also the name of the city shall be Hamonah. Thus shall they cleanse the land. [17]And, thou son of man, thus saith the Lord God; Speak unto every feathered fowl, and to every beast of the field, Assemble yourselves, and come; gather yourselves on every side to my sacrifice that I do sacrifice for you, even a great sacrifice upon the mountains of Israel, that ye may eat flesh, and drink blood. [18]Ye shall eat the flesh of the mighty, and drink the blood of the princes of the earth, of rams, of lambs, and of goats, of bullocks, all of them fatlings of Bashan. [19]And ye shall eat fat till ye be full, and drink blood till ye be drunken, of my sacrifice which I have sacrificed for you. [20]Thus ye shall be filled at my table with horses and chariots, with mighty men, and with all men of war, saith the Lord God.

As mentioned above, this is God's last big intervention. This is the last call for Jews and heathen alike before the Antichrist takes over the armies of the nations that are defeated here. The Antichrist rises in the Middle East and controls all of the nations that Gog controlled with the possible exception of Russia. Apparently, this wake-up call (the divine defeat of Gog) is wasted on a large portion of the Jews.

When the Antichrist arrives, there will be many Jews who have rejected God's New Covenant and His Savior. They believe their golden age has already arrived. God has intervened on their behalf, and now all they have to do is make peace with those heathen nations around them and be the crown jewel and apple of God's eye as the Scripture has promised. They fail to realize that God's promises are to those who receive His Messiah, Jesus, and who are looking past the end of this world and the beginning of something new in the ages to come. They may even consider the Antichrist to be their messiah.

At the same time plenty of new Christians in Israel and the countries that surround Israel will be finally convinced they are serving the wrong god and jump ship, so to speak. The God of Israel and of heaven has been sanctified in their eyes by His miraculous defeat of Gog. That defeat not only leads to a new respect for the God of the Jews, but it will cause many to search out the truths of the New Covenant and be saved by their acceptance of Jesus Christ as Lord and Savior. These saints, more than any others, will be the ones the Antichrist makes war against within the borders of his own kingdom and the ones who are killed for refusing the mark of the beast.

> [21]And I will set My glory among the heathen, and *all the heathen shall see* my judgment that I have executed, and My hand that I have laid upon them. [22]So *the house of Israel shall know that I am the Lord their God* from that day and forward. [23]And *the heathen shall know that the house of Israel went into captivity for their iniquity: because they trespassed against me*, therefore hid I my face from them, and gave them into the hand of their enemies: so fell they all by the sword. [24]According to their uncleanness and according to their transgressions have I done unto them, and hid my face from them. [25]Therefore thus saith the Lord God; Now will I bring again the captivity of Jacob, and have mercy upon the whole house of Israel, and will be jealous for my holy name; [26]After that they have borne their shame, and all their trespasses whereby they have trespassed against me, when they dwelt safely in their land, and none made them afraid. [27]When I have brought them again from the people, and gathered them out of their

enemies' lands, and am sanctified in them in the sight of many nations; [28]Then shall they know that I am the Lord, their God, which caused them to be led into captivity among the heathen: but I have gathered them unto their own land, and have left none of them any more there. [29]Neither will I hide my face any more from them: for I have poured out my spirit upon the house of Israel, saith the Lord God.

Ezekiel 39:21-29

After the fall of Gog, the Antichrist will step in and take control of the alliance formed between the nations that come against Israel. He will make a seven-year covenant of peace even as they are cleansing the dead from the land. The defeat of Gog is a supernatural provision of God that will help some of the Jews to get through the time of the Antichrist and the Great Tribulation. The seven-year period Ezekiel is talking about is Daniel's seventieth week when God finishes gathering his Jewish people unto Himself, both physically in Jerusalem and spiritually in their hearts, even in times of trouble. This will culminate with the Rapture of the entire Body of Christ, both Christians and Messianic Jews, both living and dead.

THE END OF THE WORLD

Jesus spoke the words "the end of the world" three times in Matthew: in chapter 13:39 and 49 and chapter 28:20. The disciples also used those words as they inquired of Him about the signs of His coming and the end of the world. In this book we will determine what it is they were talking about by distinguishing between events that happen before the end of the world, those that happen after the end of the world and those things and that time that mark the end of the world. This may sound strange to some, but the end of the world does not mean the end of the earth or the end of time. It does not mean a sudden end to all people living on the earth. It is more of a transition, a sudden end to the age of God's grace when sinners are no longer given the opportunity to repent and escape the wrath to come. The end of the world actually marks the beginning of God's wrath. Even after God's wrath is completed, there will be survivors on the earth who do not have the mark of the beast and did not participate in the Battle of Armageddon. These survivors will be ruled over by Christ and His saints. So, even though the world as we know it—with all of its corruption, sin and the curse—will come to an end one day, life will continue, but in a very different vein.

The Bible uses end-times phraseology pretty liberally. It speaks of everything from that final moment in time when God brings an end to His redemptive work and begins to punish sinners, all the way up to thousands of years surrounding that final moment on either side. We need to be aware of the different ways the Bible speaks about the end-times and the end of the world so we don't get confused by words that could refer to either a single day or a thousand years. When most people think of the end-times, they think of the Antichrist, the Great Tribulation, the Rapture and the Wrath of God. However, in the Bible the end-times can be just that, or it can be much more.

In Hebrews 9:26 we are told that "now once in the *end of the world* hath he appeared to put away sin by the sacrifice of himself." Jesus came to the earth two thousand years ago as a sacrifice for sin, but yet, we are told that that was a part of the end of the world. Likewise, Peter declared in 1 Peter 4:7 that "The end of all things is at hand: be ye therefore sober, and watch unto prayer." That makes it sound like the end of the world was eminent right from the beginning of the Church Age when Peter wrote these words. He also said a thousand years is like a single day to the Lord. He included the Millennial Reign and the final judgment of all mankind which occurs after the Millennium in that analogy. So for him to say that "the end is at hand" could be interpreted to mean that the final end could be ten thousand years from now, or a week to ten days from God's perspective.

We are living in the end-times just as Jesus was living in the end-times when He paid the price for our sins. As far as this book is concerned, we acknowledge that the Bible has included the last several thousand years as a part of the end-times, but we are going to be focusing on the final years of the end-times prophecies, and that pivotal point Jesus referred to as "the last day." What we really want to know is, are we about to enter those final days of the end of the world when the Antichrist will be wreak havoc, the Church will be raptured and the Wrath of God will be poured out? How close are we to the last day? Although it's obvious that we are not quite there yet, this book will help you understand how things will begin to unfold when we finally arrive at the final days of the end of the world.

The second half of Daniel's seventieth week is the Great Tribulation when the Antichrist—along with natural disasters, wars, persecution and perplexity of nations—will be causing more damage and turmoil on the earth than has ever been witnessed by man. When we think of the end, we tend to think of those last three-and-one-half years when the real trouble starts as opposed to the first three-and-one-half years, even though they are both a part of the end after the gospel has been preached to all the world. During the first half of the seven years the Antichrist will be attempting to get things started, but he will still be under restraint from God. He will not be able to accomplish his great destructive plans on the earth until God allows him to begin trying mankind at the appointed time, but he will be positioning himself for the final Tribulation through the peace accord with Israel and other means. In Daniel 8:19 an angel said these words to Daniel about a vision that he had just seen: "Behold, I will make thee know what shall be in the *last end* of the indignation: *for at the time appointed the end shall be.*" The angel was giving details of what would take place during the last end—the time of the Tribulation. When the Tribulation itself draws to an end, the Scriptures declares this to be the very end of the world when God punishes sinners. But, before He can punish evildoers, He must rescue His saints. And before they can be rescued, the Resurrection must take place.

At the very end of the Wrath of God, Jesus returns to the earth with His saints to fight the Battle of Armageddon. The purpose of this battle is to put down the military resistance that the Antichrist will mount against Him as He returns with His saints to take over the earth and to begin the Millennial Reign. This reign is a part of the end-times prophecies, but it comes after the world (as we know it) and the Wrath of God have both come to an end. We will still be on the same old planet, but the new reality of the Millennial Reign will be that God will move to the forefront of world events through Jesus Christ as He starts ruling the earth in righteousness, and Satan will be restrained in the bottomless pit. The Millennial Reign adds a thousand years to the end-times prophecies, and at the end of the thousand years, a new heaven and new earth will be created while the Great White Throne Judgment of Jesus Christ is taking place. After the White Throne Judgment is completed and the New Jerusalem descends out of the new heaven to remain on the new earth, everything that relates to the end-times is then officially over.

Matthew 24:13 and 14 both mention the end, but they differ in their meaning. Verse 13 declares that "He that shall endure unto the end, the same shall be saved." Taken at face value, we can simply say we must endure to the very end of our lives on this earth, whether that end comes by death or by Rapture. Verse 14 is a little broader. It speaks more of a process or series of events when it states, "This gospel of the kingdom shall be preached in all the world for a witness unto all nations; and then shall the end come." The "end" this verse speaks of is Daniel's seventieth week, which begins shortly after the failed attempt by Gog to destroy Israel when the Antichrist makes a seven-year peace accord with Israel. That final seven years is the last chance for mankind to make a decision between God's plan of salvation through the gospel of Jesus Christ or simply continuing on in a beggarly lifestyle that is conceived in death and will end in death without Jesus Christ. The controversy has been whether we must endure just until before Daniel's seventy weeks begins, to the middle or towards the end. Because the world has heard the gospel, does that mean we are no longer needed or required to remain on the earth? This question was already answered in the piece on Daniel's seventieth week. Daniel's seventieth week is not the Wrath of God, and it does not encompass the Wrath of God in any way. God allows Satan to try all of mankind during that time, and He uses it to shake the Jews to their very core until, as Jeremiah 30:7 says "It is even the time of Jacob's trouble; *but he shall be saved out of it.*" The rest of this book will make all these things abundantly clear.

THE DAY OF THE LORD

The following excerpt from Isaiah 13:6-13 is one of the best descriptions of the Day of the Lord in the Bible. It is clearly described as a day of punishment for sinners.

> Howl ye; for the day of the Lord is at hand; it shall come as
> a destruction from the Almighty. Behold, the day of the
> Lord cometh, cruel both with wrath and fierce anger...and
> he shall destroy the sinners thereof out of it. *For the stars of*

*heaven and the constellations thereof shall not give their
light: the sun shall be darkened in his going forth, and the
moon shall not cause her light to shine.* And I will punish
the world for their evil, and the wicked for their iniquity.
Therefore I will shake the heavens, and the earth shall
remove out of her place, in the wrath of the Lord of hosts,
and in the day of his fierce anger.

The Day of the Lord is actually much longer than just a single
day, but the first day sets the stage and the tone for what is to follow.
Whenever we read about the Day of the Lord, we see the skies becoming black as the heavenly lights refuse to shine. This absence of light
lasts only for a very short time. In the New Testament the Day of the
Lord becomes the Day of Christ, and after everything goes black,
Jesus appears in His glory as the only light. The Day of the Lord
begins as a rescue mission as Jesus removes His people from off the
planet so that the day of God's punishment of sinners can begin.
After the removal of Jesus' New Testament elect from the earth, the
lights begin to shine again, but then the world is suddenly cast into a
period of time that is known as the Wrath of God. The Day of the
Lord marks the end of the grace of God and His tolerance for unrepentant sinners and the start of vengeance.

THE LAST DAY

In John 6 Jesus informs the multitude that He is the Bread of Life
sent from the Father. During that discourse He mentions four times
between verses 39 and 54 the fact that He will raise up all who receive
Him on the "last day." In verse 40, He declares, "And this is the will of
him that sent me, that every one which seeth the Son, and believeth
on him, may have everlasting life: and I will raise him up at the last
day." In John 11:24, after Jesus arrives late for the healing of Lazarus,
Martha meets up with Him and makes it clear that she understands
what the last day is all about. After Jesus tells her that her brother will
rise again she responds by saying, "I know that he shall rise again in
the resurrection at the last day." In context Jesus is telling her that He
was going to heal Lazarus; however, Martha is a little shaky in her
faith, not expecting that Jesus will heal her brother from the grave,

but her response shows that she does understand the fact that the resurrection of believers is going to take place on the very last day of this world.

The entire chapter of 1 Corinthians 15 speaks about resurrection, beginning with the resurrection of Jesus and progressing to the resurrection of the saints. In verses 22-26 we see that all those who belong to Christ will be made alive at His coming. When we receive Him as Savior we are born again and made alive on the inside, but it's not until He comes for us that we are made alive in the flesh again, albeit, a different kind of flesh. It is a spiritual type of flesh that is incorruptible and eternal. In verses 23 and 24 we see that the end does not come until after Christ comes for us. He delivers the kingdom up to His father when He delivers His saints up into heaven to stand before the throne. The last enemy—death—is fully defeated when believers are raised from the dead with new bodies, never to die again.

> 22For as in Adam all die, even so in Christ shall all be made alive. 23But every man in his own order: Christ the first-fruits; *afterward they that are Christ's at his coming.* 24*Then cometh the end*, when he shall have delivered up the kingdom to God, even the Father; when he shall have put down all rule and all authority and power. 25For he must reign, till he hath put all enemies under his feet. 26The last enemy that shall be destroyed is death.

In the verses above we see that the Resurrection and the defeat of death occur at the coming of Christ. In the verses below we see that the dead saints will be raised and those who are still living will be changed from corruptible to incorruptible at the last trump.

> 51Behold, I shew you a mystery; We shall not all sleep, but we shall all be changed, 52In a moment, in the twinkling of an eye, *at the last trump: for the trumpet shall sound*, and the dead shall be raised incorruptible, and we shall be changed. 53For this corruptible must put on incorruption, and this mortal must put on immortality. 54So when this corruptible shall have put on incorruption, and this mortal shall have put on immortality, then shall be brought to

pass the saying that is written, Death is swallowed up in victory. ⁵⁵O death, where is thy sting? O grave, where is thy victory?

The last trump signals that last day which Jesus is speaking of in John 6—the day of the Resurrection. Verses 51-55 do not speak of the Rapture, and being changed in the twinkling of an eye does not even come close to suggesting that we will suddenly disappear. We will not! We are suddenly changed to incorruptible on the last day, but we do not disappear. However, we do see that this change will take place only after the last trump sounds to announce the coming of Christ and the end of the world. Actually two last trumps will sound in the latter days—one at the end of the Tribulation and the other at the end of the Wrath of God. The last trumpet of the Wrath of God is the last of seven trumpets of judgment. We are reassured in the Scriptures that believers are not appointed unto God's wrath, so it is not the final trump of the Wrath of God that we need to be concerned about.

First Thessalonians 4:16 and 17 declare that "The Lord himself shall descend from heaven with a shout, with the voice of the archangel, *and with the trump of God*: and the dead in Christ shall rise first: then we which are **alive and** remain shall be caught up together with them in the clouds, to meet the Lord in the air." No saints will be alive and remaining at the last trump of the Wrath of God because God Himself promised that believers will not see His wrath. The only other last trumpet sounds after the "tribulation of those days" when Jesus said that He would come to gather His New Testament elect at the sound of a great trumpet. That trumpet announces an end to our stay on this earth and an end to God's grace toward sinners.

THE SECOND COMING OF CHRIST

Much confusion exists about the second coming of Christ. Some of that confusion comes from the doctrine of a disappearing Church. It is an established historical fact that Christ first came to the earth and died on the cross. For many it is also an established fact of faith that His death on the cross was for our salvation, justification and the remission of our sins. Before His departure, He declared He would come again to receive us to Himself. Titus 2:13 calls His second coming the "blessed hope," "the glorious appearing of the great God and our Saviour Jesus Christ." This is when He appears in the clouds in His glory to gather His New Testament elect. He never sets foot on the earth during His second coming, but the Bible tells us repeatedly that this event will be witnessed by all the world, not just believers. Many theologians have turned the appearing of Jesus in the clouds into a disappearing of the Church without a trace. One reason for that is because most people do not distinguish between the second coming in the clouds and Christ's third coming on a white horse at Armageddon.

His third coming will bring a completion to the time of God's wrath as He leads His people out of heaven and back to the earth to defeat the armies of the Antichrist and to take back control of the earth. His first coming was to die for all mankind. His second coming is to resurrect believers who have already died, and rescue those who are still alive from the wrath to come. While the Wrath of God is being poured out on the earth, the wedding feast of the Lamb will be occurring in heaven with all of God's redeemed present and accounted for. As the wedding feast draws to a conclusion in heaven, so does the Wrath of God on the earth. When Jesus returns a third time, all of His saints will accompany Him on white horses, and they will bring a conclusion to God's wrath by defeating the forces of the Antichrist and establishing the Millennial kingdom of Christ.

TRIBULATION VERSUS WRATH

Both in the Bible and in general usage, the words "tribulation" and "wrath" have vastly different meanings. To understand the end-times prophecies you have to be aware of these differences as you read and study. The word "tribulation" refers to the troubles, struggles, persecutions and distresses all human beings suffer during their lives because we all live in a fallen and cursed world. Natural disasters, sickness, crime, wars, relationship and money problems are all examples of the types of tribulations that both sinners and saints might suffer in their lives. The big difference is that the saints have a whole list of heavenly promises to help get them through the tough times while sinners—who have a right to the same promises—are either unaware of them or have rejected them.

In the Bible, tribulation refers more to the struggles and persecutions that saints experience from those around them who—either through ignorance or deliberate belligerence against the gospel and those who obey it—mount varying degrees of attacks against the righteous. It also refers to attacks launched from the invisible world of spiritual wickedness. The Great Tribulation is nothing more than troubles, distresses and persecutions that engulf the whole planet at the end of the world to a degree never experienced before. The Great Tribulation is Satan's last chance to purge the planet of all that is good and godly and remake it in the image of his own darkened and perverted soul. The Antichrist will be Satan's number one emissary of evil works during the Great Tribulation. Daniel 9:26, which we read earlier, informs us that he will attack Jerusalem at the start of the Tribulation, and there will be desolations to the end of the war.

Daniel reveals in several places that the Antichrist will attack Jews and Christians in his part of the world, but that is only a part of the Tribulation. Wars, famines, pestilences and diseases will combine with what the Antichrist is doing in the Middle East to bring the worldwide death toll to a full one-quarter of mankind. God brings the madness to a close at the end of the three-and-one-half years that He has already predetermined He will allow, and then He begins to pour out His wrath on sinners.

The word "wrath" can mean a very deep heartfelt anger toward someone, but when we speak of the "Wrath of God" it becomes an action word. For thousands of years, God has been withholding His anger against those who pervert and reject His ways. At the end, when He finally unleashes His anger against sinners, it will be after the gospel has been preached to all the world and He has allowed everyone to make their final decision. He will then judge those who reject goodness. God's wrath will come as an intense flood of vengeance and punishment on a disobedient world that wants nothing to do with Him and His goodness. God's wrath is a punishment aimed at those who are evil and destructive, while tribulation comes from evil and is meant to hinder or destroy all that is good. There is a tremendous difference between the Great Tribulation and the Wrath of God. This will be made more evident as we continue in this book.

An End-Times Outline

W e will begin this study in Matthew 24 which provides a quick chronological synopsis of the end-times narrated by Jesus under the direction of the Holy Spirit. We will then move on to Revelation. Because of the importance of understanding the sequence of events, both in Matthew and Revelation and other places that touch on the end-times, a brief outline of how it all unfolds follows:

1. **THE CHURCH AGE.** Jesus speaks to the disciples as though the time has already begun. This includes the thousands of years from the time of His death up to the time the church is raptured out of the earth. The Church Age also includes the time of Jacob's Trouble and the time of the Great Tribulation.

2. **THE BATTLE OF GOG OF MAGOG.** Before any of what we consider to be normal end-times events begin to take place, Israel will be surrounded by the armies of Gog who will be defeated by God's intervention. It will take the Israelis a full seven years to burn the armaments of the army of Gog which litter the mountains of Israel. God will use this as one method of providing for the 144,000 in the wilderness as they continue to collect the spoil of Gog during the second half of this seven-year period. These seven years will be the final seven years of history when God is finishing up His work of grace. We are going to call this Gog Specific. The nations that are a part of this attack are named in Ezekiel 38 and 39. Gog will rally the forces of rebellion again at the end of the Millennial Reign, but this time it will include people from the four corners of the earth. We will call that Gog Nonspecific.

3. **DANIEL'S SEVENTIETH WEEK.** This is the final seven-year period of grace when God is still dealing with lost mankind. It

culminates with the Rapture of the Church. After the defeat of Gog, the Antichrist will rise up from the remnant of these armies and make a false covenant of peace with Israel. This seven year covenant of peace will begin Jacob's Trouble. The second half of this seven-year time period will be the Great Tribulation, which includes the time of Jacob's Trouble.

4. **THE GREAT TRIBULATION.** The time of Great Tribulation is a time when Satan and the Antichrist will cause turmoil on the earth directed primarily at the Jews, Christians and the land of Israel. It is not to be confused with the Wrath of God. The Great Tribulation is the second half of the final seven-year period when the Antichrist will break the peace agreement with Israel and set himself up in the Jewish temple as God. The Church is still on the earth and the Antichrist will persecute it, along with Israel, as he leads his evil followers in multiple wars. The Church Age and the time of the Antichrist actually overlap during the three-and-one-half-year period of the Tribulation when the temple of God is given over to the power of the Antichrist.

5. **THE RESURRECTION.** This is also known as the "last day." The last day does not bring an end to the earth, nor does it bring an end to events taking place on the earth. It is the day that the hope of God's children is fulfilled, and the despair of His enemies begins to manifest. The Resurrection will take place at the sounding of the last trump just like the Rapture, but it must proceed the Rapture of the Church, possibly by just the twinkling of an eye, to prepare believers for their journey to heaven.

6. **THE RAPTURE.** Jesus said that He would return after the Tribulation to gather His New Testament elect, which includes born-again Jews and Gentiles. The 144,000 chosen of Israel, who have been protected from the ravages of the Tribulation, will be sealed in their foreheads, and they, along with the entire Church (every born-again individual on the earth that is ready for His return), will be taken out of the earth by being caught up into the clouds with Jesus, to escape the outpouring of God's wrath and to ever be with the Lord. The Day of the Lord, so

often mentioned in the Bible, always begins with the sun and the moon and the stars of heaven being shaken and withholding their lights. The darkening of the skies is a prelude to Jesus returning to deliver those that belong to Him from the wrath that will immediately follow their departure. The shaking of the heavens, the Resurrection, the Rapture and the outpouring of the wrath of God are all a part of the Day of the Lord, although the outpouring of God's wrath will continue for a period of years, not just a day. The Wedding Feast of the Lamb will begin upon our arrival in heaven with our Savior Jesus Christ, and will last for the entire time of God's wrath.

7. **THE WRATH OF GOD** (not to be confused with the Tribulation) Several years (approximately seven) of God's wrath will be poured out on an ungodly world that has soundly rejected Him. God will not begin to pour out His wrath until after the Rapture has taken place and is completed. The Wrath of God is revealed under the final seal of the heavenly book of Revelation. That final seal reveals the seven trumpets of judgment. The seven vials, the destruction of Babylon, the 200,000 horsemen, the stinging locusts, the scorching sun and Armageddon are all a part of the Wrath of God, not the Tribulation.

8. **THE BATTLE OF ARMAGEDDON.** This is the curtain call for the Day of the Lord or the time of God's wrath when Jesus will return yet again—this time in the company of His battle-ready saints and with His angels. When He returns this time, it will be to take vengeance on all those who have rejected the ways of truth and righteousness and not for His elect who are already with Him. When we return with Him, the armies of the Antichrist will be waiting at Armageddon to do battle. With the defeat of these armies, all power and authority will be restored to Jesus, and Satan will be locked away for a thousand years.

9. **THE MILLENNIAL REIGN.** This is a thousand-year period which actually begins with the Battle of Armageddon. Jesus will begin His reign on the earth with His saints before the final judgment of God and before God comes to live on the earth

with His saints. At the end of the millennium, Satan will be released for a short time to tempt the nations once more, resulting in a final purging of evil ones. This is when Gog marshals the rebellious from the four corners of the earth. This is Gog Nonspecific.

10. **THE WHITE THRONE JUDGMENT.** Sinners and saints are separated, and everyone receives their just rewards. This is the only time sinners will ever get a glimpse of heaven. The new heavens, new earth and New Jerusalem will be created at this time.

11. **GOD COMES TO EARTH.** The heavenly New Jerusalem, which is called the Bride of the Lamb, comes down from heaven with God in residence to ever be with His beloved saints on the new earth.

*A special note to help keep things straight in our minds as we read this book. The Tribulation ends, the skies go dark, Jesus appears in the clouds, the Resurrection and the Rapture occur, and the Wrath of God begins all on the same day. That day is called the Day of the Lord and the Last Day.

MATTHEW 24

The Bare Essentials

After my conversion I did something remarkable. Remarkably stupid in retrospect. After reading a few key Scriptures—the red ones where Jesus is speaking—I asked a few questions of teachers at my old Baptist church just to see how they would answer them. I know some accepted the Bible at face value at that church, but for some reason I always ended up with those who wanted to "spiritualize" everything. "Yes, He is going to prepare you a place in heaven. No, He is not going to do anything for you while you are on this earth, other than the blessing of salvation and to bless your spirit in the midst of your manifold turmoils. He allows those turmoils to test you until the day you die and go to heaven. Don't even ask Him to intervene and change things, and certainly don't even ask Him to heal your body. He just doesn't do those things anymore." This, of course was contrary to what I was reading and what was burning in my heart. And there was more to it. They seemed to be serving a god who wasn't a god, someone tucked safely away in heaven while we—His children, His creation—suffered here below. I wanted nothing to do with this kind of religion. I was a teenager, and teenagers are supposed to rebel, or so it seems. I informed my mother that I would not be attending that old Baptist church anymore. "I quit!" I wasn't going to be subjected to all of those lies. The only problem was that I didn't read my Bible and pray and seek out another church that was more inclined to teach the truth. I didn't have a way to get to another church anyway. I didn't have a driver's licence, and I didn't have a plan. Over time the life of God that was in me began to wither.

———————

Matthew 24 is one of the most logical places to start a linear study of the end-times because it is a chronological dissertation of the end-times straight out of the mouth of Jesus Himself. His response to the inquiries of His disciples was meant to provide a countdown of events that would lead up to His appearing and the end of the world. That was, indeed, what they were asking Him. "When shall these things be?" and "What is the sign of your coming and the sign of the end of the world?" He began by reciting a list of events such as wars and earthquakes that will reoccur with an increasing frequency before the end-times ever begin, and yet, have no value in alerting us to when the end has actually arrived. After describing a few things that would take place along the way on that long journey to the end of the world, He began to tell them about certain things that would occur right before the world, as we know it, comes to an end.

The end of the world is not the end of the earth. It will not be a global meltdown or a terrestrial implosion. It is the world system, controlled by Satan, that will be violently thrown into the Wrath of God. It is God taking back control of the earth from Satan through His Son Jesus Christ and putting those who serve Satan with deceit, anger and wickedness through a much greater torment than what they have heaped upon the righteous and innocent. However, it does not happen in an instant; it is a series of events that happen over a short multi-year timeframe.

We need to understand Matthew 24 in the order that it was written to get the full gist of what Jesus is trying to convey to us. Many who read these verses miss some of the pivotal points Jesus is making. Without properly understanding Matthew 24, we will not be able to fully comprehend the Book of Revelation or the other end-times prophecies. By the same token, a misunderstanding of Matthew 24 will cause us to misinterpret the other prophecies. If we overlook the broad view of what God is saying in Matthew 24, we end up over-analyzing every sentence and every little word to the point of confusion. It's time to stop looking for a hidden message between every syllable and start listening to what God is saying. Even the prophecies are easy to understand when you do that.

We will begin by looking at selected verses from Matthew 24. The reason these particular verses are being pulled out is because they are like a skeleton upon which the flesh is wrapped. They give structure to the whole chapter and make it clear as to what order the different events of the end-times will occur. Most of the other verses that surround the ones below are warnings and/or encouragements for the time of the end. Jesus inserts His admonitions in various places, but they have no bearing on how things will transpire. In other words, at the same time Jesus is laying out the course of future events, He is giving us certain warnings of what we should or should not do while those events are unfolding. As far as prophecy is concerned, the verses that are not included here are just filler. They do not help us to understand the chronology of the end-times. But, because of His compassion for us, Jesus is speaking to us words that will help us be victorious in the midst of the many trials the future will bring.

If you read these verses carefully, you will never read Matthew 24 in the same way again. As you read, pay close attention to all the words that refer to relational timing such as "when," "then" and "after." Those words reinforce for us the fact that Jesus is speaking these things in the order in which they will occur. He is speaking rationally, intentionally and chronologically and not in some ethereal spiritualistic way that just kind of floats from one subject to another without any direction or consideration for timing. One thing Jesus does not mention in Matthew 24 is the armies of Gog that will come and be defeated by God before the rest of the end-time events begin to unfold, unless He was referring to them as a "rumor of war" in verse 6. You'll recall that Gog fills the mountainous areas of Israel with troops in anticipation of total victory, but God intervenes with a great slaughter even before war breaks out.

Among all of the things that will happen before the end begins, the most important is that the gospel will be preached in all the world. Only after that will the end-times start in earnest as a process or series of events. The first thing that will happen after the gospel has been preached is that we will see Gog humiliated in defeat and then the Antichrist rise up to take over the defeated ten-nation alliance of Gog. A few short years after he ascends to power, the

Great Tribulation will begin. In verse 29 Jesus finally gets around to answering the most important part of the disciples' question: "What is the sign of your coming and of the end of the world?" He explains that while the Tribulation is still in full progress God will interrupt things by darkening all the lights in the sky. After the lights go dim, verse 30 says that the "sign of the Son of man" will appear in the skies. The absence of light from the heavenly bodies signifies Christ is going to appear at any moment. Jesus Himself is the sign that the very end of the world has come. He will then gather His New Testament elect into the clouds and take them away from the wrath that is about to begin. He does not describe the Wrath of God because that was not a part of the disciples' question. He simply states that it will be exactly as in the days of Noah. Noah was lifted above the flood in the ark, and all those who were left had to go through the flood. And, so shall it be when Jesus returns. He will rescue His elect and leave the others for wrath. With that short explanation, let's read it as it is written in God's Word.

> ³ᴮTell us, when shall these things be? and what shall be the sign of thy coming, and of the end of the world?
> ⁵For many shall come in my name, saying, I am Christ; and shall deceive many. ⁶And ye shall hear of wars and rumours of wars: see that ye be not troubled: for all these things must come to pass, *but the end is not yet*. ⁷For nation shall rise against nation, and kingdom against kingdom: and there shall be famines, and pestilences, and earthquakes, in divers places. ⁸*all these are the beginning of sorrows*. [Verse 13 is not included because it is a warning/abomination to believers and not a chronological pronouncement.]
> ¹⁴And this gospel of the kingdom shall be preached in all the world for a witness unto all nations; AND *then shall the end come*. ¹⁵*when ye therefore shall see the* abomination of desolation, spoken of by Daniel the prophet, stand in the holy place, (whoso readeth, let him understand:)
> ²¹*FOR THEN SHALL BE GREAT TRIBULATION*, such as was not since the beginning of the world to this time, no, nor ever shall be.

*29IMMEDIATELY AFTER THE TRIBULATION OF THOSE
DAYS* shall the sun be darkened, and the moon shall not
give her light, and the stars shall fall from heaven, and the
powers of the heavens shall be shaken: *30AND THEN
SHALL APPEAR THE SIGN OF THE SON OF MAN IN
HEAVEN*: and then shall all the tribes of the earth mourn,
and they shall see the Son of man coming in the clouds of
heaven with power and great glory. *31And he shall send his
angels with a great sound of a trumpet, AND THEY
SHALL GATHER TOGETHER HIS ELECT FROM THE
FOUR WINDS*, from one end of heaven to the other.
*37BUT AS THE DAYS OF NOAH WERE, SO SHALL ALSO
THE COMING OF THE SON OF MAN BE.
40THEN SHALL TWO BE IN THE FIELD; THE ONE
SHALL BE TAKEN, AND THE OTHER LEFT.*
Matthew 24:3B 5-8,14-15,21,29-31,37,40

Now that you have finished reading these verses, you may want to
read them again until it becomes clear what Jesus is saying to us. He
is basically giving us the schedule to doomsday. Tough times will get
tougher, however, the gospel will finally be preached throughout the
earth despite those tough times. The Antichrist will then appear, and
the Tribulation will begin. However, the Tribulation will be cut short
when Jesus comes to gather His elect, and then the Wrath of God
begins. If you open your Bible and read this whole chapter again, you
will see that it still says the same things. The only difference is that the
full text contains many warnings to the Church, which will include
many Jews during the end-times before Jesus returns. If you have
believed in the past that the Rapture takes place prior to the
Tribulation, Matthew 24 does not say that. The Revelation has been
wrongly interpreted to accommodate that belief, and it has caused
great confusion to the Church. We are going to see that it communi-
cates something very different as we reread it in the order that it is
written and accept what it has been saying all along. Some prophetic
scriptures are hard to understand because of the way they were written, but we are going to see over and over again that the key to understanding Revelation and other prophecies is accepting what Jesus said
in Matthew 24, which is 1) we go through the Tribulation, 2) we are
raptured and 3) those who are left must face the Wrath of God.

Now, let's start over at the beginning where the disciples question Jesus about the end-times.

> [1]And Jesus went out, and departed from the temple: and his disciples came to him for to shew him the buildings of the temple. [2]And Jesus said unto them, See ye not all these things? verily I say unto you, There shall not be left here one stone upon another, that shall not be thrown down. [3]And as he sat upon the Mount of Olives, the disciples came unto him privately, saying, Tell us, *when shall these things be*? and *what shall be the sign of thy coming, and of the end of the world*?
>
> *Matthew 24:1-3*

One of the first things we want to look at is what, exactly, are the disciples asking Jesus. The second half of their question—the sign of His coming and the end of the world—shows they already accept the fact that Jesus will be returning in the future, and that His return is somehow inextricably tied to, and in fact, will bring an end to this current world system. They didn't ask what are the signs—plural—but rather, what is "the" sign that will alert us to Your return at the end of the world? To them, His return is a sign in and of itself that it was all over. They want to know how we will be able to know when His return and the end of the world are imminent.

Their question is twofold: "When?" and "What is the sign?" Their focus is on the very end. They assume that "all these things" Jesus said will be destroyed are going to be destroyed at the end when He returns. They didn't ask, "When will the temple be cast down" and "Oh, by the way, not to change the subject, but we also would like to know when You'll be returning, and how will we know when the end of the world is approaching?" They considered His coming and the end of the world to be a single event that would somehow be tied into the leveling of the temple and the other buildings they could see there. The end they were questioning Him about was the last day we talked about in preparing for this study when God withdraws His grace and starts to pour vengeance on those who hate Him, and not the events that lead up to the end. However, from verse 4 to verse 28, Jesus reveals to them all the things that will happen before that last great sign of His return and the end of the world. He didn't want us to get discouraged over all the horrible events that would be coming to pass as though those events would somehow bring the world to an end. Some of those events become minor signs when we understand them in the context of what He is saying. It's not until verses 29 and 30 that He discloses to us what that final one great sign will be.

Jesus begins His reply in verses 4-14. What He says in these verses can be applied in a general sense to all of church history—from the time of His earthly ministry up to the completion of time, or the "last day" when the Resurrection and Rapture occur just before the Wrath of God begins. His words can also be applied specifically to the final years of world history just prior to the time of the Antichrist and His return. However, even though the following verses speak of tragic events, they do not make up the time of Great Tribulation, Daniel's seventieth week or Jacob's Trouble. Jesus proclaims in verse 6 that these tragic things "must come to pass, but the end is not yet." He doesn't mention the Great Tribulation until verses 15-29. The last thing that must take place before we officially enter into the end times which lead into the Great Tribulation is that the gospel must be fully preached to all the world (verse 14 below). That final preaching will reach every last person who is old enough to understand it in such a way as to be convicted of sin and convinced of God's grace and mercy. The events of Ezekiel 38 and 39, which speak of Gog of Magog coming against Israel for war, are not mentioned specifically in verses 4-14 but will take place at about the same time the gospel is being proclaimed to the final outposts and heathen nations of the earth.

> [4]And Jesus answered and said unto them, Take heed that no man deceive you. [5]For many shall come in my name, saying, I am Christ; and shall deceive many. [6]And ye shall hear of wars and rumours of wars: see that ye be not troubled: for all these things must come to pass, but the end is not yet. [7]For nation shall rise against nation, and kingdom against kingdom: and there shall be famines, and pestilences, and earthquakes, in divers places. [8]All these are the beginning of sorrows. [9]Then shall they deliver you up to be afflicted, and shall kill you: and ye shall be hated of all nations for my name's sake. [10]And

then shall many be offended, and shall betray one
another, and shall hate one another.

Matthew 24:4-10

In Mark 13:4 the disciples' question was recorded like this: "Tell us, when shall these things be? And what shall be the sign when all these things shall be fulfilled?" Again, the second part of the question is seeking for a single sign, but it's worded a bit differently. They asked for "the sign when all these things shall be fulfilled." They were lumping the destruction of the temple to the return of Christ at the end of the world. And they were right.

In verse 6 Jesus said there would be "wars and rumours of wars, but the end is not yet." In 70 a.d. the destruction of the temple occurred at the hands of the Roman army. A small group of people believe that all of the prophecies have already been fulfilled in the past when the Roman army destroyed the temple, but it is quite a stretch to make the Word of God confirm that to be true. You have to jump around from one verse to another and really contort things to make the Bible say that the Church was raptured in 70 a.d. It is an even greater stretch of the imagination to conclude that the world has already come to an end, and that we are living in a new and different world of a different dispensation. No historical evidence exists that there was any kind of appearing of Christ or catching away of believers in 70 a.d. On top of all of that, the western wall remains standing to this day—one stone upon another—a silent testimony to the fact that the prophecy concerning all of the buildings being cast down has not been fulfilled.

In John 11:24, Martha says she knows her dead brother will rise again in the resurrection at the last day. That is exactly where the minds of the disciples are focused—on the end-times, the Judgment, and the Resurrection. The temple has already been destroyed once, but for the rest of Matthew 24 and the rest of the end-times prophecies to be true, the temple must be rebuilt just as surely as Israel had to become a nation again. Without a new temple, the daily sacrifice cannot be resumed only to be interrupted again by the Antichrist, the Antichrist cannot seat himself in the temple professing himself to be God and the two witnesses of God in Revelation 11 cannot prophesy from it for three-and-one-half years. However, there is no indication from Scripture that the final temple will be destroyed again until such time as God creates a new heaven and new earth. There is too much going on in the temple during the end-times before and after Jesus returns for it to be destroyed at His second coming.

The Gospel of Luke reaffirms what verse 10 above tells us about many believers being betrayed by those closest to them. It also teaches us that if any of us should be delivered up for our faith, we should not put our trust in our own abilities and wisdom but in the Lord Jesus. All of the things Jesus spoke of in these verses have come to pass and will continue to come to pass with greater intensity right up to the time when we enter into the Great Tribulation. The fact of the matter is that the things which Jesus enumerates above are pre-Tribulation atrocities. They constitute tribulation in the lives of those who experience them; however, they are not the Great Tribulation. The majority of the Church seems to be in denial over the idea that God will allow His Church to go through "The Tribulation," even though it suffers tribulation everyday all over the world. However, the Tribulation will force people to rethink their priorities, and it will open the eyes of many to their need of a savior, deliverer and provider. The Tribulation will actually be the catalyst many need to get them saved, and the Church will be right there to either assist them in their decisions or to be an example of suffering in the name of the Lord. In verse 16 below, we are told that some of us will be put to death. We are going to look closer at how probable that might be as we get further into this book.

> ¹⁴Settle it therefore in your hearts, not to meditate before what ye shall answer: ¹⁵For I will give you a mouth and wisdom, which all your adversaries shall not be able to gainsay nor resist. ¹⁶And ye shall be betrayed both by parents, and brethren, and kinsfolks, and friends; and *some of you shall they cause to be put to death.* ¹⁷And ye shall be hated of all men for my name's sake.
>
> *Luke 21:14-17*

Jesus was speaking directly to His future Church when He laid out the end-times to His apostles, giving them warnings and instructions for the times to come. He was not speaking to the unsaved Jews of Israel, nor was He speaking to a bunch of left-behind Christians. He was speaking to the born-again Jews and Gentiles who would make up His Church as one body of believers. He also was speaking to all of us who call upon the name of the Lord from pure hearts when He said in essence, "Don't let your heart become distracted, discouraged or fearful by the evil things you see taking place all around you, but keep your attentions directed towards God, His Word and His promised return. Or, at the very least, focus on your martyr's reward." We are told repeatedly that many true believers will be put to death. That is the message Jesus sends us repeatedly every time He speaks in the Gospels about the end-times. He never tells us that the Church is going to mysteriously disappear without ever seeing any kind of tribulations in the end-times. He is, in fact, preparing us—the one and only body of Christ—for the final chapter of this world controlled by sin, after the gospel has been fully preached and both sin and righteousness come to their fullness.

The world will be experiencing its darkest hour as the hearts of men become increasingly deluded and they take on a boldness in their sin, openly practicing those things that were once done only in secret and under the cover of darkness. At the same time, the Church will be experiencing its greatest hour as those who love God and have been taught in the fullness of His Word draw ever closer to Him through necessity because of the persecution that will come from those who hate goodness and light. The result will be a Church that is more radiant and full of good works than anything that was present in the early Church. Romans 5:20 informs us that where sin abounds, grace does much more abound, and abound it will during the end of time.

Bear in mind that those things Jesus has described so far are the things that will take place before the end-times ever begin. Those who believe God would not allow the Church to go through the final Great Tribulation have only to look around the world right now to see that His people are going through great tribulation right now—not to be confused with the Great Tribulation. We can see all around the world how calamities are coming against God's people everyday, and how they are suffering persecution and being put to death for the things which they believe. In free and open societies the persecution can be conducted in a very "civilized" and sometimes even in a low-key manner through political actions, legal actions, stereotyping, false reporting, distorted educational systems and so on. In other parts of the world where governments are not strong enough to protect the people, Christians sometimes become a target of persecution and annihilation, albeit, they are not necessarily the only target of hateful attacks. And finally, there are those countries where Christianity is an outlaw religion, which is punishable by prison, torture or death.

> And many false prophets shall rise, and shall deceive many.
> *Matthew 24:11*

Many false prophets have already risen in the world. Whether it is John Smith, David Koresh or the prophet Mohammed, each of these men taught things contrary to what the Bible says. Yet, at the same time, they all claimed close ties to the Bible and the God of the Bible. However, that's nothing compared to what is going to happen after the Antichrist is revealed by his seven-year peace contract with Israel. In the coming verses we will see that false prophets and false christs proliferate after the Antichrist shows His face.

There is nothing prophetic or chronological about verse 13. It is not speaking of the "last day" of the Resurrection and Rapture. It's not speaking of a disappearing Church either. It is simply one of the many warnings and admonitions Jesus gives while leading into the final response to the disciples' questions. Jesus emphasizes that all who endure to the end shall be saved. We can safely assume that He is speaking of the end of all things that we must endure while in this world. Furthermore, we can logically assume that when He raptures the Church, that will bring a conclusion to the things we must endure because we will no longer be in the world after we are escorted into heaven. But, we have to remember that the Bible uses the same words to speak of different moments, events and collections of events that are all a part of the end-times. Jesus is not telling us that we must endure to the beginning of the end when the Antichrist will make his seven-year covenant of peace with Israel and then we will be gone. He is telling us that we must endure to the final end when God blows the whistle on the Antichrist and the rest of the world and declares the saints to be the victors. The end is when the final trumpet sounds, the dead in Christ are raised and the entire Church is caught up into the clouds with Jesus. The end is when God begins to punish the earth with His wrath. This is not the final judgment where all of mankind must stand before Jesus Christ to be judged for those things that we do in this body; instead, it is when God determines that all living souls have come to that place of conviction in their hearts where they have decided between serving sin or righteousness.

Not all of those who start out serving Christ will continue with Him. The love of many of the saints will grow cold as their hearts become hard, and they, along with the rest of the world, will reject the One who bought them. At the same time, many who have refused to give Jesus the time of day will finally see the unmasked difference between good and evil, and it will be evident that Almighty God and the evil one are battling it out in the earth over the souls of men. Many will give their hearts to Christ. Daniel's seventieth week is the final call for the grace of God. In the midst of great adversity, the Jews of Israel, along with everyone else, will be cast headlong into the final valley of decision. Everyone will be forced to make a final choice that will determine their eternal destiny. God will use this time to purge His Church of those who are really wolves in sheep's clothing which is the only way Jesus will be able to come for a Church that is truly without spot or wrinkle. This purging will be one reason why the Church will be at its finest hour, because those who hinder the flow of God's spirit will be separated from the true believers by their own choice. Also at this time, the troubles and persecutions the Church endures will purge away sin and pride from the hearts of believers.

> [12]And because iniquity shall abound, the love of many shall wax cold. [13]But he that shall endure unto the end, the same shall be saved.
>
> *Matthew 24:12-13*

The end that Christ speaks of in verse 13 is the end of the Great Tribulation when the tried and purified Church will be raptured. That will be the end of this current age of grace that began when the Word of God dwelt among us in the person of Jesus Christ, full of grace and truth, and will continue until the Church is finally removed from the earth. God has positioned His people on the earth to proclaim and live out the gospel before all mankind. He has left us to be beacons of light, even in the darkest of nights. Because of the darkness that will engulf the earth at the end of this age, the Church will be more purified and moving in more power and supernatural provision than ever before. As Jesus said in John 14:12, "The works that I do, will you do also, and much greater works because I go unto the Father." Just as in the time of Jesus' earthly ministry, the world will see the moving of God in such a powerful way they cannot deny it is from God. They will either have to accept it and embrace it or reject and fight against it with all their might just like when Jesus was here in person. They either accepted Him as Lord, or they rejected Him and rejoiced over His crucifixion.

Verse 14 informs us that the gospel must be preached everywhere and to everyone before the end can even begin. This is not talking about a sudden end when the Church is removed from the earth and the world is suddenly cast into the Wrath of God. That's what verse 13 is referencing. Verse 14 is talking about the final week, or seven years, of Daniel's seventy-week period that God has determined upon Israel to bring a completion to His work of redemption. That seven-year period begins with the identity of Antichrist being revealed as he makes a seven-year false peace accord with Israel. Verse 14 is talking about the final events of world history before God calls it quits and begins pouring out vengeance in the fullness of His anger. God uses Daniel's final week—after the gospel has been preached to all the world, which would include Israel—to shake the Jews and many others awake. After the truth of salvation, the judgment of God and the end of time have been preached to all, the Antichrist will appear, and many will give their hearts to the Lord because of him. Incidentally, the final preaching of the gospel is in no way a sign that the end has come, because we have no way of knowing when the job of getting the gospel to all the world has been completed. Only God knows that. On the other hand, the appearing of the Antichrist with a seven year peace deal is a sign that the gospel has been fully preached.

> And this gospel of the kingdom shall be preached in all the world for a witness unto all nations; and then shall the end come.
>
> *Matthew 24:12-13*

One thing we want to notice at this point is that which is missing from Jesus' outline of the signs of the end-times. It leaves such a gaping hole in the Scriptures that it needs to be addressed. If the Church is supposed to be raptured or simply disappear before the Tribulation, shouldn't it be mentioned in the Scriptures as a sign? And what a sign it would be. The gospel is preached to all the world, and then millions of Christians suddenly disappear just before the Antichrist comes on the scene and causes great tribulation. After all, that is what the disciples asked Jesus for—the signs of His appearing and of the end of the world. But it's just not there. It never has been and never will be. Jesus made no mention of His appearing before verse 15 where the Abomination of Desolation is mentioned. That empty void is like the black hole of pre-Tribulation Rapture theology. The one and only Rapture, the one where Jesus appears in the sky and gathers His elect, takes place in verses 29-31 after the Tribulation—at least that is where Jesus insists it will take place. If Jesus is articulating the signs of His return and the end of the world, why would He keep the vanishing of His Church such a big secret if that is what's going to happen? That would indeed be one of the greatest signs of His return since it cannot be classified as a rapture or catching up of believers like the Rapture that occurs in verses 29-31. He's never been shy about laying everything out for everyone to see, and He definitely will not be overcome by bashfulness when He appears in His glory for every eye to see when He comes for His elect. He is laying things out as they will occur, and the only thing He leaves out is the date and time because He was not privy to that information. There will be no Rapture until after the Tribulation.

Many have interpreted verse 13 to mean that if we endure to the time when the opening events of the end-times begin to unfold, we will be taken out of here before any of those events take place. These people believe that Jesus just sort of sneaks in on a top secret mission and causes His followers to fade into the spirit world, and nobody knows what has happened to them until someone stumbles upon the answer in "Gramma's old Bible." First of all, the gospel has just been preached to all the world; the Rapture and Wrath of God are a part of the gospel, so everyone is going to know what is taking place. Secondly, nowhere in the Bible does it say that we are going to suddenly disappear. If you are thinking "changed in the twinkling of an eye," those words are not talking about the Rapture; they are talking about being instantly changed from mortal to immortal during the Resurrection. All of the events Jesus is enumerating here—even the Antichrist and the Tribulation—are simply world events, the final events that will take place on the earth before God begins to pour out His wrath. As such, they become signs to us that the final end is fast approaching when Jesus will appear for His elect. The Bible repeatedly tells us that we must suffer much persecution and tribulations for the Word's sake, but that God has excused us from His wrath, which is meant only for His enemies. The Tribulation we suffer at the hands of God's enemies is the reason for His wrath upon them.

Mark 13 is similar in some ways to verses 13 and 14 above, but it is also strikingly different. Verse 10 declares that the gospel must be published before the end will come. Verse 13 declares that we must endure to the end. And then, verse 14 immediately draws us back into the Tribulation with the words "But, when ye shall see the abomination of desolation...." Many people want to reserve those words and warnings for the Jews or left-behind Christians; however, if we do that here we must do the same elsewhere. In John 17:20 Jesus said, "Neither pray I for these alone, but for them also which shall believe on me through their word." Do we believe on Him through the Epistles? Was He speaking only to Jews in the Gospels, or was He speaking to all future generations? When He said "I am the vine and you are the branches," was He excluding the Church from that statement? If we are the branches we will see the Antichrist and the Tribulation.

> [13]And ye shall be hated of all *men* for my name's sake: but he that shall endure unto the end, the same shall be saved. [14]But when ye shall see the abomination of desolation, spoken of by Daniel the prophet, standing where it ought not, (let him that readeth understand,) then let them that be in Judaea flee to the mountains.
>
> *Mark 13:13-14*

In Revelation 3:21 Jesus said, "To him that overcometh will I grant to sit with me in My throne, even as I also overcame and am set down with my Father in his throne." Jesus did overcome, and His ultimate victory came through His death on the cross. If Jesus had to die for truth before He could gain the final victory, why is it so hard for Christians, particularly those in free societies, to believe that they perhaps may be required to lay down their own lives one day as the only way left to them by their adversaries to reject anything other than the truth of the gospel. Christians die everyday all over the world because they refuse to deny the one who died for them. During the Tribulation, which the entire Church must go through, many will have to put their lives on the line. Satan will require it of them as he tries them to see whether they are really willing to endure to the very end—the end being that final breath they draw before passing into eternity with a crown of righteousness waiting for them, which they will wear for their faith, courage and obedience. That final breath before eternity can occur just before they die or before they are raptured.

Wherever the Rapture is mentioned in the Bible, it is described as a visible event. In Titus 2:13 the Rapture is called a "glorious appearing." In Acts 1:9-11 Jesus was caught up before the eyes of the disciples and received into a cloud. "While they beheld, he was taken up; and a cloud received him out of their sight." Two angels appeared while they continued to gaze into the sky and said, "Ye men of Galilee, why stand ye gazing up into heaven? This same Jesus, which is taken up from you into heaven, shall so come in like manner as ye have seen him go into heaven." The angels were speaking of the Rapture, when we will be caught up into the clouds in the very same manner as He was. When He again comes in the clouds, Revelation 1:7 proclaims, "Behold, he cometh with clouds; and every eye shall see him, and they also which pierced him: and all kindreds of the earth shall wail because of him. Even so, Amen." Not only those who pierced Him, but "they *also* who pierced him." That means that not only the saints who are awaiting His blessed and glorious appearing will see Him appear, but every human being who is guilty of the sin that necessitated the crucifixion of Jesus Christ. Luke 21:27-28 tells us to "Look up" for our redemption because He is "coming in the clouds." It also makes clear that the other inhabitants of the earth will also see Him coming in the clouds. Verse 30 of Matthew 24 corroborates that fact. They will see Him coming in the clouds and mourn. Verse 31 reveals the purpose of His coming is to gather His elect. The sign of the darkening of the skies that precedes His appearing is the same sign that precedes the day of God's wrath. Before Matthew 24 concludes, Jesus makes it clear that He is gathering His elect to save them from this day.

THINK ABOUT IT!

— Does Jesus provide a timeline of the future in Matthew 24?

— Are the words "when, then, after, beginning and not yet" pertinent in this chapter or should we just ignore them?

— Does Jesus tell us that the church will disappear at anytime?

Selah

And he said, Unto you it is given to know the mysteries of the kingdom of God: but to others in parables; that seeing they might not see, and hearing they might not understand.

Luke 8:10

Matthew 24

Tribulation Warnings

As I grew through my teen years with no real spiritual underpinnings, Satan began to slowly steal the life away from the inside of me. I was still born again, but I didn't know how to resist his evil intrusions. I found myself very depressed. I'd wake up every day to a miserable day. One day as I stood looking out the window of my room, I felt an irresistible need to just say the words, "I am so depressed." I was told that you cannot speak unto the mountain, you cannot cast out devils and that there was no real power in your words, but at that moment it was working in reverse. It was then I realized that the depression had always been an oppression that came from the outside. When I spoke those words though the oppression dropped down to the inside of me and it seemed as though there was a chuckle as it entered. I know that some Christians believe that Christians cannot have demons, but there I was, a young teenage Baptist boy with a spirit of depression inside of me. I tried to tell it to leave. I tried to repent and reverse things. I cried out to God. And then, I just cried.

The world has experienced tribulation from the time of Adam until now but never to the magnitude of what will be experienced during the end-times. Tribulation is not judgment from God, but rather the calamitous effects of the workings of evil. The Tribulation could be called the wrath of god (with a little "g") since Satan is the god of this earth and the time of Great Tribulation comes from him. Revelation 12:12 informs us that the devil is cast out of heaven and down to earth having great wrath because he knows his time is short. We see in Revelation that he is cast to the earth before the Wrath of God begins and that he is the one who causes the Tribulation. Events such as the great flood are not a proper comparison because that was a judgment from God, while tribulation is the persecution and troubling that comes from Satan and those who practice his ways. In John 16:33 Jesus said, "In the world you shall have tribulation: but be of good cheer; I have overcome the world." He didn't say He would keep us from tribulation or deliver us out of the world so we could avoid tribulation altogether. He assures us that He will be there to help us in the midst of tribulation with the victory He obtained at the cross. He gave us the Holy Spirit as our comforter, helper, teacher and victor so that with Him we can always come out a winner, in spite of all the troubles we must endure.

> When ye therefore shall see the abomination of desolation, spoken of by Daniel the prophet, stand in the holy place, whoso readeth, let him understand.
>
> *Matthew 24:15*

The Church has not been raptured yet. Jesus is talking to the real Church about seeing the abomination of desolation; He's not talking to a left-behind band of tagalongs. In verses 22-27 of this chapter Jesus instructs the elect, which again is the real Church, concerning His return. The Church is not raptured until verse 30. Everything from verse 15 to that point is talking about the Tribulation. Verses 29-31 signal the end of the Tribulation and the beginning of the Day of the Lord when true believers are taken from the earth so the Wrath of God can be poured out on those who have been judged to be unrighteous and unrepentant.

Daniel 9:27 mentions the abomination of desolation, which refers to the Antichrist, the statue that is made in his honor, or the combination of the two, and then both of them being destroyed after Daniel's final seven-year period in the consummation. Consummation simply means an end, a conclusion, an outcome carried to the utmost extent or degree, and it is referring to the Wrath of God. (Isaiah 10:22,23 and 28:22 also mention the final consumption or destruction.) In just one verse, Daniel lays out the same series of events that Jesus laid out in Matthew 24. The Antichrist rises to prominence after the gospel has been preached to all the world. The seven-year peace accord he engineers is the first sign that the end-times have begun. He will not step into the temple of God until the midpoint of the seven-year peace plan, and that is when the Tribulation begins. This means that the Church would have to magically disappear three-and-one-half years before the Tribulation begins and a full seven years before the Wrath of God begins, if Matthew 24:13 is referring to Christians evading the Antichrist and the events leading up to God's wrath at the end of the world. The final words of this verse speak of the wrath of God, which has already been predetermined and will be poured out on the desolate ones who follow after sin and the Antichrist after the seven-year period is completed and the Church is gone.

> And he shall confirm the covenant with many for *one week*: and in the midst of the week he shall cause the sacrifice and the oblation to cease, *and for the overspreading of abomina-tions he shall make it desolate*, even until the consummation, and that determined shall be poured upon the desolate.
>
> *Daniel 9:27*

In 2 Thessalonians we see that the Antichrist seats himself in the temple of God and proclaims himself to be God. In verse 3, God is alerting us through Paul to "let no man deceive you by any means." Deceive us concerning what? Deceive us concerning that day when Jesus comes to gather us unto Himself. That day absolutely will not come until after the Antichrist is revealed before our very eyes and seats himself in the temple of God. Many people believe that the Antichrist will not come until after the Church is gone and that we are the ones who are restraining him by our presence and great power. That's nonsense. God is the one who is restraining him until it is time for him to be revealed at his appointed time in the end-times. We will be here, we will see him and we will recognize him for who he is.

[1]Now we beseech you, brethren, *by the coming of our Lord Jesus Christ, and by our gathering together unto Him,* [2]That ye be not soon shaken in mind, or be troubled, neither by spirit, nor by word, nor by letter as from us, as that the day of Christ is at hand. [3]Let no man deceive you by any means: for *that day shall not come* [that day mentioned in verses 1 and 2 when Jesus comes to gather us to Himself], except there come a falling away first, and that man of sin be revealed, the son of perdition; [4]Who opposeth and exalteth himself above all that is called God, or that is worshipped; so that he as God sitteth in the temple of God, shewing himself that he is God.

2 Thessalonians 2:1-4

The main subject of this chapter in Thessalonians is the coming of the Lord Jesus Christ for the Church at the Rapture. The description of the man of sin in this passage is not the main subject, but rather relates back to the subject of Jesus returning for His Church. Verse 6 also refers back to the Rapture in Verse 1, and it is speaking of Jesus and not the Antichrist. Paul is saying, "Now you know what is restraining Jesus from being revealed in His time because I just told you in the first three verses." Jesus will not appear until after the man of sin is revealed and the falling away of the Church occurs. We know that the preaching of the gospel has to be accomplished in all the world before any of the rest of these things take place. Then the Church of Jesus Christ and the Antichrist will face off for the final seven years before the Rapture, the final three-and-one-half years being the Great Tribulation when sinner and saint alike will have to make their final decision on who they will fear and who they will serve, God or Satan. All of mankind will have to make a choice between saving their skin or saving their souls in the persecution of the Tribulation, and then comes the Rapture for those who call upon the name of Lord in faith, and His wrath for those who reject Him.

Verse 7 refers back to the man of sin in verses 3 and 4. It informs us that "he who letteth," or more accurately "he who restrains" will restrain until he is taken out of the way. The same Greek word translated as "letteth" here is translated in other places as "seize," "held," "keep," "possessed," "withhold," "retain" and "hold fast," along with other uses. In context, the old English word means that the Antichrist is being restrained from being revealed. It is not talking about the Church restraining the Antichrist because it has not been raptured at this point; otherwise, Jesus and Paul would have no business talking to us about seeing the man of sin when he is revealed if we are not going to be here. When the Church is raptured, it is not taken out of the way for the man of sin to finally be revealed, but rather taken out of the way so that God's wrath can begin to fall on the man of sin and all other sinners after causing great tribulation on the earth. The Book of Revelation tells us that the beast—which is how the Antichrist is frequently referred to in the Bible—is being restrained in the bottomless pit until his time at the end of the world has arrived. Just like Jesus, he is alive as a spirit being, and just like Jesus he is just waiting to be released to come and get us at his appointed time. The only difference is that Jesus wants to get us to take us away to safety and the Antichrist just wants to get at us to destroy us. Obedience is the only thing that prevents Jesus from coming to take His Church away. If the man of sin were not being restrained by force, he would be here right now causing an unparalleled amount of deception, terror and destruction all over the earth. An angel stands guard over the bottomless pit, and that is who restrains or "letteth," "until he be taken out of the way."

> [5]Remember ye not, that, when I was yet with you, I told you these things? [6]And now ye know what withholdeth that He [Jesus] might be revealed in his time. [7]For the mystery of iniquity doth already work: only he [the angel of the bottomless pit] who now letteth [restrains] will let [restrain], until he be taken out of the way. [8]And then shall that wicked be revealed, whom the Lord shall consume with the spirit of His mouth, and shall destroy with the brightness of His coming: [9]Even him, whose coming is after the working of Satan with all power and signs and lying wonders, [10]And with all deceivableness of unright-eousness in them that perish; because they received not the love of the truth, that they might be saved.
>
> *2 Thessalonians 2:5-10*

The Antichrist is not consumed by the spirit of the Lord's mouth or the brightness of His coming when Jesus comes to rapture the Church. The Antichrist will not be consumed until Jesus returns a second time at the Battle of Armageddon. Several years of wrath will occur between the time Jesus appears in cool, white clouds to gather His people unto Himself and when He returns a second time on His white horse to do battle and bring an end to the Wrath of God and the rule of Satan on the earth.

Second Thessalonians 2:3 states that there will "come a falling away first, and that man of sin [will] be revealed" before the return of Jesus for the Church. It is not clear, however, whether Paul is saying that the falling away will occur first—before the Antichrist arrives—or if both of these things occur first at about the same time and, perhaps, in conjunction with one another. However, they both must occur before Jesus comes for us. There may possibly be a falling away of believers before the Antichrist arrives, but that seems unlikely since the final push to get the gospel to all the earth will be taking place just before the Antichrist is revealed. That, coupled with the fact that God speaks in numerous places about His glory and His Word filling the whole earth, suggests that the falling away is a direct result of the calamitous atmosphere that Satan and the Antichrist will be fostering across the face of the earth after the gospel has been preached. There will be a falling away of believers associated with the arrival of the Antichrist as many will have the faith scared out of them. On the other hand, there will be many who will finally turn to the Lord because they will be faced with the reality that they have nowhere else to turn. They will know by the gospel that Jesus will be returning soon, and if they don't act quickly, they are going to be left to suffer wrath with those who are causing great tribulation.

Jesus informs us in the parable about the sower of the Word of God that Satan challenges every individual who ever receives this word in their heart to see whether they are going to hold on to God's Word and stand firmly upon it, or be offended by it and let it go. In Luke 8:12 Jesus also said that the seed that had fallen by the wayside represents those who hear the Word and "then cometh the devil, and taketh away the word out of their hearts, lest they should believe and be saved." In Mark 4:17 Jesus, referring to the seed sown on stony hearts, characterizes people who hear the Word and receive it immediately with gladness but have no root in themselves as enduring "but for a time: afterward, when affliction or persecution ariseth for the Word's sake, immediately they are offended." Satan's demonic thugs always attempt to steal God's Word away. After the final great outpouring of the Spirit of God, when all the world has heard the gospel, the Great Tribulation will simply be the final outpouring of the spirit of affliction and persecution against those who have heard the Word of God. Since the whole world has heard the gospel, the whole world will be on trial to see who will stand by the truth of God's Word and who will surrender to the lies of Satan.

It must be made clear that the Bible does not say the Antichrist will take over an apostate church (those fallen away from the Christian faith) and rule as a high church official such as the pope. The Antichrist will be a warrior first, a political leader second and then a spiritual leader to some in a perverse and destructive way, but it won't be under the guise of pretending to be a Christian. The fact that the Antichrist seats himself in the temple of God has nothing to do with Christianity or Judaism. It is just one step on a trail of lies, deception, fear and destruction that the Antichrist will take as he attempts to rule the earth with a "rod of iron" to fulfill prophecy that was meant for Jesus. Satan apparently thinks he has gained a great victory if he seats his man in the temple, and those who follow after him can quote the Bible and the Koran for support as he lives out a life that is in complete contrast and contrary to the true Christ. Many followers will worship him, but they will not make any direct claim to the Christian faith and, in fact, will oppose Christians. The followers of the Antichrist will carry guns and other weapons as they follow the Antichrist on a holy jihad against Christians and Jews. The Scriptures do not say that Christians will fall away from the faith and then the Antichrist steps in to lead them. Anybody can choose to follow after the Antichrist, but they will have to deny Christ, the Church and the truth of Holy Scriptures to do so. There is absolutely nothing to support the theories of the Antichrist ruling a worldly Christian Church.

Having said all that, there is one way the theory of the Antichrist leading an apostate church could come to pass indirectly. As we will see later, the Antichrist will rule the nations surrounding Israel where Christianity first took root. Those nations are definitely not Christian anymore. There remains a small remnant of believers in these nations, but the vast majority of the people have fallen so absolutely and completely away from the Christian faith that they are now diametrically opposed to the faith by holding to another religion, which is Antichrist at its very core. Currently Islam reigns supreme in those nations, which just happens to be a religion that is Antichrist, anti-Jew, Antichristian and very militant, despite the many objections to that fact, and designed to control governments. Many Muslims are also looking for a return of Jesus, but they believe He will return as a mortal man who will lead them against Jews, Christians and someone who they call antichrist. (More on this later.)

This next reference is a sneak preview of Revelation, but it helps us to understand what the Tribulation is all about. In Revelation 12 we see a future event where Michael finally receives clearance to throw Satan out of heaven for good. He is cast directly to the earth, and the time of Tribulation ensues, which is actually the wrath of Satan according to verse 12. There is a tremendously huge difference between the wrath of Satan and the Wrath of God. After Satan is cast to the earth, the Antichrist will be loosed from the belly of the earth to do his thing. They will work in tandem in the full fury and intense hatred of Satan to cause as much trouble on the earth as possible until their time runs out. They are fully aware that Jesus is about to bring an end to Satan's reign as the god of the earth, lock him away in the pit and put Christians in charge. When Michael casts Satan out of heaven and to the earth, it is simply a short layover for Satan on his way to hell.

> [7]*And there was war in heaven: Michael and his angels fought against the dragon; and the dragon fought and his angels,* [8]And prevailed not; *neither was their place found any more in heaven.* [9]*And the great dragon was cast out, that old serpent, called the Devil, and Satan, which deceiveth the whole world: he was cast out into the earth, and his angels were cast out with him.* [10]And I heard a loud voice saying in heaven, Now is come salvation, and strength, and the kingdom of our God, and the power of His Christ: for the accuser of our brethren is cast down, which accused them before our God day and night.

> [11]And they overcame him by the blood of the Lamb, and by the word of their testimony; and they loved not their lives unto the death. [12]Therefore rejoice, ye heavens, and ye that dwell in them. *Woe to the inhabiters of the earth and of the sea! for the devil is come down unto you, having great wrath, because he knoweth that he hath but a short time.*
>
> *Revelation 12:7-12*

In verses 10-12, we see the final promise of salvation begins in heaven when Satan is booted out. Just like everything else related to the end-times, the final salvation promised to us by God is a process or series of events. Heaven rejoices first because the evil one has been removed. Verse 8 tells us that his place in heaven will no longer be found. However, the earth, on the other hand, is about to be plunged into its darkest hour of despair. The devil who was allowed to maintain his abode in heaven itself and cause long-distance trouble is now on the earth ready to do some on-site harassment of Jews, Christians and anybody else that even looks innocent. Verse 11 says that the saints will overcome him by the blood of the Lamb, and that they are willing to give up their lives rather than give up the word of their testimony.

Notice in this next verse that after Michael stands up, there will be the worst time of trouble the world has ever seen, and then those in the Book of Life will be delivered. If you read verse 1 from Daniel 12 by itself, it may appear that the people are delivered when the time of trouble begins, but when you look at the whole chapter you again see the same pattern of Tribulation, Rapture and then Wrath. The time of trouble begins, and the saints are delivered at the very end of that trouble before the punishment of God begins. The reason that trouble erupts when the protector of Israel stands to his feet is because he is getting ready to throw Satan out of heaven. He is cleaning house so that when the saints arrive, there will no longer be anyone there to accuse them before God, but they must face his accusations on the earth for a little while longer.

> [1]And at that time *shall Michael stand up*, the great prince which standeth for the children of thy people: *and there shall be a time of trouble, such as never was since there was a nation even to that same time*: and at that time thy

people shall be delivered, every one that shall be found
written in the Book.

Daniel 12:1

The next few verses from the same chapter of Daniel are talking
about the elect being tried and purified and coming to the end of the
Tribulation which is that time of trouble. Everywhere we read in the
Scriptures about the Tribulation, we see believers being purged, purified and overcoming. Sometimes the only way left to be purified is for
one to lay down his life for the gospel's sake. Daniel assures us that
there is a blessing to those who are still around on the thirteen hundred and thirty-fifth day after the daily sacrifice is taken away. The
Tribulation will be raging during that time, and the blessing we wait
for is the appearing of Jesus in the clouds to collect His purified
saints. Those who die in the Lord are no less blessed because they will
pop out of their graves at the final trump and will be carried by God's
mighty angels, along with those who are alive and remain, up into the
clouds to be with the Lord. The Resurrection of those who are written in the Lamb's Book of Life occurs just before the Rapture so that
both the dead and the living are able to leave the earth at the same
time and with immortal bodies.

> [10]*Many shall be purified, and made white, and tried*; but the
> wicked shall do wickedly: and none of the wicked shall
> understand; but the wise shall understand. [11]And from the
> time that the daily sacrifice shall be taken away, and the
> abomination that maketh desolate set up, there shall be a
> thousand two hundred and ninety days. [12]*Blessed is he that
> waiteth, and cometh to the thousand three hundred and five
> and thirty days.*
>
> *Daniel 12:10-12*

As Jesus continues in Matthew 24, He begins to issue warnings to
His elect in Israel. That would include the 144,000 born-again Jews
who are servants of Jesus Christ, and who are the firstfruits of the
earth unto God. God will have a select group of 12,000 saints from
each of the 12 tribes of Israel who serve Jesus as their Lord during the
final days of this earth, and who also will hold a special place in God's

future kingdom. However, His warning to flee Jerusalem is to anyone who will obey His command. The 144,000 will heed His directive, but the Bible is silent concerning any others who may wish to join them. Those who remain in the city will face the wrath of the Antichrist. Luke 21:23 states, "There shall be great distress in the land, and wrath upon this people." After so much time and so many signs and warnings from God, not everyone in Israel is going to repent and turn to the living God and His covenant of peace. Jesus continues with warnings right up to verses 29 and 30 where the Great Tribulation ends with the Rapture of God's people. Verse 22 informs us that God will keep the days of Great Tribulation short for the elect's sake. He will not allow it to go beyond the three-and-one-half years that He has already proclaimed in various places. Why would Jesus warn His people (born-again saints of Jewish and Gentile lineage) and keep the days short for all of us if we are not going to be here during the Tribulation? The only answer is that we *will* be here.

One thing that must be understood is that God is issuing an alert to those in Judea, which is the countryside around Jerusalem, and to those in Jerusalem itself, to flee into the mountains and wilderness. This is not a worldwide alert for all believers to flee and hide out during the entire Tribulation period. The Antichrist will live and rule in the Middle East, and his first order of business will be to take Jerusalem and persecute those who are right under his nose. Therefore, the people of Jerusalem who do not submit to the Antichrist are in imminent danger. Anyone who does not flee will likely die. God does not tell believers around the world to go into hiding because this is going to be the last and best opportunity to witness to others about the difference between serving God and serving Satan. In relation to the time of the Antichrist, Daniel 11:32 proclaims that, "Those who know their God shall be strong and do exploits." Hopefully, many nations will stand up against the advances of Antichrist in the last days. The Bible clearly indicates that it is a time of wars. If the whole world were submitted to the Antichrist, there would be no need for the wars that he embarks on. If the Church were gone at this time, there would be no saints for the Antichrist to war against either. God has promised that none of His people would have to go through His wrath, but this is not His wrath; it is Satan's wrath poured out on the innocent in the form of Great

Tribulation. Until that time comes, we do not know how things are going to unfold in the rest of the world outside of the Middle East because the Bible does not tell us. There may be strong persecution all around the world, but that does not necessarily mean we all go into hiding.

> ¹⁶Then *let them which be in Judaea flee into the mountains*: ¹⁷Let him which is on the housetop not come down to take any thing out of his house: ¹⁸Neither let him which is in the field return back to take his clothes. ¹⁹And woe unto them that are with child, and to them that give suck in those days! ²⁰But pray ye that your flight be not in the winter, neither on the sabbath day: ²¹*For then* [after we see the abommination of desolation as stated in verse 15] *shall be great tribulation, such as was not since the beginning of the world to this time, no, nor ever shall be.* ²²And *except those days should be shortened, there should no flesh be saved*: but *for the elect's sake those days shall be shortened.*
>
> *Matthew 24:16-22*

Many people take the verses we just read to mean that the Great Tribulation is going to be less than the three-and-one-half years that God has stated over and over again in His Word it would be. God is only allowing the Antichrist three-and-one-half years of Great Tribulation, and then He is going to cut His own work short in righteousness by removing the Church from the earth and judging sinners who are participants in the Tribulation, along with all those who are complacent. The goal of Satan and the Antichrist is to rule the entire world, but since Satan knows that his days are numbered, his secondary goal is to destroy as many as he can before his own end. Given enough time and with his own end in sight, he will be able and more than willing to preside over the total destruction of all mankind if God does not intervene. God allows them only a short time period of three-and-one-half years to try and frighten people into giving up the gospel that has been preached to all the earth and submitting to terrorism instead. All of mankind will have one clear and final choice between the grace and love of God or the vicious and destructive hatred of Satan. Matthew speaks in the future tense of how those days will be shortened, while the same account in Mark 13:20 is stated in the past tense. God is telling us that the time has already been predetermined and shortened to only three-and-one-half years from whatever amount of time it would take Satan and the Antichrist to destroy all flesh.

> And *except that the Lord had shortened those days*, no flesh should be saved: but for the elect's sake, whom He hath chosen, He hath shortened the days.
>
> *Mark 13:20*

> For He will finish the work, *and cut it short in righteousness*: because a short work will the Lord make upon the earth.
>
> *Romans 9:28*

Many Christians seem to believe that the Rapture will occur before the Great Tribulation, and they hold out hope that they will be able to escape the horrors and hardness of those times. They labor feverishly to form their doctrine to fit that desire. Others have mistakenly lumped the Tribulation and the Wrath together as a single event or overlapping events, and because God has promised to deliver us from the wrath to come, the assumption is that we will not see the Tribulation. God's wrath and the Tribulation are two totally and distinctly different things or events. We will see the Antichrist and the Great Tribulation, and God does allow His people to go through bad times as a purifying experience because of His compassion for all mankind. As others witness the peace and assurance we possess and our total trust in God—even to the point of death, if necessary—many will turn to Christ. Most of the horrible things we read about in the Book of Revelation from chapter 8 and beyond are judgments of wrath which we will not experience; but tribulations are something we must go through in this life with Jesus at our side and the Holy Spirit on the inside.

Below is an example of how God left Israel in bondage to the Egyptians for 400 years before delivering them and leading them back to the Promised Land. He did not leave them in Egypt because they were such rotten sinners, or to judge them; He left them there to take care of them until it was time for them to take possession of their own land. The inhabitants of the Promised Land were not ready to be judged. Verse 16 below informs us that the iniquity of the Amorites was not yet full. God was not willing to judge any of the nations in the Promised Land until the sin of every last one had come to a place of total hardness and unrepentance. Rahab of Jericho repented immediately when the Hebrews showed up in her city to spy out the land and her family was delivered because she acted in faith instead of fear. The remainder of the city was destroyed. Israel's stay in Egypt eventually ended up in misery. They suffered much affliction at the hands of the Egyptians, but God did not judge Pharaoh and His people without giving them ample opportunity to repent and obey Him.

After God delivered the Israelites from Egypt, they still did not enter the Promised Land for another forty years; this time it was because of their own sin and rebellion. All those who were afraid to enter the Promised Land and who doubted and complained while they were in the wilderness remained in the wilderness in graves. God purged out all those who feared everything else but Him and His mighty power and compassion. During the Tribulation, God will be doing the same type of work in His church in the midst of terrible persecution—cleansing the hearts of those who draw ever closer to Him and rejecting those who reject Him and, hopefully, bringing many "Rahabs" to a place of salvation in Christ in the process. Ephesians 5:27 reminds us that Jesus will present to Himself a Church without spot or wrinkle. He will scrub out all the spots through adversity and iron out the wrinkles by the things which we suffer. It will occur in that vast wilderness called the Great Tribulation because He is not willing that any should perish. There won't be many weak and fainthearted ninnies going up in the Rapture, but at the same time, He has designed His Church to look out for the needs of those who are weak, as long as they continue to call upon the name of the Lord and heed His words. Jesus gives us these advance warnings so that we will not become faint in our hearts and give up, and also so we can look after our weaker brothers and sisters to make sure they make it all the way to the end.

> [12]And when the sun was going down, a deep sleep fell upon Abram; and, lo, an horror of great darkness fell upon

him. ¹³And he said unto Abram, Know of a surety that thy seed shall be a stranger in a land that is not theirs, and shall serve them; and they shall afflict them four hundred years; ¹⁴And also that nation, whom they shall serve, will I judge: and afterward shall they come out with great substance. ¹⁵And thou shalt go to thy fathers in peace; thou shalt be buried in a good old age. ¹⁶But in the fourth generation they shall come hither again: *for the iniquity of the Amorites is not yet full.*

Genesis 15:12-16

Luke gives us a different perspective of what is taking place in Israel during the Tribulation and why believers need to flee Jerusalem. The man of sin is anxious to get to the temple of God—the crown jewel for a lying impostor who wants to claim to be God. This is several years after the defeat of Gog. The Antichrist has taken control of the armies of the ten nations that were a part of the Gog alliance. He has whipped them into shape and into a frenzy, and now they are ready to try their luck against Israel once more. Revelation 13:4 tells us that those who worship the beast do it by saying, "Who is like the beast? who is able to make war with him?" He is the ruthless and vicious ruler that this large empire of nations has been praying to lead them against the tiny little nation of Israel that they hate so passionately. He is the one that is empowered from on high to wipe out their most hated enemy. The only problem is the fact that he is empowered by the ruler of the principalities and powers of the air and not by God. He will be allowed by God to come in and destroy those Jews who still reject their Messiah, even at the end of the world. Because they reject their true God, they will either have to choose the Antichrist by receiving his mark in their flesh, be taken into slavery or die. The Antichrist and his followers are not all that fond of Jews anyway; thus, he may not extend to them the offer to take his mark and serve him. The bright side to this darkened horror is that some of them will reject the mark and receive Jesus with their dying breath.

The Antichrist will put a stop to the daily sacrifice and enter into the temple for a quick peek at his new place of self-exaltation before the Tribulation ever begins. This will occur as a result of his dealings with the reprobate Jews. Daniel 11:30 explains that he will have intelligence with them that forsake the holy covenant, and then in verse 31 he is shown taking away the daily sacrifice. Daniel 8:25 reveals to us that the Antichrist will "cause craft to prosper in his hand; and he will magnify himself in his heart, and by peace shall destroy many." He will use his false peace to gain access to the hearts and minds of unbelievers through flatteries and lies. Then he will gain access to Jerusalem, and finally he will gain access into the temple without ever firing a shot. Verse 20 of Luke 21 informs us that we will see Jerusalem surrounded by armies. This will probably be a part of the peace plan—one big lie about providing security for the Jews from their Arab Muslim aggressors by putting up a perimeter around the temple mount so that he can keep his people in line. The plan will be for Jews to freely and securely worship at their temple alongside the Muslims who will be free to worship at the Dome of the Rock on the same mount. While all of this is being put into place, a window of opportunity will be provided for believers to leave Jerusalem in relative security to God's refuge in the wilderness.

The Antichrist's first entry into the temple, when he "stands" only to look around and glory in his evil accomplishment (see Matthew 24:15), is the only sign Jesus gives to His people to leave. The Antichrist won't seat himself and declare himself to be God on his first entry, and the statue of his likeness will not be set until much later. It won't be long after his first trip to the temple before he will make his move to destroy the remnant of God's chosen people in Jerusalem. However, those who are truly chosen and have chosen God through faith and the truth of His Word will flee to the mountains of Israel to escape the torment of the Antichrist as Jesus has instructed them to do. God will care for them in the wilderness as the last days of the Tribulation play out. Afterwards, they will be raptured with the rest of the Church. It's interesting to note that the armies of the Antichrist will not go into the mountain regions where the believers will be located as the armies of Gog did. Perhaps they remember what happened to their brethren who were destroyed in the mountains of Israel and will want to avoid the same fate.

Verses 22 and 23 declare that these are the days of vengeance on this people, and refer only to the people of Israel who have rejected their Messiah. Even before God starts to pour out His wrath on mankind, He is allowing, one last time, the stiff-necked and rebellious from among His people to fall by the sword of their enemies. This is just one last time for the Jews to be slaughtered and go into slavery for their own sinfulness and their rejection of God's holy covenant as the whole world watches on. Not until after all of this takes place do the redeemed of the Lord see the Son of man coming. Not on His white horse with a sword, but on a cool, white cloud to deliver His people before God's wrath begins.

> [20]And *when ye shall see Jerusalem compassed with armies, then know that the desolation thereof is nigh.* [21]*Then let them which are in Judaea flee to the mountains*; and let them which are in the midst of it depart out; and let not them that are in the countries enter thereinto. [22]For these be the days of vengeance, that all things which are written may be fulfilled. [23]But woe unto them that are with child, and to them that give suck, in those days! for there shall be great distress in the land, and wrath upon this people. [24]And they shall fall by the edge of the sword, and shall be led away captive into all nations: and Jerusalem shall be trodden down of the Gentiles, *until the times of the Gentiles be fulfilled.* [25]And there shall be signs in the sun, and in the moon, and in the stars; and upon the earth distress of nations, with perplexity; the sea and the waves roaring; [26]Men's hearts failing them for fear, and for looking after those things which are coming on the earth: for the powers of heaven shall be shaken. [27]And *then shall they see the Son of man coming in a cloud with power and great glory.* [28]And when these things *begin to come to pass*, then *look up*, and lift up your heads; for *your redemption draweth nigh.*
>
> *Luke 21:20-28*

Verse 24 declares that the desecration of Israel and the Jews will continue until the time of the Gentiles is completed. Their time comes to an end in verse 27 after Jesus turns out all the lights in the sky and appears on a cloud to take His people home. He warns His people in Luke and in Matthew that the only place to look for Him will be overhead and in the clouds. In verse 27, we see once more that the redeemed are not the only ones who will see Jesus coming. "They" in verse 26, who are looking at the things that are coming on the earth and having heart failure, will see Him coming also. In verse 28, we are told to "look up, for *our* redemption draweth nigh." The Scriptures repeatedly tell us to maintain a watchful attitude, but it is really more than just an attitude. When things seem as though they could get no worse on the earth, when we witness the full fury of the Antichrist against fellow believers and Jerusalem has fallen to the enemy, then it is time to start looking to the eastern sky at the cloud formations. One of them may have more than just a silver lining. It may be the glory of the Lord as He approaches to carry us away.

The preaching of the gospel will continue through the Tribulation period as the saints minister to each other and as they reach out to others for their salvation. There will also be an army of false christs and false prophets who see that the end really is near this time. It doesn't take much to bring the nuts out, and they will be out in full force as the world declines into chaos. It won't take much either for these fakes to draw away the simpleminded, faithless and fearful who are looking for that instant spiritual gratification of having their Christ on demand. The Antichrist is a false christ himself, but he is different from all the rest. Many false christs will think they really are Jesus and will convince others to follow them. They will quote and misquote the Scriptures and insist that those who follow after them live their lives exactly the way they tell them to do.

The Antichrist, on the other hand, will despise the Scriptures and everything about God. If he does quote the Scriptures, it will be only for the purpose of intentionally leading the hearers to their own destruction by twisting and distorting God's Word in the same manner as Satan. He will claim to be God in the flesh. He may even go by the name of Christ, Jesus or Isa (as the Muslims call their version of the returning Christ). He may claim to be the fulfillment of all prophecies from all religions. But, he will despise Christians and Jews most of all. He is Satan's alter ego version of the true Christ. He will not seek to lead the Church or Christians, but he will demand their submission or destruction as infidels and traitors against a god who is not the one true Almighty God.

23Then if any man shall say unto you, Lo, here is Christ, or there; *believe it not.* 24*For there shall arise false Christs, and*

71

false prophets, and shall shew great signs and wonders; inso-much that, if it were possible, they shall deceive the very elect. 25Behold, I have told you before. 26Wherefore if they shall say unto you, Behold, he is in the desert; go not forth: behold, he is in the secret chambers; believe it not. 27*For as the lightning cometh out of the east, and shineth even unto the west; so shall also the coming of the Son of man be.*

Matthew 24:23-27

The following verse means two things: First, Jesus is making a fig-urative statement similar to when we say, "Where there's smoke, there's fire." He simply means, "That's just the way it's going to be, and you can count on it." Second, and more particularly, He is refer-ring back to the false christs and false prophets who will be attempt-ing to prey on the weak, uncommitted and confused members of the body of Christ in the same way that vultures gather to a dead carcass.

For wheresoever the carcass is, there will the eagles be gathered together.

Matthew 24:28

The Tribulation is drawing to a close at this point, and Jesus will be coming in the clouds for His saints very soon. The end of the Tribulation, the Rapture and the beginning of the Wrath of God are almost simultaneous events. The only thing separating the Tribulation from the Wrath of God is the time it takes Jesus to come back and take His Church away. Jesus does not give a detailed accounting of the Wrath of God in this conversation with His disci-ples because that was not what they had asked Him about. They wanted to know when this world would be brought to an end by the punishment of God, and how would they be able to know when it was drawing near. The events He has articulated to them so far are in direct response to their questions. The gospel must be preached in all the world, the Antichrist must be revealed to the Church—since it is the Church that is going to recognize the Antichrist, and the Tribulation must run its full course before the end comes. Jesus makes only an indirect mention of the Wrath of God beginning in verse 37 as He speaks of those who are taken away so that they might escape the wrath and those that are left behind to suffer vengeance. We get a pretty full rundown of the events that take place during God's wrath in the Book of Revelation—with the rivers turning to blood, the locust with scorpion stings, 200,000,000 horsemen from the bottomless pit that kill one third of mankind and so on. The Antichrist will still be present during the wrath, but he won't be causing tribulation any longer. He will be on the receiving end of God's wrath along with other sinners.

Jesus has finished answering the first part of the disciples' question: "When shall these things be?" And now He is about to answer the second part of their question: "What is the sign of your coming and the end of the world?" The Great Tribulation begins shortly after the Antichrist enters into the temple of God in verse 15. In verse 29 God brings a sudden conclusion to the Tribulation by shaking the powers of heaven and turning the lights in the sky into darkness. When the sun, the moon and the stars stop shining their lights, that is the one final sign that Jesus is about to appear and light up the skies with His own glory as He returns for His elect. All the other events of the end-times are signs that the final end is approaching, but they are not "the "sign of *His* coming and the end of the world." Jesus divulges some of the activities Satan will be sponsoring in the end-times so when they do take place, we will not become discouraged or disillusioned as though the world were going to come to an end as a result of the violent actions of the Antichrist or anyone else other than God Himself. God has reserved the right to judge and to bring an end to the world with His own violent punishment. He is going to interrupt the destruction of the Antichrist, remove the Church and then punish the Antichrist along with all of those who could not find room in their hearts for the One who first created them and then sent His Son to die to free them from the grip of Satan and their own sinful and destructive ways. The sign of His coming will be the lights going dark as they pay homage to the true Light of the world "after the tribulation of those days."

> *Immediately after the tribulation of those days* shall the sun
> be darkened, and the moon shall not give her light, and
> the stars shall fall from heaven, and the powers of the
> heavens shall be shaken.
>
> *Matthew 24:29*

Mark gives the same sign of Jesus' coming—the skies become darkened after the Tribulation of those days, and then He appears. The clouds He arrives on are not the sign of His coming; they are a sign that He has already arrived. While everything else is engulfed in darkness, the clouds will be very noticeable because His glory will be emanating from all around them. When verse 26 declares that "they" will see Him coming, it is talking about *everybody*. We have already seen that that is the case, and we will see it repeatedly as we continue reading. In the description of His first appearing we never see Jesus anywhere but in the clouds. He remains in the clouds and does nothing more than send His angels to collect His people.

> [24]But in those days, *after that tribulation*, the sun shall be darkened, and the moon shall not give her light, [25]And the stars of heaven shall fall, and the powers that are in heaven shall be shaken. [26]And *then shall they see the Son of man coming in the clouds* with great power and glory. [27]And then shall He send his angels, and shall gather together His elect from the four winds, from the uttermost part of the earth to the uttermost part of heaven.
>
> *Mark 13:24-27*

Paul tells us in 1 Thessalonians 1:10 that Jesus has already delivered us from the wrath to come. He did that when He died on the cross—pure and sinless in body, soul and spirit—and then was made victorious over sin and death and the iron grip of Satan by the power of God. He paid the price for our sins through His obedience as the Lamb of God. In a legal sense, we are no longer guilty for the sins we have committed because of the righteousness He has bestowed upon us. Because of that, God had to devise a plan to get us out of here before He pours His wrath upon those who slaughter the Lamb daily with their sinful disobedience. He does it by sending our Savior once again, but this time He saves us by catching us up out of here before His wrath begins, but only "after the tribulation of those days."

> And *to wait for his Son from heaven*, whom he raised from the dead, even Jesus, *which delivered us from the wrath to come*.
>
> *1 Thessalonians 1:10*

God has never before judged a people until after they are so hardened by sin that they are beyond repentance. That is the grace, the mercy and the long-suffering of God. The same will be true in the end. The world will be so enslaved to sin, the only thing left for God to do will be to bring judgment, but first He must deliver His people. He will not leave any of His children behind to suffer His vengeance. He has already purged His Church by the things they suffer in the Tribulation. God never causes tribulations and trouble for His people, but He does allow Satan to try our faith and test our allegiance to Him. God is right there during every trial to help us in our time of need, but in the end, it is up to us to cling to Him and His Word or to surrender to the pressure Satan brings against us. We succeed or fail by the decisions we make deep down in our hearts. After we have all made our decisions, it is time for God to punish those who reject Him.

THINK ABOUT IT!

— In John 17:20 Jesus said, "Neither pray I for these alone, but for them also which shall believe on me through their word." Do you suppose it is possible that when Jesus spoke to the disciples about seeing the Abomination of Desolation, the Tribulation of the latter days and His appearing in the clouds, He could have been speaking of and to those who believe through their words?

Selah

These things I have spoken unto you, that in me ye might have peace. In the world ye shall have tribulation: but be of good cheer; I have overcome the world.

John 16:33

After Those Days

Perhaps a year later, I was standing at that same window in my room, watching some of the girls from the neighborhood. I think I had a crush on every one of them, but I was shy. I have always had trouble putting sentences together in conversation, and with girls it was nearly impossible. I got scared and wobbly kneed if I even thought about speaking to a girl. Then the thought started coming to me. "All my friends are male, and they are pretty good friendships at that. I feel a closeness with my buddies. A real camaraderie. Maybe I shouldn't even be thinking about girls at all. Since all my friends are male, maybe I'm gay." That's when it hit me. Those words were not my thoughts. It was another demon spirit trying to get my lips moving, saying the wrong things. Suddenly I remembered the red words I had read in my Bible. I remembered my time in that old Baptist church. I wasn't going to allow Satan to lure me into another trap. I opened my mouth and told that spirit that I knew who he was and that he was not welcome. I told him to leave in Jesus' name. That was it. It was gone. To this day, I have to watch my thoughts when it comes to the ladies; they're so cute and sweet. There never really was a desire for men. It was all just a lie of the enemy, one that probably would have destroyed me.

The Antichrist was introduced in verse 15, and the Tribulation begins immediately afterwards. God interrupts the Tribulation of the Antichrist in verse 29 by turning the lights out on him—both to stop the wars, persecutions and bloodshed and to let everyone know that time is up. It is the sign the whole world will recognize because the whole gospel has been preached to all the world, including the good news of Jesus' triumphant return in the clouds to deliver His people. In verse 30, Jesus finally arrives in the clouds. Every eye will see Him—those who pierced Him, those who beat Him, those who mock His name, those who hate His righteous believers, those who cast His words to the ground and trample over them and, of course, those who love His appearing.

> *Looking for that blessed hope*, and *the glorious appearing* of the great God and our Saviour Jesus Christ.
>
> *Titus 2:13*

Jesus, who is frequently referred to as the Son of man in the Scriptures, appears in the heavens as He approaches in the clouds. Jesus Himself is called a sign in verse 30 because He is the final and unmistakable sign that the end of the world has arrived. It will be a sign of joy for believers who are about to be transported into the presence of God, but it will also be the sign of troubles to come for those who will have nothing to look forward to but vengeance. God's mercy may allow for a road-to-Damascus-type conversion when He appears. In Acts 9, Jesus confronted Paul as he was on his way to Damascus to persecute and kill Christians. Paul, knowing the predicament he was in, immediately submitted himself to Jesus, calling Him Lord. Paul went on to live a miraculous life of service to the Lord as opposed to being judged and condemned by God because of his fervent actions against the Church. The Holy Spirit had been attempting to convict Paul's heart of the sins he was committing, but Paul was unable to repent because of the rigorous religious training he had received. He repented quickly after Jesus confronted him and entered into a strong relationship with Him.

There may possibly be many death-bed-type conversions at the appearing of Jesus Christ in the clouds as the world is denied the luxury of denying His lordship any longer. Those who have been struggling in their own hearts between the anointing of the gospel they have heard and the other things they have been taught all their lives may get one last chance. However, because the Resurrection takes place at the sounding of the same last trump that announces the coming of Jesus and lasts for only one blink of an eye, this theory about last-minute conversions at the appearing of Jesus may not be anything more than just a theory. Anyone who decides to wait and see whether He really does appear in the sky is waiting too long.

> And *then shall appear the **sign** of the Son of man in heaven*:
> and *then shall all the tribes of the earth mourn*, and *they*
> *shall see the Son of man coming in the clouds of heaven with*
> *power and great glory*.
>
> *Matthew 24:30*

In Acts 1:9-11, the angels said to those who had just witnessed Jesus being taken up into a cloud that He would return "in like manner"—in a cloud. It may be the same cloud He left in, but this time it is bringing Him back, and we will be the ones gathered into the cloud. Revelation 1:7 tells us point blank that when He does return in the clouds "every eye shall see him, and they who pierced him." The Rapture will not be a mysterious disappearance of millions, leaving behind only shoes, ties, jackets and Bibles, but it will be openly witnessed by the whole world— sinner and saint alike—and everyone will understand what's going down, or in this case, who is going up and who is not.

> Behold, *he cometh with clouds*; and *every eye shall see him*,
> and those also which pierced Him: and all kindreds of the
> earth shall wail because of Him. Even so, Amen.
>
> *Revelation 1:7*

A shout, a trump and clouds again. In the following verses concerning the one and only Rapture, we see the heavens shaken, the final trumpet sounding and Jesus coming in the clouds to gather His own to Himself. First Thessalonians clearly illustrates that when He returns in the clouds, it is solely for the purpose of gathering His elect, both those who have already died and those who are still alive at His return. The word "we," which appears twice in verse 17, is referring to *us*. Regardless of whether we are passed away or still alive, *we* are the ones who will be caught up to the Lord in the air when He appears in the clouds for all to see. The word "we" is not referring to some other poor souls who just weren't quite good enough to make the first Rapture, so they were left behind after the really good Christians disappeared before the Tribulation started. That just doesn't happen.

> ¹³But I would not have you to be ignorant, brethren, concerning them which are asleep, that ye sorrow not, even as others which have no hope. ¹⁴For if we believe that Jesus died and rose again, even so them also which sleep in Jesus will God bring with Him. ¹⁵For this we say unto you by the word of the Lord, that we which are alive and remain unto the coming of the Lord shall not prevent them which are asleep. ¹⁶For the Lord Himself *shall descend from heaven with a shout, with the voice of the archangel,* and *with the trump of God:* and *the dead in Christ shall rise first:* ¹⁷Then *we* which are alive and remain shall be caught up together with them *in the clouds,* to meet the Lord in the air: and so shall *we* ever be with the Lord. ¹⁸Wherefore comfort one another with these words.
>
> *1 Thessalonians 4:13-18*

One problem with the pre-Tribulation Rapture theory is that if Jesus did take Christians out of the world before the Tribulation, they would not be a part of the gathering of God's people together at the final trump. Jesus comes for all of those who have passed away and are buried in the ground, and He comes for all of those who are still alive on the earth. If there were disappearing saints before the Tribulation began, they would not belong to either of these groups. They would be in scriptural limbo somewhere because the Bible never even suggests that there is a third group of believers that take part in the catching away, and it never implies that anyone is secretly snatched away.

The sound of the final trumpet. This trumpet is shown in 1 Thessalonians 4:16 and Matthew 24:31 and 1 Corinthians 15:52. This trumpet is different from the seventh and final trumpet in Revelation 11:15, which signals the final events of God's wrath. There are seven different trumpets in Revelation, chapters 8-11, that are used to signal various aspects of the judgment of God. They don't begin to sound until all of God's people are removed from the earth. The last of these seven trumpets is never called the "last trump" or "the trump of God." In fact, all that is said of it is "the seventh angel sounded," and then it goes on to point out that the time of wrath is coming to an end and the time for Jesus to take back control of the earth has come. On the contrary, what we are seeing here is God rapturing His elect at the end of the Great Tribulation and delivering them from that wrath which is ready to come bursting forth on the scene. This trumpet signals the end of the Gospel Age and God's final calling of His redeemed to Himself. If this were the final trumpet of God's wrath from Revelation 11:15, it would mean that the saints will have to go through the entire Wrath of God to get to that last of seven trumpets before being raptured. What would be the point then? Go through the Wrath of God, which God has promised to deliver us from, to get to the Rapture? It's not going to happen! No Christians will go into or come out of the Wrath of God.

In verse 31, we are told that Jesus sends out His angels to gather His elect. In the Old Testament, the word "elect" was used only four times in Isaiah. In each context, it referred to either Israel or those who would be saved through Israel. In the New Testament the Greek word translated as "elect" was translated as "elect" sixteen times and as "chosen" the remaining seven times. Oddly enough, the word means elect *and* chosen. It is used to refer to angels, individuals and the Church as a whole. The following three verses spell out just exactly what God is conveying to us when He mentions the New Testament elect.

> Who shall lay any thing to the charge of God's *elect*? It is God that justifieth.
>
> *Romans 8:33*

> *Elect* according to the foreknowledge of God the Father, through sanctification of the Spirit, unto obedience and sprinkling of the blood of Jesus Christ: Grace unto you, and peace, be multiplied.
>
> *1 Peter 1:2*

> But ye are a *chosen* generation, a royal priesthood, an holy nation, a peculiar people; that ye should shew forth the praises of him who hath called you out of darkness into his marvellous light.
>
> *1 Peter 2:9*

When Jesus sends for His New Testament elect, He is sending for those who are chosen, justified, sanctified, blood bought and obedient. He is not sending for a special group of 144,000 Jews. He is not sending for the elect half of His body and leaving the unelect half of His body behind. He is sending for His whole body of believers—the Church, the resurrected saints, the living and the dead. Any attempt to turn the elect into anything other than the whole and complete Church is wrong.

> And *he shall send his angels with a great sound of a trumpet,* and *they shall gather together his elect* from the four winds, from one end of heaven to the other.
>
> *Matthew 24:31*

Whenever we read about the Rapture, we read about being caught up or gathered together unto Christ in the clouds in full view of the whole world. We don't read about instantly disappearing, never to be seen again. First Corinthians 15 states that we will be changed instantly. That doesn't mean we will just suddenly disappear but, rather, that our mortal bodies will be changed instantly to immortal or eternal. After that, we are lifted up from the earth in the same manner Jesus was in Acts 1 as He was taken up into a cloud in full sight of all who were present to be delivered unto the Father. Our corruptible flesh cannot partake in the Rapture of the glorious Church of the Lord Jesus Christ; therefore, it must go through a transformation before it is able to be transported into heaven. At the final trump of this age (not to be confused with the final trump of the Wrath of God), the dead in Christ are raised up out of the ground with new bodies which are immortal, incorruptible, and spiritual. At the same time, those saints who are alive when Jesus returns are changed instantly to that same immortal, incorruptible and spiritual type of human being. Then we are all caught up together in full sight of the whole world into the clouds where Jesus awaits to escort us into the presence of the Father for the greatest family reunion of all eternity.

First Thessalonians 4:16, which we just read, says that the dead in Christ will rise first. The dead saints do not rise into the skies before those who are still alive; they are raised up from out of the earth first in the Resurrection, and then we are all raised up off of the face of the earth together to meet the Lord in the air. In other words, the Resurrection takes place moments before the Rapture so that we have the right equipment for traveling through space and living in heaven. That equipment is our resurrected bodies. The whole fifteenth chapter of 1 Corinthians is about resurrection. It begins with Paul speaking of the Resurrection of Jesus. As he continues his monologue, he speaks of the resurrection of our bodies. In verse 13, he makes a hapless observation about the sad state we would find ourselves in if there were no such thing as the resurrection of the dead. If that were the case, then Christ died like the rest of us and He is still in His grave. In verse 20, he declares that Christ is indeed risen from the dead, and that He is only the first of many who will come out of the graves. In verse 23, Paul makes it as plain as day that the Resurrection takes place at the same time Jesus arrives to take His Church away. Christ was risen from the dead first, and then many years afterwards all of those who belong to Him will be supernaturally pulled out of their graves at His appearing.

In verses 24 through 26, Paul makes several statements of fact upon which all end-times theology rests. The first statement is quite simple—"then cometh the end." After making that statement, he elaborates a bit on what the end entails. Jesus will reign from heaven until He has put down all rule, authority and power, other than that which was granted to Him by God. The last power He will conquer is death. When He returns for His Church, He will have the power to free our bodies from the dust of the earth and set us on our feet again in new and revised bodies, bodies that will never again have to taste of death. He already possesses that power, but He does not yet have the go ahead from God to accomplish it. Our resurrection is His victory over death once and forever. Before that happens, Satan will be cast out of heaven as a first step towards bringing an end to all opposing authority. Satan and the Antichrist will both be forcing their authority in the earth right up to the end when Jesus delivers His people, and then Jesus will exercise full authority over the earth by releasing wrath on those who deserve it. After He lands a knockout blow to death and gets us out of here, He will show the disobedient rebels who refused His pleas of compassion that He really is boss. Every knee will bow, and every tongue will confess that Jesus Christ is Lord.

¹³But *if there be no resurrection of the dead, then is Christ not risen*: ¹⁴And if Christ be not risen, then is our preaching vain, and your faith is also vain. ¹⁵Yea, and we are found false witnesses of God; because we have testified of God that He raised up Christ: whom He raised not up, if so be that the dead rise not. ¹⁶For if the dead rise not, then is not Christ raised: ¹⁷And if Christ be not raised, your faith is vain; ye are yet in your sins. ¹⁸Then they also which are fallen asleep in Christ are perished. ¹⁹If in this life only we have hope in Christ, we are of all men most miserable. ²⁰But now is Christ risen from the dead, and become the firstfruits of them that slept. ²¹For since by man came death, by man came also the resurrection of the dead. ²²For as in Adam all die, even so in Christ shall all be made alive. ²³But every man in his own order: *Christ the firstfruits; afterward they that are Christ's at his coming.* ²⁴*Then cometh the end, when he shall have delivered up the kingdom to God,* even the Father; *when he shall have put down all rule and all authority and power.* ²⁵For he must reign, till he hath put all enemies under his feet. ²⁶*The last enemy that shall be destroyed is death.*

1 Corinthians 15:13-26

In verse 24, another prerequisite for the end is that Jesus must deliver up the kingdom to God. Because the kingdom of God is more of a spiritual kingdom at this time made up of spiritual people who have made themselves subject to the dictates of God's Word, Jesus needs only to rapture His people and escort them into the presence of God to deliver up the kingdom. Eventually, the kingdom of God will literally fill and control the earth, but only after God has punished those who reject Him. After the wicked are punished, Jesus will bring the saints back to the earth to rule with Him. This happens when He returns to the earth a second time with the saints of God at His side for the Battle of Armageddon after the seventh trumpet of wrath sounds. His second return is on a white horse and not in the clouds. It will be years after the Tribulation and not "immediately after the tribulation of those days" like when He comes to collect the saints. When the end does come, it is a process that is called the Wrath of God, and it takes several years for that wrath to complete. Jesus has full control over the earth, the Antichrist and even death during the outpouring of God's wrath, but He does not physically step in to defeat the armies of the earth and reign over the nations who sent those armies until He is good and ready, and that is after the Marriage Supper of the Lamb, and after the sounding of the seventh trumpet of wrath.

The next two verses from 1 Corinthians 15 inform us that we will be changed at the last trump of the age of grace. This is the same trump from Matthew 24:31 that announces the coming of the Lord in the clouds. The change we go through is the conversion from mortal to immortal. It is the same change the dead go through when they are "raised" up out of their graves. The word "raised" is used twenty times in 1 Corinthians 15, and it carries the same meaning as the word "resurrection" which is used just four times. It is used exclusively in describing the raising of the dead from the ground. The word "raised" is not used in describing the Rapture in 1 Corinthians 15 at all, but we can see that it takes place before the Rapture can take place. There will not be any mortal bodies going into heaven; they wouldn't be able to stand the trip. These verses are not telling us that the Rapture will occur in the twinkling of an eye; it is the changing of our bodies which will take place that fast, and then we are caught up to the Lord in the clouds as those clouds approach our current location on the earth wherever we may be. In verse 52, the dead are not being raised *off* the earth, they are raised *out of* the earth and then go through the Resurrection transformation before they can become airborne, along with those who are alive and remain. Verse 26 above declares that the last enemy to be destroyed is death. Verse 54 below informs us that death will be swallowed up in victory during the Resurrection. "Then cometh the end" of this world when He shall subdue all things unto Himself, including death at the Resurrection, when He returns in the clouds to remove His people from a condemned world.

> [51]Behold, I show you a mystery; We shall not all sleep, but *we shall all be changed,* [52]In a moment, in the twinkling of an eye, *at the last trump: for the trumpet shall sound,* and the dead shall be raised incorruptible, and we shall be changed. [53]For this corruptible must put on incorruption, and this mortal must put on immortality. [54]So when this corruptible shall have put on incorruption, and this mortal shall have

put on immortality, then shall be brought to pass the saying that is written, *Death is swallowed up in victory*.

1 Corinthians 15:51-54

In John 6:39,40,44 and 54, and again in John 11:24, we learn from
Jesus' conversations with Martha that the day of the Resurrection is
the "last day." Between verses 23 and 52 above, we learn that the
Resurrection and the Rapture occur at the last trump, and all three of
these things alert us to the fact that the last day has arrived. As mentioned, this is the same trumpet that sounds in verse 31 of Matthew 24
to discharge the angels of God into the earth to gather Christ's elect.
The last trump of the Gospel Age calls the dead saints out of the
ground and sends the angels to gather the whole body of Christ. This
all happens as Jesus swoops in low on the clouds to rescue His fan
club. In John 12:48 Jesus declares that His word will judge those who
reject it when the last day arrives. That statement is much broader in
that those who reject His word will be severed from those who have
received it when the last trump sounds, and they will be left behind to
suffer God's wrath. The same word will judge them a thousand years
later as they stand before the Lord at the White Throne Judgment.

The next two verses communicate once more that the Rapture is
something that will be seen. Verse 20 reminds us to look for Him to
return from the heavens. We have nothing to look for if His return is
to be in an invisible stealth fashion. Verse 21 confirms that the
Resurrection takes place at the same time as the Rapture and that it
is a part of the end when He will subdue all things unto Himself.

> [20]For our conversation is in heaven; *from whence also we
> look for the Saviour*, the Lord Jesus Christ: [21]*Who shall
> change our vile body, that it may be fashioned like unto his
> glorious body*, according to the working whereby he is able
> even to subdue all things unto himself.
>
> *Philippians 3:20-21*

God is not the great game show host of the sky giving us a choice
between Rapture number one, Rapture number two or Rapture
number three. We do not get a choice between disappearing before
the Tribulation or being caught up after the Tribulation. There is not

one Resurrection for "pre-Trib" saints and another for "post-Trib" saints. There is not one Rapture for Gentile Christians and something different for Jewish Christians. We are all of the same body. God does not deliver the good guys before the Tribulation and leave the not-so-good guys to suffer in the Tribulation and Wrath until they finally get it right and become worthy of some kind of secondary Rapture. There is only one Rapture and one Resurrection—not two, not many—just one of each, and they both follow the Tribulation and precede the Wrath. After the Tribulation, Jesus will appear in the sky just as the Resurrection is taking place. He will have His angels pick the saints up off of the earth, one by one, and carry them up into the clouds to ever be with Him.

Jesus will appear in the skies a second time approximately seven years later on a white horse at the Battle of Armageddon to bring a conclusion to the time of God's wrath and to bring in everlasting righteousness and peace by taking control of the earth. When He arrives from heaven on His white horse, the same saints that He is rapturing right here in Matthew 24 after the Tribulation will be returning with Him and His angels after enjoying the Wedding Feast of the Lamb. There will not be any new saints to rapture after the Wrath of God. We will take on the armies of the earth and prevail against them, and everyone else who is left on the earth will come under the immediate and absolute rule of Christ and His saints for the thousand-year reign. The Bible never tells us that these people are saved but, rather, that they are hardened and unrepentant.

> Now learn a parable of the fig tree; When his branch is yet tender, and putteth forth leaves, ye know that summer is nigh.
>
> *Matthew 24:32*

At several places in the Scriptures, the fig tree represents Israel, but that is not necessarily the case here. If it is the case, then we have only fifty or so years left before all these things must be completed. However, the same account in Luke 21:29 says "the fig tree and all the trees." Jesus is just making the point that from the beginning of these events to their conclusion, the time will be short, and when we begin to see them come to pass, it won't be long until the end. The same thought is continued in the next four verses. In verse 34, the generation that shall not pass away until all these things happen is the last days generation and should not be mistaken for the generation Jesus was conversing with at the time, as some people believe. Verse 33 explains that we will see all of these things come to pass before the return of Christ and the end of the world. The Church has to be here if we are going to see all these things come to pass. If we disappear right after the gospel has been preached in all the world, we will not be here to see any of it. We won't see the Antichrist, we won't see the Tribulation, and we won't see the sign of the heavens going dark just before Jesus appears to catch us all away. In other words, if we disappear too soon, we are going to miss the Rapture.

> 33So likewise ye, *when ye shall see all these things*, know that
> it is near, even at the doors. 34Verily I say unto you, This
> generation shall not pass, till all these things be fulfilled.
> 35Heaven and earth shall pass away, but my words shall not
> pass away. 36But of that day and hour knoweth no man, no,
> not the angels of heaven, but my Father only.
>
> *Matthew 24:33-36*

Just because Jesus said that no man knows the day or the hour of His return and the end of the world, it doesn't mean we are supposed to ignore every sign He has given us and play ignorant when these things begin to come to pass. In verse 33, He explains that when we see these things begin to happen around us we will know that it is right upon us. In fact, He emphasized that we would *see all these things*" before the day of His arrival. When He said that no man knows the hour, He was simply saying that God had not revealed it to anyone, not even to His Son. That statement was made in the past, but it is still very true today. God has still not revealed the day or the hour to anyone yet, but that does not preclude us from knowing that approximately—in fact, nearly to the day—seven full years after Israel makes a peace accord with a ten-nation alliance led by one who is immediately revealed to us as the Antichrist by the peace accord, He will return to catch His people away.

We can see that great progress is being made in preaching the gospel around the world, but only God can determine when the job is done. After He has determined that the job is completed to His liking; then He will cast Satan out of heaven and allow him to test those who have just received the Word of God. After that testing begins, we can believe all the signs written in the Bible concerning the end-times, and we will know when the day of His return is almost upon us. We don't know the day or the hour of His return, but we will be able to predict within a few days or weeks after these things begin. The Bible tells us that the Tribulation begins in the middle of the seven-year peace accord and will last for the entire second half of it. Jesus just told us that He will return immediately after the Tribulation. There's not much math to do here. All we have to do is make it to the end of that three-and-one-half years, and then wait.

The Church seems to have adopted a philosophy that any interpretation of the end-times prophecies that allows the Church any awareness of Christ's imminent return must be false, because if we see any of the signs of His return, then we will be able to know with reasonable certainty the day that He will appear in the clouds. After all, no man knows the hour of His return. However, nothing could be further from the truth. Jesus has made it clear, as do the rest of the Scriptures, that He will return for His elect after the Tribulation. The elect Jesus will return for is all the elect of God who are justified by God. He is not returning for just a part of the Church. He is not returning for Jews only. He is not returning for just 144,000 Jews. He is returning for all those who have died in faith, and all those who are still living by faith when it is time for His return.

Even if there was a pre-Tribulation Rapture, we have to be honest enough to admit that with the gospel being preached to all of the world, and with many formerly enlightened but yet totally uncommitted Christians not included in that Rapture, all of this information will have already been disseminated to those who are left behind. They would be able to immediately recognize from the peace covenant, the desecration of the temple or any of the other signs how much more time they have. There will not be a pre-Trib Rapture, but if there was, it does not mean that the minds of all of those left behind are suddenly drained of intelligence. They would be able to figure it out, which means that the denial the Church has been in has only robbed us of the truth. Jesus was simply saying that God is not going to post the date ahead of time because He does not want the Church sitting around on their duffs waiting for that day, and living it up along the way. There would be even less commited Christians if the date was posted ahead of time. As the signs begin to unfold before our eyes, we will be able to use that as evidence and a wake-up call to people around us to get them saved. That is, if we are awake and abiding in the light ourselves.

Paul insists in 1 Thessalonians that those who are awake and sober and watchful are not going to be caught by surprise when Jesus returns. Why? Because all the signs to watch for were given to us by Jesus. Verse 9 below has been a comfort through the ages. Paul asserts that those of us who are following Jesus with a committed heart are not appointed to—will not see, experience or go through—the Wrath of God. As we differentiate between the Wrath and the Tribulation, we can see that going through the Tribulation—which is simply the worst time of turmoil caused by Satan that the world has ever known—is not the same as going through the Wrath of God, which is His punishment for all the turmoil caused by sin and sinners. Despite the massive degradation of world stability through an increase of violent and sinful behavior—most notably that initiated by the Antichrist—we can still go through the Tribulation with the assurance that God has not forsaken His people, and that His deliverer is only three-and-one-half years away from the start of the Tribulation; then the Wrath of God will come.

> [4]*But ye*, brethren, *are not in darkness, that that day should overtake you as a thief.* [5]Ye are all the children of light, and the children of the day: we are not of the night, nor of darkness. [6]*Therefore let us not sleep, as do others; but let us watch and be sober.* [7]For they that sleep sleep in the night; and they that be drunken are drunken in the night. [8]But let us, who are of the day, be sober, putting on the breastplate of faith and love; and for an helmet, the hope of salvation. [9]*For God hath not appointed us to wrath, but to obtain salvation by our Lord Jesus Christ,*
>
> 1 Thessalonians 5:4-9

The Day of the Lord is mentioned quite frequently in the Bible. It is called by different names in different places, but it is always the same thing—the day God's wrath begins to fall on the wicked. The reason we want to look at the Day of the Lord at this point is because it begins with the same sign Jesus gave His disciples of His coming and of the end of the world. In Acts 2:20, Peter condensed the words of Joel 3:15 and 16 to say, "The sun shall be turned into darkness, and the moon into blood, **before that great and notable day of the Lord come.**" This is exactly what Jesus is telling us in Matthew 24 and the other Gospels. The word "come" was added after the Day of the Lord to express in one word what Joel was saying when he informed us that the Lord would roar out of Zion and be the hope of His people. The deliverance of God's people is tied together with the judgment of the heathen. Multitudes are in the valley of decision, and on day one of the Day of the Lord, God will divide between those who choose righteousness and those who choose death.

Jesus did not make things up as He was going along; He received insight from the Old Testament by the Holy Spirit and passed it on to His disciples. When He told them that the heavens would be shaken and the sun and moon and stars would cease to shine before His return, He was repeating what He had read in Joel and elsewhere. The first two verses speak about the Battle of Armageddon, which will take place as a part of God's vengeance, but it actually takes place at the very end of several years of different kinds of punishment from God. When we get into the Revelation, we will see all of the different aspects of God's wrath and how it all unfolds.

> [9]Proclaim ye this among the Gentiles; Prepare war, wake up the mighty men, let all the men of war draw near; let them come up: [10]Beat your plowshares into swords, and your pruning hooks into spears: let the weak say, I am strong. [11]Assemble yourselves, and come, all ye heathen, and gather yourselves together round about: there cause thy mighty ones to come down, O Lord. [12]Let the heathen be wakened, and come up to the valley of Jehoshaphat: for there will I sit to judge all the heathen round about. [13]Put ye in the sickle, for the harvest is ripe: come, get you down; for the press is full, the fats overflow; for their wickedness is great. [14]Multitudes, multitudes in the valley of decision: for the day of the Lord is near in the valley of decision. [15]*The sun and the moon shall be darkened, and the stars*

shall withdraw their shining. [16]*The* Lord also shall roar out of Zion, and utter his voice from Jerusalem; and *the heavens and the earth shall shake*: but *the* Lord will be the hope of his people, and the strength of the children of Israel.

Joel 3:9-16

The Day of the Lord is called "the day of vengeance" in several places. When Jesus proclaims in Luke 4:18 that the Spirit of the Lord is upon Him, He is paraphrasing Isaiah 61:2 which announces to us that He will come "to proclaim the acceptable year of the Lord, and **the day of vengeance of our God**; to comfort all that mourn." A part of the purpose of the anointing of the Holy Spirit is to preach, teach and proclaim the coming day of wrath from God Almighty, along with providing the power and guidance needed to avoid that wrath through faith. In Isaiah 63:4, God lumps the final redemption of His people and the day of His vengeance together when He declares, "For the day of vengeance is in mine heart, and the year of my redeemed is come." The reason He mentions them in the same breath is because they both take place at the same time, even though the deliverance of His people takes only a single day, while God's vengeance and wrath begin on that same day, after the Church is gone, and lasts for several years. When we get into the Book of Revelation, we are going to see just how long the Wrath of God really takes. In Jeremiah 46:10, the day of vengeance is also called the day of the Lord God of hosts. Even though it is a day of punishment for so many multitudes, God still looks forward to it with a sense of great pleasure and anticipation because it is the same day He will finally deliver His people forever from the miseries that are continually inflicted upon them by those who hate them.

In Philippians 1:10 and 2:16 and 2 Thessalonians 2:2, the day is called the day of Christ. The first two references simply mention the day of Christ in passing. They do not give any details or enlightenment concerning what the day of Christ is all about. However, 2 Thessalonians 2:2 is different. We read it earlier in this chapter where Paul gives warning to the Church that the day of Christ will not come until there is a falling away and the man of sin is revealed. That statement is in full agreement with Jesus' statement about appearing in the clouds for His elect "after the tribulation of the final days."

Isaiah 13 gives us a very clear explanation of what the Day of the Lord will be like for the heathen who reject God. We can see from this passage that the Day of the Lord is a day marked by destruction from God upon sinners. The only good thing that comes out of it is found in verse 12. God is going to make a man more precious than a wedge of gold. He does this by giving His righteous saints victory over death, removing them from the earth and destroying those who have been selling them out for a few dollars profit. We see once again that this destruction from the Almighty begins on that day when the heavens are shaken and the heavenly lights cease to shine.

> ⁶Howl ye; for *the day of the Lord* is at hand; *it shall come as a destruction from the Almighty.* ⁷Therefore shall all hands be faint, and every man's heart shall melt: ⁸And they shall be afraid: pangs and sorrows shall take hold of them; they shall be in pain as a woman that travaileth: they shall be amazed one at another; their faces shall be as flames. ⁹Behold, *the day of the Lord cometh, cruel both with wrath and fierce anger*, to lay the land desolate: *and he shall destroy the sinners thereof out of it.* ¹⁰*For the stars of heaven and the constellations thereof shall not give their light: the sun shall be darkened in His going forth, and the moon shall not cause her light to shine.* ¹¹And *I will punish the world for their evil, and the wicked for their iniquity*; and I will cause the arrogancy of the proud to cease, and will lay low the haughtiness of the terrible. ¹²I will make a man more precious than fine gold; even a man than the golden wedge of Ophir. ¹³Therefore I will shake the heavens, and the earth shall remove out of her place, *in the wrath of the* Lord *of hosts, and in the day of his fierce anger.*
>
> *Isaiah 13:6-13*

The description of the Day of the Lord varies depending on the context in which you read it. In the Old Testament the emphasis is usually on those who are going to be punished, with brief mention of those who are going to be rescued from that punishment. In the New Testament, the rescue aspect is mentioned a lot since those who are going to be rescued are the ones receiving the message. And then there's

The Revelation, which gives the most extensive description of both the rescue and the punishment of the end-times, and repeats it several times over. In Matthew 24 that rescue takes place in verses 29-31 after the Tribulation is abruptly brought to a close as the skies turn to blackness. In the remainder of Matthew 24, we see that those who remain on the earth, after Jesus takes His people away, will be the ones who will suffer loss. The Wrath of God is no less than a declaration of war against sinners at the end of the world. When a country declares war against another country, they immediately begin to pull their diplomats out of the enemy's territory for their own safety. This is what God does when He sends Jesus to pull His diplomats out of the earth. After the Church is gone, the war can begin.

THINK ABOUT IT!

— Does Matthew 24:29-31 describe the Rapture—the catching away of believers, the blessed hope, the appearing of Jesus—or does it describe some other event?

— When did Jesus say He would gather His New Testament elect?

— Does the Bible ever say that Jesus will make an invisible visit to the earth or that Christians will disappear suddenly without notice?

— Did Jesus say that He would come again for believers, or that He would come often for believers?

Selah

Beloved, now are we the sons of God, and it doth not yet appear what we shall be: but we know that, *when he shall appear*, we shall be like him; *for we shall see him* as he is.

1 John 3:2

MATTHEW 24

The Missing Wrath

As I neared my eighteenth year, I began to drink some with the guys from the neighborhood. We were beginning to expand out of the neighborhood with new friends from school and from our various jobs. I don't recall ever having a single Christian friend during this time. I did experiment with drugs, but thankfully had enough good sense not to pursue that and, in fact, I avoided drugs and those who used them. Drinking was another story. I was depressed so I drank. I would laugh so hard as we bantered back and forth, exchanging crude jokes and dirty one-liners, but inside I was crying. There was something missing. I felt so empty. Eventually drinking just made me more depressed. Just one of the many vicious cycles of sin that Satan offers to innocent and ignorant little Baptist boys.

The remaining Scriptures are still describing the Rapture as they differentiate between those who are taken and those that are left behind to experience God's wrath. Jesus likens it to the day that Noah entered into the ark which "raptured" Noah and his family up above the floods of God's judgment coming down upon the ungodly.

> 37*But as the days of Noah were, so shall also the coming of the Son of man be.* 38For as in the days that were before the

flood they were eating and drinking, marrying and giving in marriage, until the day that Noah entered into the ark, [39]And knew not until the flood came, and took them all away; so shall also the coming of the Son of man be.

Matthew 24:37-39

One interesting thing about what we just read is the fact that the ark was a sign of gigantic proportions to the people who lived before the flood, and yet, they were taken by surprise when the flood came. Second Peter 2:5 informs us that Noah was a preacher of righteousness. He didn't preach to the animals on the ark; he preached to the people before the flood. It took him one hundred years to build the ark, and the preacher Noah was not keeping any secrets. The earth was still one language, and they more than likely remained clustered around the Middle East after Adam was removed from the Garden of Eden. The natural tendency of man is to be a part of a larger group for security and companionship. God did not confuse the language of men at the Tower of Babel and separate them into nations until after the flood of Noah. For one hundred years, people came to see the ark and listened to Noah rant and rave about turning from sin and maintaining a right relationship with God. He warned the world of the coming judgment of God. His family trusted and believed him, but the rest of the world mocked him until the day the flood came.

By reading the genealogies in Genesis, we get the impression that the population of the earth was not that great. Men lived from one to two hundred years short of a full millennium before they died. We are given the names of some of their sons and informed that they had daughters also, but we do not know exactly how prolific they really were. Noah was only the tenth generation of man from Adam, and God had not as yet spread mankind over the earth. When Noah was born, anybody that was over two hundred and fifty-six years old would have known Adam and his stories of walking in the garden with God, but by the time Noah was five hundred, God was instructing him to build an ark so He could save Noah and his family as He destroyed the rest of mankind, which had become totally corrupted by sin. The flood of Noah occurred approximately seventeen hundred and eighty-six years after Adam was created, and eight hundred and fifty-six years after he died, according to the genealogical information provided in Genesis. In such a short time sin had taken over the whole thought process of every living person on earth except for Noah and his family. God had to take dramatic action if He wanted to maintain a righteous seed on the earth. If He did not eliminate the thoroughly negative influence of the rest of the world, the subsequent generations of Noah would be corrupted also. As in the days of Noah, God is going to have to judge all flesh once more and bring an end to the world as we know it. And, as in the days of Noah, the world will be warned of the coming judgment of God, but many will mock and curse the return of Jesus and the Wrath of God until the day the sky turns black. Second Peter 3:3-4 points out that the scoffers of the last days who walk after their own lusts will be saying, "Where is the promise of His coming?" "Nothing has changed. We're safe. God doesn't care what we do. He hasn't intervened yet, and He's not going to intervene." And then cometh the end!

In verse 39 above, we need to notice a few other things. When the Scripture says, "**They** knew not until the flood came and took them all away," "they" refers to the sinners not knowing that the flood was coming, but the ones who were taken away refers to Noah and his family being taken away as they were lifted above the flood inside the ark. Those who were caught off guard were overwhelmed and destroyed by the flood. Those who were not taken away in the ark were left behind to experience God's judgment, just as those who are not taken away when Christ appears for His Church will be left to experience God's wrath. While Noah was building the ark, everyone else was going happily about their lives until he finished, and then it began to rain buckets of water on the earth after Noah was secure in the ark. In the day Jesus returns to remove His chosen from the deluge of wrath that is about to begin, sinners and some very lukewarm saints will be totally caught off guard, even though the warnings will be broadcast by the Church and the signs will be evident.

Noah was not caught off guard at all when it began to rain. God had fully informed him of all of His plans. The Word of God that came to Noah and the progress he was making on the ark allowed Noah to see the day of deluge fast approaching. After driving the final stake and sealing the final seam, he knew the day had arrived, even though he didn't know the exact day or hour. After the ark was completed, God spoke to Noah again and told him that he had seven days to get the ark loaded and then it was going to rain. The parade of animals loaded onto the ark was a sign that the flood was imminent, but Noah also had a set number of days straight from the mouth of God. With all those animals on board, if it did not rain soon, Noah was going to have problems on his hands. Last, but not least, the people had to board the ship. Genesis 7:13 bears record to the fact that on the very day Noah and his family entered into the ark, it began to rain. "As in the days of Noah, so also shall the coming of the Son of man be." In the very same day we board those heaven-bound clouds, the flood of God's vengeance will begin to fall.

The preaching of the gospel, the Antichrist, the Tribulation, the blackened heavens—these will all be signs to everyone on the face of the earth. We have been given more than just signs, though; just like God gave Noah, He has given us many specific and reliable numbers that help us to know how things will unfold in the end-times and how long they will take. God has not told anybody, not even Jesus, what day these things will begin to happen, but when they do begin to take place, we will be able to count down the days just like Noah did. Many people all over the world will miss the signs; and others will choose to ignore them even as Christians are heralding the coming of the end. A preoccupation with sin or an outright rebellion against God will exclude many from the deliverance God is about to send. Just as it was with Noah, God has given us all advance warning so that we will be ready, waiting and full of hope and expectancy, rather than despair and despondency. And, just as Noah, we are to be sounding the alarm to anyone who will listen. In Noah's day, they did not know judgment was coming until the day it began because they did not believe Noah and they did not believe the sign of the ark. They thought it was the folly of a mad man. Those who ignore the warnings God has given in His word and those who dismiss the warnings as foolishness, in the end-times will be suddenly overcome by the judgment of wrath. No man knows the day or the hour, but those who heed the warnings and watch over their own spiritual welfare will know that the day is right at the door before they ever hear the sound of knocking because they will see it coming by the signs.

In the remainder of Matthew 24, Jesus is telling us to be ready always. When He does return, it will not be for sinners, and it will not be for those "Christians" who are preoccupied with sin and

97

overwhelmed by the affairs of this life. He's coming for a spotless Church, so we need to be ready. As we approach the end of the Tribulation, life will go on as usual in many parts of the world. However, as we look at world events and the things happening in the Middle East, it may seem as though He has forgotten all about us, but that is not going to happen.

> 40Then shall two be in the field; the one shall be taken, and the other left. 41Two women shall be grinding at the mill; the one shall be taken, and the other left. 42Watch therefore: for ye know not what hour your Lord doth come. 43But know this, that if the goodman of the house had known in what watch the thief would come, he would have watched, and would not have suffered his house to be broken up. 44Therefore be ye also ready: for in such an hour as ye think not the Son of man cometh. 45Who then is a faithful and wise servant, whom his lord hath made ruler over his household, to give them meat in due season? 46Blessed is that servant, whom his lord when he cometh shall find so doing. 47Verily I say unto you, That he shall make him ruler over all his goods. 48*But and if that evil servant shall say in his heart, My lord delayeth his coming; 49And shall begin to smite his fellowservants, and to eat and drink with the drunken; 50The lord of that servant shall come in a day when he looketh not for him, and in an hour that he is not aware of, 51And shall cut him asunder, and appoint him his portion with the hypocrites: there shall be weeping and gnashing of teeth.*
>
> *1 Thessalonians 5:2-4*

Jesus is not trying to convince us that the whole Church is going to be caught completely off guard along with the rest of the world when He returns. It is those servants who say in their hearts, "My Lord will not be returning anytime soon, let me see what I can get away with," who will be "cut asunder." If we are watching the signs, and it appears that the Lord couldn't possibly come for another ten or twenty years and we decide to dabble in sin, we could be overcome by that sin to the point that our spiritual senses become dull and the day approaches us while we are busy with other things. There are many signs that Jesus does not even mention in this conversation with His disciples, such as Israel becoming a nation again. The fact that it has re-emerged as a nation tells us that the day of His return is near. However, there is no temple yet, which suggests that the day is still delayed. If we use that information as a window of opportunity for sin, it will backfire on us!

We are told in 1 Thessalonians 5:2 that the Day of the Lord will come as a thief in the night, but only for those who seek for the golden age of peace and safety through political and worldly means. In other words, those who cry "peace and safety" at the signing of the Antichrist peace accord will not be looking for the physical return of Christ and, therefore, will be caught off guard. They are looking for world peace in this lifetime because they love this life filled with the lusts of the flesh, the lusts of the eyes and the pride of life. Much of the world—many Jews included—will be crying "peace and safety" after the Antichrist has taken control of his final end-times kingdom and appears to bring peace to the most volatile part of the globe through a false seven-year peace accord. He may appear to some to be the "savior" of the world, or at least his part of the world, until halfway through the seven years when he turns against the Jews, Christians and anyone else who opposes him. His followers are already convinced that the Jews are the biggest problem they face, and together they begin the final "holocaust" by attempting to eliminate them from the face of the earth. During the time of the Great Tribulation, sudden destruction will come upon the unbelieving of Israel, and according to Revelation 6:8, at least a quarter of mankind will die as the Antichrist brings sudden destruction on the earth. The Antichrist will not be allowed to complete the destruction that he intends upon the earth because God will cut His own work short in righteousness when He sends Jesus to gather His elect. Afterwards, the real "sudden destruction" will come upon the world through the Wrath of God. In verse 4, we are informed that the day will not have that same element of surprise for those who are watching and waiting for His return. We have been enlightened. We have been given all the signs. Now all we have to do is observe those signs as they begin to appear and count down to the day when Jesus finally appears.

> ²For yourselves know perfectly that the day of the Lord so cometh as a thief in the night. ³For when they shall say, Peace and safety; then sudden destruction cometh upon them, as travail upon a woman with child; and they shall not escape. ⁴*But ye, brethren, are not in darkness, that that day should overtake you as a thief.*
>
> *1 Thessalonians 5:2-4*

Jesus tells us in different places that we should watch and be ready—or watch and pray. The idea of being watchful is more than just keeping our eyes glued to the newspapers to see what is transpiring in the world or staring into the sky watching for His appearance. He wants us to watch over our own spiritual attitudes and well-being. If we don't, we slip into a spiritual slumber or blindness that allows Satan to creep in and rob us of our inheritance. We slowly wither away on the vine until God has to prune us away. At the same time, a simple awareness of the fact that Jesus is going to come again to deliver His faithful servants and cast everyone else into a flood of wrath helps us to keep our focus. Whether it appears that Jesus' return is imminent or not, we should always be ready and in an attitude of preparedness. If we become complacent about the return of the Lord, even if there are no observable signs taking place at the time, we may soon slip into a sinful lifestyle. Once a person begins to slip into a lifestyle of sin, it is hard to turn around. Repentance is always available as long as a person has not asked Jesus and the Holy Spirit to depart from their lives, but it becomes more difficult with each passing day to turn back to righteousness. For those who fall into sin and remain in sin at the return of the Lord, Peter has a simple message for them: the same message that Jesus gave us at the end of Matthew 24 in the above scripture.

> The Lord knoweth how to deliver the godly out of temptations, and to reserve the unjust unto the day of judgment to be punished.
>
> *2 Peter 2:9*

Luke makes the comparison between the days of Noah and the days leading up to the Rapture much clearer. He makes it abundantly clear that God's judgment begins to pour out on sinners on the very day Jesus removes His redeemed from the earth. The Tribulation of the Antichrist does not begin on the day Jesus appears in the sky;that is the day it comes to an end! It is the Wrath of God that begins, but only after He gathers His elect from the four corners of the earth. Verses 26-29 make it clear that on the same day that Noah entered into the ark and on the same day that Lot went out of Sodom, God's judgments came to destroy all of those who were left. The point made by both Matthew and Luke is that God's judgment always follows immediately *after* He delivers the righteous out of harm's way. After Noah and Lot were delivered, all those who remained were destroyed. Verses 30-36 tell us that at the appearing of Jesus, one will be taken into the clouds and the other left to suffer God's wrath. After Jesus delivers His Church, many will be destroyed in God's wrath, but not all. Some will remain after the wrath to populate the millennial kingdom of Jesus Christ, but it won't be people who were saved during the wrath; it will be the heathen who were spared from death in the vengeance of God. This distinction is made in Revelation and elsewhere.

> 26And as it was in the days of Noah, so shall it be also in the days of the Son of man. 27They did eat, they drank, they married wives, they were given in marriage, *until the day that Noah entered into the ark, and the flood came, and destroyed them all.* 28Likewise also as it was in the days of Lot; they did eat, they drank, they bought, they sold, they planted, they builded; 29But *the same day that Lot went out of Sodom it rained fire and brimstone from heaven, and destroyed them all.* 30*Even thus shall it be in the day when the Son of man is revealed.* 31In that day, he which shall be upon the housetop, and his stuff in the house, let him not come down to take it away: and he that is in the field, let him likewise not return back. 32Remember Lot's wife. 33Whosoever shall seek to save his life shall lose it; and whosoever shall lose his life shall preserve it. 34I tell you, in that night there shall be two men in one bed; the one shall be taken, and the other shall be left. 35Two women shall be grinding together; the one shall be taken, and the other left. 36Two men shall be in the field; the one shall be taken, and the other left.
>
> *Luke 17:26-36*

Remember Lot's wife. She was not actively involved in the sin of the city of Sodom, but she loved her life there nonetheless. She turned to look back because she was going to miss her nice home with all the fine things they had accumulated over the years and because she was going to miss the culture with all of its open sin and all the people enjoying themselves in that sin. Many Christians today who have been abundantly blessed with nice material things and who spend a good portion of the day being entertained by the sin of others on radio, TV, the Internet and elsewhere will find it hard when Jesus appears to give all that up and to surrender to Jesus for the final deliverance of their bodies and souls. They'll be more concerned with their big plans for the day, the possessions they have worked so hard for or what is going to happen on tonight's episode of "Sex and the City." If this was not the case, Jesus would not have had to issue the warning about Lot's wife to those He is coming to catch away. Remember Lot's wife and don't become attached to the things of this world. Our life is in Him, and our affections should be set on heavenly things.

Matthew 25 is actually a continuation of the final thoughts of Matthew 24. We all know the story of the five wise virgins who kept their lamps filled with oil and the five foolish virgins who ran out of oil and were not allowed to enter the wedding. We also know the story of the servants who were given various amounts of money with which to do business. Both stories are about servanthood, faithfulness and maintaining a busy and vigilant attitude while we await our master's return. We are not going to look any further into those two parables, but the third item which Jesus mentions does need some explanation. It is less of a parable and more of a description of the final judgment. When Jesus sits on His throne to judge all of mankind, He will separate those who humbly and faithfully serve Him with works of compassion and those who just couldn't seem to find the time or resources needed to serve the Lord and, in fact, overlooked every need but their own. We want to look briefly at when this judgment actually takes place.

> [31]When the Son of man shall come in his glory, and all the holy angels with him, then shall he sit upon the throne of his glory: [32]And before him shall be gathered all nations: and he shall separate them one from another, as a shepherd divideth his sheep from the goats.
>
> *Matthew 25:31-32*

From the lead-in statement Jesus made, you might think that the final judgment will take place at the same time He appears in His glory to rescue the Church. However, that is not the case. When we get to the end of Revelation, we will see that the final White Throne Judgment happens after the Millennial Reign of Christ, or more than one thousand years after Jesus returns for His Church. Jesus is making a very broad statement here which ties over a thousand years' worth of events into one sentence. Peter did the same thing when he said in 2 Peter 3:8 that "one day is as a thousand years to the Lord, and a thousand years is as one day." In verse 9, Peter speaks of the long-suffering of the Lord as He waits on all of us to come to repentance. In the very next verse he begins to speak about the Day of the Lord with the elements being dissolved and then a new heaven and new earth to replace the current heaven and earth as though they were tied together as one great big cosmic event. They are not—at least not until you begin to clump events into thousand-year intervals. Jesus (in the above scripture) and Peter (in the scripture below) were both using great liberality of speech when they viewed things from God's perspective in which a thousand years is the same as a single day. The dissolving of the heavens and the earth and the creation of new ones do not occur until after the Millennial Reign at about the same time the final judgment takes place. There are a thousand years that separate between the second return of Jesus at Armageddon and the final White Throne Judgment with a new heaven and earth, and an additional seven years if we count from His initial return to gather His elect.

> [8]But, beloved, be not ignorant of this one thing, that one day is with the Lord as a thousand years, and a thousand years as one day. [9]The Lord is not slack concerning his promise, as some men count slackness; but is longsuffering to us-ward, not willing that any should perish, but that all should come to repentance. [10]But the day of the Lord will come as a thief in the night; in the which the heavens shall pass away with a great noise, and the elements shall melt with fervent heat, the earth also and the works that are therein shall be burned up. [11]Seeing then that all these things shall be dissolved, what manner of persons ought ye to be in all holy conversation and godliness, [12]Looking for and hasting unto the coming of the day of God, wherein

the heavens being on fire shall be dissolved, and the elements shall melt with fervent heat? [13]Nevertheless we, according to his promise, look for new heavens and a new earth, wherein dwelleth righteousness.

2 Peter 3:8-13

Hopefully, taking a closer look at the thousand-year statements of Jesus and Peter will help keep us from getting too confused as we move on to Revelation. The words of Jesus in Matthew 24 have provided a solid foundation which will help us to understand Revelation in its fullness. Jesus reveals to us that after the gospel has been preached to all the world, the Antichrist will be revealed and the Tribulation will begin. The Church will suffer through the Tribulation with the rest of the world until Jesus appears in the clouds to rescue believers. On the day we depart, it will be as the days of Noah for the rest of the world. They will be suddenly and irrevocably thrown into the winepress of the Wrath of God. We can boil the entire end-times and the order of events down into just three words—Tribulation~Rapture~Wrath. Understanding Matthew 24 is like a golden key that unlocks the greater treasure of understanding the Book of Revelation and the other prophecies. So, without further delay, let's take our key and open wide the mysteries of our final redemption.

THINK ABOUT IT!

— Did the disciples ask Jesus about the Wrath of God?

— Does Jesus describe the Wrath of God in His response to their questions?

Selah

Whose fan is in his hand, and he will throughly purge his floor, and will gather the wheat into his garner; but the chaff he will burn with fire unquenchable.

Luke 3:17

Lessons from the Past

I always struggled in school. Between the depression and undiagnosed ADD, I had to work extra hard to get "nearly" good grades. I was able to appear like I had it together until I had to speak. My thought process is slower than others. I often feel like I'm pedaling a bike uphill, pulling a thousand pounds behind me, while others are driving Porsches on a downhill grade. I listen but don't always absorb what is being said. My train of thought is more like a derailment in slow motion. I test out with a slightly high IQ, but I struggle to find the right words to communicate what I want to say. I am an extreme visual learner. Therefore, I turn to writing to say what I have to say. I have always felt that I had been unfairly saddled with a life crippling disadvantage because of my slow thought process and my struggle to communicate, but I don't attribute it to God. I blame it on Satan and the curse he brought on the earth. God helps me to overcome it and succeed, despite this shortcoming, and like the apostle Paul, I glory in my infirmities that the power of Christ may rest upon me. I always knew I could understand the prophecies, and I rejoice in the fact that God can use me, despite all else.

This book does not cover the historical and instructional aspects of chapters 1, 2 and 3 of Revelation. These chapters contain warnings, instructions and encouragement to seven specific churches of Asia that were located in Turkey at the time John received the revelation from God. Jesus was addressing the spiritual condition of each church and instructing them on what they needed to do to maintain their spiritual vitality. He then pointed out the consequences, positive and negative, for obeying or disobeying the commands of God. If we take heed to the things Jesus communicated to these seven churches, those things will become spiritual guidance for our own day, both in our personal lives and in the life of the churches of which we are a part. If we learn from the successes and failures of those who went before us, we will be better prepared when Jesus returns for His spotless church, and the statement that Jesus made in Revelation 3:5 will be true in our own lives: "He that overcometh, the same shall be clothed in white raiment; and I will not blot out his name out of the book of life, but I will confess his name before my Father, and before his angels." Beyond the wisdom we are able to extract from the first three chapters, we don't find much there that adds to the prophetic revelation of the coming end-times, which is what this book is about. However, we are going to look at the following portion of Scripture from chapter 3 for some clarification. First read the verses, paying particular attention to the words in italics.

> [7]And to the angel of the church in Philadelphia write;
> These things saith he that is holy, he that is true, he that
> hath the key of David, he that openeth, and no man shut-
> teth; and shutteth, and no man openeth; [8]I know thy
> works: behold, I have set before thee an open door, and no
> man can shut it: *for thou hast a little strength, and hast kept
> my word*, and hast not denied my name. [9]Behold, I will
> make them of the synagogue of Satan, which say they are
> Jews, and are not, but do lie; behold, I will make them to
> come and worship before thy feet, and to know that I have
> loved thee. [10]*Because thou hast kept the word of my patience,*
> I also will keep thee from the hour of temptation, which
> shall come upon all the world, to try them that dwell upon
> the earth. [11]Behold, I come quickly: hold that fast which
> thou hast, that no man take thy crown.
>
> *Revelation 3:7-11*

Some people take these verses to mean that true believers are going to be raptured before the Tribulation as Jesus told these believers that He would keep them from the hour of temptation because they kept His word. The removal of saints by Rapture is not what is being conveyed here at all. The verses above do not say Jesus is going to take us out of here to avoid any temptations or hardships at all, but rather, He is going to keep us in a protective sense during the hour of temptation. The word "keep" used in verse 10 means to guard from loss or injury by keeping an eye upon, to hold fast to or to keep in safety. The word "kept" in verses 8 and 10 is the exact same word as "keep" in verse 10. He is going to *keep* us in the same way that we *keep* His Word. We *keep* His Word while we are in the midst of adversity by guarding over it, keeping our eyes upon it and by doing what it says. The Word (Jesus is the Word) *keeps* us from being consumed by adversity by guarding over us and protecting us—both externally by controlling certain events around us, and internally by holding on tight to the reins of our hearts and empowering us in our times of need. Even when you take this verse as a specific promise, it is a promise made to one of the seven churches in Philadelphia, located in the far midwestern half of Turkey, which puts it right in the midst of the empire of the beast and the nations of Gog. If this church still exists today, God is going to keep them while the world is being tried in the hour of temptation that will come upon all of the earth—the Great Tribulation.

Proverbs 7:1-5 is very similar to what we just read. Paraphrased, it reads: "*Keep* my word and my word *will keep you* from the strange woman that flatters with her lips." God's Word does not rapture us out of this world every time we encounter a whorish woman, but rather, it (Jesus is the Word) does whatever is necessary to protect us from her as long as we are in this world and abiding in the Word. Proverbs 7:1-5 is not an end-times prophecy, but it very well could be. If we keep God's Word, His Word will keep us from the end-times delusion of that great whore called Mystery Babylon that is mentioned in Revelation. Nowhere in the Bible does the word "keep" mean to remove or to avoid altogether. To the contrary, it is often used to mean to confine, as with a prison keeper. Thank God that is not the meaning being used here. God is the keeper of our souls, but He does not keep our souls by force under lock and key;

He keeps our souls safe by watching over them and helping us in our times of weakness. Consider the following verses that use the same type of language and are, in fact, saying the exact same thing. The words to "keep from" are never used to mean to "take away from" in the Bible.

> I pray not that thou should take them out of the world,
> but that thou should *keep them from the evil.*
>
> *John 17:15*

Of course, He *has* promised to come and take us out of the world, but not until the end of this age when it is time for the judgment of wrath, which is not the same as the Tribulation. Notice that this verse uses the same phrase "keep…from" that verse 10 and Proverbs 7:1-5 use. He does not take us *out of* the world to keep us from, but rather, by His power He empowers us to overcome and thus keeps us from evil, temptation and delusion while we are still *in* the world. The next three verses all use the word "temptation" in the same way Revelation 3:10 uses it. These are just three of the nineteen times that the word "temptation" is used in the New Testament. It was translated as "try" one other time, as in "the trying of our faith," but it always means the same thing—temptations and trials.

> Watch and pray, that ye enter not into *temptation*: the
> spirit indeed is willing, but the flesh is weak.
>
> *Matthew 26:41*

Verses 8 and 10 from Revelation 3 could be rephrased like this: "You are weak (a little strength), but because you keep my word and name, I'll keep you in the time of temptation." Despite the weakness of our flesh if we watch and pray always, we eventually will be rewarded because we will be kept from every hour of temptation we are faced with in this life, even up to the very end of the world.

> Blessed is the man that endureth *temptation*: for when he
> is tried, he shall receive the crown of life, which the Lord
> hath promised to them that love Him.
>
> *James 1:12*

James informs us that we will receive a crown of life after we endure temptation, so it should seem odd to us that so many people would interpret the verses above to say we will be delivered out of this world as soon as things begin to heat up a little in the end-times. If Jesus takes us out of here to avoid the trials of the Antichrist, He is, in effect, denying us the crown of life that will be ours if we endure during that time. We are going to see over and over again that the Tribulation is from Satan and the Antichrist and that God has only given us a free pass out of this world when it comes to His wrath, which will be poured out upon sinners after the Tribulation.

> And lead us not into *temptation*, but deliver us from evil:
> For thine is the kingdom, and the power, and the glory, for ever. Amen.
>
> *Matthew 6:13*

God does not lead us into temptation as Satan does, but He has left us on this earth to be tried by temptations nonetheless. We all have to decide for ourselves how committed to God we are going to be. Anybody can say they are going to live for Christ for the rest of their lives no matter what, but what really matters is how we actually behave when the real trials come our way. Are we willing to stand up for God only until it gets uncomfortable, and then we run and hide, or even worse, try to blend in with the unrighteous. Are we willing to stand even if it costs us our families, our livelihoods, our investments and retirements, our nice homes and new cars, and everything else we have invested our lives into? Are we willing to stand even if it costs us the very breath of life?

For those who think that God wouldn't do something as unthinkable as to leave us here to suffer the trials of the Great Tribulation, all you have to do is read Hebrews 11, the Book of Acts, the Old Testament or the newspaper to see that He does allow His people to go through persecutions, tortures and even death. Some He delivers, and others He just receives their spirits into heaven after they depart their tortured bodies. Keeping us from the hour of temptation is a matter of giving the strength to stand firm on the Word of God even if it costs them their lives, giving many others deliverance during the hour of temptation and, in the case of at least 144,000 in

Israel, it is giving them a place in the wilderness where they will be cared for for three-and-one-half years during the Tribulation. This is not meant to scare anybody, but it is time to wake up and accept what the prophecies have been saying to us all along. We have to decide beforehand to stand for Christ even after the Tribulation begins, regardless of the cost.

THINK ABOUT IT!

— Are these chapters speaking about the future or the past?

— Can the things written in these chapters be applied to our lives today?

Selah

Now all these things happened unto them for ensamples: and they are written for our admonition, upon whom the ends of the world are come.

1 Corinthians 10:11

Revelation 4

Enthroned in Glory

I had to leave a particular job at about age twenty, but I still needed to work. I didn't know where to look or what to do so I turned to God. Up to this point I think my life could be characterized as heathen lite. People knew me as a nice guy, but I was living a life of sin. I was a prodigal son. At times I would be out with drinking buddies or staying with a girlfriend and God would quietly speak to my heart, "What are you doing here?" My only response, "I don't really know." I still had a trickle of the life God had put in me years ago when I got saved, so I asked God for a new job, and I also asked Him to give me somebody who could teach me about Himself. After making my request directly to Him, I felt that I needed to finish the prayer properly. I had witnessed baptisms at the old Baptist church on the other side of the hill, so my first instinct was to pray in the name of the Father, the Son and the Holy Ghost. Then I remembered when I had opened my Bible and read something like, "Whatever you ask the Father in my name, I will do it," so I finished my prayer "In Jesus' Name!" and "Oh yeah, amen." I went out the next day searching for a job and found nothing, but I knew it was a done deal. God had promised and I believed His promise. When I saw my mother later that day I told her that I had a job. "That's great, where?" "I don't know but I know I have one." Soon the phone rang, and I was working shortly thereafter. Not only that, but I met a man on the job named John with red hair, a big handlebar mustache and so full of the Holy Ghost that he couldn't possibly keep it all in. God had come through for me and He has never stopped coming through ever since.

As we begin in Revelation 4, we are starting over with the same theme and sequence of events we saw in Matthew 24. The only relevance chapters 4 and 5 have pertaining to the end-times, however, is they show that there is only one Person in the universe who is worthy to open the book that reveals the coming end-times and the judgment of God. That in itself may be the most significant point of the entire Revelation, but other than that, these chapters just lead into chapter 6 where the book is opened and the end-times begin to be revealed. In the first verse of Revelation 4, John is told that he will begin to see things that will be hereafter or which is to come in the future. Everything that he saw in the previous three chapters dealt with the present situation of the Asian church at the time John wrote Revelation.

> After this I looked, and, behold, a door was opened in
> heaven: and the first voice which I heard was as it were of a
> trumpet talking with me; which said, Come up hither, and
> I will shew thee things which must be hereafter.
>
> *Revelation 4:1*

As Revelation 4 and 5 bring us into the Throne Room of God, Jesus is declared to be the only one worthy to open the book that will reveal the events of the end-time. From time to time, God allows us a little peek into heaven by way of the Scriptures. The following is a description of God seated upon His throne and the creatures that are before Him giving Him praise and honor. There are 24 elders before the throne, but there is no mention of the rest of the redeemed of the Lord. The Rapture has not yet taken place; therefore, God's redeemed have not been gathered into heaven. After this brief look into the Throne Room of God and some of the activities that take place there, chapter 5 shows God holding the book with the seven seals in His hand. That book will show us how things will unfold in the end-times just as Matthew 24 did.

²And immediately I was in the spirit: and, behold, a throne was set in heaven, and One sat on the throne. ³And he that sat was to look upon like a jasper and a sardine stone: and there was a rainbow round about the throne, in sight like unto an emerald. ⁴And round about the throne were four and twenty seats: and upon the seats I saw four and twenty elders sitting, clothed in white raiment; and they had on their heads crowns of gold. ⁵And out of the throne proceeded lightnings and thunderings and voices: and there were seven lamps of fire burning before the throne, which are the seven Spirits of God. ⁶And before the throne there was a sea of glass like unto crystal: and in the midst of the throne, and round about the throne, were four beasts full of eyes before and behind. ⁷And the first beast was like a lion, and the second beast like a calf, and the third beast had a face as a man, and the fourth beast was like a flying eagle. ⁸And the four beasts had each of them six wings about him; and they were full of eyes within: and they rest not day and night, saying, Holy, holy, holy, Lord God Almighty, which was, and is, and is to come. ⁹And when those beasts give glory and honour and thanks to him that sat on the throne, who liveth for ever and ever, ¹⁰The four and twenty elders fall down before him that sat on the throne, and worship him that liveth for ever and ever, and cast their crowns before the throne, saying, ¹¹Thou art worthy, O Lord, to receive glory and honour and power: for thou hast created all things, and for thy pleasure they are and were created.

Revelation 4:2-11

THINK ABOUT IT!

— Who is seated on the throne?

Selah

And above the firmament that was over their heads was
the likeness of a throne, as the appearance of a sapphire
stone: and upon the likeness of the throne was the likeness
as the appearance of a man above upon it. And I saw as the
colour of amber, as the appearance of fire round about
within it, from the appearance of his loins even upward,
and from the appearance of his loins even downward, I
saw as it were the appearance of fire, and it had brightness
round about. As the appearance of the bow that is in the
cloud in the day of rain, so was the appearance of the
brightness round about. This was the appearance of the
likeness of the glory of the Lord...

Ezekiel 1:26-28

Revelation 5

Worthy Is the Lamb

I watched John for a while as I got settled into my job. Whenever he opened his mouth, the Word of God came out. I approached him one day and let him know that I wanted to learn. He taught me about the baptism of the Holy Ghost and the joy of the Lord. I was still depressed and I actually tossed around in my mind about whether I should give up the misery I was so familiar with and accept the joy that comes from the Holy Ghost. Somehow good sense prevailed and soon I recommitted my life to Jesus and invited the Holy Ghost into my life. I think it was that word "joy" that kept coming back to my mind. "What is it?" I wondered. "What's it like?" I soon found out, but there was a problem. A conflicting emotion of depression still resided in my bosom.

---

¹And I saw in the right hand of him that sat on the throne a book written within and on the backside, sealed with seven seals.

There is no man found that is worthy to open the book until the risen Christ enters the room. The rest of this chapter proclaims the worthiness of Jesus Christ to take the book out of the right hand of God and to open it and declare its contents.

> [2]And I saw a strong angel proclaiming with a loud voice,
> Who is worthy to open the book, and to loose the seals
> thereof? [3]And no man in heaven, nor in earth, neither
> under the earth, was able to open the book, neither to look
> thereon. [4]And I wept much, because no man was found
> worthy to open and to read the book, neither to look
> thereon. [5]And one of the elders saith unto me, Weep not:
> behold, the Lion of the tribe of Juda, the Root of David,
> hath prevailed to open the book, and to loose the seven
> seals thereof. [6]And I beheld, and, lo, in the midst of the
> throne and of the four beasts, and in the midst of the eld-
> ers, stood a Lamb as it had been slain, having seven horns
> and seven eyes, which are the seven Spirits of God sent
> forth into all the earth. [7]And he came and took the book
> out of the right hand of him that sat upon the throne.

The twenty-four elders are presumably the twelve patriarchs of
Israel and the twelve apostles of Jesus Christ. John, no doubt, if he got
a good look, saw himself in this lineup. He would have also seen
Mathias who replaced Judas Iscariot in Acts 1:26. In verse 9, we see
that they are redeemed men, and in verse 10 that they are expecting
to reign on the earth again sometime in the future. Notice once again
that there are twenty-four elders, four beasts and many angels, but
the redeemed of the Lord are not shown until later in Revelation
when the Rapture is revealed. The Rapture will not be revealed until
Jesus opens the sixth seal of the book that He just received out of the
hand of God, and then it will be repeated from several different perspectives later on in Revelation.

> [8]And when he had taken the book, the four beasts and four
> and twenty elders fell down before the Lamb, having every
> one of them harps, and golden vials full of odours, which
> are the prayers of saints. [9]And they sung a new song, say-
> ing, Thou art worthy to take the book, and to open the
> seals thereof: for thou wast slain, and hast redeemed us to
> God by thy blood out of every kindred, and tongue, and
> people, and nation; [10]And hast made us unto our God
> kings and priests: and *we shall reign on the earth.* [11]And I

beheld, and I heard the voice of many angels round about the throne and the beasts and the elders: and the number of them was ten thousand times ten thousand, and thousands of thousands [100 million angels, and then some]; [12]Saying with a loud voice, Worthy is the Lamb that was slain to receive power, and riches, and wisdom, and strength, and honour, and glory, and blessing. [13]And every creature which is in heaven, and on the earth, and under the earth, and such as are in the sea, and all that are in them, heard I saying, Blessing, and honour, and glory, and power, be unto him that sitteth upon the throne, and unto the Lamb for ever and ever. [14]And the four beasts said, Amen. And the four and twenty elders fell down and worshipped Him that liveth for ever and ever.

Revelation 5:1-14

THINK ABOUT IT!

— Who is the lamb that was slain to redeem from every nation and tongue to God by His blood?

— Are the four beasts and twenty-four elders the only ones redeemed, or are there more to come?

Selah

Now unto him that is able to keep you from falling, and to present you faultless before the presence of his glory with exceeding joy, To the only wise God our Saviour, be glory and majesty, dominion and power, both now and ever. Amen.

Jude 24-25

The Five Seals of Tribulation

One day as I lay on my bed in the three-bedroom apartment I still shared with my drinking buddies, I read James 4:7 where it says, "Submit yourselves therefore to God. Resist the devil, and he will flee from you." Like a thousand watt beam of light shining in my heart, God spotlighted the demon that I had unwittingly allowed into my life so many years ago by the words of my mouth. Now with anger and tenacity, and a true revelation from God, I stood right up in the middle of that bed and with the words of my mouth, I resisted that demon by commanding him out in Jesus' name. As soon as I said it, I felt it pop straight up and out of me like nothing I had ever felt before. It fled all right, like a bolt of lightning in reverse, and God's river of living water flooded my soul for the first time in my life. Oh, what a feeling!

The seven seals of Revelation 6, 7 and 8 reveal to us the end-times chronology of events beginning with the time of the Great Tribulation, followed by the Rapture of the Church and, last but not least, the outpouring of the Wrath of God. The book with seven seals does not include the Millennial Reign, the final White Throne Judgment of God or any of the events that follow the Wrath of God. Seal 1 is the revealing of the Antichrist. Seals 2-5 reveal to us the nature of the Great Tribulation. Adding to the deception that the

Antichrist will be practicing, the second through fifth seals show men killing one another—presumably by war—and death by famine, which could be a result of a world engulfed in war. Seal 6 interrupts the Tribulation and precedes the Wrath of God. It shows the sealing of the 144,000 chosen of God on their foreheads. After they are sealed, the Rapture of the entire Church takes place. The Rapture is the gathering together of all of God's elect from wherever they may be and bringing them all at one time into heaven and before the Throne of God. Seal 7 shows the saints of God in heaven right after being raptured and just before God begins to pour out His wrath. Chapters 8-11 display the seven trumpets of judgment, which are all a part of the seventh seal of the heavenly Book of Revelation. Each aspect of the Wrath of God is signaled in heaven by the sounding of one of the seven different trumpets just before it is released on the earth. The seven trumpets are recorded in the order that they will occur.

It is very important that we understand the relationship between the seven seals of revelation, the seven trumpets of judgment and the seven vials of wrath, and the chronological order of each. The seven seals of Revelation, which Jesus received out of the hand of God, reveal future events that make up the entire end-times in the order they will occur. We already mentioned that the trumpets are, in fact, what the seventh seal is revealing. The seals and trumps do not parallel each other, and the trumps do not follow after, per se, but the seven trumpets of wrath are all revealed under, and as a part of, the seventh seal of the Book of Revelation. Later in Revelation we will see the seven vials being poured out, each of which corresponds numerically to a matching trumpet. The sound of the first trumpet signals the pouring out of the first vial, and so on, in order. These trumpets and vials are the wrath of God being poured out on the earth. In effect, that means that the seven vials are also a part of the seventh seal. However, for the sake of providing a much broader understanding of the end-times, Jesus starts over in Revelation 12, repeating the things that were revealed in the first half of Revelation but from a different perspective. The trumpets of judgment and vials of wrath should not be confused with the Tribulation in any way, nor should they be confused with the seals of the book. The only correlation of the trumpets and vials to the seals of the book is that they do not begin to release their wrath until the final seal is opened.

The horses and riders depicted under the first four seals are symbolic of the events that occur during the Tribulation. Much has been said and written about the horses of the apocalypse. Much of it is based on fear, misunderstanding and delusion. Many theorists make too much out of the four horses and their riders. They do not represent four different men or dispensations or anything of that nature, nor are these riders dispatched from God with the purpose of bringing wrath upon sinners. Rather, they are dispatched from Satan with the purpose of bringing tribulation on the earth from Satan. Again, the horses are symbolic or, at best, something that happens literally in the spirit realm that initiates events in the natural realm. At any rate, we will not see these horses—only the turmoil they represent. The first one represents the Antichrist, and the three that follow simply represent three different types of tribulation and turmoil that will occur after the Antichrist's rise to power during the final seven years before the Rapture. The word "apocalypse" comes from the Greek word *apokalupsis* which means a revelation or disclosure. In popular culture, Christian and otherwise, it refers to the Book of Revelation and any other writings about the ultimate triumph of good over evil, regardless of the source. The fact that the source has no relevance should cause us to be more cautious about believing everything we hear regarding the end-times and the apocalypse. The Bible is the only reliable source of information we have concerning the end.

THE TRIBULATION

[1]And *I saw when the Lamb opened one of the seals*, and I heard, as it were the noise of thunder, one of the four beasts saying, Come and see. [2]And I saw, and behold *a white horse*: and he that sat on him *had a bow; and a crown was given unto him: and he went forth conquering, and to conquer.*

Revelation 6:1-2

The first seal reveals the Antichrist going forth to conquer. The sound of thunder symbolizes the brewing storm and the rumblings his arrival will bring. His primary purpose will be to conquer and destroy, which we will clearly see as we consider all the end-times

120

prophecies together. It could have been said that he goes forth to steal, kill and destroy like his father the devil. The next four seals that will be opened display the diabolical works of Satan and his Antichrist as they cause havoc on the earth. These seals do not reveal any of God's wrath or punishments, only Satan's torment of mankind as he uses those people who serve him with anger, hatred and hardened hearts to do his will. The white horse of the first seal is symbolic of several different things. First, it symbolizes the fact that the Antichrist will come in the pretense of peace. Secondly, it symbolizes the fact that he will be the spiritual leader of the nations he controls. And finally, it illustrates the delusion that he will hold over many worldly people who perceive him as the righteous savior of Israel and all of mankind because of the peace covenant that he brokers, which appears to defuse the time bomb that has been ticking in the Middle East for many years. Even Satan can transform himself as an angel of light and that is what the Antichrist will do when he appears. 2 Thessalonians 2:11 says that God is going to allow strong delusion to come upon the world in the end-times, and the fact that the Antichrist will appear to some to be a righteous deliverer is just a part of that delusion. He wears a crown because Satan will give him rulership over the ten nation end-times empire that will be established in the Middle East and because of the spiritual power that is bestowed upon him to reap havoc. The Great Tribulation does not begin at the appearance of the Antichrist but, rather, things are beginning to fall into place as he takes his position of authority. When the time is right, the Antichrist will make a seven-year peace agreement with Israel which will, in effect, be the sign that reveals him to the Church and the rest of the world. In the middle of that seven-year accord, he will break the agreement, and thus begins the Great Tribulation.

The emergence of the Antichrist onto the world scene is just the very beginning of God's end-times Revelation. A lot of events will transpire from his rise to power until the time Jesus rides out of heaven on His own white horse down to Armageddon with His saints at His side. The second through the fifth seals show us the Tribulation (not God's wrath) with Seal 5 showing the saints under the altar of God—who have already been killed for their faith during the Tribulation—getting a little antsy like kids on a road trip asking God, "How much longer before You judge?" And then, the sixth seal shows the Rapture of the saints from the earth. Last but not least, the seventh seal reveals the Wrath of God after the Tribulation and Rapture have been completed. God's wrath culminates with the Battle of Armageddon, which is where Jesus rides out of heaven on His very literal white horse with His figurative sharp, double-edged sword—the Word of God—in His mouth. We still have quite a while from this first seal of the book before Jesus mounts His steed. We already discussed the verse from Daniel 9 which shows the seven-year false covenant of peace that gives the Antichrist the white horse appearance. Notice again as he first makes the seven-year covenant and then breaks it after the first three-and-one-half years.

> And *he shall confirm the covenant with many for one week: and in the midst of the week he shall cause the sacrifice and the oblation to cease*, and for the overspreading of abominations he shall make it desolate, even until the consummation, and that determined shall be poured upon the desolate.
>
> *Daniel 9:27*

The verse above is where the term "Abomination of Desolation" originates. It refers to both the Antichrist and the statue or image built in his honor and placed in the temple of God. The mention of the Abomination of Desolation in the verse above ties the desecration of the temple to the second half of the seven-year covenant when the daily sacrifice is halted by the Antichrist. The Antichrist will stop the Jewish temple worship several weeks before the onset of the Tribulation. He will then enter the temple himself at the midpoint of the seven years, but his image will not actually be placed in the temple until about the very end of the Tribulation. We gain this knowledge from Matthew and through some of the numbers that Daniel gives us in his prophecies, which we will look at later in this book.

> [3]And when he had opened the *second seal*, I heard the second beast say, Come and see. [4]And there went out *another horse that was red*: and power was given to him that sat thereon *to take peace from the earth, and that they should kill one another*: and there was given unto him a great sword.
>
> *Revelation 6:3-4*

The red horse symbolizes the blood that will be shed on the earth as this rider makes his journey. This will be the blood of war, terrorism and persecution. More than anything else, the Antichrist will be a warrior king despite the fact that he makes a peace treaty with Israel. He will tighten his control over the ten-nation empire that he rules by making war with—and then defeating—three of the kings of the ten nations. The Scriptures tell us that he will rule over ten nations at the time of the end rather than over all the world through a single world government as has been suggested by many. After the Antichrist gains control of these ten nations and breaks his promise of peace to Israel, it could draw the whole world into one giant world conflict, or it could provide just the right distraction for nations all over the world to embark on their own little wars. For instance, China could attack Taiwan, or Russia could attempt to take back the nations it recently lost. The Balkans and Africa could both explode with wars; Southeast Asia could descend into total chaos, and who knows what else. All these nations need is enough of a disturbance in the Middle East to distract the peacemakers of the world long enough so they can get away with their own hearts' desires—desires for war and dominance. The Antichrist will not rule the whole world, but he will certainly be on center stage and working harder than anyone else to destroy the peace. If he controlled a one-world government, there would be no one for him to war against other than Christians and Jews, but the Scriptures make it clear that he will war against other nations and face much opposition.

> ⁵And when he had opened the *third seal*, I heard the third beast say, Come and see. And I beheld, and lo a *black horse*; and he that sat on him had a pair of balances in his hand. ⁶And I heard a voice in the midst of the four beasts say, *A measure of wheat for a penny, and three measures of barley for a penny; and see thou hurt not the oil and the wine.*"
>
> *Revelation 6:5-6*

The black horse symbolizes a plague of famine that will take place after the Antichrist rises to power, but it will only be a plague of food staples such as wheat and barley and not the luxury items such as oil and wine. At the time these verses were written, a penny was a lot of money and would have paid for a good quantity of wheat in normal economic times. In Matthew 20:2, one penny was a day's wages for a laborer. In John 6:5-10, Philip said 200 pennyworth of bread would not be sufficient for five thousand people to have a few bites each. That breaks down to one penny to poorly feed a group of 25 people. A full day's wages for a laborer in our present time for a measure of wheat would make the cost of the loaves in John 6 about $10,000 or about $50 for a full day at minimum wage times 200. That same $50 will only pay for a scrap of bread during this Tribulation plague. It will basically be a poor man's famine, perhaps caused by evil rich men hoarding foodstuff to ensure their own survival or possibly by a disruption caused by war and natural disasters.

The rich, on the other hand, will continue to prosper through all kinds of trade. Revelation 18 describes a real city named Babylon located right in the heart of the kingdom of the Antichrist. This city will be a center of world commerce that will rival all other great port cities. The merchandise that flows through the port will include spices and grains, livestock, all sorts of precious stones, metals, ointments and woods, different forms of transportation, and even slaves and the souls of men. It is said that the shipowners of the world will be made rich by the commerce of the city. If the shipowners become rich, then those who ship their merchandise on the ships will no doubt also improve their financial situations. The other ports of the world will be busy places as well because they will be importing and exporting goods to and from Babylon, not to mention the trade that will go on between other nations. All of the trade that goes on in Babylon seems to be focused on sumptuous and decadent living. Those who have wealth will be paying top dollar, even for the basic food items, which may be one of the big reasons the poor are not able to afford to eat. The next seal shows us that many will starve to death, even while such luxuriant living is going on in the kingdom of the beast—and anywhere else where men bless themselves and forget about the poor.

> [7]And when he had opened the *fourth seal*, I heard the voice of the fourth beast say, Come and see. [8]And I looked, and behold a *pale horse*: and *his name that sat on him was Death, and Hell followed with him. And power was given*

unto them over the fourth part of the earth, to kill with
sword, and with hunger, and with death, and with the beasts
of the earth.

Revelation 6:7-8

The paleness of this horse symbolizes the fear that will grip the hearts of mankind because of the things coming to pass during the Tribulation. Luke 21:26, in speaking of the Tribulation, says it like this: "Men's hearts failing them for fear, and for looking after those things which are coming on the earth: for the powers of heaven shall be shaken." Death and hell have power over a fourth part of the earth, but does that mean they are confined to only one geographical quadrant of the earth where they are free to dispense different kinds of death, or is it one quarter of the world population that will be wiped out by wars, famines and plagues? If the ravages of death and hell were confined to only one quarter of the earth surface, then it would have to be the area surrounding the beast kingdom where he will be making war against nations that are a part of his own ten-nation alliance, Israel and other surrounding nations. However, it is very unlikely that only the area surrounding Israel will be thrown into Great Tribulation by Satan and his Antichrist while the rest of the earth lives in peace and tranquility. More likely, Satan will be pouring out his own brand of wrath upon the whole face of the earth, and a full one quarter of mankind will be eliminated from the face of the earth.

Those people all over the world who are in the greatest jeopardy at this very moment will likely be the first ones to die in the Tribulation. Those who live on the edge of starvation in Africa will probably lose the aid that sustains them and gets them through to see one more day. Those living on the borders of India, Pakistan and Kashmir may see a nuclear exchange. Those who are political dissidents in China, along with many born-again Christians who violate the laws against Christianity, could very well see their final day. The drug lords of South America could take over and wipe out all opposition. There's no telling what North Korea might do. And, of course, the Antichrist will be working to eliminate Jews and Christians from the Middle East. Remember Jesus said that all flesh would be destroyed by Satan in the Tribulation if God did not cut it short. Evil will rise up to rule all over the world, and the world will be cast into

Great Tribulation as a consequence—all because Satan is finally allowed to try the whole world at the same time after everyone has heard the gospel of peace in Christ Jesus. He wants to see who is really going to stand with God and who he will be able to take down to the pit with him when he is finally brought to an end himself. It has been said that there are no atheists in foxholes. The whole world will be a foxhole as it teeters on the brink of destruction, and many will finally turn to the Lord.

The Antichrist will not be causing *all* of the chaos during the Tribulation, but he certainly will be a major player in a world full of turmoil. With a full quarter of mankind being destroyed in the Tribulation, he will have to be using weapons of mass destruction if he were responsible for causing all of the destruction, but because he survives through the Tribulation and right up to the end of the Wrath of God several years later, one must assume that there is war, famine and pestilence all over the world coming from many different sources to cause such a high death rate without bringing the Antichrist and his followers to their own graves.

Seal Number 5, which follows below, reveals a number of the saints who are killed in the Great Tribulation for their commitment to Jesus Christ and the covenant of truth. They are shown waiting for the vengeance of God against the wicked by whom their lives were shortened through murderous persecution. The fact that many of them perished in the Tribulation is confirmed by the statement made in Revelation 7:14, which is referring back to these same saints. "These are they which *came out of Great Tribulation*, and have washed their robes, and made them white in the blood of the Lamb." It is important to notice exactly what these saints are saying at this point. They are asking God how much longer it will be until His promised retribution against the wicked is unleashed. In other words, they are in a place of rest after losing their lives in the Tribulation, but they are still waiting for the Wrath of God to be poured out on sinners. The response is that they need to wait just a little longer until the rest of the martyrs of Jesus Christ will be killed in the Tribulation. After that happens, the Church will be raptured, which is what the sixth seal reveals to us, and then their antagonists will be punished in the judgments of the seventh seal. This shows that there really is a difference between the Tribulation and the Wrath of God.

In verse 10 we see that God has not as yet judged or avenged the blood of His people. If these first five seals were describing the Wrath of God, the following statements would not be accurate. The martyred saints would be asking "How much longer will your vengeance last?" and God's reply would say nothing about fellow Christians being killed because they would all be gone in the Rapture. But, that is not the case. The Rapture is about to take place under the next seal of the book, and then in the final seal God's vengeance through wrath will begin to fall.

> [9]And when he had opened the *fifth seal*, I saw under the altar the souls of them that were slain for the Word of God, and for the testimony which they held: [10]And they cried with a loud voice, saying, *How long, O Lord, holy and true, dost thou not judge and avenge our blood on them that dwell on the earth?* [11]And white robes were given unto every one of them; and it was said unto them, that they should *rest yet for a little season, until their fellow servants also and their brethren, that should be killed as they were, should be fulfilled.*
>
> *Revelation 6:9-11*

Being murdered for one's faith may not be an appealing way to die, especially for those who are serving the almighty God of heaven, but if it is a choice between that and giving in to the forces of the Antichrist and suffering the Wrath of God shortly thereafter and eternal damnation after that, martyrdom doesn't seem so bad. Our life on this earth is brief at best. When we receive Jesus as our Lord and Savior, the eternal kingdom of God should become the most important thing in our lives, not just how long we can prolong our life on this earth or how comfortable God can make it for us with His blessings. Hebrews 11:38, after naming numerous Old Testament saints who excelled in their lives and overcame by faith, or who were simply tortured and killed, declares that the world was not worthy of any of them. Those saints, along with every one of us, have a greater and more glorious future awaiting us, and it begins on the day of the Resurrection. On the day God pops open the coffin lids and the dead in Christ all begin to climb out of their graves with new bodies, and

God sends His firstborn from the dead to gather us into heaven, we will literally be thrust into the fulfillment of the plan of redemption where God Himself wipes away our tears, and we become untouchable by sin and death.

Everything we just saw under the first five seals parallels exactly what Jesus said at the beginning of His response to the disciples' questions in Matthew 24. However, He also made it clear that His opening statements were not a part of the end-times but, rather, events that would come to pass on a recurring basis as we march through time on a direct course with the end of the world. He described the kind of tribulation that we have witnessed over and over again throughout history as a fallen human race struggles to survive on a cursed planet. The Great Tribulation that will be coming up on the planet in the end-times is no different from what the world has experienced on a recurring basis from the beginning of time. The magnitude and scope of it, however, will be sufficient to destroy all of mankind if left unchecked. The intensity of the Great Tribulation is magnified by several factors that have already been mentioned: the wrath of Satan as he is cast down to the earth to plot out his remaining days, the liberty he will have in testing the whole world to see who will serve God by faith in His Word or who will serve Satan in fear and torment, and the fact that those who reject God will be so consumed by wickedness that they are willing to give it their all in opposing anything good.

Not until Matthew 24:15 does Jesus begin to speak of the true end-times. After the gospel has been preached to all the world in verse 14, then the Antichrist is manifested in verse 15. The first five seals not only parallel everything Jesus said about the Antichrist and the Tribulation in Matthew 24:15-29, but they fill in the blanks and reveal exactly what the Tribulation is all about. The Tribulation is not the Wrath of God but, rather, the troubling of Satan, the warring of the Antichrist, man's rebellion against God and man's inability to live peacefully with one another. Even nature will feel the effects of the curse and react to it. The earth will not provide any bounty other than disease, pestilence and wild beasts. These will all conspire with the other forces of evil to destroy a full one quarter of mankind before God puts a stop to it, which He will do under the sixth seal.

PRELUDE TO RAPTURE

The opening events of the sixth seal coincide with Matthew 24:29-31 where the heavens are shaken and Jesus appears and sends forth His angels to gather His elect. In Matthew 24:36-41, a comparison is made between the days of Noah and the end of the world. Noah's ark was salvation, or a catching away, for the family of Noah as they entered into it on the very same day that the judgment of the flood began to destroy the wicked. The same thing is happening here under this seal. The righteous are being gathered out of harm's way as the judgment is about to begin. Notice the familiar events in the skies as all of the lights become darkened. The Day of the Lord arrives at this point, and even the heathen know it. They are the ones making the observation that the day of His wrath has arrived.

> ¹²And I beheld when he had opened the *sixth seal*, and, lo, there was a great earthquake; and *the sun became black as sackcloth of hair, and the moon became as blood;* ¹³*And the stars of heaven fell unto the earth,* even as a fig tree casteth her untimely figs, when she is shaken of a mighty wind. ¹⁴And the heaven departed as a scroll when it is rolled together; and every mountain and island were moved out of their places. ¹⁵And the kings of the earth, and the great men, and the rich men, and the chief captains, and the mighty men, and every bondman, and every free man, hid themselves in the dens and in the rocks of the mountains; ¹⁶And said to the mountains and rocks, Fall on us, and *hide us from the face of him that sitteth on the throne, and from the wrath of the Lamb*: ¹⁷*For the great day of his wrath is come*; and who shall be able to stand?
>
> *Revelation 6:12-17*

In verse 17, the wicked of the earth declare that the day of God's wrath has finally come. They knew it was coming, but they made a choice to live their lives the way they wanted, with total disregard for the commandments of God and His soon-coming judgment. The Rapture is not going to be a big surprise to anyone, only the timing of it. When it comes, sinner and saint alike will know what day it is because the gospel will have been preached to the entire world before the end begins. The gathering of God's elect before the day of God's wrath is a part of the gospel that will be preached to the world, so there will not be a whole lot of surprised individuals when it does arrive. The seventh seal, which is opened in Revelation 8:1 and continues up through the end of Revelation 11, is the revelation of God's wrath being poured out upon the earth after the Rapture. Before the events of the seventh seal can begin, though, we have to make it through Revelation 7, which describes in part the Rapture of all God's redeemed. This includes the entire Church, both living and dead, Jewish and Gentile, and the 144,000 specially chosen ones of Israel. The gathering of believers in chapter 7 is the primary focus of the sixth seal. However, the sign of the heavens becoming dark—which we just read, before the appearing of Jesus Christ—which we are about to read, is an irrefutable part of the Rapture. This is the sign Jesus told His disciples to watch for and expect before His coming and the end of the world. In the first chapter of Revelation, we are told that every eye will see Jesus when He comes in the clouds. The verses we just read clearly display a lost world witnessing the sign of the skies turning to blackness just before every eye beholds the appearing of the Lord in the clouds.

> Behold, he cometh with clouds; and every eye shall see
> him, and they also which pierced him: and all kindreds of
> the earth shall wail because of him. Even so, Amen.
>
> *Revelation 1:7*

Think about it!

— Is the purpose of the seals to initiate events or to reveal them?

— Does the sixth seal reveal the same events as Matthew 24 where Jesus comes for His New Testament elect?

— After the skies go dark in verses 12-14, what are the people listed under the sixth seal hiding from?

— Do the skies remain darkened throughout the remaining events of this book?

Selah

Howbeit when he, the Spirit of truth, is come, he will guide you into all truth: for he shall not speak of himself; but whatsoever he shall hear, that shall he speak: and he will shew you things to come.

John 16:13

REVELATION 7

Seal Six,
The Gathering of
the Redeemed

I was reading The Revelation frequently now, but it was Matthew 24 that kept pulling me back. The things Jesus was saying in those verses were so confusing to me. Then one day I received my first big revelation. *Jesus was saying what He meant.* The reason I was so confused was because I had so many false ideas in my head that were passed on from other men. Reading Matthew 24 through the filter of what I had learned made Jesus seem like He was jumping all over the place with what He was saying, without much rhyme or reason. The actual revelation was simply that Jesus would be returning after the Tribulation and that the Wrath of God would follow. After that, things began to make more sense and those little eye-opening revelations became more frequent.

Before God is willing to begin pouring forth His wrath on the wicked, the 144,000 of Israel must be sealed in their foreheads (verses 1-8), and then the entire Church, which includes the 144,000, must be raptured (verses 9-17). It has been almost universally assumed that the 144,000 are sealed and then left behind in the Tribulation and/or Wrath of God while the rest of the Church is raptured. The Bible never says that, and there are no Christians left behind for either event. Nobody goes anywhere until after the Tribulation, so no one can be considered left behind. Any that are left behind after the Tribulation are left behind because they have rejected Jesus as Lord. The 144,000 will flee Jerusalem to the mountain wilderness after they see the Abomination of Desolation enter the temple right before the Tribulation begins. They are hidden in the wilderness for three-and-one-half years during the whole time of the Great Tribulation. At the end of that time, they will be given a special mark and raptured with the rest of the saints. The special mark is placed on the foreheads of the 144,000 during the sixth seal as a transition takes place from the Tribulation of Satan to the Wrath of God.

The 144,000 are born-again Jews, which means they are Christians. They are not left behind during God's wrath to hide from the face of God. They are a part of the Church, and as such, they possess the same promise of deliverance from the wrath to come as the rest of the Church. Revelation 12:14 tells us that the reason they are in the wilderness is because God is caring for and protecting them from the fury and wrath of Satan and his Antichrist during the Great Tribulation, not from the Wrath of God. The perception has been that they are sealed *before* they are cared for in the wilderness, but the exact opposite is true. They are protected for three-and-one-half years in the wilderness, and then they are sealed right before they are raptured.

> And to the woman were given two wings of a great eagle,
> that she might fly into the wilderness, into her place, where
> she is nourished for a time, and times, and half a time,
> *from the face of the serpent.*
>
> *Revelation 12:14*

> And after these things I saw four angels standing on the
> four corners of the earth, holding the four winds of the
> earth, that the wind should not blow on the earth, nor on
> the sea, nor on any tree.
>
> *Revelation 7:1*

The four winds these angels are holding back should be considered in both a literal and a figurative sense. To have all the winds cease blowing across the whole face of the earth at the same time that the sun, the moon and the stars stop giving their light only adds one more dimension to the final sign of the coming of Jesus Christ for His Church and the end of the world. In a figurative sense, the restraining of the winds also means that all things that could cause further harm will be held in check until after the Rapture has occurred. In the following verses, 12,000 individuals from each of the tribes of Israel are sealed in their foreheads just prior to the Rapture—for a total of 144,000. Revelation 14:1-5 is the only other place that the 144,000 are mentioned, and they are once again shown before the Throne of God with the beasts and elders and being described as the firstfruits of the earth unto God. Jesus' top priority when He comes to take His church will be to collect the 144,000 of Israel and deliver them into the presence of their Maker, then He will concentrate on the rest of His Church.

> [2]And I saw another angel ascending from the east, having the seal of the living God: and he cried with a loud voice to the four angels, to whom it was given to hurt the earth and the sea, [3]Saying, Hurt not the earth, neither the sea, nor the trees, till we have sealed the servants of our God in their foreheads. [4]And I heard the number of them which were sealed: and there were sealed an hundred and forty and four thousand of all the tribes of the children of Israel. [5]Of the tribe of Judah were sealed twelve thousand. Of the tribe of Reuben were sealed twelve thousand. Of the tribe of Gad were sealed twelve thousand. [6]Of the tribe of Asher were sealed twelve thousand. Of the tribe of Naphtali were sealed twelve thousand. Of the tribe of Manasseh were sealed twelve thousand. [7]Of the tribe of Simeon were sealed twelve thousand. Of the tribe of Levi were sealed twelve thousand. Of the tribe of Issachar were sealed twelve thousand. [8]Of the tribe of Zebulun were sealed twelve thousand. Of the tribe of Joseph were sealed twelve thousand. Of the tribe of Benjamin were sealed twelve thousand.
>
> *Revelation 7:2-8*

The 144,000 are the only ones who are sealed in this chapter. This is a very significant event that sets them apart from other believers, but it is not so they can be left on the earth during God's wrath. They are sealed and set apart according to the calling and election of God. The sealing of the 144,000 is no different than the calling of the twelve disciples at the very beginning. God has special plans for these Jewish saints that we are not fully aware of at this time, but we do know He has said He will yet choose Israel and that the last will be first. The 144,000 will be leaders in the kingdom that Jesus Christ will establish on this earth when He returns a second time at Armageddon.

THE RAPTURE

Before reading the next passage, call to remembrance Revelation 6:9-11 where the slain saints under the fifth seal were waiting for their brethren that should be slain as they were. The sixth seal reveals that the wait is over. In these next several verses, among the multitudes that are shown in heaven are those very saints along with every other saint who has ever lived. Verse 14 declares that they have come out of Great Tribulation and are now worshiping God before His Throne.

> [9]After this I beheld, and, lo, a great multitude, which no man could number, of all nations, and kindreds, and people, and tongues, stood before the throne, and before the Lamb, clothed with white robes, and palms in their hands; [10]And cried with a loud voice, saying, Salvation to our God which sitteth upon the throne, and unto the Lamb. [11]And all the angels stood round about the throne, and about the elders and the four beasts, and fell before the throne on their faces, and worshipped God, [12]Saying, Amen: Blessing, and glory, and wisdom, and thanksgiving, and honour, and power, and might, be unto our God forever and ever. Amen. [13]And one of the elders answered, saying unto me, What are these which are arrayed in white robes? and whence came they? [14]And I said unto him, Sir, thou knowest. And he said to me, *These are they which came out of great tribulation*, and have washed their robes, and made them white in the blood of the Lamb.
>
> *Revelation 7:9-14*

The sixth seal revealed to us that the time of God's wrath had arrived in Revelation 6:16-17. Chapter 7, verses 1-13 describe events that make up the Rapture, and verse 14 shows us that all of this happens after the Great Tribulation is complete. In the next four chapters the Wrath of God will be revealed through the seven trumpets. The sealing of the 144,000 is completed in chapter 7, verse 8, and then immediately in verse 9 we see all the redeemed of God in heaven all at one time. There is absolutely nothing to suggest that the 144,000 are not a part of this gathering. In fact, verse 14 explains that "These are they that came out of great tribulation." This would include the 144,000 that God protects in the wilderness during the Tribulation from the wrath of Satan. There isn't even a hint of delay between the last of the Jews being sealed and all of the saints congregating together in heaven. The 144,000 are not going to be left out of the festivities described above; they will be the first to arrive!

The actual word "**tribulation**" is used 22 times in the King James Version of the Bible. In the Old Testament the Hebrew word translated as "tribulation" (in only a few cases) was used a total of 102 times, but it was also translated as anguish, adversaries, enemies, foes, troubles, distresses, afflictions, narrow pit, strait, narrow place, sorrows, distress and tribulation. In the New Testament the Greek word for "tribulation" was used 43 times and was translated into the same words as in the Old Testament with the addition of the word "burdens." The phrase "**great tribulation**" is only used three times in the Bible—Matthew 24:21, Revelation 2:22, and Revelation 7:14. In addition, Deuteronomy 4:30, Daniel 12:1, Mark 13:19 and Matthew 24:29 are the only other places that refer to the **great tribulation.** It is evident by the following scriptures that tribulation is something the Church and individual believers—and even nonbelievers—will experience on an ongoing basis. God promises to help, comfort and get us through our tribulations; He never promises that He will cause us to avoid them altogether. On the other hand, He does promise that we will avoid His wrath if we endure and hold fast to our faith, right up to the end.

Words that describe God's wrath—such as wrath, vengeance, repay, recompense and fury—are used over three hundred times in the Bible referring to God's angry judgments, particularly His final judgment of the end-times. As we read these verses about tribulation, we can see that they have nothing to do with God's wrath or judgment.

> Yet hath he not root in himself, but dureth for a while: for *when tribulation or persecution ariseth because of the word*, by and by he is offended.
>
> *Matthew 13:21*

The verse above is referring to Jesus' parable of the sower sowing the seed. In Mark 4:15, we learn that Satan comes immediately to steal the Word out of an individual's hearts after it has been planted there. The verse below is God's promise to be with us and to aid us as we go through tribulations that plague our lives.

> These things I have spoken unto you, that in me ye might have peace. *In the world ye shall have tribulation*: but be of good cheer; I have overcome the world.
>
> *John 16:33*

This next verse by itself is not proof that we go through the Great Tribulation, but it should completely decapitate the false belief that God wouldn't ever allow anything bad to happen to any of His "little lambs." Think of all the tribulation the Church has suffered throughout the ages to this very day we live in—more so in certain places on the planet than in others—and then think of the Great Tribulation as the final episode of Christians suffering in service to their Lord. It may be helpful, also, to think about the fact that the Church is being raptured here under this sixth seal, and the Wrath of God is coming up under the seventh seal. That is where the rivers of blood and the locust with scorpion tails and all of the other unimaginable tortures occur as a part of God's wrath against sinners. The Great Tribulation is just a greater degree of what we see going on around the world all the time, but because Satan and the Antichrist are allowed by God to give it all they have, people all around the world will either be afflicted all at one time, or they will be a part of those causing the affliction. Satan will attempt to take as many down with him as he can as he sees his days drawing to an end, and God will continue to build His church even as He is purging it for a spotless Rapture. Acts 14:22 below is Paul's admonition to the church at Lystra after he was stoned and left for dead. Afterwards God raised him up to continue what he had set out to accomplish: "He stood up and went on his way."

> Confirming the souls of the disciples, and exhorting them to continue in the faith, and that *we must through much tribulation enter into the kingdom of God.*
>
> *Acts 14:22*

The rest of these verses are self-explanatory. Each one reaffirms the fact that tribulation is just a fact of life, particularly for those who stand up for righteousness. The Great Tribulation is nothing more than a particular time of great affliction at the end of the world, which will involve the Antichrist.

> And not only so, *but we glory in tribulations also: knowing that tribulation worketh patience;*
>
> *Romans*

> *Who shall separate us from the love of Christ? shall tribulation, or distress, or persecution, or famine, or nakedness, or peril, or sword?*
>
> *Romans 8:35*

> Rejoicing in hope; *patient in tribulation;* continuing instant in prayer;
>
> *Romans 12:12*

> Great is my boldness of speech toward you, great is my glorying of you: I am filled with comfort, *I am exceeding joyful in all our tribulation.*
>
> *2 Corinthians 7:4*

> For verily, *when we were with you, we told you before that we should suffer tribulation; even as it came to pass,* and ye know.
>
> *1 Thessalonians 3:4*

I John, who also *am your brother, and companion in tribulation*, and in the kingdom and patience of Jesus Christ, was in the isle that is called Patmos, for the Word of God, and for the testimony of Jesus Christ.

Revelation 1:9

I know thy works, and tribulation, and poverty, (but thou art rich) and I know the blasphemy of them which say they are Jews, and are not, but are the synagogue of Satan.

Revelation 2:9

None of the Scriptures we just read promise us a blissful trouble-free existence during this life. The Bible never claims that we will bypass all troubles, tribulations and persecutions—quite to the contrary. It is not so much a promise that we are going to be attacked for our faith, persecuted for our testimony and pummeled for the Word of God we possess, but rather we are repeatedly forewarned that the devil is going to attempt to discredit and hurt us in every way possible. The Great Tribulation is just his way of telling us how special we are to God. Satan hates us with every putrid wisp of his spiritual being. He wants us destroyed, or at the very least, he wants us to give in to the persecution that comes against us and join up with his team of persecutors.

Some of the definitions of wrath are fierceness, indignation, violent passion, abhorrence, anger, punishment, vengeance and wrath. Having a tough time in our tribulations is a far cry from having God's fierce wrath being poured out on us as punishment. Thank God He has said He will deliver us from the wrath to come. One of the scriptures that was originally inspired—using the Greek word for tribulation but translated as afflictions, and ties in so well with the study of the end-times—is found in 2 Corinthians.

[16]For which cause we faint not; but though our outward man perish, yet the inward man is renewed day by day. [17]For our *light affliction [or tribulation]*, which is but for a moment, worketh for us a far more exceeding and eternal weight of glory; [18]While we look not at the things which are seen, but at the things which are not seen: for the

things which are seen are temporal; but the things which
are not seen are eternal.

2 Corinthians 4:16-18

The following paraphrase is given to make these verses even more meaningful to us as the time of Great Tribulation draws ever closer.

"For which cause we should not faint; for even though our outward man perishes a little bit each day, and could be destroyed through various means at any given moment, God continues to renew our inward man on a daily basis. For the light and insignificant tribulations which we suffer will last for only a small moment in eternity (even during the Great Tribulation), but if we endure spiritually through those tribulations with our hearts firmly committed to God, it will gain for us a far more exceeding and eternal weight of glory, blessings and great reward; while we look not at the things which we see all around us that could cause us to doubt and even fear, but we look at and focus on the things which are not seen with our natural senses, but with the eyes of our spirits or deep inside our hearts, which things we can only see by faith in God's Word: for the things which we behold with our natural senses are temporal and subject to change, and will perish with use, even our own bodies; but the things which are not seen and are invisible to our natural eyes are eternal and spiritual and will last forever and never change."

Now back to those who came out of Great Tribulation. Remember, we are still looking at the sixth seal of the Book of Revelation and we will soon open the seventh seal, which deals exclusively with the Wrath of God. John is told here by one of the 24 elders assembled before the Throne of God that the rest of the great multitude assembled before the Throne is made up of those who have come out of great tribulation. He didn't say they came out of *the* Great Tribulation but out of great tribulation, nonetheless. Every person who lives a life of righteousness on this earth suffers a certain amount of great tribulation. Jesus was persecuted constantly as He went around doing good works and healing those who were oppressed of the devil. The lawyers and priests were constantly on His trail trying to catch Him in His words or trying to find some fault in Him. Satan tempted Him in the wilderness; His enemies tried to throw Him off cliffs, and they even hired one of His own men to betray Him. He was in the midst of great tribulation on multiple occasions during His life, and God kept delivering Him—right up to the time He delivered Him to the cross. We all suffer great tribulation in our lives from time to time as Satan works feverishly in the background trying to ruin our lives and the lives of our friends and loved ones. If we stand firm in faith, God delivers, but if we falter and let our faith slip, Satan wins one more skirmish in the battle between life and death, good and evil. Those who are living at the end of days will collectively suffer more tribulation on a worldwide basis than has ever been suffered before. That's the difference between great tribulation and the Great Tribulation.

> ¹⁴And I said unto him, Sir, thou knowest. And he said to me, *These are they which came out of great tribulation*, and have washed their robes, and made them white in the blood of the Lamb. ¹⁵Therefore are they before the throne of God, and serve him day and night in His temple: and he that sitteth on the throne shall dwell among them. ¹⁶They shall hunger no more, neither thirst any more; neither shall the sun light on them, nor any heat. ¹⁷For the Lamb which is in the midst of the throne shall feed them, and shall lead them unto living fountains of waters: and God shall wipe away all tears from their eyes.
>
> *Revelation 7:14-17*

The reward for serving God faithfully in this life is that we get to serve Him faithfully in the life to come. We get to approach Him on His throne and worship and adore Him. That's a far cry better than having the flames of eternal damnation licking away at our resurrected spiritual bodies. Jesus tells us that the worms that will eat away at the damned never die. He also tells us about the rich man who died and asked Abraham to send the beggar Lazarus to dip his finger in water so that he might touch it to his tongue to quench just the tiniest portion of his thirst (see Luke 16:19-31). Another aspect of the reward for those who don't give in to sin, but rather endure to the end, is that they will be fed, their thirst will be quenched and they will never have to worry about sunburn or heatstroke any more. That's right, that's what we just read in verse 16 above. But that's not all. Verse 17 declares that God is going to wipe away the tears of our tribulations—no more pain, no more agony and no more temptations—just the joy of living the life we were created to live.

One more reward of enduring to the end is that we will become like Him when He appears. We have already discussed the fact that we will all, both living and dead, be physically changed into the physical likeness of Jesus when He appears in the clouds. First John reminds us that He will actually appear, that it is not some kind of vision, trance or spiritual hallucination that we are to look for in the clouds. Jesus does appear twice at the end of the world, but we only need to look for Him once when He comes to rescue us. The second time we will be with Him as we return together to reign over all of those who are fortunate enough to survive the Wrath of God.

> Beloved, now are we the sons of God, and it doth not yet appear what we shall be: but we know that, *when he shall appear*, we shall be like him; for we shall see him as he is.
>
> *1 John 3:2*

THINK ABOUT IT!

— Are the 144,000 redeemed by the blood of the Lamb?

— Are we told that they will be left behind?

— Does God exclude any nations, kindreds, people or tongues from the group that is gathered before His throne in this chapter?

Selah

> Fear not: for I am with thee: I will bring thy seed from the east, and gather thee from the west; I will say to the north, Give up; and to the south, Keep not back: bring my sons from far, and my daughters from the ends of the earth; even every one that is called by my name: for I have created him for my glory, I have formed him; yea, I have made him.
>
> *Isaiah 43:5-7*

REVELATION 8

Seal Seven,
The Trumpets of Wrath

My first endeavor at organizing the prophecies on paper was by employing the technologies available to me at the time—a pair of scissors and a Xerox machine. I cut pages out of an old Bible that had become otherwise useless through wear and tear, and made copies. Afterwards, I was going to cut and paste until I had all of the corresponding verses together and then add my handwritten notes to that. Remember, I am an extreme visual learner. I needed to see these things written down to remember them. I didn't get very far as I didn't have the time necessary. Then we got our first computer with a Bible software program and I could cut and paste to my hearts desire. I put Matthew 24 and the entire Revelation down in one document and went to town on it. I'm not one of those people that can recite Scripture like it's my home address, but I have it in my heart and the Holy Spirit brings things to my remembrance. The problem is that my remembrance may be only one, two or three words in a verse. I would type those words into my computer until I found the verse God was leading me to. Things were beginning to look up, but it would still take years to understand the prophecies.

The seventh and final seal which is about to be opened will reveal the fullness of God's wrath. All the events, that together make up

God's wrath, appear in Revelation, chapters 8-11. They will be repeated in chapters 16-19 as the end-times are laid out chronologically a second time from a different perspective. The time of God's wrath begins with a half hour of silence in heaven. All of the praise and worship, all of the rejoicing and celebration by the saints who have just been liberated from their mortal flesh and delivered from a world of sin, and all of the other activities of heaven stop for what amounts to a thirty-minute moment of silence before the Wrath of God begins. This half hour of silence has nothing to do with the Rapture that has already been completed under the sixth seal. The great multitude from every nation and tongue is already in heaven. Now that God has removed His people from harm's way, He is preparing to unleash the full fury of His wrath on the people of the earth below for all the things they have done against Him and His servants and for their rejection of all that is good. The half hour of silence ends when an angel takes a golden censer filled with fire, incense and the prayers of the saints and casts it into the earth. The silence is broken by the great commotion that ensues with voices, thunders and an earthquake. "Vengeance is mine," saith the Lord.

> [1]And when he had opened the *seventh seal*, there was silence in heaven about the space of half an hour. [2]And *I saw the seven angels which stood before God; and to them were given seven trumpets.* [3]And another angel came and stood at the altar, having a golden censer; and there was given unto him much incense, that he should offer it with the prayers of all saints upon the golden altar which was before the throne. [4]And the smoke of the incense, which came with the prayers of the saints, ascended up before God out of the angel's hand. [5]And the angel took the censer, and filled it with fire of the altar, and cast it into the earth: and there were voices, and thunderings, and lightnings, and an earthquake.
>
> *Revelation 8:1-5*

Each of the seven trumpets that are about to sound signify one of the seven judgments of God to be poured out upon the wicked who remain on the earth. The seven trumpets coincide with and correspond to the seven vials of Revelation 16, which have been inserted after each trumpet below for the purpose of comparison. When you read the scriptures together, you notice similarities that make it clear that the trumpets and vials correspond and relate to each other. However, we must bear in mind that the trumpets and vials are expressing things from different perspectives; thus, we should not expect them to say the same thing down to the last letter. Many have placed such stringent constraints on interpretation of prophecy that they do not allow for variations in the way that one event may be recorded differently in different places.

Seven is God's number of completion. God completed His work of recreating the world in seven days as reported in Genesis, He will allow the Antichrist seven years to complete sin and rebellion and then He will bring seven years of wrath on a disobedient world. Perhaps the seven judgments and plagues come one each from the seven spirits of God.

There is not much explaining of the following events other than to read them and take them literally. Just try to imagine for yourself what it would be like to be around when these things begin to take place—and then make sure that you're not. The judgments of the first four trumpets are aimed at only one third of the earth, but they have an effect on all of the earth. As we read through the rest of Revelation, it becomes clear that the things taking place are centered in the Middle East where the kingdom of the beast will be found, but they will have a ripple effect throughout the rest of the world, which will then be totally populated by sinners. It appears from what we are about to read that the judgment the residents of the beast kingdom will receive is much more severe than that of the rest of the world.

As we read about the trumpets in chapters 8-11, we will see a broad, or more of a worldwide, perspective to the Wrath of God, and because of that when things occur, we are told to look at that third of the world where the impact is felt the most. Later when we read about the vials in chapters 16-19, God is, in effect, using a zoom lens that takes us exclusively into the Middle East and the kingdom of the beast. Therefore, when things occur in those chapters where the vials are revealed, we are not directed to the one third of the world where the beast exerts his greatest amount of control because we have already zoomed in on that portion. Even though the vials seem broader, they are simply showing the same targeted area of judgment that the trumpets are—that one third of the world that will be most actively serving the Antichrist. So when we read the chapters that reveal the judgments of the trumpets, we are looking at the whole world and being directed to narrow our focus down to that one third of the world where the Antichrist will have his greatest influence. When we look at the vials of wrath, we are not seeing things from a worldwide perspective but, rather, an isolated view of the Middle East and environs where the Antichrist leads his loyal subjects on a killing rampage against Christians and Jews.

The first trumpet sees a third part of the greenery of the earth destroyed by fire. Where is this third of the earth? It's in the same location in which the first vial is centered—in the Middle East where the Antichrist will be dividing his time between making war and playing God in the temple of God in Jerusalem. This first trumpet/vial combination seems to have a cause-and-effect aspect to it. One third of plant life is destroyed and the people in that part of the earth come down with a very bad and very painful open sore, perhaps through a vitamin and oxygen deficiency caused by a lack of green plants. However, the sore could just be something God slaps on them, irrespective of the lack of greens.

> [6]And the seven angels which had the seven trumpets prepared themselves to sound. [7]*The first angel sounded*, and there followed hail and fire mingled with blood, and they were cast upon the earth: and *the third part* of trees was burnt up, and all green grass was burnt up.
>
> *Revelation 8:6-7*

> And *the first went, and poured out his vial upon the earth*; and there fell a noisome and grievous sore *upon the men which had the mark of the beast, and upon them which worshipped his image.*
>
> *Revelation 16:2*

The next trumpet/vial combination also shows "cause and effect," but this time it is more apparent. A great burning mountain is thrown into the sea; it becomes blood, and everything dies in the sea. These two references are not speaking of a particular sea but, rather, are being used in a generic sense to refer to all seas. At the same time, the first reference narrows things down to one third of the seas while the second reference is already narrowed to one third of the seas by virtue of the fact that the scriptural setting of Revelation 16 is such that it focuses only on that third of the world where the Antichrist rules with a rod of iron.

> 8And *the second angel sounded*, and as it were a great mountain burning with fire was cast into the sea: and *the third part of the sea* became blood; 9And the third part of the creatures which were in the sea, and had life, died; and the third part of the ships were destroyed.
>
> *Revelation 8:8-9*

> And *the second angel poured out his vial upon the sea*; and it became as the blood of a dead man: and every living soul died in the sea.
>
> *Revelation 16:3*

Next, a burning star named Wormwood falls into the rivers, fountains and springs. Wormwood means bitter, poisonous and calamity. The vial mentions the same rivers and fountains, but in addition to them becoming bitter, they turn to blood just like the seas that surround them. It's interesting to note that although the springs feed the rivers and the rivers run into the seas, the bloody waters start in the seas and progress backwards to the rivers and fountains. Perhaps God is showing off a little bit, or maybe He is just making sure that they are unable to explain things away as some type of fluke phenomenon, and they have to confess that it is the God of the Jews doing these things to punish them.

> 10And *the third angel sounded*, and there fell a great star from heaven, burning as it were a lamp, and it fell upon the *third part of the rivers*, and upon the fountains of waters; 11And the name of the star is called Wormwood: and the third part of the waters became wormwood; and many men died of the waters, because they were made bitter.
>
> *Revelation 8:10-11*

And *the third angel poured out his vial upon the rivers* and
fountains of waters; and they became blood.

Revelation 16:4

Cause and effect is presented in a whole different light in the next
judgment. (That is meant to be a pun. It will dawn on you as you read
on.) The trumpet shows that one third part of the day and night is
darkened while the vial shows the sun heating up to the point that it
scorches the occupants of the earth. At first glance, if we compare the
fourth trumpet/vial combination to the three that preceded it, we
might assume that the sun just stops shining in the one third of the
earth that is Antichrist controlled, and they live out this plague in
eight hours of darkness. However, since Revelation 16 is speaking
specifically of the Beast kingdom, we see that the sun and moon shine
there for the other two thirds of the day. That part of the day when
the sun is not shining and the Beast Kingdom is bathed in darkness
is the only time of relief these unrepentant sinners will get. The other
two thirds of the day the sun is so hot it scorches them. That's global
warming at its worst. But it comes from God, and there's nothing
they can do about it. If the waters are still blood at this time, these
people will have to submerge themselves in the hot stinky mess to
keep from broiling. It's not much of a choice—being broiled in the
hot sun, baked in an ovenlike home or simmered in blood.

And the *fourth angel sounded,* and *the third part of the sun*
was smitten, and the third part of the moon, and the third
part of the stars; so as the third part of them was darkened, and the day shone not for a third part of it, and the
night likewise.

Revelation 8:12

And the *fourth angel poured out his vial upon the sun*; and
power was given unto him to scorch men with fire.

Revelation 16:8

The verse below states that the final three trumpets will follow
after the first four are completed. In other words, everything is being

recorded chronologically. This does not mean that the entire Book of Revelation is supposed to be read as a chronological rendition of the end-times. There are three different segments of the Book of Revelation dealing with the end-times, and each of them is presented in chronological order. However, verse 13 is referring only to the trumpets and, by extension, the vials. As we begin to read about the final three trumpets and vials, or woes as they are called here, we begin to see references to the duration of certain events. We will look at the times catalogued in the upcoming chapters later in this book as we consider how long the Wrath of God really takes. It is important to know that these events are being recorded chronologically and that each one is completed before the next one begins. Using that knowledge, we are able to see how long the Wrath of God actually takes.

> And I beheld, and heard an angel flying through the midst of heaven, saying with a loud voice, *Woe, woe, woe, to the inhabiters of the earth by reason of the other voices of the trumpet of the three angels, which are yet to sound!*
>
> *Revelation 8:13*

THINK ABOUT IT!

— Are the trumpet plagues tribulation from Satan or wrath from God?

— Does Satan turn the waters to blood and darken the sun?

Selah

> For, behold, the Lord cometh out of his place to punish the inhabitants of the earth for their iniquity: the earth also shall disclose her blood, and shall no more cover her slain.
>
> *Isaiah 26:21*

Stinging Locusts and Fiery Horsemen

There came a point in my prophetic inquiries where I realized that some of the foundational truths about the end-times I had learned through various means were not truths at all. No wonder I was so confused. I would get real head-splitting headaches as I wrestled between the things God was teaching me and the things I already knew. Turns out, I didn't know as much as I thought. What I finally had to do was abandon everything I had learned in the past and allow God to teach me afresh. A new foundation was already emerging. There is a distinct difference between the Tribulation and the Wrath of God. The Tribulation comes first, the Church is still here, and God is allowing the nation of Israel to suffer mightily at the hand of Satan and his Antichrist because of their unbelief. There is no difference between Jewish believers and other believers except that God protects the Jewish believers while their nation suffers during the Tribulation, and then we are all raptured together before God's wrath begins. What really surprised me was that the Wrath of God was actually longer than the Tribulation and it doesn't even start until after Daniel's seventieth week is completed.

When the fifth angel sounds his trumpet, another angel comes down from heaven to release some very strange creatures from the bottomless pit for a period of five months. They may be a type of creature that followed Satan in his downfall or, more likely, they were created by God for this very moment in time to punish sinners. It should not seem strange that God would create something like this for the punishment of evildoers since we already know that He created hell where "their worm dieth not and their fire is not quenched" (Mark 9:44). The eternal punishment of God truly will be severe, and the temporal punishment of His wrath will not be much better. In fact, the short period of retribution that God will pour out on a world of rebellious and hateful infidels will be a sign, if you will, that He is no longer willfully and lovingly extending His compassionate mercy towards sinners but, rather, giving them all the rejection they deserve. God hates sin but loves the sinner, but the day is coming when the practitioners of sin will be cast into eternal punishment because of their unwillingness to repent. On the day God's punishment begins, they will wish that they had never been born.

The creatures described in the next two judgments should not be assumed to be anything other than what they are represented to be in the upcoming passages. In verse 6 of the first passage, it is interesting to note that men will seek death at this time, but it will flee from them. After losing every green plant, drinking from bloodied waters and being scorched by the sun (not to mention the severely depleted oxygen supply brought on by the high temperatures and lack of oxygen-producing plants on the land and in the waters), the people of the earth are exhausted and want to escape the newest torment by "giving up the ghost." But, the Savior of all mankind has conquered the last enemy named death and has removed death as an alternative at this time. Every person must live through this judgment right up to the very last day, and then death will become a very real option once again. After the five months of torment these creatures inflict upon those who remain on the earth after the Church is gone, the creatures could possibly return to the bottomless pit to greet these very same people later on when they do die. There's just nowhere to hide if you're an enemy of God.

> [1]And the *fifth angel sounded*, and I saw a star fall from
> heaven unto the earth: and to him was given the key of the
> bottomless pit. [2]And he opened the bottomless pit; *and*

there arose a smoke out of the pit, as the smoke of a great furnace; and the sun and the air were darkened by reason of the smoke of the pit. ³And there came out of the smoke locusts upon the earth: and unto them was given power, as the scorpions of the earth have power. ⁴And it was commanded them that they should not hurt the grass of the earth, neither any green thing, neither any tree; but only those men which have not the seal of God in their foreheads. ⁵And to them it was given that they should not kill them, but that they should be tormented five months: and their torment was as the torment of a scorpion, when he striketh a man. ⁶And *in those days shall men seek death, and shall not find it*; and shall desire to die, and death shall flee from them. ⁷And the shapes of the locusts were like unto horses prepared unto battle; and on their heads were as it were crowns like gold, and their faces were as the faces of men. ⁸And they had hair as the hair of women, and their teeth were as the teeth of lions. ⁹And they had breastplates, as it were breastplates of iron; and the sound of their wings was as the sound of chariots of many horses running to battle. ¹⁰And they had tails like unto scorpions, and there were stings in their tails: and their power was to hurt men five months. ¹¹And they had a king over them, which is the angel of the bottomless pit, whose name in the Hebrew tongue is Abaddon, but in the Greek tongue hath his name Apollyon.

Revelation 9:1-11

Verse 4 contains a statement that is both puzzling and confusing. The locusts are told not to hurt the trees, grass and green things, but only those who do not have the seal of God in their foreheads. This has caused some to assume that the 144,000 are still on the earth, but they're not. They are protected during the Tribulation, but they are raptured with the rest of the Church before the Wrath of God begins. Between Daniel 8 and 12, we will see that the Antichrist controls activity in the temple starting 75 days before the Tribulation begins, during the entire Tribulation and 965 days into the Wrath of God. The 144,000 will be protected from the Antichrist for the entire three-and-one-half years of tribulation, however they are seen in heaven with the rest of the Church wherever we read about the Rapture, so they could not be the ones who have the seal of God in their foreheads in verse 4 above. Either there is no one at all on the earth who has the seal of God in their foreheads at this time and all of mankind is open prey for the locusts, or the angels who sealed the 144,000 are still around sealing people who call out to God.

A third possibility is that people could take it upon themselves to seal themselves with the same mark that the 144,000 received. They were not sealed in secret. Anyone who was in close proximity would have been able to witness it. In fact, Revelation 14:1 informs us that the seal is the "Father's name." It could be a last-ditch effort by those who are too scared to take the mark of the beast who improvise the mark of God instead. If you can imagine witnessing those people who have the mark of the beast being systematically targeted by the Wrath of God, it is not that hard to imagine many of the heathen who remain on the earth at this time etching the name of God into their foreheads in an attempt to escape death. This is all speculation since there do not seem to be any scriptures that tell us who is being sealed during the Wrath of God, nor how it is done.

Under this fifth trumpet/vial combo, we are able to see more clearly that the trumpets are a much broader worldwide view of events with the beast kingdom receiving the bulk of attention, while the vials are focused on the kingdom of the beast exclusively with no regard to what is happening in the rest of the world. Verse 2 in the scripture above tells us that the sun and air are darkened by the smoke that escapes from the bottomless pit as the stinging locusts ascend from it. The description of the corresponding vial tells us that the kingdom of the beast will be filled with darkness. The plague of the stinging locust may stretch across the face of the earth, but the doorway to the bottomless pit is located in the midst of the beast kingdom. The darkness resulting from the smoke and the locusts will mix with the spiritual darkness that already engulfs the beast kingdom to darken their souls even further. The pains mentioned below are those caused by the locust stings. The statement about this vial being poured on the seat of the beast simply means that it is poured out on the very center of his kingdom and the seat or throne of his power. The Antichrist will rule from Babylon and Jerusalem alternately.

> [10]And the *fifth angel poured out his vial upon the seat of the beast*; and his kingdom was full of darkness; and they gnawed their tongues for pain, [11]And blasphemed the God of heaven because of their pains and their sores, and repented not of their deeds.
>
> *Revelation 16:10,11*

This next verse actually completes those above about the stinging locusts of the fifth seal. However, for emphasis it was saved until after the vial. The fifth trumpet and vial combined make up the first of three woes that are coming to an end right now after five full months of agony. Woe is defined as "an exclamation of grief." Five months of grief and agony that is collectively described by the fifth trumpet and vial comes to an end before the next woe begins.

> *One woe is past*; and, behold, *there come two woes more hereafter*.
>
> *Revelation 9:12*

The sixth angel is about to sound his trumpet. This trump will cover at least three years, six months, and three-and-one-half days, and could possibly stretch beyond four years and seven months. The events of the sixth trumpet will not be completed until Revelation 11:14 where the two witnesses are taken up in their own little mini-rapture. The seventh angel will not sound his trumpet to begin the final woe until Revelation 11:15, right after the two witnesses are taken up into heaven.

> [13]And *the sixth angel sounded*, and I heard a voice from the four horns of the golden altar which is before God, [14]Saying to the sixth angel which had the trumpet, Loose the four angels which are *bound in the great river Euphrates*. [15]And the four angels were loosed, which were *prepared for an hour, and a day, and a month, and a year*, for *to slay the third part of men*. [1 year, 1 month, 1 day and 1 hour][16]And the number of the army of the horsemen were *two hundred thousand thousand*: and I heard the number of them.
>
> *Revelation 9:13-16*

The number of the horsemen is 200 million. The next three verses are not a 2000-year-old attempt at describing modern warfare for the year 2020 or whenever the Wrath of God comes, but again, it is something God has prepared especially for the time of His wrath. What John is describing are real horses with heads like lions, tails like serpents and mouths that spew forth fire, smoke and brimstone. Verse 20 describes this as a plague, not an army of men equipped with sophisticated armament.

If the world population were about six billion when the Tribulation begins and we recall that one quarter of mankind was wiped out during the Tribulation of the Antichrist, that would leave a worldwide population of four-and-one-half billion. Out of that number, suppose that only 500,000,000 are raptured before the wrath begins. During this second woe of the Wrath of God, another one third of mankind will be eliminated by the horsemen; however, this time it is the wicked that are being slain and not the innocent. That would leave about 2,660,000,000 sinners on the earth at this time, assuming a limited number of people are killed during the first four trump/vial combinations and those who survive continue to copulate. This is not a bad assumption since we know that death is taken away completely during the first woe of stinging locusts. Try to imagine surviving this torment for thirteen months as you witness one third of mankind slain before your eyes by these terrible creatures. For many of those who do survive, the fear of God may finally be implanted in their hearts, which could be a type of salvation to them. They could be the ones who survive the Wrath of God and are ruled over in the Millennial Reign by the saints of Christ. Not everyone is going to have the fear of God in his or her heart, though. The sixth vial shows us that the governments operating on the earth at this time will come to the aid of the Antichrist. They have come to the political conclusion that it is in everyone's best interest to make a united stand against Jesus Christ when He returns a second time with His soldier saints at Armageddon to take back control of the earth.

> [17]And thus I saw the horses in the vision, and them that sat
> on them, having breastplates of fire, and of jacinth, and
> brimstone: and the heads of the horses were as the heads
> of lions; and out of their mouths issued fire and smoke

and brimstone. *18By these three was the third part of men killed*, by the fire, and by the smoke, and by the brimstone, which issued out of their mouths. *19*For their power is in their mouth, and in their tails: for their tails were like unto serpents, and had heads, and with them they do hurt.

Revelation 9:17-19

When the sixth trumpet and vial are released, two different things take place around the Euphrates River, which is right in the heart of the beast kingdom. The four angels and the horsemen mentioned above are especially prepared by God for the time of His wrath and are released from the Euphrates at the sounding of the trump. While they are busy doing their thing, we can see in the scriptures below that the Euphrates is being dried up as three evil spirits go out to draw the armies of the whole world together for the Battle of Armageddon. Several years have passed since the Rapture and now all the world is banding together for one last battle. With the waters of the Euphrates out of the way, the armies of countries such as Iran, China and India, and all others in those regions to the east, will be able to march straight into Israel unimpeded.

Verse 14 points out that the three spirits are devils working miracles. This is surely a miracle of hell to draw the armies of the earth to Armageddon to face the return of Jesus Christ after all that has taken place so far. This is a part of the strong deception God has allowed to come upon the earth. There will be great darkness and delusion upon those who reject the truth of the gospel before the Rapture ever takes place. However, when the Church is gone, things only get worse. At the time this starts taking place, the Church will have been gone for quite a few years before the sixth angel sounds his trumpet, and there has been no one to bring true enlightenment to the people of the earth other than the two witnesses who are a part of this woe. They will be placed in the same temple that the Antichrist occupied during the Tribulation. However, the enlightenment the witnesses bring only adds to the torment of the heathen rather than bringing salvation to them, because their testimony is about the judgment and severity of God rather than the saving grace they have already rejected internally in their hearts and externally in their actions.

> [12]And *the sixth angel poured out his vial upon the great river*
> *Euphrates*; and the water thereof was dried up, that the way
> of the kings of the east might be prepared. [13]And I saw
> three unclean spirits like frogs come out of the mouth of
> the dragon, and out of the mouth of the beast, and out of
> the mouth of the false prophet. [14]For they are the spirits of
> devils, working miracles, which go forth unto the kings of
> the earth and of the whole world, to gather them to the
> battle of that great day of God Almighty.
>
> *Revelation 16:12-14*

The following passage from Isaiah is one that covers a wide time-frame from the Battle of Armageddon to the new heavens and the new earth. Peter was probably thinking of this passage when he combined together the Day of the Lord with the re-creation of the earth. In both cases the Millennial Reign of Christ just happens to be sandwiched in between, making both Peter's statement and this passage a thousand years long and then some. Verses 2 and 8 are the most important to us at this time, telling us that God is going to gather the armies of the earth together for their destruction in the day of His vengeance. Satan and his foul spirits are the ones actually doing all the footwork, but God has a way of leading him along on a short leash to wherever He wants him to be and to do whatever He wants him to do. God does not control Satan's will, but by His omniscience He is able to manipulate him around with ease.

> [1]Come near, ye nations, to hear; and hearken, ye people: let
> the earth hear, and all that is therein; the world, and all
> things that come forth of it. [2]*For the indignation of the Lord*
> is upon all nations, and his fury upon all their armies: he
> hath utterly destroyed them, he hath delivered them to the
> slaughter. [3]Their slain also shall be cast out, and their stink
> shall come up out of their carcasses, and the mountains
> shall be melted with their blood. [4]And all the host of heaven
> shall be dissolved, and the heavens shall be rolled together as
> a scroll: and all their host shall fall down, as the leaf falleth
> off from the vine, and as a falling fig from the fig tree. [5]For
> my sword shall be bathed in heaven: behold, it shall come
> down upon Idumea, and upon the people of my curse, to

judgment. [6]The sword of the Lord is filled with blood, it is made fat with fatness, and with the blood of lambs and goats, with the fat of the kidneys of rams: for the Lord hath a sacrifice in Bozrah, and a great slaughter in the land of Idumea. [7]And the unicorns shall come down with them, and the bullocks with the bulls; and their land shall be soaked with blood, and their dust made fat with fatness. [8]*For it is the day of the* Lord's *vengeance, and the year of recompences for the controversy of Zion.*

Isaiah 34:1-8

The final two verses of Revelation 9 show us the justness of God's judgment and punishment. Notice that the rest of the men fail to repent, even after all the punishments they have gone through and even after seeing so many of their companions destroyed.

[20]And the rest of the men which were not killed by these plagues *yet repented not of the works of their hands, that they should not worship devils, and idols of gold, and silver, and brass, and stone, and of wood: which neither can see, nor hear, nor walk:* [21]*Neither repented they of their murders, nor of their sorceries, nor of their fornication, nor of their thefts.*

Revelation 9:20-21

THINK ABOUT IT!

— Do these trumpet plagues come from Satan or are they wrath from God?

— How many people die as a result of each plague?

Selah

Wherefore doth the wicked contemn God? he hath said in his heart, Thou wilt not require it.

Psalm 10:13

REVELATION 10

John's Secret Mission

It's amazing how just one word can change an entire sentence, an entire paragraph or even an entire doctrine. For years men have been rewriting the Bible, particularly in regards to the end-times prophecies because too many words interfered with what they believed. Unending research and word studies have been conducted to justify changing the words that don't support the researcher's doctrine as if the King James translators did a poor job by translating verbatim without the corrupting influence of personal opinion.

This chapter seems parenthetical to us but it was preparatory to John. It seems to have been dropped into the middle of everything else going on with a big set of parentheses surrounding it, without necessarily being connected to the flow of events. However, as we read through Revelation 10 and 11, we are going to discover that everything taking place here has to do with the sixth trumpet and the two witnesses as a part of the sixth trumpet.

John is being given a message here, and then he is told to seal it up. It's not until the last verse of the chapter that we learn why. In verse 6 John was told that time was about to come to an end. That is a very strange statement if it is declaring John's day to be the end of the world. There are places where the writers of Scripture declare that the end of the world has already come at the time they were composing the Word of God, but that is not the case here with John. As we read these next two chapters, we are going to see that this statement is made in relation to the sixth trumpet, which began in Revelation 9:13 and does not conclude until Revelation 11:14,15 where the second "woe" ends and the seventh trumpet signals God's final judgment. The things John is seeing in this chapter are all a part of the sixth trumpet which leads into the final trumpet and the end of time.

> [1]And I saw another mighty angel come down from heaven, clothed with a cloud: and a rainbow was upon his head, and his face was as it were the sun, and his feet as pillars of fire: [2]And he had in his hand a little book open: and he set his right foot upon the sea, and his left foot on the earth, [3]And cried with a loud voice, as when a lion roareth: and when he had cried, seven thunders uttered their voices. [4]And when the seven thunders had uttered their voices, I was about to write: and I heard a voice from heaven saying unto me, *Seal up those things which the seven thunders uttered, and write them not.* [5]And the angel which I saw stand upon the sea and upon the earth lifted up his hand to heaven, [6]And sware by him that liveth for ever and ever, who created heaven, and the things that therein are, and the earth, and the things that therein are, and the sea, and the things which are therein, *that there should be time no longer.*
>
> *Revelation 10:1-6*

The phrase "that there should be time no longer" makes it seem as though everything is going to come to a complete halt, leaving only a blackened void of lifeless nothing. However, as we have already discussed, God and His creation do not fall into a vacuum and cease to exist. He has an eternal future kingdom planned for those who love Him, and for those who don't, He has flames that are never quenched and worms that never die. The next verse puts this statement in a better perspective. Verse 7 declares in advance that it is the seventh trumpet that will bring an end to the mystery of God. The completion of the mystery of God, in this case, is the mystery of His wrath as declared unto us by His prophets. The mystery is completed when Jesus returns with His saints to rule. However, it won't be until Revelation 11:15 that the seventh trumpet is finally sounded. In the meantime, the two witnesses will be doing their thing for the next three-and-one-half years. In verse 11 John is told that he must prophesy again before diverse multitudes. John wasn't able to complete his mission while he was here the first time, and he wasn't supposed to. God is going to send him back in his resurrected body at the appropriate time to do the job assigned to him. When he returns, he's not going to be John the Beloved, the disciple of love who leaned against the breast of Jesus. He and Daniel both are going to have power to bring plagues against their enemies, and with fire that spews from their mouths, be able to destroy anyone who tries to harm them. Bear in mind that all of the people they come in contact with have already been judged worthy of God's wrath, so to breathe fire on those who try to harm them is not an act of rebellion against the command to love; it is just being obedient servants fulfilling their assignments in the Wrath of God.

> *7But in the days of the voice of the seventh angel, when he shall begin to sound, the mystery of God should be finished*, as he hath declared to his servants the prophets. *8And the voice which I heard from heaven spake unto me again, and said, Go and take the little book which is open in the hand of the angel which standeth upon the sea and upon the earth. 9And I went unto the angel, and said unto him, Give me the little book. And he said unto me, Take it, and eat it up; and it shall make thy belly bitter, but it shall be in thy mouth sweet as honey. 10And I took the little book out of the angel's hand, and ate it up; and it was in my mouth sweet as honey: and as soon as I had eaten it, my belly was bitter. 11And he said unto me, Thou must prophesy again before many peoples, and nations, and tongues, and kings.*
>
> Revelation 10:7-11

If you look at ten different versions of the Bible, you will likely find as many different renderings of the final statement in verse 11, and those different translations may all mean something totally different.

The reason that is true is because the translators have relied on personal interpretations to guide them, rather than translating verbatim what the original text was saying. When the different "translations" of the same verse start to conflict with each other, they render the statement meaningless and we can never be sure of what is actually being said. In one version the words prophesy "again before" many peoples reads "again over"; in another they read "yet further concerning," and in the New King James they read "again about." Each of these changes the meaning from what was intended and what was accurately translated and written in the King James Version. The newer translations make assumptions, and rather than translating, they interpret in such a way as to fit into their own beliefs. The word "again" seems to come through in each of the translations unscathed. John has to prophesy again, but is it about, concerning, over or before many people?

The Greek word in question is one that shows the physical relationship between two things. It can be translated into several different words such as on, upon, in, over, at, and against. In every case it shows the location of one thing in regards to another. In verse 11, it is meant to show the actual physical relationship of the two witnesses in regard to "many peoples" while they are prophesying to them, as opposed to showing what or who they will be prophesying about. It is not *about* many people, nations, tongues and kings, but it's *before* them. Everywhere else in the King James Version where this word is used in relation to someone giving any kind of testimony, the word "before" is used.

In the Gospels, Jesus informs us that believers will be brought "before" counsels, synagogues, rulers and kings to give a witness. In Acts chapters 23-26, Paul was brought "before" his accusers, "before" Festus and "before" King Agrippa. We are told not to go to law with a brother "before" unbelievers, not to hear accusations against elders except it be "before" two or three witnesses and Jesus gave a good confession "before" Pontius Pilate. In each of these cases, a testimony was given *in front of* someone or something and not *about* that someone or something. The same thing is true concerning John. He did not prophesy again *in front of* people, nations, tongues and kings before he died, but he will when he returns. A part of his testimony to the world of the Antichrist will be that after the seventh trumpet sounds, its alarm time will have run out on the world of sin and death.

Chapter 10 concludes with John's work order to prophesy again before many diverse groups of people. Everything that John sees in this chapter is very much similar to the vision Daniel saw and wrote about in Daniel 12. John and Daniel both saw an angel standing upon the waters with a concealed message concerning the end of time, and both were told they had a job to do at the end of time. We will look at what Daniel wrote in chapter 12 a little later in this book.

THINK ABOUT IT!

— Is there a difference between prophesying again before many nations in a literal sense and prophesying again about, concerning, unto, upon or over many nations in a figurative sense?

— Did John prophesy again and again in the Revelation or is it one continuous revelation?

— Does John still have a job to do?

Selah

For the gifts and calling of God are without repentance.

Romans 11:29

Truth Squared Equals Torment

The two witnesses always confused me, both because of their actions and because there is never any indication that they are preaching the gospel. God never uses fear and intimidation to get people saved, but yet these two guys are described as blowing smoke and speaking curses against their enemies, even before the time of God's punishment had arrived. Or so I thought. As God began to unravel things for me I could see that the two witnesses were indeed a part of His wrath. It should have been evident by everything that is written about them, and by their placement in the Scriptures. I think the greatest problem has been the tendency of people to lump the Tribulation and the Wrath of God into one big ball of string that wraps continually around itself with the beginning buried in the center, and the tail end stuffed beneath the surface. There is no clear beginning and no clear end. It wasn't until God began to open my eyes to the differences between the Tribulation and the Wrath that I was able to accept this chapter exactly as it is written and where it was written.

It has been universally assumed that the two witnesses are a part of the Tribulation. However, everything about them and their ministry maintains that they are a part of the Wrath of God. Everything in

Revelation 10 was preparatory for John, getting him ready for that time, and then Revelation 11 shows him as one of the two witnesses at work—and solidly anchored—in the Wrath of God. They are a part of the sixth trumpet of wrath, and to try and detach them from that is to distort the Word of God. They are resurrected human beings, which is evidenced by the powers they possess. They take part in the same Resurrection as the rest of the body of Christ. God does not bestow the kind of powers that these two possess upon any of His ministers of reconciliation until the door of salvation has been closed.

The first half of Revelation 11 is about the two witnesses of God who will be in Jerusalem prophesying against the inhabitants of the earth while God's wrath is being poured out. They are a part of the second woe, which concludes in verse 13 of this chapter as soon as the two witnesses are taken up into heaven. After they are taken from the earth, verse 14 immediately declares that the second woe is past and the third woe is coming quickly. These two men are the only servants of God that we know for sure are on the earth during the time of God's wrath. They are not left-behind saints, but rather, God places them back on the earth for a three-and-one-half year time of prophecy during the midpoint of the Wrath of God. They may very well be the only ones who will be worshipping in the temple at this time. Daniel 8:14 informs us that the temple will be cleansed after 2300 days, and these prophets are the ones who cleanse it. The Antichrist enters the temple 75 days before the Tribulation begins and stops the daily sacrifice. He controls it for the entire 1260 days of the Tribulation. And he continues to control the temple for another 965 days after the Tribulation ends for a total of 2300 days. The Abomination of Desolation will then be removed, and the Antichrist will be barred from entering the temple for three-and-one-half years while God's two witnesses are at work dispensing the Wrath of God. The courtyard, however, is given over to the Gentiles to tread underfoot.

During the Tribulation, which is the second half of Daniel's seventieth week, the Antichrist controls and inhabits the temple of God, and he has the Abomination of Desolation set up in the temple near the end of that time. The two witnesses do not occupy the temple of God alongside the Antichrist during the Tribulation, and it does not need to be cleansed before the Antichrist enters it. Furthermore, since the Antichrist gains control of the temple and stops the daily sacrifice

75 days before the Tribulation begins, that effectively bars us from trying to place the two witnesses into the first half of Daniel's seventieth week. They are, in fact, participants in the Wrath of God. The two witnesses actually drive the Antichrist from the temple several years after the Tribulation is abruptly halted by the Rapture of the Church and the initial onslaught of the Wrath of God is poured out. They begin their testimony of torment against the inhabitants of the earth after they kick the Antichrist out. Nowhere are we told that their testimony is an evangelistic outreach, only that they smite the earth with plagues as often as they like. At the end of their three-and-one-half year testimony, they are killed by the Antichrist, brought back to life by God and then raised back up into heaven once more. God predetermines that they must relinquish their lives a second time, and then He raises them back to life a second time. This creates a sense of false hope for the world, but it is as short-lived as the short death of the two witnesses. After three-and-one-half days, they stand on their feet again and wave bye-bye to those who are celebrating their death.

> [1]And there was given me a reed like unto a rod: and the angel stood, saying, Rise, and measure the temple of God, and the altar, and them that worship therein. [2]But the court which is without the temple leave out, and measure it not; for it is given unto the Gentiles: and the holy city shall they tread under foot forty and two months. [3 1/2 years] [3]And I will give power unto my two witnesses, and they shall prophesy a thousand two hundred and threescore days, clothed in sackcloth. [260 days or 3 1/2 years using only 30-day months] [4]These are the two olive trees, and the two candlesticks standing before the God of the earth. [5]And if any man will hurt them, fire proceedeth out of their mouth, and devoureth their enemies: and if any man will hurt them, he must in this manner be killed. [6]These have power to shut heaven, that it rain not in the days of their prophecy: and have power over waters to turn them to blood, and to smite the earth with all plagues, as often as they will.
>
> *Revelation 11:1-6*

The two witnesses are called olive trees and candlesticks that stand before the God of the earth. Olive trees are truly miraculous plants. They have regenerative cells that keep them alive and healthy for centuries. Many olive trees in the Mediterranean area are reported to be hundreds and even thousands of years old. They are trees of life, although not as potent as the tree of life that stood in the midst of the Garden of Eden. In Revelation 22:2, the tree of life that grows in the New Jerusalem bears twelve different fruits and has leaves for the healing of the nations, making it much different and far superior to the olive tree. However, the similarities are very striking.

The olive is considered a fruit, and it is the only fruit that produces oil. The fruit by itself adds health and vitality to those who consume it, while foods cooked in the oil actually become healthier for human consumption. The oil has been used medicinally, both topically and internally, to combat different diseases. Some people take a daily sip of it for their health. One of the effects of olive oil intake is reduced body fat, which in itself is a major boost to one's health. The leaves of the olive tree can be brewed into one of the most powerful anti-oxidant teas known to man.

The candlesticks are actually candleholders. They're not of much use by themselves, but when you place a candle on top, they provide light to see by. The two witnesses hold out the light of heaven as they speak the words of God. As the primary writers of the end-times prophecies, John and Daniel are the candlesticks who hold a light up to the future. They shine a light of hope into the hearts and minds of those who would otherwise see only gloom and despair. Through their prophecies, we can see that there is a path to the future that includes abundant life, and their light shines bright upon all of the troubles and pitfalls we will encounter along the way. That light is also a beacon of warning to all who would otherwise live for this life only.

During the time of their prophecy, the world will be inhabited by those who have already rejected the light because they love darkness instead and, therefore, their prophecies will be torment to those people. There may be an outreach component to the message they bring during the Wrath of God. However, we are not really told that. In Revelation 9:4, the stinging locust of the fifth seal are instructed to go after only those who have not the seal of God in their foreheads.

That's not an indirect reference to the 144,000 who have the seal of God in their foreheads but have already been taken to heaven with the rest of the Church in the Rapture. It seems to suggest that there is some form of repentance and salvation during the Wrath, even though the age of grace has already come to an end. People may seal themselves with the same seal that the 144,000 received before they were taken away, or the same angels may come to do the sealing whenever someone does call upon the Lord. On the other hand, those who have the mark of the beast are the primary target of God's wrath, and they will be totally eliminated before the Wrath reaches its conclusion.

The beast, mentioned in verse 7 below, is the Antichrist who will kill the two witnesses, but only after they finish the job they were sent to do. As a part of the second woe, which the two witnesses have a shared part in, the Euphrates River is dried up to make the way clear for the kings of the East to come to the Battle of Armageddon. The first stop for the armies may very well be at the temple of God to silence the two witnesses.

One thing that the two witnesses—John and Daniel—will do is ask, "Why didn't you believe us back when you had a chance?" They will follow that up with a great big "I told you so" to a world that has rejected the goodness of God and ignored the warnings of a judgment to come. They will then enlighten the world regarding what else lies in wait for them as the Wrath of God reaches closure. They could be delivering a warning and a message of hope to those who remain on the earth to not follow the beast or take his number if they want to survive God's wrath and be left standing after the return of Jesus Christ at Armageddon. They will more than likely have the seal of God in their own foreheads and instruct others that this is the mark they need to take if they are going to take any.

Some people believe that Enoch and Elijah are the two witnesses because they were both taken by God without experiencing death. Hebrews 9:27 asserts, "It is appointed unto men once to die, but after this the judgment." While that is true, it is also true that many saints will still be living and breathing at the return of Jesus Christ for His Church. They are not going to suddenly drop dead at the appearing of the Lord just because it is appointed unto all to die and, therefore, they must die before they can be raptured. Not hardly! They are going to be changed to incorruptible beings at the sounding of the last trump, even as those saints who have already died are raised out of the ground.

The two witnesses are described in superhuman terms, and because the Resurrection has already taken place before the two witnesses prophesy as a part of the Wrath of God, that would make just about anybody qualified for this job. For John and Daniel, their judgment would already be determined because they have already died once, and therefore, the life that they already lived would determine their judgment. It would be impossible for them to fall away during their prophecy of the end-times because they are resurrected saints. On the other hand, if Enoch and Elijah are the two witnesses, by using the argument that they are the only two who were taken to heaven without dying, they would face double jeopardy if they were placed on the earth a second time so that they could finally die—if you have to die once before your fate is sealed. More likely, God raptured these two just like He will rapture the Church in the end because their work was done and He was so pleased with them that He put them through the express checkout line—not because He was going to send them back but because He wanted to give them a special blessing for the great faith they exhibited during their lives. If you'll recall, 1 Corinthians 15:50 declared that flesh and blood will not inherit the kingdom of God. If that is so, and it is, we know Enoch and Elijah could not possibly be up in heaven walking around in flesh-and-blood bodies waiting to come back and die.

Neither of these dynamic duos should have to die since the Resurrection is already past, but die they will if they are the chosen two who carry out this mission. Because Jesus has gained full control over death at the Resurrection, you would think they wouldn't have to die at all, but God has allowed their bodies to lie in the streets for three-and-one-half days so that the world might celebrate a hollow victory and then taunt them as He raises them up again. In truth, it really matters little who the two witnesses are because this is part of the sixth trumpet judgment, and God can use whomever he desires to prophesy. Let it suffice to say that there is more than one possibility; however, John and Daniel—the two persons who received the bulk of revelation concerning the end-times—were given special insights and directives that almost assuredly places them back on the earth at the end of time.

Jesus does not return at Armageddon for a second Rapture; He returns at Armageddon to destroy those who have amassed there with weapons of war and to take control of the earth. He accomplishes these goals by completely annihilating the armies that have gathered to resist His unwanted intrusion, and then He brings the remaining occupants of the earth under His submission. He has come to live on the earth, which eradicates any need for a second Rapture. Nobody's going anywhere after He returns the second time. He will set up His Millennial Reign and, with a rod of iron, rule over all who survive. Revelation tells us in several places that those who experience the Wrath of God lack a repentant heart. That is, after all, why they are being punished in the first place. Those who survive may have nothing more than just enough sense to back off and suppress their hatred, or perhaps, they do have some type of awakening in their souls that doesn't quite get them saved but makes them realize they are getting what they deserve. Or, it could be that they are too old, too young, too lazy or too busy with other things to bother with joining the armies of the beast. Whatever the reason, their lives are spared. During what must surely be a full seven-year period, multitudes of infants will doubtless be born who will grow into Christ-loving adults during the Millennial Reign.

Before the Battle of Armageddon can take place, the sixth judgment must be completed and the seventh trumpet and vial must be released. The sixth judgment does not end until verse 14 (see scripture below) after the two witnesses are slain and then taken into heaven. After suffering so much of the Wrath of God, many of those who remain on the earth are not repenting but just waiting for the opportunity to slay the two witnesses. Verse 10 discloses the fact that the prophecy of the two witnesses actually torments the remnants of the earth. Now they are ready to silence them through death. Verse 7 declares that the beast that ascends out of the bottomless pit will lead the armies, some of which have been present in Israel since the beginning of the Tribulation, to make war against the two witnesses. Two against hundreds, thousands, maybe even millions. It's not a very fair war, but Satan is never fair. Revelation 17:8 reaffirms that the beast actually ascends out of the bottomless pit. We are going to look at that in more depth (pun intended) later on. The beast is the Antichrist, and he is being restrained at this moment in the bottomless pit.

⁷And when they shall have finished their testimony, *the beast that ascendeth out of the bottomless pit* shall make war against them, and shall overcome them, and kill them. ⁸And their dead bodies shall lie in the street of *the great city*, which spiritually is called Sodom and Egypt, where also our Lord was crucified.

Revelation11:7-8

The "great city" is referring to Babylon which spiritually is called Sodom and Egypt. All of these places symbolize the bondage and sin for which Jesus died. Egypt represents bondage. After the Israelites were delivered from the bondage of Egypt, they continually turned their hearts back to that bondage rather than receive the freedom God had given them. (Isn't that like some of us today?) Sodom represents unbridled sins of the flesh. The people of Sodom, wanting to have their way with the angels that came in to deliver Lot's family, "wearied themselves to find the door" after the angels smote them with blindness (Genesis 19:11). Even after being stricken with blindness, they were so driven by lust for new flesh that they could not give up trying to enter the house to get at these new men. Babylon represents the pride and arrogance of all those who, through any means possible, sow to themselves and hoard wealth for their own sensual pleasures while they persecute the poor and needy and righteous. Babylon is called the "great city" in Revelation 14:8; 16:9; 17:18; 18:10,16,18-19,21. Together, Babylon, Sodom and Egypt represent the fullness of sin that nailed Jesus to the cross.

Jesus was slain in Jerusalem, which, although it is meant to be a mirror of the heavenly city, also represents religion in a worldly and fleshly manner, law that convicts rather than pardons, brings bondage rather than liberty and judgment rather than grace. In a very real sense, our Lord was crucified in all these places and wherever sin is found. The heavenly Jerusalem is also called the "great city," and the holy Jerusalem as well. In verse 2 above, the earthly Jerusalem is called the holy city even though the Gentiles are allowed to tread upon the courtyard of the temple and the rest of the city. The presence of the two witnesses in the temple of God and the decree of holiness by God are what make it holy, even though at times the holy city has been corrupted. God has chosen to put His name there and declare it holy. That is enough to make it holy, despite the fact that legalism, reprobate Jews, angry heathen and the Antichrist himself will at times pollute the city and the temple. The two witnesses will be slain in Jerusalem, the holy city, and their bodies will be carried to great Babylon, the great city, for all the world to see and to celebrate their deaths.

> 9And they of the people and kindreds and tongues and
> nations shall see their dead bodies *three days and an half,*
> and shall not suffer their dead bodies to be put in graves.
> 10And they that dwell upon the earth shall rejoice over
> them, and make merry, and shall send gifts one to another;
> *because these two prophets tormented them* that dwelt on
> the earth. 11And after three days and an half the Spirit of
> life from God entered into them, and they stood upon
> their feet; and great fear fell upon them which saw them.
>
> *Revelation 11:9-11*

God's people, who are gathered from all nations, kindreds and tongues, were removed from the earth right before His wrath was released. Now, in the very depths of that wrath, people from every kindred, nation and tongue who are left on the earth are having a party—a global celebration with gifts, party hats and balloons because they have been liberated from the torment of the two saints who spoke the truth of God to them. There's no repentance, no sorrow, no guilt over the murder of the saints, only rejoicing over their brutal slaying. The party ends suddenly, however, after three-and-one-half days as the two witnesses get to their feet again and receive their own personal rapture. They are raptured in the same exact manner as Jesus when He received His own personal rapture after His resurrection in Acts 1:9. And they are raptured exactly as the rest of the Church will be when Jesus returns for His people. In all three of these raptures, those involved are received up into the clouds while everyone present watches on.

> 12And they heard a great voice from heaven saying unto
> them, Come up hither. *And they ascended up to heaven in a*
> *cloud; and their enemies beheld them.* 13And the same hour

was there a great earthquake, and the tenth part of the city fell, and in the earthquake were slain of men seven thousand: *and the remnant were affrighted, and gave glory to the God of heaven.*

Revelation 11:12-13

Not to be mistaken for praise, the only glory these people give to God is their acknowledgement that all these events, including the earthquake, originated from Him. A tenth of the city and 7000 men are destroyed in this earthquake, but another earthquake of much greater severity is yet to come after the seventh angel sounds his trumpet. Verse 14 declares that not until after the two witnesses are slain, raised up, and taken back into heaven will the second woe be past. The statement of verse 14 was not placed there inadvertently. The second woe, which is the sixth trumpet and vial combined, does not end after the Euphrates River is dried up and the 200 million horsemen of chapter 9 complete their slaughter of one third of mankind. The two witnesses, with their three-and-one-half years of ministry, are firmly anchored in the second woe. There are only three ways to remove them from between the sounding of the sixth trumpet and the sounding of the seventh trumpet. The first is dynamite and that probably won't do it. The second is a statement somewhere else in the Bible that "irrefutably" pulls them out of this context and places them somewhere else; however, there is no such statement to this effect. And the third is for convenience sake to make it fit one's own personal interpretation of Scripture. That is more dangerous than using dynamite, and it should not be done. God placed them within the confines of the sixth trumpet as part of His wrath because that is where they belong and that is where they will stay.

The second woe is past; and, behold, the third woe cometh quickly.

Revelation 11:14

The sounding of the seventh and final trumpet signals the final chapter of God's wrath and the final end of this world system, where Satan reigns as god of the earth. The final trumpet of the Wrath of God should not be confused with the final trump that sounds at the end of the age of grace when God sends Jesus to gather His people out of the earth and begins punishing those who are left behind because they have rejected Him. The Millennial Reign—where God gains back full control of the earth and locks Satan away for a thousand years—is about to begin but not before the Battle of Armageddon. The following verse tells us that Jesus will put down all rule, power and authority. He completes this when He rides back to the earth on His white battle stallion. He appears with His saints in the skies over Israel and defeats the armies that await His arrival, then He begins to rule.

> Then cometh the end, when he shall have delivered up the kingdom to God, even the Father; when he shall have put down all rule and all authority and power.
>
> *Corinthians 15:24*

When the final trumpet of the Wrath of God sounds, a great voice proclaims that Jesus will now be the Ruler of all the earth forever and ever. The last part of verse 18 declares that He will destroy those who destroy the earth. Verses 16 through 18 cannot be counted on as any type of chronological outline, however. The 24 elders are worshipping God with their mouths, and they are just speaking out in no particular order the many things that make up the final salvation of God for which they are thankful.

> [15]And *the seventh angel sounded*; and there were great voices in heaven, saying, *The kingdoms of this world are become the kingdoms of our Lord, and of his Christ*; and he shall reign for ever and ever. [16]And the four and twenty elders, which sat before God on their seats, fell upon their faces, and worshipped God, [17]Saying, We give thee thanks, O Lord God Almighty, which art, and wast, and art to come; because thou hast taken to thee thy great power, and hast reigned. [18]And the nations were angry, and thy wrath is come, and the time of the dead, that they should be judged, and that thou shouldest give reward unto thy servants the prophets, and to the saints, and them that fear thy name, small and great; *and shouldest destroy them*

which destroy the earth. [19]And the temple of God was
opened in heaven, and there was seen in his temple the ark
of his testament: and *there were lightnings, and voices, and
thunderings, and an earthquake, and great hail.*

Revelation 11:15-19

As you read about the final vial, you'll notice the exact same things
are happening there as what we read in the seventh trumpet in the
above scriptures. The temple of God is open, and there is a declaration
that the end has come (verses 15 above and verse 17 below) for those
who destroy the earth (verses 18 above and verse 19 below), and there
are voices, thunders, lightnings, a great earthquake, and giant hail
(verse 19 above and verses 18 & 21 below). This again shows us that the
trumpets and vials are different revelations of the same events.

[17]And the seventh angel poured out his vial into the air;
and there came a great voice out of the temple of heaven,
from the throne, saying, *It is done.* [18]And *there were voices,
and thunders, and lightnings; and there was a great earthquake,* such as was not since men were upon the earth, so
mighty an earthquake, and so great. [19]And the great city
was divided into three parts, and the cities of the nations
fell: and great Babylon came in remembrance before God,
to give unto her the cup of the wine of the fierceness of his
wrath. [20]And every island fled away, and the mountains
were not found. [21]And *there fell upon men a great hail out
of heaven, every stone about the weight of a talent:* and men
blasphemed God because of the plague of the hail; for the
plague thereof was exceeding great.

(Revelation 16:17-21)

God speaks! The voice from the throne is God declaring an end
to Satan's rule. But, wait…, it doesn't just suddenly end. There are still
the three frog-like evil spirits that came out of the mouth of the
dragon, the beast and the false prophet that went to gather the kings
of the earth to bring them to the Battle of Armageddon. The
Euphrates River dries up to make the way clear. In verse 13 of this
chapter, a tenth of the city of Babylon fell, killing 7000 men—that

was the first earthquake. The second earthquake was mentioned after the final trumpet and vial. In Revelation 16:19, the city is split into three parts, and the cities of other nations will fall also. But the worst is yet to come for Babylon. There are no more earthquakes; however, in chapters 17 and 18, the city of Babylon will be utterly burned to the ground before the Battle of Armageddon ever takes place.

Revelation 11 ends here, and so does the sequence of events. When we begin Revelation 12, we are starting the whole sequence of events over again but from a much earlier time. The Book of Revelation repeats the same theme and sequence of events three times: the world experiences the Great Tribulation while the Church is still around, much of the persecution is aimed at Christians and Jews and afterwards, Jesus raptures His Church before the Wrath of God begins to fall on the remaining occupants of the earth. Only after we are gone can the Wrath of God begin to fall. That is exactly what we saw in Matthew 24: Tribulation—Rapture—Wrath. In chapters 6-11, we saw this end-times sequence of events unfold as the seals of the Book of Revelation were opened to reveal the Tribulation, followed by the Rapture and then the Wrath of God. In chapters 12-17, the whole sequence is repeated but from a much earlier time and with a much greater focus on Israel. In chapters 6-11, we were looking down upon the whole earth, with the Middle East being the one third that is targeted for the main thrust of God's wrath. In chapters 12-17, we are not looking at the entire earth any more; instead, we are looking only at the one third that is directly in the cross-hairs of God's wrath—the area surrounding the Middle East. Chapters 12-17 will again take us right up to the time just before the destruction of Babylon, the Battle of Armageddon and the completion of God's plan of redemption and restoration. The only bump in the road is Revelation 14:6-20 where God uses only fifteen verses to give us the entire sequence of events once again. Verses 6-7 show the gospel being preached. Verse 8 shows the fall of Satan's domain in heaven just prior to his being cast out to the earth; verses 9-13 show the Tribulation; verses 14-16 show the Rapture; and finally, verses 17-20 show the judgment of wrath that culminates with the Battle of Armageddon. Chapters 18-22 can be added to the end of any one of the three chronological sets of Scripture to finish out the story of the end-times.

THINK ABOUT IT!

— Does this chapter speak in any way about redemption to those who hear the two witnesses?

— What is the response of those who hear the two witnesses?

— Are they a part of the second woe?

— Are they a part of the Tribulation or the Wrath?

Selah

For the wrath of God is revealed from heaven against all ungodliness and unrighteousness of men, who hold the truth in unrighteousness.

Romans 1:18

DANIEL 8

From Babylon
to Greece
to Antichrist

As I began to learn the truth about what was really going to happen at the end of the world, I felt faint. I had to fight off feelings of fear and despair. It took weeks to get past those feelings. About
a year later the terrorist attacks of 9-11 occurred. This time it wasn't
fear or despair, it was anger and frustration. Anger, because I saw
Satan at work. He was able to motivate the kingdom of the beast
before its time. Religious fervor that kills, steals and destroys. A religion based in hate and perpetuated by fear. An attack from the land
of the lost. I believe that God allowed this attack to succeed to wake
up this nation and the world. A giant warning flare of the danger
ahead. Not just one, but in the mouth of two or three witnesses let a
thing be established. Trouble up ahead. I felt so much frustration
because I knew it was coming. This attack and more, and then the
end. I knew it was coming but there was nothing I could do to stop
it. The end is coming and I cannot stop it. The leaders of the world
may be able to practice containment of the religion that conquers,
but in the end it is a simple matter of who you bow your knee to. I
often tell people that approximately 50,000 miracles occurred on that
awful day in 2001. That's how many people we are told typically pass
through the 10 million square feet that make up the World Trade
Towers. There were miracles of heroic rescues, impossible escapes
and an inordinate number of seemingly circumstantial events that

conspired to keep many, many people from making it to work on time. Those were miracles too. Even some of those who died left behind a legacy of miracles through the testimony of their actions or events that were set in place through their deaths. The Pentagon escaped maximum impact when the airplane aimed at it fell short by feet. The final plane fell short by miles. God is able to deliver now and again at the end of time.

Daniel 8 is essentially the same vision as recorded in Daniel 7 but with a renewed urgency and more focus on the rise of the Antichrist from the geographical area of ancient Greece. The vision of Daniel 7 came in the first year of Belshazzar, the king of Babylon, and the vision in Daniel 8 came two years later in the third year of his reign. In verse 1 in the scriptures below, Daniel asserts that this second vision is after the same manner as the first. In this vision, Babylon is not mentioned, but the destruction of the empire is very imminent as Daniel stands in a province of the empire that borders the encroaching Persian Empire. From where he was standing, Daniel would only have had to lift up his eyes to see the oncoming Persian ram of verse 3. The Medo-Persian Empire was displayed as a bear, or the second beast in the first vision. It had three ribs in its mouth, which were Babylon, Egypt and Lydia (Turkey). The two horns in verse 3 are Media and Persia. The taller horn is King Cyrus who united the two kingdoms into one and continued to expand the borders to the north, south and west. Coming out of the land that is now called Iran, the Medo-Persians pushed to the north to conquer Turkey, west to conquer Babylon and south to conquer Egypt. The whole Middle East and Israel fell under the control of Persia with the exception of the Saudi Arabian Peninsula. In Daniel 5, we read about the death of Belshazzar and the fall of Babylon on the same night the handwriting appeared on the wall of the palace. MENE: God has numbered your kingdom and finished it. TEKEL: You are weighed in the balances and found wanting. PERES: Your kingdom is divided and given to the Medes and Persians.

> ¹In the third year of the reign of king Belshazzar a vision
> appeared unto me, even unto me Daniel, after that which

appeared unto me at the first. ²And I saw in a vision; and it came to pass, when I saw, that I was at Shushan in the palace, which is in the province of Elam; and I saw in a vision, and I was by the river of Ulai. ³Then I lifted up mine eyes, and saw, and, behold, there stood before the river a ram which had two horns: and the two horns were high; but one was higher than the other, and the higher came up last. ⁴I saw the ram pushing westward, and north- ward, and southward; so that no beasts might stand before him, neither was there any that could deliver out of his hand; but he did according to his will, and became great.

Daniel 8:1-4

As in the first vision, the Medo-Persian Empire will only stand for a short time. Afterwards the Greeks, under the leadership of Alexander the Great, will move in and topple their kingdom. The he-goat in the following verses are the same as the leopard in Daniel 7. The notable horn between the eyes of this goat represents Alexander the Great, but rather than having four heads like the leopard, in this vision the notable horn is broken and turned into four horns. Those four horns represent the four generals of Alexander and the division of the kingdom into four parts.

⁵And as I was considering, behold, an he-goat came from the west on the face of the whole earth, and touched not the ground: and the goat had a notable horn between his eyes. ⁶And he came to the ram that had two horns, which I had seen standing before the river, and ran unto him in the fury of his power. ⁷And I saw him come close unto the ram, and he was moved with choler against him, and smote the ram, and brake his two horns: and there was no power in the ram to stand before him, but he cast him down to the ground, and stamped upon him: and there was none that could deliver the ram out of his hand. ⁸Therefore the he-goat waxed very great: and when he was strong, the great horn was broken; and for it came up four notable ones toward the four winds of heaven.

Daniel 8:5-8

The division of the Greek Empire obviously has a very important tie to the latter-day makeup of the kingdom of the beast. In the vision of Daniel 7, we see four heads on the leopard, but we are not given any further insight concerning them. Here, we are told that out of one of the four heads of Daniel 7:6, or four horns of Daniel 8:8-9, there will arise a little horn. This is the same little horn that crushes the earth into pieces and stamps the residue in Daniel 7. In verse 24, he is shown using his power to "destroy wonderfully." It's quite humorous to see God repeatedly refer to the Antichrist as the little horn, and then see the "little horn" persistently magnify himself. Clues in the Bible suggest that Satan is actually small in stature. This reference to a "little horn" may be, at least in part, a reference to his height. But, back to the point. In both chapters of Daniel, there is a time lapse of several thousand years. After seeing the break-up of the Greek Empire into four parts, the visions jump all the way to the end-times when the little horn will spring up on the earth to cause great tribulation.

Daniel 2 shows us the same exact thing but without making mention of the four generals of Alexander. Verse 39 of that chapter illustrates that a second kingdom will arise after Nebuchadnezzar when it says "after thee shall arise another kingdom inferior to thee." Even though the Medo-Persians were inferior to Nebuchadnezzar, they still overthrew Nebuchadnezzar's kingdom after he was gone. In the second half of the verse it states "and another third kingdom of brass, which shall bear rule over all the earth." The Greek Empire blanketed the Middle East, but it did not literally rule over all the earth. Europe, Asia and Africa may not have been as densely populated as the Middle East, but they were populated nonetheless, and yet they did not fall under the control of the Greek Empire. This is an important consideration when studying the end-times. Just like when Caesar Agustus made an official decree before the birth of Christ that all the world should be taxed, it only applied to those who were citizens of the Roman Empire. When the end-times prophecies speak of the reach of the Antichrist to all the world, they are speaking first of the ten-nation empire of the beast, then those nations that surround the ten nations and finally the rest of the world will feel the effects of his actions, like ripples in a pond. The further away you are, the less the ripple effect, unless the Antichrist is able to send out tsunamis to those he hates. Unfortunately for Israel, they will be right there on the front line.

After verse 39 of Daniel 2, there is a continual reference to the fourth kingdom—not many kingdoms or one kingdom of iron and one of clay; not a leg kingdom and then a foot kingdom—but one and only one kingdom. That fourth kingdom is the Antichrist's kingdom. Here, as with Daniel's other depictions of the Antichrist kingdom, the description is of that final empire and not something that stretches through the ages. It is described as a divided kingdom with the strength of iron and the weakness of clay. The clay could represent the fact that the Antichrist has to subdue three of the ten kingdoms mentioned in Daniel 7:8 and 20. In effect, the three kings and their kingdoms have feet of clay when it comes to following the Antichrist, and they try to resist. The iron part, which reflects the iron will of destruction of the Antichrist, will bring them in line with his will. To a lesser extent, the mix of iron and clay could represent some other aspects of the beast kingdom. For instance, he could have a well-equipped military manned by the weak-minded, disenfranchised, and poverty-stricken subjects of his kingdom. Or he could have a strong economy fueled by the world trading ports that will be located at the future location of the city of Babylon, while having a weak, poorly-equipped military empowered from the spirit realm. The whole iron/clay contrast could just be the fact that human beings as vessels of clay are being empowered by Satan and his demonic work force from the spirit realm.

As we read about the little horn that springs up in the end-times from one of the four quarters of the ancient Greek Empire, notice that it reads like Revelation 12 where Satan as a great red dragon casts a third of the stars to the ground. There is, however, nothing about this next passage to suggest that Satan, or anyone other than the Antichrist, is being spoken of. In Revelation 12, Satan cast a third of the angels of God down to the earth to do his will after gaining their allegiance. However, in Daniel 8, the stars and the host of heaven that the Antichrist is casting to the ground are none other than the saints of God. Daniel 12:3 tells us that those who are wise and turn many to righteousness will shine as the stars and "the brightness of the firmament" forever and ever. God considers His people as a part of the host of heaven before they ever depart the earth. Verse 11 declares that the

Antichrist will exalt himself not only to be like the Prince of this per-secuted host, which is Jesus Christ, but to take on the Prince of the host. First, he will seat himself in the temple and claim all deity and make war against those who refuse to bow to him, and then he will take on Jesus, the Prince of the host, when He returns with His embattled host to rule the earth from Jerusalem. Just to be clear about it, it does not say that the Antichrist casts a third of anybody down to the ground. Verse 10 only says *some* of them are cast to the ground. From what we have learned already, it appears that the Antichrist will have much control over one third of the earth, but that in itself does not mean he will eliminate all saints in his part of the world.

> 9And out of one of them came forth a little horn, which waxed exceeding great, toward the south, and toward the east, and toward the pleasant land. 10And it waxed great, even to the host of heaven; and it cast down some of the host and of the stars to the ground, and stamped upon them. 11Yea, he magnified himself even to the prince of the host, and by him the daily sacrifice was taken away, and the place of his sanctuary was cast down. 12And an host was given him against the daily sacrifice by reason of transgression, and it cast down the truth to the ground; and it practiced, and prospered.
>
> *Daniel 8:9-12*

There is a second host that is given over to the Antichrist in his conquests over the host of God, which is the people of his ten-nation kingdom that actively serve him. This is the same multitude of people that are described as many waters where the whore resides in verses 1 and 15 of Revelation 17. The host that the Antichrist leads is the one that provides him with the manpower for causing tribulation. It pro-vides him the military might for moving into Jerusalem to bring an end to the daily sacrifice and into other countries for dominance and destruction. Verse 12 describes the host of the Antichrist as transgres-sors. The very fact that they follow the Antichrist reveals their trans-gression and rejection of the God of heaven. The same verse declares that the people who follow the Antichrist cast truth to the ground. They don't just reject truth; they work overtime to make sure that

God's truth is abolished in their kingdom. This is already happening in the Middle East region of the old Greek Empire where the Antichrist religion of Islam rejects everything about the covenant of God.

The next two verses give us one of the most important numbers concerning the end-times as far as our overall understanding of the sequence of events is concerned. We are told that the Antichrist will eliminate the daily sacrifice for 2300 days. Because of the connection between the Greek Empire of the past and the Antichrist kingdom of the future, some have tried to partition the number between the past and the future.

After the death of Alexander the Great in 323 b.c., his empire was split into four parts between his four generals just as God had revealed to Daniel. Years later in 167 b.c., Antiochus Epiphanes, as ruler of the Syrian division of the Greek Empire, conquered Israel and dedicated the Jewish temple to Zeus Olympus. For two days short of three full years, the temple was used in pagan worship. Antiochus was, at the very least, a type of the Antichrist. The liberation and cleansing of the temple at that time is what the Jews celebrate during Hanukah.

Using thirty-day months, three years minus two days is 1078 days, which falls way short—less than half—of the 2300 mentioned above. The Antichrist of the end-times will take away the daily sacrifice for a full 2300 days. The numbers from Daniel 8 and 12 prove that the 2300 days is not split between the past and the future. In them we see that from the time the daily sacrifice ceases to the Rapture of the Church there will be 1335 days. Subtracting 1335 from 2300 leaves us with 965 days, or 32 months and 5 days. Because Antiochus was able to stop the sacrifice for 1078 days, or 35 months and 28 days, we end up with an extra 113 days when we add the 1335 days from Daniel 12 and the 1078 days of Antiochus. Those extra days prove that the time that Antiochus stopped the sacrifice, and anything else from the past, has nothing to do with the 2300 days. God has already declared that it would be 1335 days from the stoppage of the daily sacrifice to the removal of the Church from the earth. However, He did not say that the sanctuary would be cleansed at the Rapture. Quite the contrary. The Antichrist and his Gentile followers will remain after the Rapture and have free access to the temple as God begins His punishment. The temple will not be cleansed until the 965 remaining days of the 2300-day stoppage have elapsed and the two witnesses drive the Antichrist from the temple during the Wrath of God. This will be made clearer when we get to the chapter called The Length of the Wrath of God.

The remainder of this chapter reinforces in five different places that the whole purpose of this chapter and vision is to give insight into what is going to happen at the end of time. Also, if you read the declaration concerning how long the daily sacrifice will be removed, in context, exactly as it is written and without trying to manipulate it around to fit a favorite doctrine, it is clear that the 2300 days is consecutive and comes about as a direct action from the end-times Antichrist.

> [13]Then I heard one saint speaking, and another saint said unto that certain saint which spake, How long shall be the vision concerning the daily sacrifice, and the transgression of desolation, to give both the sanctuary and the host to be trodden under foot? [14]And he said unto me, *Unto two thousand and three hundred days; then shall the sanctuary be cleansed.* [15]And it came to pass, when I, even I Daniel, had seen the vision, and sought for the meaning, then, behold, there stood before me as the appearance of a man. [16]And I heard a man's voice between the banks of Ulai, which called, and said, Gabriel, make this man to understand the vision. [17]So he came near where I stood: and when he came, I was afraid, and fell upon my face: but he said unto me, Understand, O son of man: *for at the time of the end shall be the vision.* [18]Now as he was speaking with me, I was in a deep sleep on my face toward the ground: but he touched me, and set me upright. [19]And he said, Behold, *I will make thee know what shall be in the last end of the indignation: for at the time appointed the end shall be.*
> Daniel 8:13-19

Some have attempted to explain away the enormous leap from the Greek Empire to the Antichrist empire by suggesting that the world was a smaller place back then, and they would not have had any knowledge of anything to do with Rome. However, when Greece was first identified to Daniel as the nation that would overthrow the Persians, it existed only as a group of island nations that was forming settlements throughout the Mediterranean. The Greeks were a little over two hundred years away from conquering the Persians when Daniel received his vision, and the Romans were another hundred years down the road from that. Each of these future world empires had to have growing populations, thriving industries and governmental oversight for them to pull together the resources and mount the attacks that made them dominant over the most notable part of the world at that time.

Sea trade was prevalent throughout the Mediterranean, and news of all the different developments taking place would have spread fast. China, India, Africa, Europe and even the Americas have plentiful signs of civilization that date back to 3000 b.c. and even earlier. Daniel's second and third visions (Daniel 7 and 8) took place right around 550 b.c., allowing for much population and cultural growth in all of these regions. Trade grew with population growth, and as anyone knows, true salesmen love to talk. The world was small, but the world was big. God did manage to convey that Rome was a part of the dragon/beast conspiracy against Israel and the plan of God, but not as the final empire. He made it clear that the land holdings of Greece would be reunited once more as the end-times empire of the beast. The real destroyer of the small world theory is that Jesus and all of the authors of the New Testament lived right in the Roman Empire and never attempted to correct Daniel's quantum leap from Greece to beast, and they never gave any indication that the empire of the Antichrist would be anything other than a future version of the old Greek Empire.

In verse 19 in the previous scriptures, Gabriel tells Daniel that he is going to explain the vision to him, but in so doing, he points out that the vision is concerning "the last end of the indignation," and "at the time appointed the end shall be." What end is he talking about? In verse 17, it is clear he is talking about *the* end—not the end of the Greek Empire, but the end of the world. The vision was not fulfilled back then, but it will be fulfilled when the ten nations of the Antichrist kingdom join together and look astonishingly like the early Greek Empire. Gabriel is telling us that the vision is for the appointed time of the end of this world system in which God continues to tolerate the corruption of sin. God has appointed a time for the end. When Jesus appeared in Acts 1:6-7, the disciples asked Him if He would restore the kingdom of Israel. He told them that God had put the timing of all things in His own power, and they were not privy to that information. The vision Daniel is witnessing is of the final days and central events of this world before God judges it and restores all things. It's all in His timing and according to His purposes.

In the following verses, Gabriel is identifying the various images in the vision. In verse 20, the ram is identified as the Medo-Persian government, and then in verse 21 the Greeks are mentioned by name in connection with the rough goat. Notice that there are two kings mentioned in verse 21. The rough goat is called the king of Grecia, and his horn is called the first king. The goat itself represents the kingdom and the spirit king that rules it from the principalities of wickedness. The first king mentioned is, of course, Alexander the Great, the man responsible for bringing the empire into existence in our own natural world.

In the next verse, the kingdom is divided into four separate king-doms, all of which share the same heart and soul and spiritual king as the Greek Empire. Then, in verse 23, we see that quantum leap that skips over thousands of years of world and Middle East history and takes us right into the end of time. In verse 9 in the previous scrip-tures, we are told that the Antichrist will rise out of one of four sub-kingdoms of the divided Greek Empire. As Gabriel gives the interpretation of the dream, however, he broadens it again to include the whole region of Greek influence when he says "in the latter days of *their* kingdom." The reason for this discrepancy is not to confuse us, and it is not because Gabriel was confused; it is so that we might know where the ten nations of the Antichrist kingdom are located— the former Greek Empire, stretching all the way to the borders of India and China, and where the Antichrist will rise from—the Syrian portion of the divided Greek Empire where Antiochus once polluted the temple of God with idol worship.

Verse 24 points out that the Antichrist will not come in his own power, but he shall be mighty through the power that is bestowed upon him from Satan. Revelation 13:2 informs us that the dragon, who was identified as Satan, is the one who gives power unto the Antichrist. We see in these verses that his purpose is not to rule the world but to destroy his enemies. Those enemies are the holy ones who trust in the true God of heaven. Verse 25 mentions in passing the peace covenant he will use to set Israel up for an eventual overthrow. That same peace covenant will lull many all over the world into a sense of false security. Those who ignore and despise the Scriptures are the ones that sudden destruction comes upon, even as they are crying peace and security. Many high-level authorities from all over the world have already publicly stated that if a man called Antichrist were to arrive with solutions to world problems, they would gladly follow him. That does not mean that he will rule the world. It simply means that those who love lies will lend their support to him, and after it is too late, they will learn that they were simply pawns in his devious plans for destruction.

> [20]The ram which thou sawest having two horns are the kings of Media and Persia. [21]And the rough goat is the king of Grecia: and the great horn that is between his eyes is the first king. [22]Now that being broken, whereas four stood up for it, four kingdoms shall stand up out of the nation, but not in his power. [23]*And in the latter time of their kingdom*, when the transgressors are come to the full, a king of fierce countenance, and understanding dark sentences, shall stand up. [24]And his power shall be mighty, but not by his own power: and he shall destroy wonderfully, and shall prosper, and practice, and shall destroy the mighty and the holy people. [25]And through his policy also he shall cause craft to prosper in his hand; and he shall magnify himself in his heart, and by peace shall destroy many: he shall also stand up against the Prince of princes; but he shall be broken without hand.
>
> *Daniel 8:20-25*

All of these things up to the end of verse 25 take place before the Church is raptured. In verse 25, we are told that he will "stand up against the Prince of princes." That is a figurative statement relating to the time that he spends treading down the earth while targeting Christians and Jews in particular for destruction. It is also a literal statement relating to the final episode of God's wrath when Jesus returns with His saints to destroy the Antichrist and his followers. The term "broken without hand" refers to what we will read later in Revelation about the Antichrist being taken by the angels of God and cast into the Lake of Fire.

World War II is the closest thing we have to compare with the Great Tribulation. Hitler's arrogance, his ability to make war and his single-minded addiction towards killing Jews is a foreshadowing of what the Antichrist will be like. While the war was progressing, Russia signed a non-aggression treaty with Hitler only for the self-serving purpose of dividing the nation of Poland between themselves as they attacked from different fronts. At the same time, the Japanese used Hitler's war as a diversion as they simultaneous waged war in Southeast Asia in an attempt to rule that part of the globe. The rest of the world was slowly drawn into the war to help bring the unparalleled aggressions to an end. The world is a much more dangerous and volatile place now, and even without an Antichrist another world war would be devastating. World War II is just a small taste of what the final Tribulation period will be like. Throughout history it seems as though Satan, having a knowledge of the prophecies, has attempted to fulfill them on his own terms in an effort to get the upper hand and outsmart God. However, he has never succeeded and never will. Not during World War II and not at any time. God contained Satan during World War II and turned the Japanese and German people around, at least for a time. The end that is fast approaching will happen on God's terms and in His timing, and there's nothing that Satan can do to change the outcome.

Verse 23 contains an important clue as to what God is doing during this whole time of Tribulation. We are told that the sinfulness of the people in this part of the world will come to fullness. Sin will be thriving all over the world, but the kingdom of the beast will be full of people who are hell bent on destruction, both self-destruction and the destruction of others—particularly God's people—and the Antichrist will be there to lead them on that path of destruction. The world will be able to see firsthand what the kingdom of darkness is like where the gospel is forbidden and truth is cast to the ground, and contrast it to the kingdom of light, which will be on display through the Church. Most of the world will be wrapped up in their own personal sins. James addresses the sinners of the world when he asks, "Ye adulterers and adulteresses, know ye not that the friendship of the world is enmity with God?" (4:4). A self-willed, self-serving, fleshly, carnival-type attitude that lacks commitment to God and rejects righteous behavior already permeates many free and prosperous societies. But in the kingdom of the beast, things will be different.

There will be no lack of commitment to a god who turns the people against God's chosen, both Israel and born-again Christians, and against God's Holy Word. The kingdom of the beast will be filled with hatred and murder for anyone who does not conform to their way of doing things. They will hate the God of heaven, and Jesus will have to appear and rescue His followers from off the earth before the followers of the beast destroy all flesh off the face of the earth. God is going to cut His work short in righteousness. Before the gross darkness of the beast kingdom is able to snuff out the light, God will bring an end to things. Satan will bring the Tribulation with all its worldly horrors, but God will use it to turn many to righteousness as they finally see the unmasked face of evil and the very depths of sin. After He cuts the Tribulation short, He will pour forth His own righteous judgment of wrath on those who have actively opposed Him and His ways, and preserve many lesser sinners to be ruled over by the saints in the kingdom of Jesus Christ.

In the final two verses, we see first of all that the vision was for a time in the future. Earlier Daniel was told that it is for the end of time; here he is told to seal it up just as he was told to seal the vision in chapters 11 and 12. Only through the enlightenment that we receive from the Book of Revelation and other New Testament writings will the vision come alive with understanding. As that day draws ever closer and we are able to see developments in that area of the world—which will become the kingdom of the beast, our understanding grows. The second thing we see in these verses is the effect the vision had on Daniel. He has a psychosomatic episode as his body becomes physically disabled because of the mental anguish he suffers from seeing the vision. This is similar to what Jesus said in Luke 21:26 about men's hearts failing them as they see these things coming to pass on the earth. Daniel got just a small glimpse of those things to come, and it put him out of commission for a time. God is giving His people ample warning concerning the Tribulation so that we will not faint but be gallant and strong, doing the Lord's business of reaching out to sinners. As people come to understand that God's wrath will be worse by multiple magnitudes, and that the god of this earth is filled with nothing but hatred for them and all mankind, it may be the final nudge they need to forsake their own ways and get saved.

> [26]And the vision of the evening and the morning which was told is true: wherefore shut thou up the vision; for it shall be for many days. [27]And I Daniel fainted, and was sick certain days; afterward I rose up, and did the king's business; and I was astonished at the vision, but none understood it.
>
> *Daniel 8:26-27*

THINK ABOUT IT!

— What time in history does this vision point to?

— Have you ever heard an acceptable and verifiable explanation for the 2300 days of no sacrifice?

— How do you cast truth to the ground?

Selah

> Keep not thou silence, O God: hold not thy peace, and be not still, O God. For, lo, thine enemies make a tumult: and they that hate thee have lifted up the head. They have taken crafty counsel against thy people, and consulted against thy hidden ones. They have said, Come, and let us cut them off from being a nation; that the name of Israel may be no more in remembrance. For they have consulted together with one consent: they are confederate against thee.
>
> *Psalms 83:1-5*

DANIEL 11 AND 12

Antiochus Antichrist

It's amazing how simple the prophecies are when you look at the broader statements that are being made and stop trying to over-analyze every single word. We read two similar passages that are speaking of the same event, but because they are worded differently we turn them into two different events. We have been straining at a gnat and swallowing the camel.

Daniel 11 is the interpretation of another one of Daniel's visions. In Daniel 10:14, the angel Michael told Daniel, "Now I am come to make thee understand what shall befall thy people in the latter days: for yet the vision is for many days." Daniel 11 and 12 contain the enlightenment Daniel received concerning the things that will befall his people in the latter days. It is important to understand that Daniel's people include both the Jewish people who are kin to Daniel in the flesh and those who are made righteous through the covenants of God and are kin to Daniel in spirit. This vision is very specific to the nation of Israel as God reveals some of the details of their pre-wrath judgment in view of the fact that He allows them to fall into the hands of the Antichrist before His wrath begins. In more general terms, we see that even some of God's holy redeemed, which means born-again saints, will suffer at the hand of the Antichrist also, as he attempts to wipe out all vestiges of the work of God on the earth. This does not include the 144,000 who are being protected from Satan's wrath during the Great Tribulation.

Daniel 11 actually takes us back to Daniel's time in the Medo-Persian Empire. He again sees the imminent fall of Medo-Persia to Alexander's Greece. This vision is an amplification of the third and fourth empires that Daniel had already seen in earlier visions about the four great empires that emerge on the earth. It shows great detail about the divided Greek Empire up to the time of Antiochus Epiphanes, and then jumps to the final Antichrist empire that emerges from the modern-day region of the former Greek Empire. The first four verses of chapter 11 explain that the Babylonian Empire had already passed, and Daniel was now a resident of the Persian Empire. After the Persians try to overthrow the region of Grecia, Alexander the Great will turn things against them with his conquests, which give birth to the Greek Empire while bringing demise to the Persian Empire.

> ¹Also I in the first year of Darius the Mede, even I, stood to confirm and to strengthen him. ²And now will I shew thee the truth. Behold, there shall stand up yet three kings in Persia; and the fourth shall be far richer than they all: and by his strength through his riches he shall stir up all against the realm of Grecia. ³And a mighty king shall stand up, that shall rule with great dominion, and do according to his will. ⁴And when he shall stand up, his kingdom shall be broken, and shall be divided toward the four winds of heaven; and not to his posterity, nor according to his dominion which he ruled: for his kingdom shall be plucked up, even for others beside those.
>
> *Daniel 11:1-4*

After Alexander establishes the Greek Empire, he passes away and the kingdom is divided into four. Verses 5-20 are omitted here, but for those interested, the topic they cover can be further studied in an encyclopedia or in other books that touch on the subject. Those verses foretell the rise of the four sub-kingdoms that emerged from the Greek empire. However, the focus is on the two that battled between themselves and traded control of Israel back and forth. They both brought a Greek influence to the region. The first kingdom was the Seleucids of the north who ruled from Syria, and the second kingdom was the Ptolemies of the south who controlled Egypt. The reason they are mentioned is because God used them in judgment against Israel when they were in sin. More importantly, though, is the fact that Antiochus Epiphanes, from the Seleucid kingdom, foreshadowed the Antichrist by entering the holy place and placing a statue of Zeus Olympus in God's temple to be worshipped. It was during his reign that the Maccabean revolt began. The Maccabeans were devoted Jews who were finally fed up with what was going on in the temple in particular, and in Israel in general, and started to fight back. They recaptured the temple, but only after the daily sacrifice had been prohibited for two days short of three years according to history. Hanukkah, or the Feast of Dedication, is observed in celebration of the cleansing of the temple at that time.

It is difficult to pick a place and say this is where Antiochus ends and this is where the final Antichrist begins. However, when we get to verse 21, the remainder of the prophecy begins to focus primarily on just one king. The final king in all of Daniel's prophecies has been the Antichrist, and it is no different here. God is showing us many of the moves that the Antichrist will make in the latter days. The rivalry that existed during the Seleucids and the Ptolemies of ancient Greece will be resumed by the Antichrist as he attempts to bring the king of the south under his control. However, much of what is written from verse 21 to verse 39 can be applied to Antiochus *or* the Antichrist. It seems to be a double or extended prophecy dealing with both the earlier Antichrist and the end-times Antichrist. In verse 30, the ships of Chittim can be traced back to Roman interference when Antiochus attempted to conquer Egypt, but it is written of the future king who will again make the same attempt. It appears that many of the steps Antiochus took will be repeated in the future. The reason that overlap occurs could be to alert us to the fact that a European alliance containing many of the European nations that once made up the former Roman Empire—and possibly including the U.S. and other nations—will attempt to stand against the beast as he works to spread his borders.

In the next several verses, we see that the Antichrist will arise from within the northern kingdom and be rejected at first, and then he will use peace, flatteries, war and whatever other means he has at his disposal to gain control of the kingdom. We are told that he has only a small following at first, but then he uses his great deceptive abilities to gain a toehold into the kingdom offering peace so he can then gain full control, strengthen and enrich himself for the conquests to come. This is somewhat different from some of the theories of a great charismatic leader that appears out of nowhere and is immediately accepted because of his great wisdom in dealing with world problems.

> ²¹And in his estate shall stand up a vile person, to whom they shall not give the honor of the kingdom: but he shall come in peaceably, and obtain the kingdom by flatteries. ²²And with the arms of a flood shall they be overflown from before him, and shall be broken; yea, also the prince of the covenant. ²³And after the league made with him he shall work deceitfully: for he shall come up, and shall become strong with a small people. ²⁴He shall enter peaceably even upon the fattest places of the province; and he shall do that which his fathers have not done, nor his fathers' fathers; he shall scatter among them the prey, and spoil, and riches: yea, and he shall forecast his devices against the strong holds, even for a time.
>
> *Daniel 11:21-24*

Verse 25 shows the Antichrist reviving the ancient rivalry against the king of the south after gaining firm control of the northern kingdom by coming against the great army of Egypt. There will be a great slaughter, but neither king will prevail even though the generals and advisors of the Egyptian king turn against him and aid the Antichrist in his efforts. In verse 27, it appears that either the life of the Egyptian king will be spared or one of those who sold him out will take his place and hatch devious plans with the Antichrist. Their plans are to overthrow Israel, conquer many nations, destroy Christians and Jews and enforce on many their own narrow and ungodly way of thinking. These are the great plans of the beast in his end-times kingdom. His plans, however, do not come to fruition because it is not yet the appointed time of the end. By the way, the only thing that lies between the king of the north in Syria and the king of the south in Egypt is Israel.

> 25And he shall stir up his power and his courage against the king of the south with a great army; and the king of the south shall be stirred up to battle with a very great and mighty army; but he shall not stand: for they shall forecast devices against him. 26Yea, they that feed of the portion of his meat shall destroy him, and his army shall overflow: and many shall fall down slain. 27And both these kings' hearts shall be to do mischief, and they shall speak lies at one table; but it shall not prosper: *for yet the end shall be at the time appointed.*
>
> *Daniel 11:25-27*

None of what we have just read from Daniel 11 is a part of the Great Tribulation. The appointed time of the end has not yet come. The Antichrist will be in power before the Great Tribulation for at least the first three-and-one-half years of the false covenant of peace he establishes with Israel. The actions described above could be during that time, or they could even predate the false covenant. The Antichrist may not even be what we consider to be the Antichrist at that time. If these actions are those of a mere man, and it requires the infilling of the unholy spirit from the bottomless pit to make him the Antichrist, then he won't fully become the Antichrist until the appointed time when he begins his demon empowered earth ministry, which is meant to be an exact opposite—and in opposition to—the true Christ. It's interesting to note that there is no mention here of the deadly wound that was healed or the beast from the bottomless pit bringing a perverted form of life back into his body.

The Antichrist will return to his land and later come against Egypt again, but the ships of Chittim—most likely NATO—will repel him. In his despair he will return to his own land and begin conspiring with the Jewish traders of the covenant. Afterwards, he will enter Jerusalem and take over the temple, put a stop to the daily sacrifice and set up the Abomination of Desolation. These things will not happen all at once but will be spread over time. The Tribulation is approaching fast.

²⁸Then shall he return into his land with great riches; and his heart shall be against the holy covenant; and he shall do exploits, and return to his own land. ²⁹At the time appointed he shall return, and come toward the south; but it shall not be as the former, or as the latter. ³⁰For the ships of Chittim shall come against him: therefore he shall be grieved, and return, and have indignation against the holy covenant: so shall he do; he shall even return, and have intelligence with them that forsake the holy covenant. ³¹And arms shall stand on his part, and they shall pollute the sanctuary of strength, and shall take away the daily sacrifice, and they shall place the abomination that maketh desolate.

Daniel 11:28-31

The reprobate Jews will be taken in by the lying flatteries of the Antichrist and conspire with him. Those who know the true and living God and who cling to the Lord of the New Covenant will flee Jerusalem. They will also be busy doing great works for God by instructing others to escape the trap of submission to the beast by submitting to Jesus Christ instead. Many of the true servants of God will lose their lives for their opposition to the Antichrist, but they will not lose their souls. As a result of their faithfulness and their testimony, many new converts will walk the streets of gold in the city of God.

The Great Tribulation will not be a time for God's people to faint and draw back but will be a time to serve God gallantly and do exploits in His name. Any adversity we suffer during the Tribulation will serve to purge and purify us if we are following the Lord. The following verses are given for our admonition. You can almost hear the voice of Jesus in these verses. "Fear not, only believe." Verse 32 declares that the people who "know their God shall be strong, and do exploits." Shadrach, Meshach and Abednego are perfect examples of men who knew their God and did exploits. At the end of time, some of us may be ordered to bow down to a golden image of the beast as they were. They refused to do so, and so must we if we are going to serve the living God. The words they spoke must be in our mouths if we are counted among those who are confronted by the servants of the beast: "Our God is able to deliver us from this fiery furnace, but if he chooses not to, we still will not bow to your gods." This is particularly true of those who live in the Middle East.

> [32]And such as do wickedly against the covenant shall he corrupt by flatteries: but the people that do know their God shall be strong, and do exploits. [33]And *they that understand among the people shall instruct many*: yet they shall fall by the sword, and by flame, by captivity, and by spoil, many days. [34]Now when they shall fall, they shall be holpen with a little help: but many shall cleave to them with flatteries. [35]And *some of them of understanding shall fall, to try them, and to purge, and to make them white, even to the time of the end: because it is yet for a time appointed.* [36]And the king shall do according to his will; and he shall exalt himself, and magnify himself above every god, and shall speak marvelous things against the God of gods, and shall prosper till the indignation be accomplished: for that which is determined shall be done.
>
> *Daniel 11:32-36*

The indignation of verse 36 that has been predetermined is the desecration of the temple during the Great Tribulation, along with open rebellion against God by the followers of the Antichrist. Much of the persecution described above takes place on a continuing basis even now, but it will escalate to an all-time high after the Tribulation begins. Both the persecution and the work of the saints during the Tribulation are described, but the Tribulation doesn't begin until verse 40. In verse 38, we see the Antichrist in an act of reverence to the god of forces. The word "forces" speaks of strength, primarily of a military nature. The same word is used in verse 39 to describe the strongholds. The Antichrist is giving glory to Satan, the one who empowers him to make war and to reign by terror.

> [37]Neither shall he regard the God of his fathers, nor the desire of women, nor regard any god: for he shall magnify himself above all. [38]But in his estate shall he honor the god of forces: and a god whom his fathers knew not shall he

honor with gold, and silver, and with precious stones, and
pleasant things. [39]Thus shall he do in the most strongholds
with a strange god, whom he shall acknowledge and
increase with glory: and he shall cause them to rule over
many, and shall divide the land for gain.

Daniel 11:37-39

The time of the end has finally come. The three-and-one-half year Great Tribulation begins in verse 40 as the king of Egypt rebels and attacks the Antichrist. The Antichrist wipes him out, along with many other nations to the south, and he shall take Israel at this time also. According to Daniel 12, the daily sacrifice is taken away 75 days before the Tribulation begins. In this chapter, the daily sacrifice is taken away in verse 31 after the Antichrist is repelled by the ships of Chittim, which would be an alliance of the European portion of the former Roman Empire. Within 75 days he attacks, is repelled and attacks again to successfully conquer Egypt, along with other nations.

In verse 43, we are told that Libya and Ethiopia are at his steps. This seems to convey a sense of closeness. In all of the activities of the Antichrist, we never see him venturing far from his homeland. Libya and Ethiopia are also named as a part of the Gog alliance that forms before the rise of the Antichrist with the single-minded objective of ridding the world of a nation called Israel. They could represent a much larger portion of North Africa, or they could be just lonely outposts that are a part of the Middle East beast empire. That is, until the Antichrist takes Egypt, along with other North African countries. The Libyans and Ethiopians may even send troops to assist in the capture of Egypt, which has successfully resisted the Antichrist up to this point.

Only three little mountainous areas between Israel and Jordan east of the Dead Sea will escape the final southern thrust of the Antichrist— Edom, Moab and Ammon. Edom is the land that Esau settled. Moab and Ammon are the lands of the two children of Lot. This may be where the 144,000 are hiding safe and secure during the Tribulation. God will obviously blind the Antichrist to the whereabouts of the 144,000 select Jews; otherwise, he would be there to destroy them.

[40]And *at the time of the end* shall the king of the south
push at him: and the king of the north shall come against

him like a whirlwind, with chariots, and with horsemen, and with many ships; and he shall enter into the countries, and shall overflow and pass over. ⁴¹He shall enter also into the glorious land, and many countries shall be overthrown: but these shall escape out of his hand, even Edom, and Moab, and the chief of the children of Ammon. ⁴²He shall stretch forth his hand also upon the countries: and the land of Egypt shall not escape. ⁴³But he shall have power over the treasures of gold and of silver, and over all the precious things of Egypt: and the Libyans and the Ethiopians shall be at his steps.

Daniel 11:40-43

With the conquest of Egypt, the Antichrist will gain great wealth and a stockpile of military hardware. With one problem resolved and becoming stronger because of that victory, the Antichrist can set his sights elsewhere. If the Antichrist is ruling from Jerusalem at this time, the news from the east could be coming from Jordan, Iraq, Iran or any part of Asia, including China. Tidings from the north could be Syria, Turkey, Russia or even Europe to the northeast. The news he receives will cause him to return back to protect his home base of ten nations and possibly to push further into other lands, and he does it with great fury. Whoever it is that counterattacks and causes him to go into this fit of rage will not prevail against him. The tidings from the east could actually be that revival is breaking out in the lands that are under his control, as many of the people are finally forced to deal with the reality that they are serving the wrong god.

Daniel 11:33 declares that those of understanding among God's people will instruct many, yet many of them will still fall by the sword. Because the gospel of Jesus Christ has already been preached throughout the kingdom of the Antichrist before the end-times begin, and now, after seeing the brutishness of the one who claims to be their god, there could be millions of converts right under the nose of the beast as he is rejected by many. God wants His people on the earth at this time for several reasons, two of which are: 1) to bring them to a place of purity where they stop loving this world so much and are ready to lay everything on the line. After all, Jesus is coming for a spotless Church. And, 2) to complete the reaping phase of the great commission. All over the world people will be forced to face their own destiny and examine their loyalties. God wants us here to reach out for the final harvest of souls.

Verse 45 states that the beast will rule from Jerusalem until he comes to his end; however, his end will not come from the armies of the earth. At about this time, Jesus will throw a bucket of cold water on things by rapturing the saints. This removes one of the biggest objectives of the war plan of the beast. He owns Israel at this time, and God has already given the reprobate Jews into his hands, but now there are no Christians left for him to persecute to death. He will continue to rule from Israel during the time of God's wrath, and will gather a great army at Armageddon to take on the armies of heaven at the end of the wrath. He will then be taken and cast into the Lake of Fire, and none shall help him. That final statement is the only one that makes any reference to the Wrath of God. Everything else is either a view of the activities of the Antichrist leading into, and including, the Tribulation at ground zero—the lands of the former Greek Empire—or a historical view of some of the turmoil that took place during that earlier empire. The Great Tribulation, more than anything else, will be military actions in the Middle East that the world cannot afford to ignore. In the same spirit of war that has been a part of Middle East history from the very earliest days, the Antichrist will resume a more recent quest for world domination under the banner of Islam and will be very successful until God interrupts things with His wrath.

> [44]But tidings out of the east and out of the north shall trouble him: therefore he shall go forth with great fury to destroy, and utterly to make away many. [45]And he shall plant the tabernacles of his palace between the seas in the glorious holy mountain; *yet he shall come to his end, and none shall help him.*
>
> *Daniel 11:44-45*

Daniel finishes with his vision of the end-times in chapter 11 and then begins a grand overview of the end-times in chapter 12. After seeing the Antichrist come to his end in chapter 11, the first thing Daniel does is jump way back to a time just before the beginning of the Tribulation. Chapter 12 is not a reliable outline of the end-times and will only add confusion to those who attempt to make it that. This chapter is simply highlighting a few important points which help us to understand the overall end-times prophecies.

Verse 1 tells us that the Tribulation, which is described as a time of trouble unlike the world has ever seen, will start after Michael stands up. That doesn't make much sense until you realize that he is standing up at God's appointed time to cast Satan out of heaven for good. We see that in Revelation 12 where Michael and his angels fight against Satan and his angels and cast them to the earth. Satan immediately goes forth with great anger to make war with the seed of Abraham as he sees his own time drawing to an end. The second half of verse 1 identifies Daniel's people as those who are written in the book. That book is the Lamb's Book of Life and those in it are the same New Testament elect that Jesus gathers into the clouds of Matthew 24. The saints of God will receive their final deliverance at the end of that time of trouble just before the start of the Wrath of God. Verse 2 speaks of the resurrection of some to everlasting life and some to shame and everlasting contempt; however, the resurrection of the ones to everlasting life actually takes place a thousand years before those resurrected to shame and everlasting contempt. During the first resurrection, those who have died in Christ are raised from their graves first so that all of God's people may participate in the Rapture together. Then at the end of the Millennial Reign, those who have died outside of Christ are raised just in time for the White Throne Judgment.

> ¹And *at that time shall Michael stand up*, the great prince which standeth for the children of thy people: *and there shall be a time of trouble, such as never was since there was a nation even to that same time*: and at that time thy people shall be delivered, every one that shall be found written in the book. ²And many of them that sleep in the dust of the earth shall awake, some to everlasting life, and some to shame and everlasting contempt.
>
> *Daniel 12:1-12*

If you read verse 1 by itself, it may appear that the Rapture occurs at the beginning of or before the Tribulation. However, it does not say that. It does not say whether Daniel's people are delivered before or after the time of trouble; it simply states that they will be delivered sometime in the future when that time of trouble has come upon us. Not until we arrive at verse 7 are we told that God will not deliver His people until after the time of trouble in which the Antichrist persecutes and scatters the righteous for three-and-one-half years. The opening statement about Michael standing up and the time of trouble beginning immediately afterwards is not talking about Michael standing up to rescue the saints. That's not really his job—it's Jesus' job to rescue the saints. Daniel's name is written in the Lamb's Book of Life, and those who are listed in the book alongside him will be delivered in the Rapture. Those words are not referring to the Jewish nation that is divided between sinners and saints.

God is not going to deliver His people out of the world to keep them from being persecuted. If He was going to do that, we would already be out of the world, or at least, those saints that are suffering persecution right now would have to be removed from the earth. Jesus said in John 16:33, "*In the world you shall have tribulation*: but be of good cheer; I have overcome the world." Then in John 17:15, He said, "I pray not that thou shouldest take them out of the world, but that thou shouldest keep them from the evil." He didn't overcome the world and leave us here just to turn around later and snatch us out because things are getting a little too rough for our liking. He left us here to continue the work of salvation, which He began, right up to the end of the Tribulation. People still have an opportunity to get saved during the Tribulation as long they are not already sporting the mark of the beast.

Persecution is like a tool that the Holy Spirit uses to get people saved. Paul got saved as a direct result of the persecution he was bringing against the Church—and Stephen in particular. Any time a person persecutes one of God's children, he must face the conviction of the Holy Spirit. If the conscience of the individual has not been hardened and seared by hatred and denial, he will be faced with the choice of either repenting and giving in to the Spirit of the living God like Paul did or continuing down a path of spiritual destruction. All the world will be on trial during the time of Daniel's trouble. The saints will be tried by Satan to see if they are truly committed to God, while sinners will be convicted by the Holy Spirit to see if they will repent unto salvation or continue unto damnation. This trial of hearts will continue right up to the end of the Tribulation when Jesus will remove us from the earth before God's wrath begins. Verse 10 explains that many will be tried and purified during this time of trouble, but the truly wicked will continue to do wicked deeds. Verse 12 again points out that many blessed ones, referring to the saints, will come to the end of this time of trouble before they are finally delivered.

The next two verses just provide us with general information. Verse 3 describes the glory that will be bestowed on those who live contagiously and lead many to Christ, especially during the Great Tribulation. Verse 4 tells us two different things. First, that the words of this book were sealed up until the time of the end. The Book of Daniel became unsealed when John completed the Revelation and was told in Revelation 22:10 to "seal not the sayings of this book: for the time is at hand." It is through Revelation, the Holy Spirit and the remainder of the New Testament that we receive the insight we need to understand Daniel and the rest of the Old Testament prophecies. The second thing we see in verse 4 is a sign of the end-times. There will be a great increase in travel and in knowledge. These are signs that are being fulfilled in our time and will continue to escalate as we move into the limited amount of future that remains.

In verse 7, the one time plus two times plus a half time equals three-and-one-half years—each time being a year—which is the duration of the Great Tribulation. The second half of the verse explains that the Antichrist will only be allowed to persecute believers without any apparent restraints for that amount of time. For the first three-and-one-half years of Daniel's seventieth week Christians and Jews will more or less be off limits to the Antichrist, but when the Tribulation begins in the second half of the week, he will overrun Jerusalem and put a death sentence on Christians, Jews and anyone who refuses the mark of the beast. During that time, he will disrupt all organized Christian endeavors that fall within the reach of his ten-nation war machine and attempt to kill as many Christians as he is able. His reach will be extended considerably through the export of war and terror. At the end of the Tribulation, the Lord will descend from heaven and remove all Christians from the reach of the Antichrist forever through the Rapture. Daniel does not use the words "rapture," "catching away" or any other words that would describe the lifting of the Church from the earth. However, in verse 12 he does refer to the Rapture as simply a blessing. After the Church is gone, the wrath can begin.

> 5Then I Daniel looked, and, behold, there stood other two, the one on this side of the bank of the river, and the other on that side of the bank of the river. 6And one said to the man clothed in linen, which was upon the waters of the river, How long shall it be to the end of these wonders? 7And I heard the man clothed in linen, which was upon the waters of the river, when he held up his right hand and his left hand unto heaven, and sware by him that liveth for ever that it shall be *for a time, times, and an half*; and when he shall have accomplished to scatter the power of the holy people, all these things shall be finished. 8And I heard, but I understood not: then said I, O my Lord, what shall be the end of these things? 9And he said, Go thy way, Daniel: for the words are closed up and sealed till the time of the end.
>
> *Daniel 12:5-9*

Daniel is told a second time in verse 9 that the words he has just finished writing down are to be sealed spiritually from human understanding until the time of the end when they will be made complete by the additional information provided by The Revelation. When he is told to be on his way, he is essentially told to be involved with the present and not worry about what the future will bring. He was given a partial revelation of what the future holds because of his intense interest in the matter, but it would have been a complete waste of time and cerebral resources for him to try to understand it. If he had attempted to figure it out without the Spirit of God and the future revelations of God to rely upon, Satan would have led him down the same crooked path that he leads many of the modern-day "experts" who believe the teachings of men, their own mental prowess and the baseless "revelations" that continually come to them more than they believe the Word of God.

Verse 10 shows us once more one of the reasons why the Church will go through the Tribulation. We have already seen in Daniel 11:32-35 that those who know their God intimately through the covenant that He has established with them will do great exploits in reaching the lost. At the same time, those who are not one hundred percent sure of where they stand will be tried and purified as they reject all hope in this life and lay their lives down for the eternal kingdom of Jesus Christ. By the same token, some will spare their own lives for a short while longer by either outright rejection of Christ or gradual embracing of the ways of the world and the will of the Antichrist. There will be many Christians who are Christians by the new birth but not by their actions or lifestyle. Many sinners will exhibit traits of righteousness but remain sinners simply because they have not taken the step of faith into the body of Christ. The Tribulation will make it clear that there is no middle ground to stand on. You are either for Christ, or you are against Him. You are either for the Antichrist, or you are against him. You are for the God of hope, salvation and life, or you are for the god of despair, murder and death. The choice will be forced upon all living souls by Satan and allowed by God before He closes the door on the age of grace. There is a price to pay regardless of which way you decide. Choosing the true Christ could cost you everything in this life, including life itself, but the eternal reward makes that choice the right one. Choosing the Antichrist will only keep a person alive for a short time longer—maybe—with nothing but despair and misery as an eternal reward.

> [10]Many shall be purified, and made white, and tried; but the wicked shall do wickedly: and none of the wicked shall understand; but the wise shall understand. [11]And from the time that the daily sacrifice shall be taken away, and the abomination that maketh desolate set up, there shall be a thousand two hundred and ninety days. [12]*Blessed is he that waiteth, and cometh to the thousand three hundred and five and thirty days.*
>
> *Daniel 12:10-12*

Now, if we look at verse 12 in the scripture above, the number 1335 is given, which is 75 days or two-and-a-half months longer than the Great Tribulation using thirty-day months. Because we have established that the Rapture will occur at the end of the Tribulation, the last day of the 1335 days must be the Rapture. What other "blessing" could

God be referring to at that time? It is the same blessing or "blessed hope" for which we are looking to this very day. Daniel 9:27 declares that the daily sacrifice is taken away in the midst of the seven-year peace plan which makes up Daniel's seventieth week. However, from the verses above we see that it is not actually the dead center of the seven years but rather 75 days before the middle of the seven-year week. That means the Antichrist stops the sacrifice 75 days before the Tribulation begins, and it will be 1290 days from that point before the Abomination of Desolation is set up; then only 45 days later the Rapture will occur.

Matthew 24:15-21 states that when we see the Abomination of Desolation stand in the holy place, the Great Tribulation will begin. Second Thessalonians 2:4 says that "he as God sitteth in the temple of God, showing himself that he is God." By these verses, it appears that the Antichrist will march into Jerusalem 1335 days before the Rapture and bring an end to the daily sacrifice. He may even enter the temple and stand there as a sign to believers in Jerusalem to flee into the wilderness. At 1260 days before the Rapture he will enter the temple to seat himself as God and the Tribulation will officially begin. It won't be until the last 45 days that the image of the beast is erected in the temple, which is what the 1290 days after the sacrifice is stopped in verse 11 is referring to. And on the final day, Jesus will come for His redeemed. The name "Abomination of Desolation" is used interchangeably between the beast and his image.

When we add Luke's portrayal of the beginning of the Tribulation from Luke 21:20 and 21, we see that 75 days before the Tribulation ever begins the Antichrist will have Jerusalem surrounded by armies, put a stop to the daily sacrifice and enter the temple probably to curse God and magnify himself as God. That means the believers in Jerusalem will have about that much time to leave the city as the Antichrist basks in his own grandiose glory before the real trouble begins. The Tribulation has an appointed time, both in its timing and duration, however, due to the urgency of Jesus' warning to His people when He instructs them to drop everything and don't look back, it must be assumed that the Antichrist will be in a killing mood as soon as he arrives. Working in conjunction with the reprobate Jews, he will very likely be attempting to eliminate any known believers in the city from the very outset.

God does not allow the three-and-one-half years of the actual Tribulation to begin until the appointed time. Everything that happens before that time will cause tribulation, anguish and anxiety, mixed with a false sense hope for many throughout the world, but it will not be the full unleashed fury of the Antichrist until after he is loosed by God to fulfill his evil destiny. The second half of Daniel 9:26 provides us with a snapshot of what the Great Tribulation is all about. "The people of the prince that shall come shall destroy the city and the sanctuary; and the end thereof shall be with a flood, and unto the end of the war desolations are determined." The Antichrist will be making war against all things godly.

As we have seen, the war will not be confined to just Israel or Jerusalem. It will be scattered throughout the Middle East and North Africa, and then it will turn north, perhaps reaching Russia and Europe as the end of the war approaches—when the Rapture interrupts everything. The Antichrist's mission is to tread down the earth, stamp out the residue and destroy all flesh, targeting Christians and Jews first. God will allow him to overrun Israel as a final pre-wrath judgment against those Jews who ignore the Savior's warning to flee the city. For many others, it will be a wake-up call to abandon their resistance to the gospel that has been preached to them and embrace the true Christ, before dying at the hands of the Antichrist. God is always able to use those things that Satan intends for our hurt and destruction and turn them around for our good. The Tribulation is no different. Many will be saved as they come face to face with the one whom Christians call Antichrist.

When it is time for the Wrath of God, the only warning will be the skies turning to momentary darkness just before the appearing of Jesus Christ in all of His glory, and then there will be nowhere left to flee. The war of the Antichrist will end in total destruction of all mankind without the intervention of Jesus Christ to rescue His people. But Jesus will suddenly appear in the skies to personally gather His people and take them away to a place of safety called heaven. After the Rapture, Satan's war ends as the Wrath of God begins to fall on the ungodly.

In the final verse, Daniel is told to be about his business again, but in this last passage he is told that he will rest until the time of the end. And not only that, but he is told that he would stand in his lot or destiny at the end of days. Whether he understood it or not, he was being told that he will be one of the witnesses. Daniel died hundreds of years before the Greeks arrived and approximately four hundred years before Antiochus Epiphanes desecrated the temple with a statue of Zeus Olympus. He was not around for either of those events, and he was not resurrected in a.d. 70 when the Romans demolished the temple. He has not fulfilled his duty to God at the end of days yet, but when the time comes he is going to be right there, shoulder to shoulder with John the Beloved, proclaiming the goodness and severity of God to a world that has passed from grace unto judgment.

> But go thou thy way till the end be: for thou shalt rest, and
> stand in thy lot at the end of the days.
>
> *Daniel 12:13*

John and Daniel can be assumed to be the two witnesses who torment the earth during the Wrath of God. In Revelation 10 John was given a book to eat, along with some commentary about the book from the seven thunders that came out of heaven. After swallowing the book, he was immediately told that he would prophesy again before many nations, peoples and tongues, which he did not accomplish before his death. Daniel was not told that he would prophesy again, but he was told in Daniel 12:13, which we just read, to go his way till the end and that he would stand in his lot (destiny) at the end of days. There are so many similarities between the two prophecies that both John and Daniel must have been given basically the same vision but in such a way as to make it personal to each of them.

We are still not privy to the information that was recorded in the book John swallowed in Revelation 10, nor are we aware of what the seven thunders uttered, but all of the rest was written for us to understand. For 2000 years the veil has been lifted from the Revelation. Daniel had only limited insight into the things of the end-times. He had pieces of the puzzle, but it wasn't until John recieved the final pieces that we could finally understand it. The Old Testament was given as a prophetic mystery that was sealed from the understanding of man until the last days, which we are now living in. Our understanding of the prophecies must be squarely based on the newer, eye-opening revelations of the New Testament. By the same token, Daniel's prophecies are neccesary to be able to fully understand New Testament prophecies such as Matthew 24 and the Book of Revelation, and indeed, agree fully with them.

THINK ABOUT IT!

— Is the king of the north the beast from Daniel's other visions?

— Does the king of the north rule or even make war with the whole world?

— Does Michael cause the great time of trouble by standing up?

Selah

Pride goeth before destruction, and an haughty spirit before a fall.

Proverbs 16:18

You Don't Say

I have often wondered why so little is written about the 2300 days in which the daily sacrifice is cut off. It doesn't really matter what perspective the writer is coming from, ie: pre-Trib, mid-Trib, post-Trib or past-Trib, the 2300 days is either missing or the things that are written don't add up mathematically, are totally unfounded and speculative or they are just downright silly. After discovering the simple truth, I realized the answer to that question was quite simple. The 2300 days do not agree with any of the prevailing doctrines. It's like a stick in the spokes, a rip in the main sail, a loose shoestring that trips everything up. People often would rather hold to the doctrine they first fell in love with than to go back to the very beginning and start from scratch. If you rebuild an engine and end up with extra parts left over you can either discard them, or you can start over and try again. It's the same with prophecy. If you don't deal with everything that Daniel says about the 2300 days, your doctrine is not going to work right.

Before going any further, we are going to look at how long the Wrath of God actually lasts. We just used the numbers from Daniel 12 to get an idea of how things will unfold during the Tribulation. Now we are going to use those same numbers to get an idea of how long the Wrath of God will last. Along with those numbers, we will look back at the time that it took for several of the trumpet plagues, and add one other number found in Daniel 8. We'll start by recalling that the first four plagues of the Wrath of God did not give any time references. It does take time to burn up a third part of the green vegetation, turn a third of the waters to blood and to darken a third part of the sun while heating up the other two thirds of the same. But we are not given any time limits or duration for any of these plagues. Each of these events could be implemented in an instant, so it's actually the amount of time they will last that is important. Because God seems to be taking His good old sweet time about the whole matter of His wrath, we can assume that these things will not be sprints but marathons.

Revelation 9:10 reveals to us that the fifth punishment, which is the first of the three woes we read about, will last five months as the locusts with scorpion stings discharge their duty of tormenting mankind for that time period. Revelation 9:12 then states very matter-of-factly that the first woe is past and the other two will follow, thus showing the chronological nature of the plagues. Revelation 9:15 asserts that the next punishment, which involves the 200 million horsemen that kill one third of mankind, will last one year, one month, one day, and one hour—not a minute more. But the second woe does not end with that. In Revelation 11:3, the second woe continues as the two witnesses of God show up in the middle of God's wrath to torment the earth with their prophecies of doom for 1260 days, or three-and-one-half years. After that, Revelation 11:9 declares that after they have finished their three-and-one-half year prophecy, they will be slain and will lie in the streets for three-and-one-half days before they are taken into heaven. That makes a total of 1263.5 days just for the two witnesses to complete their part of the seven plagues of wrath. It is not made clear whether this 1263.5 days follows or overlaps the one year, one month, one day and one hour time frame given for the 200 million horsemen, but they are both a part of the second woe because that woe does not end until Revelation 11:14. Chapter 11, verse 14 establishes as fact that the second woe does not end until after the two witnesses are taken up into heaven. Certain aspects of how the second woe is described strongly suggest that the horsemen and the two witnesses fulfill their ministries consecutively rather than simultaneously. We will look at some of those reasons as we go along.

The final woe does not give a time reference, but it has to be long enough for the Battle of Armageddon to take place. The minimum time span for the whole outpouring of wrath has to be at least three years, eleven months, three-and-one-half days and a half an hour, which is the five months of the first woe, a minimum of three-and-one-half years and three-and-one-half days of the second woe, and the half hour of silence that was observed before the wrath began all added together. This does not include the one year, one month, one day, and one hour of the second woe, the Battle of Armageddon in the final woe or any time allowance for the first four trumpets and vials. If the one year, one month, one day and one hour of the 200 million horsemen takes place before the three-and-one-half years of the two witnesses, then adding that time to the equation gives us five years, four-and-one-half days, and a half hour.

Now, if we look at the numbers Daniel gave us, we see that the time of wrath is longer than either of these numbers. We need to start with the numbers that deal with the Tribulation. We see consistently throughout the prophecies that the time of Tribulation will last for three-and-one-half years. In the verses from the end of Daniel 12, we saw that the daily sacrifice will be taken away 1335 days before the Rapture occurs, and since the Tribulation only lasts 1260 days and Jesus has told us that His return will be "immediately after the tribulation of those days," we know that the sacrifice is taken away 75 days before the Tribulation begins.

> [11]And from the time that the daily sacrifice shall be taken away, and the abomination that maketh desolate set up, there shall be *a thousand two hundred and ninety days.* [12]*Blessed is he that waiteth, and cometh to the thousand three hundred and five and thirty days.* [13]*But go thou thy way till the end be: for thou shalt rest, and stand in thy lot at the end of the days.*
> Daniel 12:11-13

We also determined that since the Abomination of Desolation is set up 1290 days after the daily sacrifice is taken away, that leaves only 45 days until the return of Christ for His people. That's the 1335 days from when the sacrifice is stopped to the Rapture minus the 1290 days until the Abomination is set up. What really helps us to understand the duration of the Wrath of God is something Daniel was told in chapter 8. He was being shown a vision of the end-times when the

Antichrist rises to power and takes away the daily sacrifice. As part of the vision, Daniel heard two individuals speaking to each other. The first asked how long would the sacrifice be discontinued and the temple polluted by desolations. The second individual responded that it would be 2300 days, and then the temple would be cleansed. If it had been left to Daniel to ask the question, it may not have been asked, but God wanted us to know the duration for this transgression against His holy temple for a reason—so that we can keep things straight when it comes to the end-times prophecies.

> [11]Yea, he magnified himself even to the prince of the host, and by him the daily sacrifice was taken away, and the place of his sanctuary was cast down. [12]And an host was given him against the daily sacrifice by reason of transgression, and it cast down the truth to the ground; and it practiced, and prospered. [13]Then I heard one saint speaking, and another saint said unto that certain saint which spake, *How long shall be the vision concerning the daily sacrifice, and the transgression of desolation, to give both the sanctuary and the host to be trodden under foot?* [14]And he said unto me, *Unto two thousand and three hundred days; then shall the sanctuary be cleansed.*
> [19]And he said, Behold, *I will make thee know what shall be in the last end of the indignation: for at the time appointed the end shall be.*
>
> *Daniel 8:11-14, 19*

The last chapter in the Book of Daniel explains that the daily sacrifice will be discontinued 1335 days before the Church is removed from the earth. Daniel 8 informs us that it will be 2300 days before the temple is finally cleansed of the abominations of the Antichrist. Verse 19 is included because it clearly states that this vision is one that concerns the appointed time of the end. Everything in the chapter points to the end of time when the Antichrist is out and about causing great tribulation on the earth.

If we subtract the 2300 days it takes to cleanse the temple from the 1335 days that the temple is polluted before the Rapture takes place, we end up with a negative number—minus 965. That's because the temple is not cleansed until long after the Church is gone from the earth, and the Wrath of God has been in full swing for 965 days. If we use thirty-day months again, the two witnesses will appear on the scene to kick the Antichrist out of the temple and to begin their prophecy two years, eight months and five days after the Rapture. Their prophecy will last for three-and-one-half years after they take back the temple and cleanse it. Therefore, by adding those two numbers together, we can see they will not complete their prophecy until after a full six years, two months and five days of God's wrath have elapsed. The Wrath of God does not end with the conclusion of their prophecy. If you will recall, the Euphrates River was dried up to allow for a much swifter and easier troop deployment into Israel. The foul spirits that ascended out of the river are working to draw the armies of nations to Israel to ambush Jesus and His saints when they return at Armageddon.

The Wrath of God will very likely be a full seven years to equal the seven years that the Antichrist will reign in his part of the earth prior to the Rapture. (Remember the seven-year truce that he makes and then brakes in the midst of the seven years, thus causing Great Tribulation.) That would leave nearly ten whole months for the armies of the world—refusing to believe the Word of God right up to the end—to join up with the Antichrist in Israel for the overwhelming destruction that has been prophesied upon them. If you consider that the people remaining on the earth chose to follow after tribulation and persecution along with the Antichrist rather than the peace and salvation God was offering them, seven years of wrath makes perfect sense. Seven is God's number of completion or wholeness. God is doing everything in sevens: seven seals, seven vials, seven trumpets, seven candlesticks, Daniel's seventieth week, seven days a week, seven Spirits of God, and so on. The judgment just wouldn't be complete if it was not seven full years.

Prophecy teachers have been trying for years to squeeze the Tribulation and the Wrath of God into the same seven-year period that the Antichrist first makes and then breaks his peace covenant with Israel. That is why it is of the utmost importance that we realize the Tribulation and the Wrath of God are two entirely different set of circumstances during entirely different time periods. The Antichrist will be present for seven years *before* the Wrath of God, and he will be present for seven years *during* the Wrath of God before he is cast into the flames of eternity. We saw in Matthew 24 the separation of the Tribulation and the Wrath of God by the Rapture. We also made a transition from the Tribulation to the Wrath as we moved from the first five seals of the book (not to be confused with trumpets or vials) into the sixth seal where the Church was raptured, and finally the seventh seal, which is the fullness of the Wrath of God. Tribulation comes first, then the Rapture, and then the Wrath: Tribulation—Rapture—Wrath.

Bible scholars are never going to fit everything into one seven-year period because the Tribulation begins in the middle of the seven-year period and ends three-and-one-half years later when God's wrath begins. His wrath is longer than the three-and-one-half year Tribulation, and it follows after it. We just saw that the wrath will last beyond six years and two months, and that is without adding any time for the final trumpet and vial, which signal the end of time—the end of God's wrath and the Battle of Armageddon. According to the timetable of some Bible scholars and prophecy teachers, to make things fit together properly, God's wrath would have to begin several years before the Tribulation begins. No one has ever been successful at compressing all the different components of the Wrath of God that are revealed to us into the seven years of Daniel's troubles and have everything make sense. The Bible never limits the time of the Antichrist to just seven years. He makes a seven-year covenant and is limited to three-and-one-half years of Tribulation from the midpoint to the end of those seven years, but it is a misunderstanding of Scripture to remove him from the face of the earth after just seven years or to try to overlap or combine the Tribulation and the Wrath of God.

It is important to reaffirm the fact that although God has said that Jesus' return would be as a thief in the night and that no man knows the day or the hour of His return, He also states in 1 Thessalonians 5:4 that we are not in darkness that the day should come upon us as a thief. The fact that He numbered the days of the Tribulation and gave us other signs and indicators of His return shows us that He wants us to, at least, be in the ballpark when it comes to estimating the day of His return, but only after things begin to happen. When we see Israel sign a seven-year peace accord and then notice that it is broken in the middle of the seven years and suddenly a large number of Israelites have headed for the mountains right before the fall of Jerusalem, you have some clue that His return is eminent—in fact, approximately seven years from the signing of the treaty and three-and-one-half years from the time the Antichrist crowns himself God. Those Jews that are flee-ing to the wilderness know they only have three-and-one-half years to wait before their Redeemer comes to rescue them; the rest of the Church will know also, except for those who are willfully ignorant and those who are deceived. We should not be afraid to believe the num-bers God has freely provided to us. Jesus did say that no man knows the day or the hour of His return, but that does not mean we will be totally caught off guard. God has given us more than enough information to zero us into the approximate day and hour, but only after things begin to unfold. After the signing of the treaty, we don't know for sure whether to use thirty-day months or calendar years to determine the end of the seven-year period, which would coincide with His return date. That alone causes over a month of variation. There are also other small variables that prevent us from knowing the exact day or hour, but God is not going to leave us here squirming in our seats for too long. Immediately after the Tribulation of those days, He will return. The world has chosen to disregard this information, and as a consequence, they will be caught totally by surprise.

THINK ABOUT IT!

— Does God expect us to ignore all of the numbers and other information that He gave us through the truth of His word and be caught off guard like the rest of the world?

— When Jesus tells us to watch, is He telling us to watch the unfolding of events as well as watch over our own spiritual condition?

— Does 1 Thessalonians 5:4 say that we are not in darkness that that day should overtake us as a thief.

Selah

Behold, the former things are come to pass, and new things do I declare: before they spring forth I tell you of them.

Isaiah 42:9

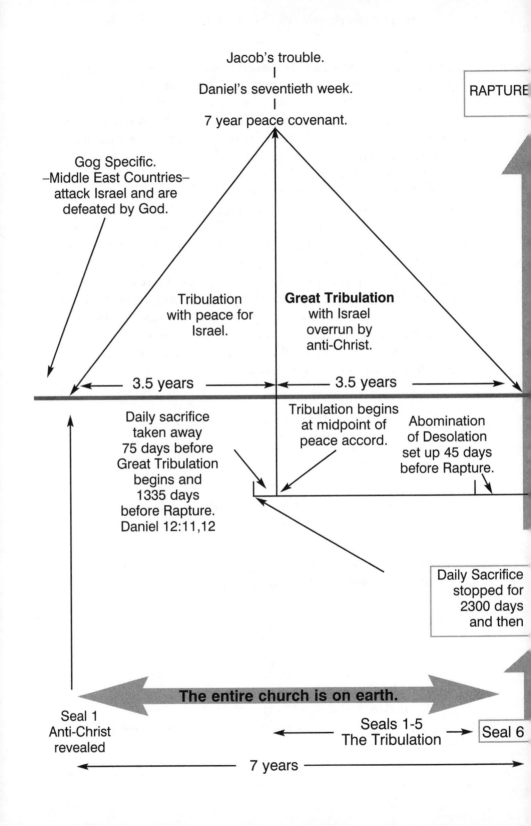

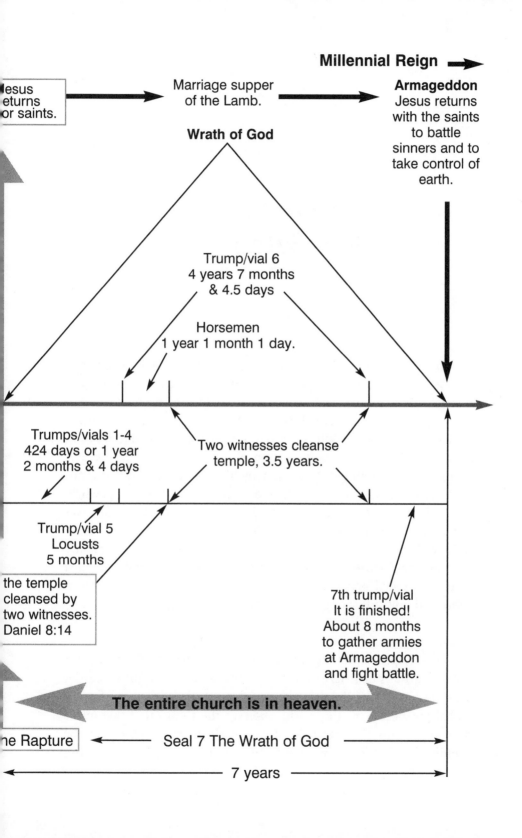

REVELATION 12

Where in the World Does Satan Live?

I guess I grew up with the idea that Satan lived in hell from where he would cause calamities and influence the corrupt actions of men. As God continued to open my eyes to the simplicity of His Word, I began to see that hell is the last place on earth Satan wanted be. In fact, he doesn't really want to be on earth at all. He doesn't want just the earth, he wants all of creation. He is a part of creation—a part that has been corrupted completely by his own unbridled and ignorant pride. Satan is after the throne of God. Man is just a pawn to him. Adam was created in the likeness of God and made to rule over the earth, but Satan was able to get him to act on his lies and forcefully took over as the illegitimate god of mankind. Most of Satan's time is spent before the throne of God bringing accusations against God's redeemed believers, but he is going to have to leave heaven soon, and boy, is he going to be mad then.

This chapter starts the whole end-times sequence of events over again from a much narrower perspective and from a much earlier time. The previous chapters showed the unveiling of events from a global perspective as the world observes the things that take place over approximately one third of the world that is centered in the Middle East. In this chapter the focus is on Israel, the beast kingdom that surrounds Israel, and Satan's attempts to destroy Israel, with no regard to what is happening in the rest of the world. Revelation 12 concentrates on God's plan of redemption from the very beginning of time up to the time Satan is cast out of heaven. That plan started with Abraham and proceeded with Israel, from Israel to Jesus, and from Jesus to the Church. It shows the war that has been raging between the God of creation and the forces of Satan over the fate of Israel and all of mankind from the very beginning when God first started to implement His plan of salvation. It also reveals how Israel remains in the middle of this conflict to the very end with Satan right there every step of the way, trying to stop the plan of God from being fulfilled. Revelation 12 takes us right up to the time of the Great Tribulation, which is the subject of Revelation 13.

This chapter seems to take on a conversational tone and should not be relied upon as a totally accurate verse-by-verse sequential telling of events. In other words, if a person were to say, "A dog bit me when I got out of my car at the park," the sequence is totally opposite from the way it was told. The person first had to drive to the park, then get out of the car, and then the dog bit. This chapter is essentially in order, but some things are out of place. Verses 6 and 14 are both foretelling the same event but mixed in at different places in the chapter. To understand the timing of what is happening, this chapter has to be compared to all of the rest of Scripture. The entire content of this chapter does, however, take place before chapter 13 and actually leads into that chapter where the Tribulation begins. What's being said here is that there is already war in heaven and eventually Satan is going to be cast out, having great anger, and then the Tribulation will begin. That is when certain special citizens of Israel will be cared for in the wilderness.

Verses 1 speaks of a woman, which is Israel, and the crown of twelve stars are the twelve tribes of Israel. Verse 2 describes Jesus the Messiah being birthed into the world through the nation of Israel. God uses the sun, the moon and the stars in describing the woman to show the high esteem in which He holds Israel, not because of who they are, but because of the covenant of faith Israel accepted from God. Abraham believed God, and Jacob followed in that faith, even to the point of changing his name in obedience to God.

> [1]And there appeared a great wonder in heaven; a woman
> clothed with the sun, and the moon under her feet, and
> upon her head a crown of twelve stars: [2]And she being
> with child cried, travailing in birth, and pained to be deliv-
> ered. [3]And there appeared another wonder in heaven; and
> behold a great red dragon, having seven heads and ten
> horns, and seven crowns upon his heads.
>
> *Revelation 12:1-2*

In verse 3 we see a dragon with seven heads. The dragon is Satan, and the seven heads represent seven empires that Satan brings into existence at different times throughout history for the express purpose of destroying Israel and putting a stop to the plan of God. The ten horns are a league of ten nations that give their power over to the Antichrist during the end-times after the seventh and final empire is established. The Antichrist will use this ten-nation empire as a base of operations in his quest to destroy Christians, Jews and Israel, resulting in the Great Tribulation which will affect the whole world. The first of the seven heads take us all the way back through history to the time when Egypt oppressed the Jews and was judged by God because of that oppression and Pharaoh's refusal to obey God. Along with seven particular empires that Satan controlled, the dragon also symbolizes thousands of years of attempts by Satan to destroy the work of God by destroying Israel through any means available. The crowns on the heads of the dragon not only symbolize the rule of the seven empires, but also Satan's desire to rule as the most high.

Verse 4 shows Satan as he leads the one third of all angels that chose to follow him in his fall from grace and his failed attempt to kill the Christ at his birth. Satan's fall with one third of the angels actually occurred before God breathed the breath of life into Adam's nostrils, so chronologically, this should be the first thing to occur in this chapter. The time between Satan's fall from grace and his attempts to snuff out the life of the Christ Child could be anywhere from a few thousand years to billions of years. We don't know how long he's been around, nor do we know when he fell. Despite the fact that a few things are technically out of place in this chapter, when you take the chapter as a whole, it shows a logical progression leading up to the Tribulation.

Satan doesn't actually lead the angels from here. Verse 4 reports that he cast them down to the earth to do his dirty work as he remains in heaven. He knew that Jesus, God in the flesh, the Messiah, would be born out of Israel, and he wanted to celebrate His birth with the gift of death. This verse announces the birth of Christ despite Satan's attempts to destroy Him at or before His birth. Verse 5 also reminds us of the fact that even though Satan did crucify Jesus, God later passed on to Jesus a judgment of righteousness, resurrected Him from the grave, and seated Him at His right hand to lead the Church from His throne in heaven. God used Jesus as a decoy in His plan of redemption to save the humble and bring judgment against Satan, his angels and sinners, and it worked marvelously.

> ⁴And his tail drew the third part of the stars of heaven, and did cast them to the earth: and the dragon stood before the woman which was ready to be delivered, for to devour her child as soon as it was born. ⁵And she brought forth a man child, who was to rule all nations with a rod of iron: and her child was caught up unto God, and to His Throne.
>
> *Revelation 12:4-5*

Verse 6 speaks of the 144,000 elect of Israel being cared for in the wilderness for 1260 days during the Great Tribulation. This three-and-one-half years of wilderness protection that is mentioned right after the resurrection and glorification of Christ and before Satan is cast out of heaven in verse 9, is mentioned again in verse 14 right after Satan is cast out of heaven. Obviously, it is not meant to be taken as an exact chronological ordering of events. Instead, it should be taken in the broader context of the historical countdown in the war between good and evil. This chapter unveils Satan's part in bringing the world to a point of "Great Tribulation" before it ever gets underway. So far, the beast has not been mentioned in this chapter, and he's not mentioned until the beginning of Revelation 13. The Tribulation does not start and the redeemed of Israel are not protected in the wilderness until after the beast, who is the Antichrist, is revealed.

And the woman fled into the wilderness, where she hath a place prepared of God, that they should feed her there a thousand two hundred and threescore days.

Revelation 12:6

In Job, chapters 1 and 2, we see that Satan still has access to heaven and the throne of God as he accuses Job before God and tries to find opportunity to bring harm upon him. Satan not only enjoys access to heaven, but as the next four verses point out, he has his own place of residence there. Verse 10 informs us that he is continually bringing accusations against the saints. After that, he starts barking commands to his angels and demons whenever he finds an opening as he did with Job. Verses 7-10 speak of a final battle in heaven when Satan and his angels will be cast out of heaven for good. Those verses then point out that "their place" in heaven will not be found any more. If "their place" can be found now, it is only because it is a real place in the real heaven which is located in the real spiritual realm. In Ezekiel 28:18, God declares that Satan has defiled his sanctuaries by the multitude of his iniquities. In Isaiah 14:12-17, God reads Satan the riot act with a prophecy about his eventual arrival in the pits of hell, despite Satan's proclamation that he would exalt his throne and his rule above God's. Satan does have a throne, he does have sanctuaries, and he does have a place in heaven right now. However, he will lose it all when he is thrown out of heaven and to the earth just prior to the Great Tribulation.

7And there was *war in heaven: Michael and his angels fought against the dragon*; and the dragon fought and his angels, 8And prevailed not; *neither was their place found any more in heaven.* 9And the great dragon was cast out, that old serpent, called the Devil, and Satan, which deceiveth the whole world: *he was cast out into the earth, and his angels were cast out with him.* 10And I heard a loud voice saying in heaven, Now is come salvation, and strength, and the kingdom of our God, and the power of His Christ: for *the accuser of our brethren is cast down, which accused them before our God day and night.*

Revelation 12:7-10

Daniel 12:1 shows us a picture of Michael seated, but when he does stand up, it is for the purpose of casting Satan down to the earth, and the time of trouble—which is the Great Tribulation—immediately ensues. However, Michael has not been instructed to throw the old serpent out of heaven yet, and he will not be instructed to do so until it is time to finish up on the job of salvation and judgment. This verse does not tell us whether those in the Book of Life shall be delivered before, after or during the time of trouble, but from the rest of Daniel 12 and the rest of Scripture, we know that the saints will be delivered after the time of trouble is cut short by the appearing of Jesus Christ.

> And at that time shall Michael standeth up, the great
> prince which stinted for the children of thy people: and
> there shall be a time of trouble, such as never was since
> there was a nation even to that same time: and at that time
> thy people shall be delivered, *every one that shall be found*
> *written in the book.*
>
> *Daniel 12:1*

Verse 12 is a warning to all those who are alive on the earth when "the devil is come down unto you, *having great wrath*, because he knows that he hath but a short time." There will be great calamity and woe to the inhabitants of the earth because Satan will be full of fury as he fights his last battles and tries to take down as many with him as he is able. The woe of verse 12 should not be confused with the three woes of the Wrath of God. When the Wrath of God does begin, all the people who remain on the earth will have to deal with the three woes of God's wrath, along with anything else Satan might throw at them. We have not arrived at the Tribulation in this sequence of events, which began at the start of Revelation 12. Revelation 13 shows the Tribulation; Revelation 14 and 15 describes the Rapture and then we will see the vials of wrath again in Revelation 16. This chapter is still about Satan and the time leading up to the Tribulation. In verse 11, we notice that even though the saints do overcome Satan, and eventually the Antichrist, they do not necessarily get to keep their lives. To the contrary, many will have to lay down their lives for Christ's sake in order to keep their eternal lives and to fully overcome Satan.

[11]And they overcame him by the blood of the Lamb, and
by the word of their testimony; and they loved not their
lives unto the death. [12]Therefore rejoice, ye heavens, and ye
that dwell in them. Woe to the inhabiters of the earth and
of the sea! for the devil is come down unto you, having
great wrath, because he knoweth that he hath but a short
time. [13]And when the dragon saw that he was cast unto the
earth, he persecuted the woman which brought forth the
man child.

Revelation 12:11-13

Verses 7-13 tell us how the Great Tribulation gets started. Satan is finally booted out of heaven for good and has great wrath because he knows his time is short. His great wrath eventually translates into Great Tribulation for those who inhabit the earth—sinner and saint alike—but the main thrust of his anger is directed at Israel and the saints. As we read the different prophecies of the end-times, we can see that Satan uses those people who have rejected God's holy Word as agents of his wrath and tribulation. In other words, the people who make up the armies and governments, and even the general population of the end-times, will be the ones causing all the trouble. In verse 13, we see that when Satan is cast out of heaven, his attention is turned toward persecuting the woman, which is Israel.

Verse 14 again explains that God will protect His Jewish saints for three-and-one-half years. God doesn't protect them twice, and it is not until the Tribulation begins that He does protect them. What's interesting about verse 14 in the scripture below, and Matthew 24 where Jesus warns those in Israel to flee to the wilderness, is that the 144,000 are never mentioned. The invitation to a wilderness stronghold is never limited to any specific number. Apparently, anyone who finds themselves in Jerusalem and surrounding environs is welcome to join the crowd. God does, after all, honor faith that acts. The 144,000 Jewish saints are a special group of Israelites who find favor and positions of authority in the future kingdom of God, but God never excludes anyone else from the safety of His prepared place. In fact, the invitation is to the woman, which is all of Israel, but only those who obey it will benefit from it.

The last six words in this verse clues us in to something very important. God is not protecting His people from His own wrath. He's protecting them from the face of the serpent and from the wrath of the serpent. This is just one more verse that helps us to divide between the events of the Tribulation and the events of the Wrath of God.

> And to the woman were given two wings of a great eagle,
> that she might fly into the wilderness, into her place, where
> she is nourished for a time, and times, and half a time,
> *from the face of the serpent.*
>
> *Revelation 12:14*

After repeating His commitment to protect those Israelis who heed His warning, God begins to reveal to us what will happen after Satan is cast out of heaven. Verses 15 and 16 are describing Gog of Magog from Ezekiel 38 and 39. This will be Satan's first attempt of the end-times to totally destroy Israel by using the armies of the ten-nation alliance, which the Antichrist will eventually rule over. At the start of this book, we saw that the alliance will be made up of most, if not all, of the Middle East nations, Pakistan and Afghanistan, portions of North Africa and a few of the small states that sit between the Middle East and Russia. He will bring the great army of this alliance against Israel, but God will help His chosen nation by using the elements of the earth to defeat the enemy. Only one sixth of the army of this Gog alliance will survive and retreat. Israel is not in the wilderness at this time. They are resting securely in their homes with God looking out for them. Ezekiel says in verse 38:23 and elsewhere that God will magnify and sanctify Himself in the eyes of the heathen and many nations when He protects His people, and they will know that He is God. Ezekiel 39:22 states that Israel shall know that He is their God from that day forward forever. This all occurs before the Tribulation and is a great final sign from heaven that will turn many to God just prior to the appearance of the Antichrist.

The only time that the earth, or God for that matter, defends Israel against an attack in the end-times—which is what the flood from the serpent's mouth represents—is when Gog of Ezekiel 38 and 39 attempts to attack Israel. In that attack, the armies of Gog never get past the mountain wilderness of Israel, so if God's chosen were hiding there at that time, they would be right in the midst of the great destruction of Gog's armies. On the other hand, after the earth defeats Gog and the provisions of the armies of Gog are left behind in the mountainous regions of Israel, those who depart Jerusalem when the Antichrist enters the temple can hide in the wilderness for three-and-one-half years with all of their needs met by their enemies. Ezekiel 39:9-10 declares,

"They that dwell in the cities of Israel shall go forth, and shall set on fire and burn the weapons, both the shields and the bucklers, the bows and the arrows, and the handstaves, and the spears, and *they shall burn them with fire seven years*: so that they shall take no wood out of the field, neither cut down any out of the forests; for they shall burn the weapons with fire: and *they shall spoil those that spoiled them, and rob those that robbed them*, saith the Lord God."

There is a seven-year supply of goods outside the cities just waiting to be used up, and there will be plenty left over for those who flee Jerusalem to the wilderness.

> [15]And the serpent cast out of his mouth water as a flood after the woman, that he might cause her to be carried away of the flood. [16]And the earth helped the woman, and the earth opened her mouth, and swallowed up the flood which the dragon cast out of his mouth.
>
> *Revelation 12:15-16*

This is not the Battle of Armageddon; the saints are still on earth, and it will soon be given to the Antichrist to make war with them. The seven-year period, when the people of Israel are consuming the spoil of Gog, is Daniel's seventieth week. The second half of that week, or seven-year period, will be the Great Tribulation. Daniel's whole 70 week, or 490-year period (7x70), was a time when God was bringing salvation and deliverance to Israel, even in times of great persecution. The first 69 weeks (483 years) began with a command to rebuild the temple, and it ended when Christ died for our sins. The final seven years is also referred to as the time of Jacob's Trouble.

> Alas! for that day is great, so that none is like it: it is even
> *the time of Jacob's trouble*; but he shall be saved out of it.
>
> *Jeremiah 30:7*

After the prophecy of Ezekiel 38 is fulfilled, the seven-year time of Jacob's Trouble will begin. Ironically, it will begin with a covenant of peace for Israel. During the first part of this time, the Antichrist will begin to marshal all the forces at his disposal, which will include the remainder of the defeated armies of Gog, along with new recruits who now have an even deeper hatred of Israel because of what her God did to their brethren, and millions of children who have three-and-one-half years to mature into warriors just before the Great Tribulation begins.

The final verse of Revelation 12 shows us the reaction of Satan to the defeat of his faithful warriors. He becomes exceedingly angry with Israel, and prepares for a second onslaught with another flood of humanity. About this time the Antichrist arrives on the scene, and Satan and the Antichrist will work as one to destroy Israel, capture the temple and kill Christians along the way. The remnant of her seed are those who receive Jesus as Lord and Savior.

> 17 And the dragon was wroth with the woman, and went
> to make war with the remnant of her seed, which keep the
> commandments of God, and have the testimony of Jesus
> Christ.
>
> *Revelation 12:17*

The Antichrist is not mentioned at all in this chapter. The spotlight has been on Satan throughout the chapter as the dragon, the serpent, the devil, and Satan. This whole chapter is dedicated to describing the actions of Satan leading up to the final seven years before the Wrath of God. After the fall of Gog, the Antichrist will step in and take control of the alliance that was formed between the nations that came against Israel. He will make a seven-year covenant of peace even as they are cleansing the dead bodies from the land. When the Antichrist does show up in the next chapter, Satan will be squarely behind him as he makes a false covenant of peace and then breaks it as he brings Great Tribulation on the earth.

The seven-headed dragon with ten horns in this chapter will suddenly become the seven-headed beast with ten crowns in the next chapter as the Antichrist takes center stage and begins to fulfill the will of Satan on the earth.

THINK ABOUT IT!

— In Luke 10:18, after the seventy disciples returned from casting out devils and healing the sick, Jesus said, "I beheld Satan as lightning fall from heaven." Was that a literal or figurative statement?

— When Satan is cast out of heaven in this chapter, is it literal or figurative?

Selah

Be sober, be vigilant; because your adversary the devil, as a roaring lion, walketh about, seeking whom he may devour.

1 Peter 5:8

DANIEL 7

Lions and Leopards and Bears, Oh My

Y ou cannot change history. When it comes to prophecy, you cannot change the historical aspects. You just have to figure out how it is that they are supposed to relate to the future. Many of the end-times prophecies began to be fulfilled in the distant past. The reason being that part of the past is tied to the future, and it teaches us things we need to know about the future. Antiochus of Syria fulfilled portions of those prophecies in the past which have yet to be completed by the Antichrist in the future. There is such a smooth transition between the two, and then we are told that the beast who was in the past will be again in the future. Could they be the same?

Revelation 13 starts off with John viewing a vision of a seven-headed beast rising out of the sea. Before reading about this vision, we are going to look at a very similar vision seen through Daniel's eyes in Daniel 7. Although they are different in some ways, the Spirit of God was conveying a unified message to these two men. By the time John saw his vision, a good bit of Daniel's prophetic vision was already history. However, both of the visions were for the purpose of enlightening us to the same things related to the Antichrist in the end of time. Rather than seeing one beast with seven heads as John did, Daniel saw a series of four beasts, each of them distinct one from the other. In the first verse, we notice that this vision took place before the fall of ancient Babylon. The reason this is an important point is because the first beast he saw represented Babylon.

> ¹In the first year of Belshazzar king of Babylon Daniel had a dream and visions of his head upon his bed: then he wrote the dream, and told the sum of the matters. ²Daniel spake and said, I saw in my vision by night, and, behold, the four winds of the heaven strove upon the great sea. ³And four great beasts came up from the sea, diverse one from another. ⁴*The first was like a lion*, and had eagle's wings: I beheld till the wings thereof were plucked, and it was lifted up from the earth, and made stand upon the feet as a man, and a man's heart was given to it.
>
> *Daniel 7:1-4*

The lion perfectly describes Babylon, particularly with Nebuchadnezzar at the helm. Nebuchadnezzar was the gold head on the great figure in the second chapter of Daniel. However, in Daniel 3, he was given the heart of a beast and made to eat grass like an oxen for seven years, and his hair grew to be like eagle feathers. Afterwards, he was lifted back up and given a man's heart again and returned to his former glory after giving glory to God.

> And behold another beast, *a second, like to a bear*, and it raised up itself on one side, and it had three ribs in the mouth of it between the teeth of it: and they said thus unto it, Arise, devour much flesh.
>
> *Daniel 7:5*

The bear is the Persian Empire after it has fought with and then united with the Medes under Cyrus the Persian. The three ribs in the mouth of the bear represent the combined armies of Babylon, Egypt and Lydia (Turkey) which were conquered by the Medo-Persian Empire.

> After this I beheld, and lo *another, like a leopard*, which had upon the back of it four wings of a fowl; the beast had also four heads; and dominion was given to it.
>
> *Daniel 7:6*

The leopard is the Grecian Empire led by Alexander the Great. This beast symbolizes the swiftness of Alexander's conquests. The four heads are the four generals that divided the kingdom after Alexander's youthful demise.

> [7]After this I saw in the night visions, and behold *a fourth beast, dreadful and terrible,* and strong exceedingly; and it had great iron teeth: *it devoured and brake in pieces, and stamped the residue with the feet of it:* and it was diverse from all the beasts that were before it; *and it had ten horns.* [8]I considered the horns, and, behold, there came up among them another little horn, before whom there were *three of the first horns plucked up by the roots:* and, behold, in this horn were eyes like the eyes of man, and a mouth speaking great things.
>
> *Daniel 7:7-8*

The fourth beast represents the empire of the Antichrist, which will arise in the end-times. Many have assumed that the fourth beast represented the ancient Roman Empire that arose after the Greeks, and/or a revised Roman Empire that the Antichrist will rule over. That is not the case at all. The iron of the teeth is the only thing from this description that could possibly be applied to the Roman Empire, and only if those teeth symbolized the conquering power of Rome that it derived from a strong military. Nothing else about the fourth beast fits Rome. The fact of the matter is that the teeth do not represent the strength of Rome or revised Rome at all but rather the vicious, blood-thirsty and beast-like nature of the Antichrist as he devours in war. Many of the people he rules over in his ten-nation empire will be so destitute of the truth, the life and the love of God that they too will be like brute beasts. Those who reside in the Beast Empire—who do not share the attributes of the beast and still have some humanity left in them—will be among those devoured by the iron.

As we continue, we are going to pay close attention to the fact that whenever the beast or his end-times kingdom are mentioned, the focus is on death and destruction and the destructive abilities of the beast. In contrast, although Rome was a very successful conquering empire, it did bring stability and unity to its part of the world without bringing total destruction and brutality as the Antichrist will do. The ten horns—which represent ten nations—exist today, while the ten kings that will rule over them may or may not now be alive, and they certainly have not as yet joined their kingdoms together as one nation. These are not ten nations of a past or future Roman Empire, but rather, the nations of the future Antichrist Empire, which will be located in the Middle East. Verse 8 in the scripture above states that three of these nations will fall to the Antichrist, and the others will give their power over to the beast whether willingly or through fear.

If Daniel's fourth beast was Rome, it seems reasonable that God would have portrayed it as the beast that slew the Messiah, but He doesn't do that. Nor does He give any other conclusive evidence that leads us to believe that this is indeed Rome. Furthermore, we are talking about "The Revelation of Jesus Christ, which God gave unto John, to shew unto his servants things which must shortly come to pass" (Revelation 1:1). Jesus never said that the beast had anything to do with the Roman Empire or a revision of the Roman Empire, and John had nothing to say either even though Rome was the reigning empire at the time he gave his end-times prophecies. Daniel's prophecies always jump from Greece to the end-times beast just like his seventieth week is separated by thousands of years from the first sixty-nine weeks. Daniel 2:40 declares that the iron legs and iron mixed with clay feet are all a part of the fourth kingdom, which is the kingdom of the Antichrist. Each of his prophecies makes that leap from the Greek to the Antichrist empire. Each subsequent prophecy gives a little more detail, allowing us to finally realize that it is the area of the Greek Empire the Antichrist will rule over.

After the Antichrist is revealed in verses 7 and 8, verses 9-14 show the real Christ rapturing the Church, overcoming the Antichrist, and sitting for the final judgment. These things are not presented in a clear and concise manner, and they appear in a mixed order. The slaying of the Antichrist and the final White Throne Judgment, which happen about a thousand years apart, are shown in reverse order here, followed by the Rapture. When we get to the second half of Daniel 7, the explanation Daniel receives from the angel will help to straighten things out. Verse 12 tells us that the first three beasts lose their kingdoms, but yet, have their lives prolonged for a season.

Babylon survives as the nation of Iraq, Persia as Iran and Greece as Greece. The area that each of these empires control is what is important to us in this prophecy, particularly the area that Greece covered.

> [9]I beheld till the thrones were cast down, and the Ancient of days did sit, whose garment was white as snow, and the hair of his head like the pure wool: his throne was like the fiery flame, and his wheels as burning fire. [10]A fiery stream issued and came forth from before him: thousand thousands ministered unto him, and ten thousand times ten thousand stood before him: the judgment was set, and the books were opened. [11]I beheld then because of the voice of the great words which the horn spake: I beheld even till the beast was slain, and his body destroyed, and given to the burning flame. [12]As concerning the rest of the beasts, they had their dominion taken away: yet their lives were prolonged for a season and time. [13]I saw in the night visions, and, behold, one like the Son of man came with the clouds of heaven, and came to the Ancient of days, and they brought him near before him. [14]And there was given him dominion, and glory, and a kingdom, that all people, nations, and languages, should serve him: his dominion is an everlasting dominion, which shall not pass away, and his kingdom that which shall not be destroyed. [15]I Daniel was grieved in my spirit in the midst of my body, and the visions of my head troubled me. [16]I came near unto one of them that stood by, and asked him the truth of all this. So he told me, and made me know the interpretation of the things.
>
> *Daniel 7:9-16*

After asking for an explanation of what he had just seen, the individual Daniel was speaking to gave him a whole two-sentence reply that left Daniel a little less than satisfied. He was told that the beasts represent four kings that rise out of the earth, and then the saints of God would rule. Daniel immediately requested more information about the fourth beast. Before we look at that, though, we are going to consider the four kings. We have already identified four kingdoms, but what about the kings?

If these beasts represented the mortal kings that ruled each empire, there are many to choose from in each empire. However, the most significant ruler of the Babylonian Empire would be Nebuchadnezzar. Nebuchadnezzar presided over the fall of the Syrian Empire at about 609 b.c. and established the Babylonian Empire as the reigning world power. In 586 b.c., Jerusalem fell to the Babylonians and many of the people were scattered. Daniel was among a group of highly skilled and intellectual Jews who were taken captive into Babylon which eventually fell to Cyrus the Persian in 539 b.c. The Medo-Persian Empire became the great empire of the world under Cyrus. He allowed many of the Jews to return to their land with the vessels of the temple of God, and he even gave wealth from the king's treasure to help rebuild the temple. The third king would be Alexander the Great who led the Greeks to complete victory over the Persian Empire at about 330 b.c. Greece then became the great ruling power in the Middle East. The fourth king is the Antichrist who will rule over a ten-nation empire made up of nations that were a part of these other empires in the past.

The great mortal kings of these empires lived short lives and were replaced by successive kings until their empires crumbled and vanished. Nebuchadnezzar and Cyrus actually gave honor and service to God, but each of the empires was eventually judged and defeated by the empire that followed. Each empire was guilty of various sins which were topped off by mistreatment of the Jews. In Daniel 8 we saw the spirit rulers that work in the realm of the invisible as they war in the spirit realm to bring changes in the natural world. More than likely these are the kings to which we need to pay attention. However, when we read about the Antichrist, he seems to be a hybrid—a cross between flesh and spirit just like Jesus. In Revelation 11:7 and in Revelation 17, the Antichrist is called the beast that ascends out of the bottomless pit, but yet, he walks the earth as a man. His ability to survive is similar to that of the two witnesses except he doesn't display the same type of powers as they do. What we do know is that he does come from the pit, and he is empowered and protected by Satan as he deceives and makes war.

> [17]*These great beasts, which are four, are four kings,* which shall arise out of the earth. [18]But the saints of the most

High shall take the kingdom, and possess the kingdom for
ever, even for ever and ever.

Daniel 7:17-18

Any attempt to make Rome a part of these *four* (not five) beasts
is an exercise in futility. We end up missing the main points that are
being made in the prophecies if we turn the fourth beast into some
kind of revised Roman Empire. Revelation 17 will make this much
clearer. Rome does fit into the picture but not as one of these four
beasts. Rome is one of the heads of the seven-headed dragon.

Revelation 12 is recorded in more of a conversational style which
sometimes makes it a little more difficult to get a feel for the timing
of events. Daniel 7 is another example of how recording things that
way can be confusing. As Daniel first records things concerning the
fourth beast, it is difficult to get a good sense of how things are actually progressing. But when he asks for a clarification about the fourth
beast, he seems to slow down and describe things just exactly as he
saw them. A terrible fourth beast—after devouring everything in his
path, even three of the nations that are supposed to be on his side—
goes after the people of God. He prevails against them *until* the
Ancient of Days comes, and the kingdom is given to the saints. After
asking the question, the response Daniel gets provides even more
detail, but to fully understand the whole thing, we need to look at all
of the elements of this chapter.

For instance, in Daniel's initial description of the vision, in verses
13 and 14, he speaks of the Son of Man coming in the clouds. The
only problem is that He is not coming to earth; He is coming in the
clouds as He approaches heaven, and then He is taken before the
presence of God. After arriving there, He is given dominion over all
people. What's happening is that He is returning to heaven with the
saints whom He has just raptured out of the earth. They will remain
there while the Wrath of God is dispensed on the earth, and when it
is time to return for the Battle of Armageddon, Jesus will already have
the authority to rule all the earth, which is granted to Him after com-
pleting the Rapture. We are witnessing the tail end of the Rapture in
the verses above, but when we look at the next four verses, we see the
beginning of the Rapture when Jesus comes to rescue His people and
put a stop to the Great Tribulation, which is spinning out of control.

Jesus said in Matthew 24:22 that He would keep the days of Tribulation short for the elect's sake; otherwise, no flesh would survive. That means that the dominion and kingdom Jesus receives from God would only include the saints if no flesh survived. But God has other plans. He is going to pour His wrath out after we are gone, and when we return, there will be nations of heathen to rule over for a thousand years.

> [19]Then I would know the truth of the fourth beast, which was diverse from all the others, exceeding dreadful, whose teeth were of iron, and his nails of brass; which devoured, brake in pieces, and stamped the residue with his feet; [20]And of the ten horns that were in his head, and of the other which came up, and before whom three fell; even of that horn that had eyes, and a mouth that spake very great things, whose look was more stout than his fellows. [21]I beheld, and *the same horn made war with the saints, and prevailed against them*; [22]*Until the Ancient of days came*, and judgment was given to the saints of the most High; and the time came that the saints possessed the kingdom.
>
> *Daniel 7:19-22*

The remaining verses constitute the final explanation Daniel received concerning his vision. The Antichrist is the little horn that arises after the first ten. Again, he is shown ruling over only ten nations. Verse 24 makes it clear that the original ten horns are present before the Antichrist arrives. This is important because it shows us that the ten-nation alliance the Antichrist rules over will come together before he ever shows his face. He does not form the alliance himself, and he must subdue three of the kings that give the force of their kingdoms into this alliance in order to either take over the alliance or to hold it together after he does take charge.

He is shown devouring the earth. That does not mean he rules over a one-world government. To the contrary, he is destroying governments and people, targeting Israel and Christians above all. Daniel 9:26, in speaking of the Tribulation, says there will be desolations to the end of the war. The Antichrist will drag the whole world into war and will devour and destroy many nations and the resources of those nations through war. In Revelation 6:8, after the fourth seal has been opened, we see that one fourth of mankind has been destroyed by war and famine and also the beasts of the earth. This is no ordinary war, though; the Antichrist will lead millions of devoted followers who have been waiting for someone strong enough to lead them in a holy jihad against Israel and all other infidels.

Verse 25 reveals the Antichrist prevailing against the saints of God. This happens not because people were left behind in the Rapture but because the Rapture has not yet occurred. Jesus tells us that He will return for His elect after the Tribulation. In Verse 22, Daniel makes it clear that Jesus does not return as the Ancient of Days, who was in the beginning with God and was God, until after the Antichrist makes war against them.

Again, in verse 25, a time, times and the dividing of times is three-and-one-half years, or forty-two months, as described in Revelation 13:5. In the same verse, the Antichrist thinks to change time. He will no doubt desire to set the calendar back to year one, signifying his arrival on the scene. The laws that he changes will be a combination of governmental and spiritual laws that reflect the god and religion he serves.

Verse 23 shows us that the kingdoms, which are represented by the beasts, are more important than the kings who rule over them. It is not important to identify any single king for each of these kingdoms or convey any type of special significance to them until we get to the fourth kingdom and the little horn that rises to lead that kingdom in world war, thus causing the final Tribulation and trying of mankind. In verse 26, the term "the judgment shall sit" refers to the entire judgment of the last days, beginning with the time God separates His righteous from all sinners in the Rapture continuing through the Wrath of God and ending with the White Throne Judgment a thousand years later. Between verses 26 and 27, we see the Beast Empire destroyed when the saints return with Jesus at Armageddon and their subsequent rule in the Millennial Reign.

> [23]Thus he said, *The fourth beast shall be the fourth kingdom upon earth*, which shall be diverse from all kingdoms, and *shall devour the whole earth, and shall tread it down, and break it in pieces.* [24]And *the ten horns out of this kingdom*

are ten kings that shall arise: and *another shall rise after them*; and he shall be diverse from the first, and *he shall subdue three kings*. ²⁵And he shall speak great words against the most High, and *shall wear out the saints of the most High*, and think to change times and laws: and they shall be given into his hand until a time and times and the dividing of time. ²⁶But the judgment shall sit, and they shall take away his dominion, to consume and to destroy it unto the end. ²⁷And the kingdom and dominion, and the greatness of the kingdom under the whole heaven, shall be given to the people of the saints of the most High, whose kingdom is an everlasting kingdom, and all dominions shall serve and obey him.

Daniel 7:23-27

Many people today are expecting the Antichrist to rule over a one-world government, but that is not the case at all. There are certainly many forces at work, not only now but all during history, that have been trying to bring about a one-world government. Many Christians point to verses like the ones above where it mentions the whole earth in the same breath as the Antichrist to make their case. However, the beast is not described in terms of reigning over the whole earth, but rather stomping, breaking and devouring it. The first seal of the Book of Revelation reveals a rider on a white horse and wearing a crown. The simple presence of a crown does not tell us that he will rule the world, just that he will be a ruler of something. The only nations we know he will rule over are the ten nations that will form a Middle East alliance that purposes to overthrow and destroy Israel. When the Antichrist arrives, it will be a perfect marriage between the nations that both surround and detest Israel and the one who will finally lead them to victory over Israel. The Antichrist will overthrow some nations, but rather than actually ruling over those nations, he will be on a path of destruction like a giant devastating hurricane. However, Israel will be one exception. The Antichrist will destroy the people, but he wants the temple and the land for his own evil purposes.

Rather than coming in meekness and compassion and to destroy the works of the devil as Jesus did, the Antichrist will come in pride-filled arrogance and loathing and to destroy the works of righteousness through a world war conflict. Just as Nazi Germany, was the base from which Hitler launched his destruction, the Middle East Empire of the beast will be a base of destruction for the Antichrist. Any nation that clings to righteousness will be a primary target for the Antichrist. Many scriptures suggest that there will be good nations in the end-times that will stand up against the Antichrist. There will also be those that God will judge even beyond the time of wrath by eliminating them as nations altogether. If we consider the different types of nuclear, chemical and biological warfare that some Middle East nations—along with the terrorists that they support—and other aggressor nations are working on, it's not hard to see how all of mankind can be wiped out in a very short time if God does not intervene.

Part of God's purpose in allowing the Tribulation is to send a resounding wake-up call to unsaved Jews, sleepy Christians and those people who live in the Middle East who serve another God. As those people begin to see the unbridled terror of their religious leader who claims to be their god, many will begin calling upon Jesus Christ and the God who loves them. Many millions of them will pay for that decision with their lives. As the rest of the world observes not only the brutality of the Antichrist in the Middle East but the general mayhem that will grip the earth as nations rise up against each other, along with a sense of hopelessness coupled with lawlessness in many cities around the globe, the Church will be a beacon of light to guide many to salvation. Many—perhaps most of those who perish during the Tribulation, particularly in the Middle East—will be Christians, but not all. With wars, famine and pestilence adding to the death toll, death will hit hardest in areas where there is war or where poverty already keeps people on the precipice of eternity every single day. But because people will see and know that the end has arrived, millions will be saved around the world. If only one quarter of the people who remain on the earth are born again at the appearing of Jesus in the clouds, that would mean over a billion Christians will be caught up into the clouds to be with Jesus. Assuming a starting point of six billion (our current world population), and one quarter of those dying during the Tribulation, that would leave about three billion people for the wrath that follows.

Think About It!

— Is there a connection between the end-times empire of the beast and ancient Greece?

— Even if Daniel had no knowledge of the beginnings of Rome, why did God skip over it completely without even a cursory mention of it?

— Is the beast the Antichrist?

— Is he described more as a ruler or a warrior?

Selah

And in the days of these kings shall the God of heaven set up a kingdom, which shall never be destroyed: and the kingdom shall not be left to other people, but it shall break in pieces and consume all these kingdoms, and it shall stand for ever.

Daniel 2:44

REVELATION 13

Profile of the Beast

I think that some people experience bondage to their prayer closets. They go in determined to learn the answer to a particular question and don't come out until they have it. That is only inviting trouble. Sometimes it take years for God to lay out a foundation that will allow you to finally understand the answer to your question. If you enter your prayer closet seeking the answer to a question, and there are a hundred other things you need to understand before God can give you the answer you seek, it will take time and patience to wait on Him to develop your overall understanding. I don't have a prayer closet, per se. Most of the time I pray when I'm alone. Sometimes in my car, sometimes on my bed, walking down the street, on a fishing pier or in a crowd of people. Nobody knows that I'm praying. I speak to God in my heart. I know that I will get an answer, but I don't try to force it. It will come in God's time and in God's way. If you try to force it, you may end up reasoning your way to an improper conclusion. Of course, there are many lying spirits who would just jump at the chance to mislead you. I have learned that I can ask God questions and cast the care of it over on Him, and as I go through my day, the answers come. I have received answers while bathing and while cleaning the bathtub, at work and at play, while eating and while dreaming at night. God gave me the answer to one particularly puzzling question one time while watching

"Little House on the Prairie." It always comes from the heart first, and then it changes the way your head thinks.

The word "beast" is used fifteen times in Revelation 13. Fourteen of those uses are in reference to the Antichrist. Once, in verse 11, we see "another beast" rise up out of the earth, which is the false prophet who exalts the Antichrist. The name Antichrist is never used in Revelation; it is always "the beast." The name Antichrist comes from the little Johns. Both names are very fitting. The name "beast" refers to his beastly nature that completely lacks humanity, while the name Antichrist implies that he is the complete antithesis of the true Christ. The very nature of their beings is diametrically opposed to each other. They are so completely opposite, they possess no qualities or characteristics that are the same. First John 2:18,22; 4:3; and 2 John 1:7 all mention the name Antichrist. First John 4:3 tells us that "every spirit that confesses not that Jesus Christ is come in the flesh is not of God: and this is that spirit of Antichrist, whereof ye have heard that it should come; and even now already is it in the world." Many people believe in Jesus as a saintly character who went around doing good, but they do not believe He was the anointed Christ or the Son of God. The simple denial of the deity of the man Jesus Christ is Antichrist according to 1 John 2:22, but there is one who is yet to come who thinks, acts and is a total violation of the true Christ—he is the Antichrist.

Revelation 13 serves several purposes. It begins to familiarize the saints with the Antichrist so that when we see him, we will be able to recognize him. While we are being shown some detail about the Antichrist and how the Tribulation will be played out, we are introduced to the false prophet and the Mark of the Beast. We also see a link between the Antichrist and Satan. The last thing we saw in Revelation 12 was Satan going to make war with the offspring of Israel who keep the commands of Jesus Christ. In this chapter, we see that the Antichrist is the emissary of Satan on this earth who is given the job of making war with the saints. In fact, the great red dragon with seven heads from the previous chapter is morphed into the seven-headed beast of this chapter.

The dragon was identified as the old serpent named the Devil and Satan in verse 9 of the last chapter. The seven heads always represent seven empires, which he exerted great control over and which he used to persecute Israel as he attempted to stop the plan of salvation. Those empires, in order, are Egypt, Syria, Babylon, Persia, Greece, Rome and the Antichrist Empire. Whenever we read about the beast, we are reading about the Antichrist, and by extension, his end-times kingdom. The end-times kingdom of the beast will provide Satan with one last chance to interfere with the work of God. He will attempt to put a stop to the preaching of the gospel through fear and intimidation and the mass murder of all those who oppose him. This plan will backfire because many people draw closer to God in times of tragedy and persecution, and many will get saved, which will lead him to plan B—the destruction of all flesh. Plan B will be thwarted, however, by the appearing of Jesus to rescue His saints. The first two verses of this chapter link the Antichrist and his kingdom to the past while at the same time showing us what is yet to come.

> ¹And I stood upon the sand of the sea, and saw a beast rise up out of the sea, having seven heads and ten horns, and upon his horns ten crowns, and upon his heads the name of blasphemy. ²And the beast which I saw was like unto a *leopard*, and his feet were as the feet of a *bear*, and his mouth as the mouth of a *lion*: and *the dragon gave him his power, and his seat, and great authority.*
>
> *Revelation 13:1-2*

Lions and leopards and bears, oh my! These are the same three animals Daniel saw in his vision that represented world empires which arose upon the earth to rule. The lion represented Babylon, the bear was Persia and the leopard was Greece. All three animals are used to describe the end-times beast, suggesting that the fourth kingdom, which is the Antichrist kingdom, will have all the power and fierceness of the previous kingdoms combined. The Antichrist will also rule over the same geographic areas as those previous empires, particularly Greece. We learn this from Daniel 8 where we see Alexander the Great lead the Greeks against the Persians with spectacular success, only to die and have the kingdom divided between his four generals in Daniel 8:22. Then, in Daniel 8:23, we are told that in the latter time of their kingdom, transgressors will come to a fullness just before the Antichrist steps in to reign. The Greek Empire actually has little to do with the nation of Greece and much to do with the Middle East, including Turkey, Afghanistan, Pakistan and parts of North Africa.

The end-times beast will be like a leopard, suggesting great speed and agility, quickness and stealth. His feet are like a bear—strong and powerful, able to kill with a single blow, supporting the full weight of the bear and crushing anything that gets in its way. The mouth of the beast is that of a lion. The king of the jungle is able to rule with just a roar, but if that is not enough, his jaws are powerful enough to tear the flesh of any foe. Not only is the mouth of the beast like a lion, but, as Daniel said in Daniel 7, his teeth are like iron, which symbolizes the cold and destructive power the Antichrist receives from Satan until Jesus intervenes to take the kingdom at the appointed time. The amalgamation of all these characteristics into one beast makes for an extremely powerful, capable and destructive adversary. This is what the end-times beast will be. The end of verse 2 says that the dragon, who is Satan, is the one who gives the beast the power to make war and a kingdom to rule. Daniel 7 proclaims that God will eventually give Jesus the victory over the beast, and He will give Him the kingdom to rule forever but not until after Satan delivers it over to the Antichrist for a short time at the end of time.

In the next verse, we see one of the heads of the beast receive a death blow, followed by a full recovery back to life again. The heads of the beast represent different empires and could represent the primary kings of those empires. In the case of the Beast Empire, the supreme leader of the ten-nation alliance—that comes together before the Antichrist ever rises to power—would be the most likely candidate for a death blow and subsequent Antichrist indwelling, if that is what is happening here—which may very well be. As we have already seen in Revelation 11:7, the beast is described as literally ascending out of the bottomless pit. This is reaffirmed later in Revelation. Of course, the Antichrist himself, as a mortal man, could be the one slain and then revived with no other personalities involved. We will look at this further when we get to Revelation 17 where we find more information about the Antichrist, the seven heads of the beast and the ten kings.

> ³And I saw one of his heads as it were wounded to death; and his deadly wound was healed: and all the world wondered after the beast. ⁴And they worshipped the dragon which gave power unto the beast: and they worshipped the beast, saying, Who is like unto the beast? who is able to make war with him?
>
> *Revelation 13:3-4*

The end of verse 3 states that the world will marvel after the beast. The fact that those words are tacked onto the end of verse 3 does not mean that the world will marvel over the rising from the dead of the Antichrist. It could simply be a stand-alone statement that has nothing to do with his near death experience. There are many reasons why the world will wonder after the Antichrist: 1) He will be the most visible world leader of his time; 2) his arrogance and his desire to instill fear into the hearts of men will drive him to remain in the spotlight; 3) people will wonder after him because of his crude nature as he rises to power by trickery and force; and 4) the world will be amazed by his claims of deity just like they were amazed by Jesus' claims of deity. People will either love him and his destructive ways, or they will disdain him.

Back in Revelation 11:13 when we were looking at the Wrath of God, we saw that the same people who are worshipping the beast here were giving glory to God by their acknowledgement that God is the one bringing wrath upon them at that time. This type of worship is not praise; it is simply an acknowledgement. Regardless of whether a person is a follower of the beast with a heartfelt hatred for all of God's people, or one who has rejected God, has no hope in God, wants nothing to do with God and yet rejects the Antichrist also, they will all make the same acknowledgement: Who is able to stand against the beast? If you'll recall, Matthew 24:21 declares the beginning of the Tribulation, and then verses 23 and 24 declare that there will be false christs and false prophets out to deceive all who will listen to them, even the elect of God if they give in to the lies. Those false christs will worship the beast along with others as they speak of the great power of the beast and then demand submission to themselves from the simpleminded. The Church—those who are written in the Lamb's

Book of Life—will continue to magnify Jesus and minister salvation to any who are willing to receive.

When anyone willingly worships and serves the beast and all that he stands for, they are, in effect, worshipping the dragon, which is Satan. This does not mean that there will be an outbreak of Satan worship across the face of the earth. Many will deny any connection between the Antichrist and Satan, but the truth is, if you worship the beast, you worship the serpent that sent him. The kind of worship the beast generates from people is different from the loving admiration and adoration that Jesus engenders. The world will worship the beast by saying things like, "Who is like unto the beast? Who is able to make war with him?" Rather than accolades of joy, the Antichrist will generate utterances of disdain and fear. For those who love disdain and fear, the worship will be genuine, but for all others it is only a verbal acknowledgement that the Antichrist is indeed someone to be reckoned with. Any statement that recognizes the brutal warlike nature of the beast, and particularly those statements that give support to his actions, is worship to the Antichrist. Second Thessalonians explains that strong delusion will accompany the Antichrist. Many will love his lies and his disregard for the truth. Daniel 8:12 declares that those who actively support and follow after the Antichrist in his kingdom will cast truth to the ground. They will be the true worshippers of the beast; all others will simply fear him. If you'll recall, the chapters of Revelation we are reading now are the ones that accompany the vials and are focused around the Middle East exclusively, with Israel right in the middle of things. If there is an abundance of true worship for the beast in this region of the world by those who look upon him as the messiah who has come to destroy Israel, that should in no way be mistaken for a worldwide worship service for the beast.

> [8]And then shall that Wicked be revealed, whom the Lord
> shall consume with the spirit of his mouth, and shall
> destroy with the brightness of his coming: [9]Even him,
> *whose coming is after the working of Satan with all power*
> *and signs and lying wonders,* [10]And *with all deceivableness*
> *of unrighteousness in them that perish*; because they
> received not the love of the truth, that they might be saved.
> [11]And *for this cause God shall send them strong delusion,*

that they should believe a lie: [12]That they all might be damned *who believed not the truth, but had pleasure in unrighteousness.*

2 Thessalonians 2:8-12

God, by His omniscience and omnipotent power, is able to control Satan and cause him to do things within His own timing. In other words, when verse 11 says that "God shall send them strong delusion," it is not God doing these things or forcing Satan to do these things. Rather it is God knowing what Satan's plans are, knowing Satan's nature and how he is going to react in any situation (knowing the end from the beginning) and then restraining, circumventing, tricking and basically pushing Satan's buttons and jerking his chain to the point that He actually brings Satan's actions in line with His own timing and plans.

Verse 5 is one of the many places we see the time limitation put on the Antichrist for causing Great Tribulation—forty-two months, or three-and-one-half years. His reign will exceed that number by years. But for forty-two months, he will have the full power of Satan at his disposal and will be completely unrestrained by God from causing all the trouble that he can (except that God will continue to deliver those who trust in Him and His covenant, which will still be in effect). He will begin his reign sometime before he is able to get the seven-year peace treaty put into effect and will continue to be the ruler of a devastated kingdom after the Wrath of God begins. He will survive right up to the end of God's wrath and will be successful in turning world opinion against the God of heaven and the soon-returning king of all nations—Jesus Christ. The words of blasphemy he speaks will be a part of the strong delusion he will bring to all those who refuse the gentle leadings of the Holy Spirit and who refuse to believe the truth.

[5]And there was given unto him a mouth speaking great things and blasphemies; and power was given unto him to continue forty and two months. [6]And he opened his mouth in blasphemy against God, to blaspheme His name, and His tabernacle, and them that dwell in heaven.

Revelation 13:5-6

It is apparent from the verses below that the saints will still be on the earth during the Tribulation. We have already seen in Matthew 24 and in the first half of the Revelation that the Church is not raptured until after the Tribulation. That is exactly what we are seeing here once more. The Rapture will not take place in this chronological setting until we get to the beginning of Revelation 14, and even then it is divided into two stages—the 144,000 firstfruits from Israel and then the rest of the Church. God's wrath is not discussed in the following verses; His wrath does not begin until Revelation 16.

There will be a circle of death surrounding Israel where deception and a love of lies are so deeply ingrained in the people that many will not even be able to recognize truth. Those that are resident in this area of the world, and have received the truth and a love for the gospel, will reach out to others with the Word that is sharper than any two-edged sword and cut through some of the delusion. There will be revival, but the Antichrist will make war against the saints, against revival and against the Word of God. There will be plenty of distress to deal with, no matter what part of the world you live in, but the nations surrounding Israel will see the very worst of it. Those who live outside the circle of death need to start praying now for the salvation of all those who belong to God inside those nations. The gospel will be preached throughout all of the ten nations where the Antichrist will rule before the end comes. Pray for those who are called as missionaries, pastors and laborers to these nations.

In verse 7, we read about the Antichrist having power over all nations and tongues. Because we are also told that he rules over ten nations, it must be assumed that he does not rule over all nations directly but has some other power by which he is able to either influence or control other nations. That influence and control is six-fold: 1) He will have the power of Satan working in his life to accomplish his goals; 2) he will have the disruptive power of a world war, which puts him at the center of world affairs as other nations rush in to put a stop to his madness; 3) he will have the power of religious zeal working in the people who serve him and the false prophet who exalts him; 4) he will have the power of terrorism; 5) he will have shock value and confusion when he seats himself in the temple of God and claims to be God; and 6) he will have enormous control over the wealth flowing through his kingdom by way of the city of Babylon.

He will have power over all of the earth without actually reigning over all the whole earth—all he has to do is cause great tribulation.

In Job, chapter 1, Satan gained power over all Job had and he used that power not to rule over Job's family and possessions, but to destroy them. For years Job trusted God and God built a protective hedge around him. Satan, knowing he was unable to penetrate that hedge, didn't even try anymore. Instead, he went whining to God. Satan may or may not have noticed that Job was offering sacrifices continually in fear, as opposed to offering one sacrifice a year in faith as prescribed by God. Because Job was no longer in faith, God had to release him into the hands of Satan. In the end the Antichrist will use those who submit to him to destroy those who don't, and God will determine who He delivers and who He will allow to be tried by death. During the Tribulation, the power of the Antichrist will be concentrated in his kingdom first, over those nations which he conquers second and then will flow to all the earth to the proportion he is able to rally evildoers by his deception. His power is not to rule over all the earth but to cause havoc and destruction.

> ⁷And *it was given unto him to make war with the saints, and to overcome them*: and power was given him over all kindreds, and tongues, and nations. ⁸And all that dwell upon the earth shall worship him, whose names are not written in the book of life of the Lamb slain from the foundation of the world. ⁹If any man have an ear, let him hear. ¹⁰He that leadeth into captivity shall go into captivity: he that killeth with the sword must be killed with the sword. Here is the patience and the faith of the saints.
>
> *Revelation 13:7-10*

God gives us a warning in the tenth verse about how we are to conduct ourselves during the end-times—and any time for that matter. The Antichrist and a good portion of the world may be at war against the saints, but the saints are not at war against the world, or at least, they are not supposed to be. With the end so near, there is no reason to fight for our survival. We will all be included in the Rapture—dead or alive. Our primary concern should be what our Lord wants from us, and our secondary concern should be how many of our antagonist we can take to heaven with us. Stephen was willing to lay down his life for Christ, and that act of faith and obedience, coupled with his testimony, eventually led to Paul's salvation. Paul went on to lay his life on the line multiple times, and God delivered him every time. The Book of Acts will continue to be written in the end-times with millions of Stephens giving up their lives as a testimony to others, and millions of Pauls who just don't know when to quit and who put their lives on the line every day for the eternal lives of others. Belonging to any type of civil or national defense occupation brings a high level of responsibility with it to protect others, and God has ordained these ministries of protection. He doesn't expect law enforcement and military to lay down their arms and allow evil to have free rein.

We are introduced to the false prophet in the next two verses. His job is to point the way to the Antichrist with deceiving miracles and signs. The two horns the false prophet exhibits more than likely represent two additional nations the false prophet has power over that are not included in the original ten nations the Antichrist will rule. This will make him a political and spiritual figure and possibly a warlord just like the Antichrist. The addition of two more nations would make twelve altogether, which would mimic the twelve tribes of Israel that together make one nation. Satan is very unoriginal and always copies and perverts the things God does—even down to this dirty dozen.

> [11]And I beheld another beast coming up out of the earth; and he had two horns like a lamb, and he spake as a dragon. [12]And he exerciseth all the power of the first beast before him, and causeth the earth and them which dwell therein to worship the first beast, whose deadly wound was healed.
>
> *Revelation 13:11-12*

The false prophet gets the attention of the world by performing miracles and wonders, which will be scientifically unexplainable miracles. These are not the modern miracles of technology put to use by a team of animation experts, but rather, the simple working of demons as they manipulate the natural realm to deceive human beings. You'll recall from 2 Thessalonians, chapter 2, that the Antichrist will come after the working of Satan with all power and signs and lying wonders to deceive. We learned from verse 12 that the false prophet possesses and exercises all the same powers the Antichrist possesses. In Revelation 16:13 and 14, we see the words "the spirits of devils working miracles." It will be the power of demons and the power that Satan bestows upon him that causes these things to come to past.

> [13]And he doeth great wonders, so that he maketh fire come down from heaven on the earth in the sight of men, [14]And deceiveth them that dwell on the earth by the means of those miracles which he had power to do in the sight of the beast; saying to them that dwell on the earth, that they should make an image to the beast, which had the wound by a sword, and did live. [15]And he had power to give life unto the image of the beast, that the image of the beast should both speak, and cause that as many as would not worship the image of the beast should be killed.
>
> *Revelation 13:13-15*

Antiochus Epiphanes, the king of the Syrian portion of the old Greek Empire, took over Jerusalem in 167 b.c., and set up a statue of Zeus Olympus in the temple of God and forbade the worship of God. However, before that, he entered the Holy of Holies himself and put a stop to the daily sacrifice for nearly three years. Antiochus may be more than a type of the Antichrist. He lived over a hundred years before Jesus ever spoke of the abomination that would stand in the temple in the latter days, and he did fulfill some of the prophecy that is written of the Antichrist, but, by no means, not all. We'll discuss Antiochus and the abomination later.

When the false prophet calls for the people of the earth to make an image of the beast, it will be similar to when God called upon the Israelites to give a freewill offering for the building of the temple. So much was given that a second decree had to be made to get the people to stop giving. At the same time, it will be like Aaron taking the offerings of gold to build a calf for the wayward Jews. The beast image might very well be constructed of gold just like the calf. People from all over the kingdom of the beast and from other parts of the world will send the resources needed to form the image of the beast. It will be a dumb idol with the likeness of the false god who has taken over the temple of God until the false prophet empowers the dumb idol to speak. That empowerment will be coupled with the command that all who are not giving true knee-bending, soul-surrendering worship to the beast should be killed. In the kingdom of the beast, mothers will finally have no choice but to turn in their sons who have rejected the beast over to the magistrates, and daughters will have to snitch on their fathers who have given their hearts to the Lord, or face death themselves. And, because it's a talking idol that comes to life, it must be God doing it. Right? Wrong! The power comes from the false prophet who receives his power from Satan.

The following verses warn us of the Mark of the Beast. The mark is described in very simple terms because it is a very simple thing—a permanent mark like a tattoo or a brand. There are three different markings to choose from, and it may be placed on the forehead or the right hand. A person may choose between the name of the beast—the number 666, which is described as the number of his name, or a mark which is not described but is probably some type of emblem or logo that may or may not be unique to the beast but will show one's allegiance to the beast.

> [16]And he causeth all, both small and great, rich and poor, free and bond, to receive a mark in their right hand, or in their foreheads: [17]And that no man might buy or sell, save he that had the mark, or the name of the beast, or the number of his name. [18]Here is wisdom. Let him that hath understanding count the number of the beast: for it is the number of a man; and his number is six hundred three-score and six.
>
> *Revelation 13:16-18*

God forewarns us not to take the mark, the name or the number of the beast. God wants us to know about it now so that when it is happening, we will be able to avoid it even if it costs us our lives. If God had given us the number 777 for the real Christ, we would say that seven is God's number of completion and it also represents the seven spirits of God. Because it appears three times, which is God's perfect number, it represents the fullness of the perfection of the Godhead. Verse 18 explains that 666 is the number of a man and because six appears three times, this man is perfect in his ungodliness and rebellion toward God. Six is one half of twelve, which is a number God uses frequently in reference to His redeemed. Maybe God is saying that despite all the earthly and devilish wisdom the Antichrist possesses, he is still just a halfwit compared to those who have the wisdom to follow after and submit to the God of heaven. It is important to remember in these times, as in any other time, that God is well able to deliver and provide for His people. If we are among those who keep their lives until the return of Jesus, that doesn't at all mean we will continue in our jobs, remain in our fine homes or enjoy any creature comforts. The 144,000 of Israel will be hiding in the mountains of Israel, and things may not be much better for the rest of us. We need to be prepared for anything and be willing to give up everything.

Having said that, in the year that Jesus was born, a decree went out that "all the world should be taxed" (Luke 2:1); however, we know that the decree was to the people of the Roman Empire and did not affect people in places such as China, India or anywhere outside the empire. Likewise, when the decree goes out for all people to receive the Mark of the Beast, until the time has come and gone, we will not know how far-reaching it will be. It will likely only be in the ten-nation kingdom of the beast and will affect those who wish to trade with these nations. Any nation that is overrun by the Beast Empire will fall under this rule which will be used to eliminate all Christian and Jewish opposition in those nations.

Many theories have sprung up about the Mark of the Beast being some type of microchip implant, a smart card, a bar code or some other technology that the Antichrist will use to track individuals and information about them. However, the Scriptures do not imply anything like that at all. It is a pretty far stretch for a mark to become an implant. Here, and in the remainder of the Revelation, the Mark of the Beast is always talking about a visible mark. Chapter 14:11b says, "whosoever receiveth the *mark of his name*." For many, the name of the Antichrist will be written onto their flesh by tattooing it, stamping it with some type of permanent method or even by burning it into the flesh as you would brand a cow. Knowing the nature of the Antichrist and the completely fallen nature of those who serve him, suffering the pain of being branded will more than likely be the method of choice. Something quick would be preferable also because the false prophet will probably not be promoting the beast until after he enters the temple of God at the middle of the seven-year treaty when the Great Tribulation has already begun. That would leave less than three-and-one-half years to mark perhaps billions of people during the chaos of war. We can expect the name of the beast to be written in Arabic since he will be ruling his ten-nation empire in the midst of the Arab world.

The Mark of the Beast will actually aid the true worshippers of the beast in following out the orders to kill all of those who refuse to worship the image of the beast. Those who do not have the Mark of the Beast on their bodies will be the ones who stand out like sheep in a den of hungry lions. Whether you are on a crowded street or on an elevator with just one other person, everyone knows who has submitted to the beast and who has not because you either have the mark or you don't. This is actually scarier than an implant because it makes it impossible to walk down that crowded street without detection. A simple mark is the most practical and the most diabolical way to turn the population into a singleminded mob, doing the work of the Antichrist. Fear of persecution and death will transform many peace-loving uncommitted citizens of the beast kingdom into soldiers for their lord. The absence of the mark will make Christian and Jewish believers ready targets for persecution and death.

Verse 15 in the previous scriptures makes clear that those who refuse to receive the Mark of the Beast and worship him will be killed. From that statement it may appear that only unbelievers will survive the Tribulation since Christians will be avoiding and refusing his mark and thus putting their lives at risk. However, we need to remember that the chapters we are reading now are the ones that focus on the kingdom of the beast in the Middle East and not the whole world. We need to remember that Jesus will not come for His elect until after the Tribulation. We also need to remember that there are 144,000 Israelites who are born again and protected in the wilderness from the wrath of Satan during the Tribulation. Jesus will return to an earth full of saints who are alive and remain unto the coming of the Lord. There will be a worldwide Church purged of all those who turn away from God because of fear, as they see the things that are coming on the earth and as their own faith is put to the flame and consumed. Many millions will also turn to the Lord because of the things that are coming on the earth. They will finally see Satan unmasked and will not like what they see, so they will turn to the Lord for refuge. For those who believe in the doctrine of "once saved, always saved," receiving the mark of the beast will prove that doctrine to be a lie.

The Tribulation will be the worst time of persecution the Church as a whole has ever known, but it will also be the Church's greatest hour. The covenant of faith will still be in effect, and God will still be delivering many of His people through the daily tragedies that will befall them. At the same time, however, many will have to lay down their lives during the trial of their faith. Verses 7-10 of this chapter reveal the Antichrist targeting the saints for destruction and overcoming many, but the ones who overcame relied on their faith and patience and not retribution or self-defense. Revelation 12 explains that "they overcame him by the blood of the Lamb, and by the word of their testimony; and they **loved not their lives** unto the death." Many will have to lay down their lives for the Lord. Daniel 11:32 and 33 put everything into perspective. Bear in mind that the epicenter of the Tribulation will be in the Middle East.

> [32]And such as do wickedly against the covenant shall he corrupt by flatteries: but the people that do know their God shall be strong, and do exploits. [33]And they that understand among the people shall instruct many: yet they shall fall by the sword, and by flame, by captivity, and by spoil, many days.
>
> *Daniel 11:32-33*

Many of the early saints, and even Jesus Himself, make excellent examples of going through trials of persecution. Stephen was a man who laid down his life for the Lord without regret, without guile and, in fact, without pain. He didn't die an agonizing death at the hands of his persecutors; he simply fell asleep as they threw stones at him.

> [58]And cast him [Stephen] out of the city, and stoned him: and the witnesses laid down their clothes at a young man's

feet, whose name was Saul. ⁵⁹And they stoned Stephen, calling upon God, and saying, Lord Jesus, receive my spirit. ⁶⁰And he kneeled down, and cried with a loud voice, Lord, lay not this sin to their charge. And when he had said this, *he fell asleep.*

Acts 7:58-60

Before Jesus laid his life down at the cross, God delivered him at various times as the religious Jews tried to kill Him before His time. Twice He walked right through the middle of angry mobs as they tried to end His life.

⁵⁸Jesus said unto them, Verily, verily, I say unto you, Before Abraham was, I am. ⁵⁹Then took they up stones to cast at him: but Jesus hid himself, and went out of the temple, *going through the midst of them,* and so passed by.

John 8:58-59

²⁸And all they in the synagogue, when they heard these things, were filled with wrath, ²⁹And rose up, and thrust him out of the city, and led him unto the brow of the hill whereon their city was built, that they might cast him down headlong. ³⁰*But he passing through the midst of them went his way,*

Luke 4:28-30

Paul went through an awful lot of persecution (tribulation) and kept on going, all the way to prison to witness to Caesar.

²⁴Of the Jews five times received I forty stripes save one. ²⁵Thrice was I beaten with rods, once was I stoned, thrice I suffered shipwreck, a night and a day I have been in the deep; ²⁶In journeyings often, in perils of waters, in perils of robbers, in perils by mine own countrymen, in perils by the heathen, in perils in the city, in perils in the wilderness, in perils in the sea, in perils among false brethren; ²⁷In

weariness and painfulness, in watchings often, in hunger and thirst, in fastings often, in cold and nakedness.

2 Corinthians 11:24-27

[19]And there came thither certain Jews from Antioch and Iconium, who persuaded the people, and, *having stoned Paul, drew him out of the city, supposing he had been dead.* [20]Howbeit, as the disciples stood round about him, *he rose up, and came into the city:* and the next day he departed with Barnabas to Derbe.

Acts 14:19-20

Paul knew that he had a choice between living or laying down his life as a martyr. After finalizing his decision in the verses below to continue on and live for the ministry to the saints, they could have stoned him on a daily basis, and he would have just kept on getting up and going on.

[21]For to me to live is Christ, and to die is gain. [22]But if I live in the flesh, this is the fruit of my labour: *yet what I shall choose I wot not.* [23]*For I am in a strait betwixt two, having a desire to depart,* and to be with Christ; which is far better: [24]*Nevertheless to abide in the flesh is more needful for you.* [25]And having this confidence, *I know that I shall abide and continue with you all* for your furtherance and joy of faith;

Philippians 1:21-25

THINK ABOUT IT!

— From where does the beast derive his power?

— Does the beast exhibit all of the attributes of Satan?

— When the beast is given power over all kindreds, tongues and nations, does that mean he will rule over the entire earth or could that power be more in the form of wars, deception and tribulations?

— If the beast rules a one-world government, does mean that the false prophet also rules a one-world government when he exercises all the power of the first beast?

Selah

A righteous man regardeth the life of his beast: but the tender mercies of the wicked are cruel.

Proverbs 12:10

REVELATION 14

Firstfruits First and a Short Chronology

This is my favorite chapter, perhaps because it is the last one I finally really understood. Or, perhaps because I have a deep appreciation for how God hid His truth so craftily under our noses. The way the prophecies are written is such that anybody can come up with any scenario they want and prove it with Scripture. The problem is, just because you string various scriptures together does not mean you are dealing with the truth. For God's truth, you must approach Him for the answers. You must wait on Him for the answers. And when you do, you develop a strong relationship with Him that is hard to shake. Everything seemed like it had fallen into place for me. It all made perfect sense—except for one little thing. Babylon was out of place in this chapter. Why was it there? "Why, God?" And then He sent the answer. I still laugh about it, the way that He hides things right in front of us. He's like the master magician using smoke and mirrors. Illusions of the mind. But yet, He is God—all-knowing and a fountain of wisdom and understanding to those who love Him.

The Tribulation ends as chapter 13 concludes, and then the first five verses of chapter 14 begin to show the Rapture of the Church once again. There is no talk about clouds and trumpets or being caught up to meet Jesus in the air in these verses; instead we are see-ing the concluding moments of the Rapture as the first group of believers are brought before the Throne of God for the very first time. We only catch a glimpse of the first group of believers in these five verses; the second and final group does not arrive in heaven until Revelation 15. In verse 1, the first arrivals are identified as the same 144,000 that were sealed in their foreheads just before they were raptured in Revelation 7. In the same verse, the seal in their foreheads is identified as the name of God, which could be Jehovah, Yahweh, El Shaddai, I Am or any of the other names of God. In Verse 4, the 144,000 are called the firstfruits unto God, and as such, they are delivered up to heaven before anyone else. Finally, in verse 1 their location is identified as on Mount Zion, and in verse 5, it is nar-rowed down to a very special area on Mount Zion—before the Throne of God.

In Hebrews 12:18-22, we are told in regards to our salvation and the New Covenant that we are come "unto **Mount Zion** and unto the **city of the living God**, the **heavenly Jerusalem**, and to an innumer-able company of angels," as opposed to the Old Covenant where the earthly mountain burned with fire and produced only a law that was impossible for man to keep. In other words, the Old Covenant is based in earthly practices and the New Covenant is based in heaven in the very city of God where grace flows from Mount Zion to the heirs of the promise. There is no reason why the Mount Zion in verse 1 should be taken as anything other than the heavenly Mount Zion of Hebrews 12:22, which is the location of the city of God in heaven. The 144,000 have just gone through forty-two months of Great Tribulation in chapter 13, and now they are before the Throne of God as the "firstfruits" of God. The beasts and elders that were before the Throne in Revelation 4 and 7 are stationed before the Throne here also, which gives further proof that these saints are indeed in heaven and not just part of some elaborate imagery designed to relay a point other than what we are actually seeing.

The 144,000 are not firstfruits in name only. They are raptured about two steps ahead of everyone else, or at least, they are the first ones who are allowed into the presence of God. They are delivered out of the Tribulation of chapter 13 just before God's wrath begins in chapter 16. If you'll recall from Revelation 6:12, the sixth seal of the Book of Revelation was opened and the Rapture was revealed. The first thing that happened was that the 144,000 from all the tribes of Israel were sealed, and then we saw the redeemed of every tribe, tongue and nation gathered into heaven before the throne of God. There is something special about the 144,000, and God makes that clear by allowing them into the throne room first with a song that only they can learn and then He drops fifteen verses of chronological commentary into the passage that follows to separate the 144,000 and the rest of the Church which is raptured in Revelation 15.

Just as Moses heeded the advice of his father-in-law Jethro in Exodus 18:13-27 and appointed a functional chain of command, so will the new earth have a system that works, makes sense and has a chain of command. For instance, although we may all freely approach God at times in heaven, when it comes to making things work in an orderly fashion, the twelve apostles and the twelve Jewish patriarchs will likely answer directly to Jesus with the 144,000 answering to the twenty-four elders, and the rest of us taking orders from the 144,000. God has chosen them for His own special purposes, not because they are more righteous than anyone else, but solely by His election and because of His promises to Abraham and His natural seed. A secondary purpose for rapturing the 144,000 first could be to put terror into the heart of the Antichrist and his closest followers who seem to have an affection for the city of Jerusalem and the temple of God.

> [1]And I looked, and, lo, *a Lamb stood on the mount Sion, and with him an hundred forty and four thousand,* having his Father's name written in their foreheads. [2]And I heard a voice from heaven, as the voice of many waters, and as the voice of a great thunder: and I heard the voice of harpers harping with their harps: [3]And they sung as it were a new song before the throne, and before the four beasts, and the elders: and no man could learn that song but the hundred and forty and four thousand, which were redeemed from the earth. [4]These are they which were not defiled with women; for they are virgins. These are they which follow the Lamb whithersoever he goeth. These were redeemed from among men, being the first fruits unto God and to the

Lamb. [5]And in their mouth was found no guile: for they are without fault *before the throne of God.*

Revelation 14:1-5

These verses suggest to us that Jesus will make his first stop of the Rapture in the mountains of Israel to take the 144,000 who are being protected by God during the Tribulation. Jesus does not set foot on the Mount of Olives or any other part of the earth during His first return visit. The sole purpose of His first trip will be to remove all of those who belong to Him from the earth so that sinners may be punished.

A BIBLICAL TIMELINE

The 144,000 are called the firstfruits but never the only fruits. The rest of the redeemed follow immediately after the 144,000, but as far as putting it all down on paper, God chose this place to insert a quick chronological rundown of the end-times in verses 6-20. This rundown begins with the final preaching of the gospel, which is exactly what Jesus said would have to happen before the events of the end-times would ever begin. The final event recorded in these fifteen verses is the Battle of Armageddon. In just fifteen verses, God shows us again the entire end-times in the order things will transpire. If we were to remove verses 6-20 of Revelation 14, then the first five verses of that chapter—where the 144,000 of Israel have been gathered into heaven before anyone else—would flow perfectly and logically right into chapter 15 where the rest of the Church is finally united with the firstfruits before the throne of God.

This short section of Scripture is the only significant break in the flow of events from Revelation 12 to the end of the Revelation. However, it does repeat and reinforce the same theme and sequence of events we saw in chapters 6-11, and those we are currently studying in chapter 12 through the end of the book, but in a condensed form. God makes five main points in these verses that serve to further enlighten us concerning things which will come to pass, but they also serve as a written timeline of the end-times that cannot be ignored.

The first point comes as a reminder to all the earth that they must heed the gospel. Why? Because the day of wrath is fast approaching.

Anyone who has not acted upon the gospel of salvation will soon find themselves reacting to the Wrath of God. Jesus is coming for those who have accepted His loving substitution at Calvary and who embrace Him as the Son of God. The failure of any one person to heed God's word is going to affect everyone else around them in a negative way. Someone has to be the strong one who steps up to the plate regardless of what others think. Needless to say, there will be many evil people who are not going to repent of their evil, but there are also a lot of frightened people who need help in being brave. Those who hold back because of fear will be a negative influence on all those around them who want to get saved, while those who are brave will be like towers of strength to those who are scared. The following warning precedes the Rapture because afterwards, as the Bible repeatedly states, there will be no more repentance nor any desire by those remaining on the earth to do so.

> 6And I saw another angel fly in the midst of heaven, having the everlasting gospel to preach unto them that dwell on the earth, and to every nation, and kindred, and tongue, and people, 7Saying with a loud voice, Fear God, and give glory to him; for the hour of his judgment is come: and worship him that made heaven, and earth, and the sea, and the fountains of waters.
>
> *Revelation 14:6-7*

When verse 6 refers to "another angel," it is simply referring back to all the other angels John has already seen during the unfolding of the entire Revelation. No connection is made between them other than the fact that this is just one more angel bringing enlightenment to him from God. However, this is the first of three angels in this setting that is going to fly across the skies and proclaim a message. The second angel is referred to as "another angel" and the third one is referred to "the third angel," making these three a unique group in a unique setting. Two other angels complete this chronology as each comes out of the temple of God in heaven to deliver their messages.

Verse 8 declares the fall of Babylon, but this is not the fall of a worldly Babylon. If this verse was talking about the earthly city of Babylon that is destroyed in Revelation 18, then it would have been placed near the end of these fifteen verses where the time of God's wrath is drawing to a close with the Battle of Armageddon. In fact, verse 8 relates back to Revelation 12 where Satan and his angels fought against Michael and his angels, and Satan was cast out of heaven. This is "MYSTERY, BABYLON," which we will look at in further detail when we get to Revelation 17 and 18. In a nutshell, Isaiah 14 calls Satan "the king of Babylon" and declares that he will be brought down to the pit of hell. If you thought he was already there, think again. The Bible doesn't say that. There is a literal spiritual city which God refers to as Babylon that is located in heaven itself just like the literal spiritual city of God. Satan rules the earth from there by dispatching his angels to do his dirty work. Satan has a throne of his own, and it doesn't just float through outer space or sit at the bottom of the pit of hell. It is in the spiritual city of Babylon, which God calls the great whore in Revelation 17. Satan is also called the prince of the power of the air and the supreme ruler of spiritual wickedness in high places (Ephesians 2:2, 6:12). Jesus called him the prince and the god of this world (John 12:31; 14:30; 2 Corinthians 4:4). In chapter 12, Satan and his angels were cast out, and **their place was found no more in heaven.** The destruction of "their place" in heaven is what's being described in verse 8. Afterwards, their place will be found on the earth after they are cast out of heaven, and it will be in the midst of the kingdom of the beast. They will cause Great Tribulation from there.

> ⁸And there followed another angel, saying, Babylon is
> fallen, is fallen, that great city, because she made all nations
> drink of the wine of the wrath of her fornication.
>
> *Revelation 14:8*

Verses 9-13 are a reminder to all during the Tribulation, which occurs before the Rapture, not to follow after the beast and not to take his mark. If you will recall, Revelation 12:12 said that after Satan is cast out of heaven, he is come down to the earth having great wrath because he sees that his time is short, and then the Tribulation begins, which is what we see here. He is cast out of heaven in verse 8, and then we immediately see the Antichrist in verse 9 demanding that all people take his mark. As we have seen everywhere else, the beast will come bringing Great Tribulation before the Wrath of God is poured out on those who receive the Mark of the Beast. Verses 9-13 clearly tell us that if we are faced with a choice between serving the beast and taking his mark, or serving Jesus Christ even if it means death, death is the proper choice to make. It needs to be pointed out that the Antichrist will be prominent on the earth for three-and-one-half years before the Tribulation, three-and-one-half years during the Tribulation and for about four to seven years after the Tribulation during the time of wrath. Therefore, it must be assumed that he will more than likely still be requiring people to take the mark after the Church is gone. If you should find yourself on the earth during the time of wrath, don't take the mark. It is clear from the verses below, and from the first and fifth vials, that those who follow the beast and have his mark will be targeted above all others for wrath. Some people are going to survive the Wrath of God, but those with the Mark of the Beast have a bull's-eye right in the middle of their foreheads.

> [9]And the third angel followed them, saying with a loud voice, *If any man worship the beast and his image, and receive his mark in his forehead, or in his hand,* [10]*The same shall drink of the wine of the wrath of God, which is poured out without mixture into the cup of his indignation; and he shall be tormented with fire and brimstone in the presence of the holy angels, and in the presence of the Lamb:* [11]*And the smoke of their torment ascendeth up for ever and ever:* and they have no rest day nor night, who worship the beast and his image, and whosoever receiveth the mark of his name.
>
> *Revelation 14:9-11*

From everything we read in the Scriptures, there appears to be no need to witness to those who sport the Mark of the Beast because it is a final submission to Satan from which there is no repentance. God declares that all who receive the mark will drink of His wrath. He doesn't leave any leeway for those who might want to try it out and get saved later or for those Christians who take the mark to keep from being killed, thinking that God will understand that their hearts are right towards Him and that they will serve Him once the heat dies down. There is no wiggle room. Anyone who takes the mark seals their fate at the same time. There is never any indication of any of these people ever repenting or being in heaven afterwards. They all end up in hell.

On the other hand, there will be great pressure and even fervor on the part of those who wear the mark to "convert," persecute or even kill those who do not wear the mark. As mentioned elsewhere in this book, this phenomenon will take place in the Middle East and may spread beyond the ten-nation kingdom of the Antichrist, but it is by no means clear as to how far it may go around the globe. It is very unlikely that the mark will be a legally required mandate beyond the borders of the Beast Empire and the nations that are conquered by the beast. However, a few nations that have the same kind of heart and mentality as the beast nations may be included, but much of the rest of the world will resist the beast through war.

In the end-time Tribulation, you have a right to trust the Lord for deliverance, and you have the right to die for Him. But you do not have a right to fight back and defend yourself from persecution for your faith in Jesus Christ. This does not void the right of nations to defend their citizens from persecution for their faith through police or military actions. God says in Luke 21:15, "I will give you a mouth and wisdom, which all your adversaries shall not be able to gainsay nor resist," but that does not mean they will repent and get saved. They are adversaries after all; they are there to cause trouble. Revelation 13:10 states, "He that leadeth into captivity shall go into captivity: he that killeth with the sword must be killed with the sword." However, the following verses inform us that those who keep the commandments and faith of Jesus Christ might possibly die in the Lord. We need to be trusting God for supernatural deliverance and at the same time be prepared for martyrdom. Above all else, we need to do what the Lord tells us to do by His Holy Spirit. The next two verses are a continuation of the previous scriptures concerning the Mark of the Beast. They are all a part of the Tribulation.

> [12]Here is the patience of the saints: here are they that keep the commandments of God, and the faith of Jesus. [13]And I heard a voice from heaven saying unto me, Write, Blessed are the dead which die in the Lord from henceforth: Yea,

saith the Spirit, that they may rest from their labours; and
their works do follow them.

Revelation 14:12-13

The third angel has completed his message. So far, the first three
angels have shown us a consecutive flow of events that map out the
end-times. The gospel must be preached first before the end-times
begin. Satan will be violently defeated in heaven, his place of abode
will be destroyed and he and his angels will be cast out of heaven and
down to the earth. And then the Tribulation begins with wars, persecution and the Mark of the Beast. The remaining two angels will proclaim their messages in the chronological order in which they occur.

One thing that needs to be clearly understood as we read the rest
of this chapter is that Jesus is going to return twice in the end-times.
The first time will be in the clouds to gather His elect after the
Tribulation, and the second time will be years later to tread the winepress of the Wrath of God and to take charge of the earth forever.
There is only one reaping of believers, which is the Rapture. After that
comes the reaping of sinners in the Wrath of God. When Jesus
returns the second time, He will be on a white horse prepared for battle. His purpose then will be to complete God's wrath and to bring in
everlasting righteousness. Verses 14-16 give us a different description
of the Rapture, and once again, it is positioned between the
Tribulation, which occurred in the preceding verses, and the Wrath of
God in verses 17-20, which complete Revelation 14.

> ¹⁴And I looked, and behold *a white cloud*, and upon the
> cloud one sat like unto the Son of man, having on his head
> a golden crown, and in his hand a sharp sickle. ¹⁵And
> another angel came out of the temple, crying with a loud
> voice to him that sat on the cloud, Thrust in thy sickle, and
> reap: for the time is come for thee to reap; for the harvest
> of the earth is ripe. ¹⁶And *he that sat on the cloud thrust in
> his sickle on the earth*; and the earth was reaped.
>
> *Revelation 14:14-16*

If the one who is sitting on the cloud is not the Son of man, it is
meant to represent Him as He reaps the saints from the earth in the

Rapture. Jesus explains in the Gospels that He will be returning in the clouds with His angels to reap the earth of His elect. Daniel 7:13 also shows Him coming in the clouds. The three verses we just read are definitely depicting the Rapture. Verses 17-20 give another view of the time of God's wrath with the symbolic reaping of the sinners of the earth during the final Battle of Armageddon. Again, these are two different reapings. The first one is the reaping of the saints from the earth for deliverance *from* God's wrath, and the second one is the reaping of the wicked for destruction *in* God's wrath. The final verse explains that the blood flow of that final Battle at Armageddon will be about two hundred miles long and five to six feet deep. This could be a literal flow of blood at Armageddon, or it could be descriptive of the total amount of blood that will be shed around the globe as Jesus puts down all rebellion. After verse 20, we are going to be done with this short timeline of the end-times and back into the chronology that began in Revelation 12. When we get to Revelation 19, we will again see this same scene, and it will be made very clear that Jesus is the one who returns at the end of the Wrath of God to tread out the winepress of wrath, smite the nations and rule with a rod of iron.

> [17]And another angel came out of the temple which is in heaven, he also having a sharp sickle. [18]And another angel came out from the altar, which had power over fire; and cried with a loud cry to him that had the sharp sickle, saying, Thrust in thy sharp sickle, and gather the clusters of the vine of the earth; for her grapes are fully ripe. [19]And the angel thrust in his sickle into the earth, and gathered the vine of the earth, and cast it into the great winepress of the wrath of God. [20]And the winepress was trodden without the city, and blood came out of the winepress, even unto the horse bridles, by the space of a thousand and six hundred furlongs.

THINK ABOUT IT!

— Does Jesus come back only once, or does He return twice?

— If twice, what does He come for on each return?

— Has this chapter confused you in the past?

— Does it make sense to remove verses 6-20 and allow verses 1-5 to flow into chapter 15?

Selah

Israel was holiness unto the Lord, and the firstfruits of His increase: all that devour him shall offend; evil shall come upon them, saith the Lord.

Jeremiah 2:3

REVELATION 15

The Saints in Heaven and the Wrath Below

I think about heaven a lot, but not the way some people do. I know that there will be continual praises to God and overwhelming peace, but I also think about the other things that take place. Jesus said that He was going to prepare a mansion for us in His Father's house. Is He providing the blueprints for exactly what each of us want, and having the angels do the work? Is the apostle Paul present with the Lord, and setting marble columns or laying carpet? Is the city of God created or built? Are the gates of pearl handcrafted and do they come from real oysters? Do the transparent street of gold have to be refined in a furnace? If God gave us shadows and images of heavenly things in the Bible, is everything and every activity on earth a shadow and image of heaven? Is heaven a round planet with gravity? I'm going to find out for sure one day.

Now that the fifteen-verse synopsis of the end-times is completed, Revelation 15 resumes with the Rapture of the Church. This chapter is a view of heaven after the entire Rapture has been completed. All the rest of the redeemed of the Lord are now gathered into the Throne Room to join the 144,000 firstfruits we saw earlier in chapter 14:1-5. They have finished singing their special song of praise to God that no other man is allowed to hear or learn. Now the rest of the Church is all present and accounted for, and everybody begins to sing the song of Moses and the song of the Lamb. The words of that song are given below, thus demonstrating that it is not the song of the 144,000 of which no other man could learn. After the entire Church is completely removed from the earth, the next event will be the release of the seven vials of the Wrath of God on the earth as recorded in Revelation 16. As you read the following verses, notice that the seven angels having the seven plagues of the Wrath of God are in the same heaven, in the same Throne Room at the same time as all the redeemed of the Lord. Not until after the saints have been raptured are these angels allowed to leave the Throne Room and pour forth God's wrath upon those who are left on the earth. Also notice in verse 2 that many of these new occupants of heaven had to have been on earth during the Great Tribulation and the time of the Antichrist because they had gained the victory over the beast and had not taken his number.

> ¹And I saw another sign in heaven, great and marvelous, seven angels having the seven last plagues; for in them is filled up the wrath of God. ²And I saw as it were a sea of glass mingled with fire: and them that had gotten the victory over the beast, and over his image, and over his mark, and over the number of his name, stand on the sea of glass, having the harps of God. ³And they sing the song of Moses the servant of God, and the song of the Lamb, saying, Great and marvelous are thy works, Lord God Almighty; just and true are thy ways, thou King of saints. ⁴Who shall not fear thee, O Lord, and glorify thy name? for thou only art holy: for all nations shall come and worship before thee; for thy judgments are made manifest. ⁵And after that I looked, and, behold, the temple of the tabernacle of the testimony in heaven was opened: ⁶And the seven angels came out of the temple, having the seven plagues, clothed in pure and white linen, and having their breasts girded with golden girdles. ⁷And one of the four beasts gave unto the seven angels seven golden vials *full of the wrath of God*, who liveth for ever and ever.

⁸And the temple was filled with smoke from the glory of God, and from his power; and no man was able to enter into the temple, till the seven plagues of the seven angels were fulfilled.

Revelation 15:1-8

By excluding the brief synopsis of the end-times events which we just identified in verses 6-20 of chapter 14, we can see that things are continuing in the same order as in three other places—Matthew 24, the fifteen verses from chapter 14, and Revelation 6–11. Revelation 12 is a historical look at Satan's struggles as the seven-headed red dragon as he attempts to abort God's plan of salvation. Satan was finally cast out of heaven having great wrath, and the red dragon was morphed into the seven-headed beast who is Antichrist of Revelation 13. The beast causes tribulation by making war in general, and against Israel and the saints in particular. The events in that chapter are the same as the first five seals of the book Jesus opened, which revealed the Antichrist coming forth and causing great tribulation. Revelation 14:1-5, combined with this chapter, show the Rapture or the gathering of all of God's family into heaven at one time after the Tribulation and just prior to the Wrath of God. This view of the Rapture is similar to Revelation 6 and 7 where the sixth seal was opened, and now Revelation 16 is a restatement of the seventh seal of the book, where the trumpets signaled the release of the different events of the Wrath of God.

THINK ABOUT IT!

— This chapter shows those who went through the Tribulation without submitting to the beast positioned in heaven right before the Wrath of God is released. Do you think the Tribulation and the Wrath of God are the same thing?

— Could victory over the beast be symbolic of all saints who gain victory in this life?

Selah

For thou art not a God that hath pleasure in wickedness:
neither shall evil dwell with thee. The foolish shall not
stand in thy sight: Thou hatest all workers of iniquity.
Thou shalt destroy them that speak leasing: the Lord will
abhor the bloody and deceitful man. But as for me, I will
come into thy house in the multitude of thy mercy: and in
thy fear will I worship toward thy holy temple.

Psalm 5:4-7

REVELATION 16

Vials of Wrath

Back in the dark ages of my youth, there was one particular guy who seemed to like picking on me. He may have been a general all-purpose bully picking on anyone who was smaller than himself, but all I knew was that he was picking on me. I hated him. I wanted to kill him. I had a plan to go to his house one night and douse the front porch with gasoline, light it and run. Again, better sense prevailed. I let him live. I didn't want to kill innocent people, but mostly I didn't want to get caught. The truth is, I hated a lot of people. I hated my parents and everyone else. My brothers were the only ones I still had some positive emotion for, but I felt that slipping away too. I knew I needed to do something soon. That's when I asked God for a new job and a spiritual guide. I am slow now to judge people. I was there. Caught in a trap. Depressed, full of hatred and murder, a brush with a homosexual demon; if not for the grace of God I would have fallen all the way. That's why I'm slow to judge. I know that Satan's demons prey on young Baptist boys who lack spiritual knowledge. And not only Baptist boys, but Catholic girls, Methodist men, Jewish rabbis and anyone who has any spiritual inclination at all. Those evil spirits want to turn the most innocent into murderers and liars, addicts, rapists, witches and atheists. Anything but the likeness of God.

At the end of chapter 15, the seven angels are coming out of the temple of God carrying seven vials which contain the seven plagues of God's wrath. These are not the seven last plagues which follow after the seven trumpets but the same exact plagues that are revealed at the sounding of the trumpets. This, of course, happens after the saints have all arrived in heaven where it is impossible for them to be harmed by the Wrath of God. We already looked at the vials as they were compared to the seven trumpets; therefore, we will not spend a lot of time analyzing the specific events a second time. However, we do want to look at a few things.

First of all, just to drive home a point, the seven trumpets and seven vials of Revelation are all listed under, and are a part of, the seventh seal of the book that Jesus opens in heaven. That is the only seal that deals with the Wrath of God in any way. If you try to match the other seals to the trumpets and the vials, you will end up with a confusing mess. We already compared the trumpets and vials to each other, but the same comparison cannot be made with the seven seals.

You'll notice that each vial that is poured out has a different target area. Starting with the first and progressing to the last, the targets are the earth, the seas, the rivers, the sun, the seat of power of the beast, the Euphrates River and the air. Although the target shifts slightly, the aim is always the same—the punishment of sinners in general but those who serve the beast in particular. If you'll recall, the vials we are reading about are a part of the Revelation that has been focused on the kingdom of the beast, as opposed to the trumpets which are more global. Every aspect of the lives of those who live in the kingdom of the beast seems to be affected by the judgments God releases on them—the earth they walk on; the water they drink, fish in and navigate; the air they breath, the natural source of life known as the sun; and even the governmental powers they trust in. They have nowhere to turn except to the beast since they have totally rejected God, and that is exactly what they do when they regroup and join forces again as they prepare for the return of Jesus Christ in the air.

> [1]And I heard a great voice out of the temple saying to the seven angels, Go your ways, and pour out the vials of the wrath of God upon the earth. [2]And *the first went, and*

poured out his vial upon the earth; and there fell a noisome and grievous sore upon the men which had the mark of the beast, and upon them which worshipped his image. ³And *the second angel poured out his vial upon the sea; and it became as the blood of a dead man*: and every living soul died in the sea. ⁴And *the third angel poured out his vial upon the rivers and fountains of waters; and they became blood.* ⁵And I heard the angel of the waters say, thou art righteous, O Lord, which art, and wast, and shalt be, because thou hast judged thus. ⁶For they have shed the blood of saints and prophets, and thou hast given them blood to drink; for they are worthy. ⁷And I heard another out of the altar say, Even so, Lord God Almighty, true and righteous are thy judgments.

Revelation 16:1-7

Many people, Christians included, find it very difficult to accept that God would actually allow people to spend eternity in hell. As we read this chapter, we get a crystal clear, undistorted understanding of the unyielding, unrepentant hearts of so many people in this world. One of three things would have to happen for these people to go to heaven. First, God would have to break their wills by force and make them obey Him. However, we can see by the surrounding verses that that doesn't work. It is repeatedly stated throughout Revelation that the harsh punishment being directed at these sinners does not cause any repentance at all from their evil deeds. Second, God could change their hearts and take away their free wills by His divine power, thus making them nothing more than puppets on a string, obeying God because they have no choice to do otherwise. God's love toward us is so much greater because of this thing called "free will." He chose to love us despite our shortcomings and sinfulness, and because He saw what we could be through Him. God wants no less from all of us. He wants us to love Him by our own choosing, because we appreciate Him for who He is and not because He forces us to or because we have no will to do otherwise. God's third option would be to fill heaven with sinners, making it no different from the earth with all the corruption, lying, murders, adulteries, thefts and other evil that they would bring with them.

It was God's decision to give us the free will to choose to love, serve and obey Him, or to choose to disobey Him and serve sin. It's His decision how He will judge those who rebel. As we read on, we notice in verses 9 and 11 that there is no repentance by the people who are the recipients of God's wrath, and that is why they are the recipients of His wrath. Later in verse 21, we see that men are cursing God for the judgments they receive for their own sins. The only way for God to deal with sinners, whose spirits He created to exist forever and who have made the choice to remain sinners, is to permanently incarcerate them in a place where they are unable to have any effect on the rest of creation. That place of incarceration is hell first and then the Lake of Fire. That is the only way for real peace to ever exist on the earth and in heaven.

> 8And the *fourth angel poured out his vial upon the sun*; and *power was given unto him to scorch men with fire.* 9And men were scorched with great heat, and blasphemed the name of God, which hath power over these plagues: and *they repented not to give* Him glory. 10And the *fifth angel poured out his vial upon the seat of the beast*; and *his kingdom was full of darkness; and they gnawed their tongues for pain,* 11And blasphemed the God of heaven because of their pains and their sores, and *repented not of their deeds.* 12And *the sixth angel poured out his vial upon the great river Euphrates*; and *the water thereof was dried up, that the way of the kings of the east might be prepared.* 13And I saw three unclean spirits like frogs come out of the mouth of the dragon, and out of the mouth of the beast, and out of the mouth of the false prophet. 14For they are the spirits of devils, working miracles, which go forth unto the kings of the earth and of the whole world, *to gather them to the battle of that great day of God Almighty.* 15Behold, I come as a thief. Blessed is he that watcheth, and keepeth his garments, lest he walk naked, and they see his shame. 16And *he gathered them together into a place called in the Hebrew tongue Armageddon.*
>
> *Revelation 16:8-16*

Again, the seventh vial, just like the seventh trumpet, declares the end of the Wrath of God. Babylon is judged and divided into three parts by a great earthquake and the Battle of Armageddon will soon begin and end. The sixth vial shows only the gathering of troops to Armageddon. The actual battle will not take place until the last vial is released in the air. Consequently, Jesus will come riding through the air on a white horse to do battle. Jesus' arrival is not shown immediately in the release of either the last trumpet or the last vial, but He must come back to complete the wrath and take control of the earth. The events of the final trumpet/vial combination are revealed later in Revelation.

The same thunder, lightnings, earthquake and hail of the seventh trumpet are shown here. Five places in Revelation speak of earthquakes. These are all different earthquakes except for the two that are paralleled between the final trumpet and vial. The first earthquake is in Revelation 6:12 under the sixth seal. It occurs at the same time that the skies become black in anticipation of the arrival of Jesus in the clouds to gather His elect. The second is under the seventh seal in Revelation 8:5 as an angel cast the golden censer filled with fire from the altar of God down to the earth. As this is taking place, the seven angels with the seven trumpets of the Wrath of God are preparing to sound. This is important because the next two earthquakes are revealed under the trumpets as part of the Wrath of God. In Revelation 11:13, we are told that in the same hour the two witnesses are slain, an earthquake topples a tenth of the city of Babylon and kills seven thousand men. The very next verse in that chapter tells us that the second woe ends with that earthshaking event, and the third woe is ready to begin. The final earthquake occurs as a part of the third woe in verse 19 of Revelation 11, which just happens to be the same earthquake we see here under the seventh vial.

Each of these earthquakes mark significant events as when Jesus died on the cross and there was a great earthquake that tore the veil of the temple into two halves, and again when the angel rolled the stone away from Jesus' tomb to show that He was no longer there. In Revelation, the first earthquake happens at the Rapture of the Church. It may, in fact, be the result of the dead saints rising up out of the ground during the Resurrection, although that is only conjecture. The second one follows immediately on the heels of the first as the Wrath of God is put into motion. The third takes place when the two witnesses are resurrected and raptured sometime close to the end of the Wrath of God. The fourth earthquake signals that the Wrath of God is nearing a conclusion and that Jesus will soon appear a second time in the skies—but this time on a white horse prepared for battle.

> [17]And *the seventh angel poured out his vial into the air; and there came a great voice out of the temple of heaven, from the throne, saying, It is done.* [18]And there were voices, and thunders, and lightnings; and there was a great earthquake, such as was not since men were upon the earth, so mighty an earthquake, and so great. [19]And the great city was divided into three parts, and the cities of the nations fell: and great Babylon came in remembrance before God, to give unto her the cup of the wine of the fierceness of His wrath. [20]And every island fled away, and the mountains were not found. [21]And there fell upon men a great hail out of heaven, every stone about the weight of a talent: and *men blasphemed God because of the plague of the hail;* for the plague thereof was exceeding great.
>
> *Revelation 16:17-21*

Many Christians believe that sinners will be saved during the time of God's wrath. That is in part due to the confusion over the difference between the Tribulation and the Wrath of God. As we have seen over and over again, the Tribulation and the time of God's wrath are two separate events. During the Tribulation many people will be saved and many others will fall away. Although there is absolutely no indication of anyone repenting during the time of wrath, there will be survivors who are not slain during the time of God's wrath who will remain on the earth during the millennium to be ruled over by the Lord and His saints. Perhaps these are the ones who were less proactive in resisting God. They acknowledge the glory and power of God in the things transpiring all around them, but yet, without true repentance and salvation. It may be no more than a begrudged surrender to the fact that God is going to win this battle, and Satan and the Antichrist are on their way to defeat. They no longer try to resist God, and they refuse to join the Antichrist as he continues to maintain his claims of deity. They also refuse to take the Mark of the Beast and join in with those who are congregating in the Middle East at Armageddon to take on the armies of Jesus Christ when they descend from heaven. All those who fight in this war and all those who wear the Mark of the Beast will be destroyed. Everyone else will have a fighting chance because of their refusal to fight. God could be out to destroy all those who serve another god who is an evil aberration of Himself, while those other sinners who love life in the flesh to the point of abuse may end up being spared.

In Daniel 8:12, we are told that the host, or very large multitude of people, who serve the beast cast truth to the ground. Second Thessalonians 2:9-12 declares that they love not the truth but take pleasure in unrighteousness. The second half of Romans, chapter 1, has been included below so that we might see the reasons God judges the earth. In verses 19-21 and 28, we see that God has not only put inside all of us a deep understanding of Himself and who He is, but in verse 32, we find that He has also put in us the knowledge of His judgment against all those who commit sins against the goodness of His creation.

> ¹⁸For the wrath of God is revealed from heaven against all ungodliness and unrighteousness of men, *who hold the truth in unrighteousness;* ¹⁹Because *that which may be known of God is manifest in them; for God hath shewed it unto them.* ²⁰For *the invisible things of him from the creation of the world are clearly seen, being understood by the things that are made, even his eternal power and Godhead; so that they are without excuse:* ²¹Because that, *when they knew God, they glorified him not as God,* neither were thankful; but became vain in their imaginations, and their foolish heart was darkened. ²²Professing themselves to be wise, they became fools, ²³And changed the glory of the uncorruptible God into an image made like to corruptible man, and to birds, and four-footed beasts, and creeping things. ²⁴Wherefore God also gave them up to uncleanness through the lusts of their own hearts, to dishonour their own bodies between themselves: ²⁵*Who changed the truth of God into a lie,* and worshipped and served the

creature more than the Creator, who is blessed for ever. Amen. ²⁶For this cause God gave them up unto vile affections: for even their women did change the natural use into that which is against nature: ²⁷And likewise also the men, leaving the natural use of the woman, burned in their lust one toward another; men with men working that which is unseemly, and receiving in themselves that recompence of their error which was meet. ²⁸*And even as they did not like to retain God in their knowledge, God gave them over to a reprobate mind, to do those things which are not convenient;* ²⁹Being filled with all unrighteousness, fornication, wickedness, covetousness, maliciousness; full of envy, murder, debate, deceit, malignity; whisperers, ³⁰Backbiters, haters of God, despiteful, proud, boasters, inventors of evil things, disobedient to parents, ³¹Without understanding, covenant breakers, without natural affection, implacable, unmerciful: ³²*Who knowing the judgment of God,* that *they which commit such things are worthy of death, not only do the same, but have pleasure in them that do them.*

Romans 1:18-32

As we saw earlier when we compared the trumpets and the vials, one third of the earth will be judged more harshly than the rest of the earth. That part of the earth is centered around Israel in the Middle East, North Africa and possibly Russia. Despite the fact that sin is rampant all around the globe and people choose to seek after the pleasures of sin, only one third will follow after the Antichrist as their god. Just like the one third of the angels that followed Satan in his fall, only one third of the earth will become so irrational and corrupt in their thinking that they would willingly serve a god with all the attributes of Satan. Consequently, that one third of the earth will get clobbered with the brunt of God's wrath while the other two thirds escape the worst of it. Those that escape are sinners in a very self-centered way to be sure, but that will not compare in magnitude to the god-whoremongers of the latter days in this one third of the earth. Most sinners know who the God of heaven is, and they understand Him to be a God of love. Although they are self-serving, they do have a concept of good and evil, and they do not bow their knees in worship to other gods as do those who worship the Antichrist and the devil that sent him.

Think about it!

— Do the vials of this chapter have to match up exactly with the trumpets of earlier chapters to be speaking of the same events or timeframes?

— Who is suffering this wrath?

— Are there any clues that draw us into a particular geographical area?

Selah

The Lord is in his holy temple, the Lord's throne is in heaven: his eyes behold, his eyelids try the children of men. The Lord trieth the righteous: but the wicked and him that loveth violence his soul hateth. Upon the wicked he shall rain snares, fire and brimstone, and an horrible tempest: this shall be the portion of their cup. For the righteous Lord loveth righteousness; his countenance doth behold the upright.

Psalm 11:4-7

REVELATION 17

———◆———

Of Kings and Kingdoms

Most of what I have learned about the prophecies came about as God showed me that I could read what was written in His Word and accept that it is true. Face value. What you see is what you get. He did this by leading me to related scriptures that were saying the same exact thing. Most of Revelation is literal and easy to understand if you realize it is meant to be divided into sections. However, once in a while you get to something that defies a literal interpretation. Those things usually become obvious as you read the surrounding text. The one thing to remember is that the interpretation of the figurative things is always based in Scripture. Somewhere God has left the answers and clues that bring understanding to the figurative statements, and they always make perfect sense. Maybe not right away, because they are not always in line with how we are used to thinking, but with time, it makes sense.

———◆———

Chapter 17 of Revelation introduces us to a woman called MYSTERY, BABYLON THE GREAT. The comma that appears after the word "MYSTERY" in the Bible text is being dropped from the name because it was added by the translators who had the chore of punctuating everything they converted from Greek to English. In this book, we will simply call her Mystery Babylon because the context and interpretation strongly suggest that Mystery is a part of the name of the whore. We are also introduced to the beast she rides upon with seven heads and ten horns. We have already seen this beast as the red dragon, which is Satan, and as the beast, which is the Antichrist. This woman has remained a mystery for many years, but we are going to solve that mystery once and for all in this chapter.

One of the first things we want to notice is that one of the angels involved with emptying the seven vials on the earth comes forward to instruct John about the great whore. More than likely it is the angel that emptied out the final vial, since that judgment is not complete until the great whore is judged and Jesus returns to the earth. The final vial does not conclude until the second half of Revelation 19 where Jesus leads the saints out of heaven on white horses prepared for war against the armies of the earth that are gathered at Armageddon. Jesus' departure from heaven and the Battle of Armageddon both take place after the Wedding Feast of the Lamb.

> ¹And there came one of the seven angels which had the seven vials, and talked with me, saying unto me, Come hither; I will shew unto thee the judgment of the great whore that sitteth upon many waters: ²With whom the kings of the earth have committed fornication, and the inhabitants of the earth have been made drunk with the wine of her fornication. ³So he carried me away in the spirit into the wilderness: and I saw a woman sit upon a scarlet colored beast, full of names of blasphemy, having seven heads and ten horns. ⁴And the woman was arrayed in purple and scarlet color, and decked with gold and pre-cious stones and pearls, having a golden cup in her hand full of abominations and filthiness of her fornication: ⁵And upon her forehead was a name written, MYSTERY, BABY-LON THE GREAT, THE MOTHER OF HARLOTS AND ABOMINATIONS OF THE EARTH. ⁶And I saw the woman drunken with the blood of the saints, and with the blood of the martyrs of Jesus: and when I saw her, I won-dered with great admiration.
>
> *Revelation 17:1-6*

MYSTERY BABYLON

It may be stating the obvious, but the woman described above is not a real woman at all. Like the seven-headed beast she rides on, the woman is a spiritual illusion representing something much greater. The name Mystery Babylon gives us a clue as to what she represents. Mother of Harlots and Abominations of the Earth lets us know that she has great influence on the earth to prostitute others. That is what verse 2 is telling us when it declares that the kings of the earth have fornicated with her. Verse 15 of this same chapter informs us that "The waters which thou sawest, where the whore sitteth, are peoples, and multitudes, and nations, and tongues." After the kings of the earth climb into the bed of prostitution with her, they turn and seduce the people of the earth who use the corrupt world system that the kings model after that of the great whore.

What is being described, in part, is a world political and economic system based on corruption, lust, exploitation and unrighteousness. The image of the woman is an image of decadent wealth, and the only thing that interferes with her fully enjoying her abominable lifestyle is the saints of God and, by extension, the woman we saw in chapter 12 that gave birth to the sons and daughters of God—the nation of Israel.

Mystery Babylon goes way beyond a corrupt world system; it reaches from heaven all the way down to the earth. Mystery Babylon first began to manifest on the earth shortly after Noah and his family dry-docked their boat in the mountains of Ararat. Genesis 11 informs us that the whole earth had one language and consisted only of the offspring of Noah's family. Verse 2 declares that "they" journeyed to the east to a plain in Shinar. (Shinar is in Iraq, which means that the mountains of Ararat are to the west towards Iran and not Mount Ararat in Turkey.) As soon as they arrived at Shinar, Nimrod—who was the son of Cush, who was the son of Ham, who was the son of Noah—began to build a city and a tower to reach unto heaven, or so they thought. They would have failed in building a tower of brick up to heaven; nevertheless, God scattered them and confused their language because, as He said, "Nothing will be restrained from them which they have imagined to do." What was it that man had already imagined to do? Just like in the Garden of Eden, they imagined to be like God.

God slowed things down by confusing the language of mankind; but as the world comes together, there is very little that man has not imagined to do and he has accomplished much of it. But what about Shinar? The tower that was being built was the Tower of Babel, and those people who were not scattered from Shinar remained under the leadership of Nimrod who continued to build the city of Babel. Eventually Babel became Babylon, and it ruled much of the earth under King Nebuchadnezzar. Babylon was later overthrown by the Medo-Persian Empire, but the story doesn't end there. A great city of trade is going to arise in the Middle East once more, and it will be a very integral part of the end-times scenario of the Bible. In fact, the U.S. and the rest of the world may be at work building that city for the Iraqis right now as we rebuild Iraq.

This is all very interesting, but what does it have to do with Mystery Babylon? The answer to that question goes to the very heart of the tower, the empire and the city. That heart is the one who inspired and, to a large degree, controlled this reoccurring Babylon. Satan is the mastermind behind each of these endeavors, and his purpose is to have a base of operations from which to control the whole world. In each case—at the beginning with the tower of Babel, in the middle with the Empire of Babylon and in the end-times with the city of Babylon—Satan will attempt to bring the whole world under a single ruler who answers directly to him. However, there's more to this story. Satan remains in heaven to this very day in a place God refers to as Mystery Babylon.

Back in chapter 12 we saw Satan residing in heaven and spending much of his time in the face of God accusing the saints of God just like he did with Job. God finally allowed Satan to test Job in the areas where he had lost his faith—his children and his wealth. Job said it himself, "The thing that I greatly feared is come upon me, and that which I was afraid of is come unto me." After Job stopped trusting God and started fearing the worst, the hedge of protection that surrounded him for so long was no longer in place. Satan is going to be cast out of heaven one day and he won't be able to snivel and whine directly to God any more, but he will go out in full force to challenge everything and everyone that belongs to God.

The highest order, if you will, of Mystery Babylon is found in heaven. In Revelation 14:8, after the gospel has been preached to the whole world and before the Tribulation ever begins, a declaration is made concerning Babylon—"Babylon is fallen." That statement is made in regards to the fall of Mystery Babylon in heaven. It is not just a fall, but rather, it is cast down by force as Michael and the other angels of God are given orders to get rid of Satan and his angels for good, and to destroy the place they have been calling home. Revelation 12:8 tells us that after Satan and his angels are cast out of heaven, "their place" will no longer be found there. When Satan is cast down to the earth, he will take up residence in the city of Babylon, one of the most godless and evil cities on the earth. After he arrives, the city will only get worse.

The great whore, which is the roost of the devils in heaven, could be referred to as the bride of Satan or the bride of Antichrist. No scriptures say that outright, but when we combine the description of Mystery Babylon from this chapter to that of the end-times city of Babylon in chapter 18 and all that we know about Babylon of the past, we end up with something completely contrary to the holy city New Jerusalem. New Jerusalem is called the bride of the Lamb in chapter 21 of Revelation. John gives the physical description of that city as he observes it descending out of heaven to the new earth where it will be situated among mankind for the rest of eternity. Mystery Babylon, no doubt, shares many of the same physical characteristics as New Jerusalem, but while the city of God will be adorned in righteousness, full of goodness and lit by the glory of God, the city of Satan is most assuredly adorned by wickedness, covered with darkness and filled with the works of unrighteousness. Because Satan does not possess the power to lift his unholy city up out of heaven and lower it to the earth in the same manner that God does New Jerusalem, he will have a replica city built here for his eventual habitation. Satan leaves no stone unturned when it comes to copycatting God. The only problem is that all of his mimicry is corrupt to the point of abomination.

Satan exerts some level of corrupt control over all of the cities of the earth as he rules from Mystery Babylon in heaven. Much of his time is spent bringing accusations against the saints before the Judge of the whole earth. This city in heaven, which rules in the affairs of man, attempts to maintain full control over every earthly city by replicating itself over and over again as the mother of harlots. The problem (or should I say the good news) is that after the covenant of God was established in the earth, God is able to gain different levels of influence in governments wherever men pray and observe this covenant. Unlike God, Satan cannot be everywhere at once, so he has his hands full trying to corrupt every city; however, with the fallen nature of man being so prevalent on the earth, he is able to make great strides in polluting the earth by polluting the very center of power in each city. Nevertheless, even at the end of the world when he is cast out of heaven and down to the earth, he will only be able to directly control a small empire of ten nations with Babylon as the capital. The rest of the world will be at war against him as they either come to Israel's aid, attempt to prevent the expansion of the beast kingdom or fight against the servants of the beast as they export terror to the rest of the world.

First Timothy 6:10 declares that "the love of money is the root of all evil, which, while some coveted after, they have erred from the faith, and pierced themselves through with many sorrows." In the scriptures below from Ezekiel 28, we discover that Satan's fall began as the love of money took root in his heart. In the first ten verses of Ezekiel 28, God declares His judgment on an earthly king as He speaks to the prince of Tyrus. Tyrus had become too much like Mystery Babylon. It was one of Satan's proudest accomplishments— a harlot offspring that was nearly identical to her mother. The prince of the city exhibited all of the characteristics of Satan himself. He was so filled with pride that he declared himself to be God, yet he was just a man. As we read these verses, we want to note that the prince of Tyrus is actually the king of the earthly city. This becomes more obvious as we read the second half of the prophecy, which is directed at Satan as the king of Tyrus. The prince is declared to be wiser than Daniel; however, unlike Daniel, he uses his wisdom to satisfy his love of money and the power that it brings, and rather than maintaining humility like Daniel, his pride became his destruction. Verses 4 and 5 tell us that he used his wisdom for the purpose of trafficking. (Traffic is a word that refers to trade, commerce and merchandise and often refers to illegal trade.)

¹The word of the Lord came again unto me, saying, ²Son of man, say unto *the prince of Tyrus,* Thus saith the Lord God; Because thine heart is lifted up, and thou hast said, I am a God, I sit in the seat of God, in the midst of the seas; *yet thou art a man,* and not God, though thou set thine heart as the heart of God: ³Behold, thou art wiser than Daniel; there is no secret that they can hide from thee: ⁴With thy wisdom and with thine understanding thou hast gotten thee riches, and hast gotten gold and silver into thy treasures: ⁵By thy great wisdom and *by thy traffick hast thou increased thy riches, and thine heart is lifted up because of thy riches*: ⁶Therefore thus saith the Lord God; Because thou hast set thine heart as the heart of God; ⁷Behold, therefore I will bring strangers upon thee, the terrible of the nations: and they shall draw their swords against the beauty of thy wisdom, and they shall defile thy brightness. ⁸They shall bring thee down to the pit, and thou shalt die the deaths of them that are slain in the midst of the seas. ⁹Wilt thou yet say before him that slayeth thee, I am God? *but thou shalt be a man, and no God, in the hand of him that slayeth thee.* ¹⁰Thou shalt die the deaths of the uncircumcised by the hand of strangers: for I have spoken it, saith the Lord God.

Ezekiel 28:1-10

When we get to the second half of the chapter, we see that God is speaking of someone who was in the Garden of Eden and who was created, not born. God is speaking to Satan as the king of Tyrus. We know that Satan was in Eden because he tempted Eve there. The king of Tyrus is that wicked spirit Satan who controls principalities and powers and who rules the darkness of this world. He is the leader of spiritual wickedness who inhabits high places.

The word "traffick" is used again in relation to Satan's activities, along with the word "merchandise." Satan was involved with trade, the peddling of goods and the exchange of money before he ever tempted Eve in the garden. Just like the earthly king of Tyrus, Satan increased his riches by his great wisdom and his trafficking to enrich himself, all for the purpose of bringing more controlling power to himself. He became proud and called himself God. In verses 15 and 16, we see that Satan's illegal trade is what corrupted his heart, thus making his love of money the root out of which all other evil sprang. God created all things to reproduce by seed. He never created seed for the purpose of producing evil things. In Satan's kingdom, sin first takes root and then starts to grow like a weed wherever it is able to take hold. There had to be a system of trade in operation before God created man for Ezekiel 28 to be true, and Satan was in charge of that system. After seeing the power that he wielded in trade, instead of giving glory to God and being thankful, he became proud. He thought more highly of himself and the power that he gained through the control and use of money and trafficking than he did of God.

The final and most important thing we want to look at in the context of Revelation 17 and Mystery Babylon is found in verse 18, which declares that Satan corrupted his sanctuaries by his evil merchandising, and the full range of his iniquities sprang out of the desire for more monetary power. A sanctuary is a consecrated place. The sanctuaries of Satan were either consecrated for his service to God as the anointed cherub until he corrupted himself and polluted the sanctuaries, or he may have taken it upon himself to build them to honor himself after his fall. The word "sanctuary" also refers to a palace-like structure. You'll notice that the word is plural in verse 18, alerting us to the fact that there are more than one. All of these things happened to Satan before God created man. In heaven, Satan had his own sanctuaries from where he lived and worked. Revelation 12:8 refers to these as "their place."

> [11]Moreover the word of the Lord came unto me, saying,
> [12]Son of man, take up a lamentation upon *the king of Tyrus*, and say unto him, Thus saith the Lord God; Thou sealest up the sum, full of wisdom, and perfect in beauty. [13]Thou hast been in Eden the garden of God; every precious stone was thy covering, the sardius, topaz, and the diamond, the beryl, the onyx, and the jasper, the sapphire, the emerald, and the carbuncle, and gold: the workmanship of thy tabrets and of thy pipes was prepared in thee *in the day that thou wast created.* [14]Thou art the anointed cherub that covereth;

and I have set thee so: thou wast upon the holy mountain of God; thou hast walked up and down in the midst of the stones of fire. *¹⁵Thou wast perfect in thy ways from the day that thou wast created, till iniquity was found in thee. ¹⁶By the multitude of thy merchandise they have filled the midst of thee with violence,* and thou hast sinned: therefore *I will cast thee as profane out of the mountain of God: and I will destroy thee,* O covering cherub, from the midst of the stones of fire. ¹⁷Thine heart was lifted up because of thy beauty, thou hast corrupted thy wisdom by reason of thy brightness: I will cast thee to the ground, I will lay thee before kings, that they may behold thee. *¹⁸Thou hast defiled thy sanctuaries by the multitude of thine iniquities, by the iniquity of thy traffick;* therefore will I bring forth a fire from the midst of thee, it shall devour thee, and I will bring thee to ashes upon the earth in the sight of all them that behold thee. ¹⁹All they that know thee among the people shall be astonished at thee: thou shalt be a terror, and never shalt thou be any more.

Ezekiel 28:11-19

Verse 17 above says that Satan's wisdom has been corrupted. That does not mean he is stupid. Satan has vast knowledge and cunning craftiness which he uses to destroy. The very best of us are no match for Satan in our own abilities, but with God's abilities and the Holy Spirit as our helper, we are more than conquerors and more than a match for Satan.

If we were to combine Matthew 24:24 and Thessalonians 2:11, it might say that God is going to send strong delusion in the end-times, and that if it were possible, the very elect will be deceived. In Revelation 17:6, John observed the decadent filth of "the mother of harlots of the earth," and he said, "I wondered with great admiration after seeing her drunk on the blood of the saints." Then in verse 7 below, the angel asks him why he marveled at her. If John can be so dazzled by the great whore while he is in the spirit, then God help the rest of us in the flesh. If you sit in front of the TV watching these things as they unfold, you might find yourself marveling and desiring and wanting. The new Babylon will likely be more lavish and wealthy than anything we have ever seen before, and the Antichrist will have a charisma that will transcend all of his destructiveness. For those who hate righteousness, his charm will be that destructive nature that seeks to eliminate all that is godly, particularly Christians and Jews. The Adolpf Hitlers and Ayatollah Khomeinis of the world are not able to draw the whole world by their charisma, such as it is, but they are able to draw enough followers after them to cause trouble for everyone. For the rest of us, there's an allure to the things of sin that needs to be guarded against before we ever get to the end. The wealth, the fornication and even the bloodshed of nameless faces have a way of reaching into the depths of hearts with corruption. That's what has made Hollywood so successful. They give people what they lust after. If we allow our eyes and ears to linger on those things for too long, our hearts and then our feet will soon follow.

> [7]And the angel said unto me, Wherefore didst thou marvel? I will tell thee the mystery of the woman, and of the beast that carrieth her, which hath the seven heads and ten horns. [8]The beast that thou sawest was, and is not; and shall ascend out of the bottomless pit, and go into perdition: and they that dwell on the earth shall wonder, whose names were not written in the book of life from the foundation of the world, when they behold the beast that was, and is not, and yet is. [9]And here is the mind which hath wisdom. The seven heads are seven mountains, on which the woman sitteth. [10]And there are seven kings: five are fallen, and one is, and the other is not yet come; and when he cometh, he must continue a short space. [11]And the beast that was, and is not, even he is the eighth, and is of the seven, and goeth into perdition. [12]And the ten horns which thou sawest are ten kings, which have received no kingdom as yet; but receive power as kings one hour with the beast. [13]These have one mind, and shall give their power and strength unto the beast.
>
> *Revelation 17:7-13*

The beast that carries the whore called Mystery Babylon is more important than the whore herself. You'll recall from chapter 12 how the red dragon was identified as the old serpent, the Devil, and Satan. As we moved into chapter 13, the dragon became a beast that resembled the dragon in every way. The beast is the Antichrist that will arise after Satan is cast out of heaven. Satan has always been the heart and soul of the seven-headed dragon, but in the end-times, the Antichrist will be the manifestation of it on the earth as he rules over the ten kings and their kingdoms which form the final destroying empire. Satan will no longer rule from that spiritual city called Mystery Babylon in heaven, but he will be behind the scene in that earthly city called Babylon where the Antichrist will rule. The name of the earthly city may be something other than Babylon, but more than likely as the world comes together to develop a world trade zone in Iraq, they will surely dredge the Euphrates and develop ports near ancient Babylon, then transfer the name Babylon to the new city that springs up.

TEN HORNS

The ten horns of the beast are rather easy to understand. In fact, verses 12 and 13 nearly sum them up for us. The ten horns represent ten kings who will be giving the power of their kingdoms over to the Antichrist in the end. Revelation 13:1 shows a crown on top of each horn, which verifies that each horn represents a king and his nation. If we could enter into John's vision and look at the seven-headed beast alongside him, the ten horns more than likely appear all on one head because only one of the heads of the beast actually represents the end-times ten-nation empire of the Antichrist. The others have all come and gone, never to be again.

Daniel saw the same ten horns on the final beast in his vision in Daniel 7:7-8: "And behold a fourth beast....and it had ten horns. I considered the horns, and, behold, there came up among them another little horn, before whom there were three of the first horns plucked up by the roots." The Antichrist is the little horn that rises up among the other ten. The fact that they are already present and he rises up among them tells us that they have already joined their nations together as a league of nations that are in cooperation for some reason. The Antichrist will be the eleventh king to take part in that group of nations as he disposes of three of the original kings.

That brings us to the study of Gog of Magog mentioned at the beginning of this book. We established that the group of nations making up the armies of Gog come together before any of the other end-time events take place. Their purpose is to overrun, rob and then destroy Israel, but their purpose is foiled as God marshals the forces of nature against them. After the armies are defeated, the Antichrist will rise up out of the masses to take over as the supreme leader of the ten nations. The fact that he rises among the ten nations could suggest that he is not a ruler of any of the nations, but gains a following of mercenary soldiers who assist him in overthrowing three kings before the empire is given into his hands.

SEVEN HEADS

The next thing we want to look at is the seven heads of the beast. We mentioned that one head represents the empire over which the Antichrist will reign, and the other heads have some kind of historical significance. Verse 9 explains that the seven heads are seven mountains upon which the woman sat—not all at once but over the course of history. Verse 10 tells us that there are seven kings that coincide with the seven mountains. In verse 10 we learn that there are historical aspects to all of this. At the time John was writing Revelation, one of the kings was in existence and five others had already come and gone. The one that was ruling during John's time was the spirit king of Rome. The other five kings were the spirit kings of Egypt, Syria, Babylon, Medo-Persia and Greece. These are the empires named in Daniel's prophecies and elsewhere.

There is one more king with his mountain-like kingdom, or empire, that is still yet to come to this day. It is the Antichrist ten-nation empire, and the spirit king that brings it into existence. We are told that he will continue for just a short time after his arrival. The reason for the short reign of the seventh king is because the Antichrist will take over the seventh empire from the seventh king and reign in his stead as the eighth king. Verse 11 tells us that the Antichrist is the eighth and is of the seven. The seventh king, who arises just before the Antichrist, serves a twofold purpose. The first purpose is to bring together ten nations of the end-times in an attempt to destroy Israel. These are the nations of Ezekiel 38 and 39 that join together with Gog of Magog to make Israel a spoil. Gog may even be the name of the spirit king that brings together this alliance. After the first attack is thwarted by God, with the destruction of all but one sixth of the armies of Gog, the Antichrist will take his place with a seven-year covenant of peace. The same seven years in which Israel consumes the spoils of Gog.

These seven spirit kings answer directly to Satan, and each king is responsible for bringing his particular empire into existence and then ruling it from behind the scene. Although these kings answer to Satan, God has used each of these kingdoms in His own divine plan as He deals with Israel and the rest of the world. When necessary, He was able to gain influence in these kingdoms by dealing with the individual mortal kings. These kings invariably bring judgment against their respective empires because of their ill-treatment of Israel—with one exception. That exception was Rome which we will look at later. We saw in verse 12 above that the Antichrist will be number eleven among the kings involved in the final empire, In verse 11 he is number eight among the seven spirit rulers. The Antichrist will be an antitype of the true Christ, who was God in the flesh. The Antichrist will not be Satan, but he will be a perfect ringer for the real thing. He is a being from the spirit realm that will possess a body as he operates in the natural realm, and as such, he is mimicking the life of Christ but with perverseness and deception.

Verse 8 from the above scripture tells us that the beast "was, and is not, and yet is" and that he will "ascend out of the bottomless pit." These words reveal to us that the Antichrist was present on the earth, and was a part of world affairs at some time before John lived. When it says that "he is not," it just means that he is not being allowed access into this life even though he still exists, restrained in the bottomless pit. Verse 11 verifies that the beast "was, and is not," and after he ascends out of the bottomless pit, he is described as the eighth king, and of the seven. The Antichrist does exist today as a spirit being that is being restrained in the bottomless pit. He may even be a human a spirit in the pit. If so, he would have to be resurrected to take his place in the future. He would be the firstfruits of the resurrection of the dead, just as Jesus is the firstfruits of the resurrection of life. You can almost hear Satan in heaven whining about getting his opportunity to raise one of his own from the dead. He will exist in the near future as a man when he presents himself as the eleventh king who over-throws three nations of the first ten and takes over the ten-nation empire. We may not understand how he can be a man and a spirit from the bottomless pit at the same time, but he will be. In Revelation 9:1-11, the fifth trumpet of the wrath of God sounds and the locusts are released from the same bottomless pit. In Revelation 20:3, we are told that Satan will be bound in the bottomless pit for a thousand years while the Millennial Reign is taking place. In the same manner, the Antichrist is being restrained right now and will be loosed when his time comes.

The prophecies of Daniel always jump from the past into the future whenever he speaks of the Antichrist or his kingdom because it is the same Antichrist past and future. These double or extended prophecies are common in the Bible as God deals with Satan in the spirit world and the men who serve his purposes so well in the natu-ral world. We see this phenomenon in Daniel's seventy weeks with the final or seventieth week separated by thousands of years from the first sixty-nine weeks. We also see it every time he speaks of those great kingdoms springing up during Daniel's time, only to skip ahead thousands of years from that time to the time when the Antichrist will rule. In Daniel 8:23, we see the jump from the Greek Empire to the Antichrist Empire by the words "in the latter time of their king-dom." In Daniel 11:35, we shift from the Syrian portion of the Greek Empire where Antiochus ruled to the time of the Antichrist with the words "at the time of the end." And in Revelation 18, we see the city of Babylon being destroyed at the end of time. These references give the impression that one of these empires will be revived and repeated at the end. However, that is not what the loosing of the beast from the pit is speaking of. The beast that ascends out of the bottomless pit is referred to as a "he," and that is what he will be, not a city and not an empire, but a he. The final empire will be sort of a kaleidoscope of the former empires, but the beast is, and will be, the Antichrist who rules that empire.

We know from Scripture that angels are able to manifest and live in the natural realm when it serves their purpose. Hebrews 13:2 tells us that we may be dealing with angels when we deal with strangers. Abraham prepared a meal for two angels and the Lord in Genesis 18 as they were on their way to investigate the sinfulness of Sodom.

Afterwards, when the two angels entered Sodom to rescue Lot and his family, the men of the city sought to rape them. So we know that at least some spirit beings are able to take on flesh-like bodies. We see in Revelation 13:3 that one of the seven heads of the beast is wounded and then healed. We know by the context that this is speaking of the Antichrist, but since the seven heads represent the spirit kings, it tends to blur our understanding of what is truly happening. The best explanation is that out of the ten kings, one is recognized as the supreme leader of the ten-nation alliance. If he is slain and the Antichrist rises from the pit and takes over his body, that may be how the Antichrist is both human and a spirit from the bottomless pit. These are just two theories on how the Antichrist exists now in the bottomless pit and will exist later on as a man, and how he can be the spirit king and earthly king at the same time. He either possesses the ability to manifest in the flesh, or he takes over someone else's flesh.

We are able to see in Daniel 10 some of the behind-the-scenes activity of these spiritual kings as they war in the heavenlies for the right to control what takes place on the earth. After fasting twenty-one days as he sought understanding from God, Daniel was greeted by an angel sent to enlighten him. That angel would have arrived on the very first day that Daniel began to seek understanding if he had not been hampered by the spiritual prince of the kingdom of Persia. Persia was the reigning empire at the time this struggle took place, and it took the military intervention of Michael, the spiritual prince of Israel, to get the messenger angel past the resistance of the prince of Persia. After delivering his message, the angel had to enter once more into conflict with the prince of Persia, but before leaving, he alerted Daniel to the fact that the spiritual prince of Grecia was on his way.

> [12]Then said he unto me, Fear not, Daniel: for from the first day that thou didst set thine heart to understand, and to chasten thyself before thy God, thy words were heard, and I am come for thy words. [13]*But the prince of the kingdom of Persia withstood me one and twenty days*: but, lo, Michael, *one of the chief princes, came to help me*; and I remained there with the kings of Persia. [20]Then said he, Knowest thou wherefore I come unto thee? *and now will I return to fight with the prince of Persia*: and *when I am gone forth, lo, the*

prince of Grecia shall come. ²¹But I will shew thee that which is noted in the scripture of truth: and *there is none that holdeth with me in these things, but Michael your prince.*

Daniel 10:12,13 & 20

Daniel had already been informed that the Medo-Persian Empire would take over the Babylonian Empire, and the Greeks would follow after that. He received that foreknowledge in Daniel 8 in the third year of Belshazzar, the king of Babylon. That prophecy concerned the end-times and spoke primarily of the spirit kings. We see the spirit kings of Media and Persia that joined together to make the Persian Empire. After that the spirit king of Grecia arrives. We know it is the spirit king because the second half of Verse 21 differentiates between the spirit king and Alexander the Great who turned out to be the only real king of the unified Greek Empire. Alexander is described as a great horn between the eyes of a rough goat, and the rough goat is the spirit king that empowered him to establish his kingdom so rapidly. After his death the empire was divided into four smaller kingdoms. We know that the Greek Empire was divided between the four generals of Alexander, but what is more important to understand is that there were four spirit kings working in the background of the spirit world to make the four-way division a reality. Verse 23 then jumps thousands of years into the future to the time when ten kings from the general boundaries of the former Greek Empire join together in an attempt to overwhelm Israel and eventually give the power of their kingdoms over to the Antichrist.

¹⁹And he said, Behold, *I will make thee know what shall be in the last end of the indignation: for at the time appointed the end shall be.* ²⁰The ram which thou sawest having two horns are *the kings of Media and Persia.* ²¹And the rough goat is *the king of Grecia:* and *the great horn that is between his eyes is the first king.* ²²Now that being broken, whereas four stood up for it, *four kingdoms shall stand up out of the nation,* but not in his power. ²³*And in the latter time of their kingdom, when the transgressors are come to the full, a king of fierce countenance, and understanding dark sentences, shall stand up.*

Daniel 8:19-23

The seven heads of the dragon are seven mountains that represent empires. Each empire is similar in that they all surrounded Israel, they all held Israel captive at some time, they all fell under the direct control of Satan and all but one is judged by God for the way they treat Israel. In the Bible, when we read the word "mountain," more than likely it is referring to a mountain. However, at times it is referring to more than just a physical mountain. The mountains of Revelation 17 refer to empires in a manner similar to that in Daniel 2 where Daniel is giving the interpretation of the king's dream concerning the image of gold, silver, brass, iron and clay. The image was used by God to tell of several future kingdoms Satan was to establish on the earth to oppose Israel. Those same kingdoms are represented by four of the seven heads of the beast. In verses 34, 35, 44 and 45 of Daniel 2, we see a stone cut out without hands that smites the image and grounds it to dust, and then the stone becomes a great mountain that fills all the earth. That mountain is the millennial kingdom of God, or it could be called the empire of Jesus Christ on earth. Christ's empire will take over and destroy the empire of the Antichrist at the end of this age. Or, in other words, Christ's mountain will squash Satan's seventh mountain just as the other six mountains were squashed, and the mountain of Christ will remain as the final mountain. This is not talking about the spiritual kingdom of God that comes without observation and that we participate in right now, but rather, the earthly kingdom Jesus will establish after the Battle of Armageddon and at the outset of the Millennial Reign.

> [34]Thou sawest till that a stone was cut out without hands, which smote the image upon his feet that were of iron and clay, and brake them to pieces. [35]Then was the iron, the clay, the brass, the silver, and the gold, broken to pieces together, and became like the chaff of the summer threshing floors; and the wind carried them away, that no place was found for them: *and the stone that smote the image became a great mountain, and filled the whole earth.*
>
> *Daniel 2:34-35*

One thing we didn't look at when we read Ezekiel 28 at the start of this chapter was verse 16 regarding the mountain of God. We saw earlier that the heavenly Jerusalem is situated on a heavenly mount

Sion (Zion). Even the reigning city of God in heaven is built on a mountain, a literal mountain at that, but the very mention of the mountain of God stirs in us a figurative image of a city and throne elevated above all of creation and a nation that is limitless in its breadth. The following verses from Micah speak of the last days when the nations turn their weapons into farm tools, but that will occur after the Wrath of God and the return of Christ to the earth, because only then will this prophecy be fulfilled. In verse 1, two mountains are mentioned with one being established upon the other. This is the seat of power of the empire of Jesus Christ being set up in the mountains of Jerusalem. These mountains are both literal and figurative.

> ¹But *in the last days it shall come to pass*, that *the mountain of the house of the* Lord *shall be established in the top of the mountains*, and it shall be exalted above the hills; and people shall flow unto it. ²And many nations shall come, and say, Come, and let us go up to the mountain of the Lord, and to the house of the God of Jacob; and he will teach us of his ways, and we will walk in his paths: for the law shall go forth of Zion, and the word of the Lord from Jerusalem. ³And he shall judge among many people, and rebuke strong nations afar off; and *they shall beat their swords into plowshares, and their spears into pruninghooks: nation shall not lift up a sword against nation, neither shall they learn war any more.*
>
> *Micah 4:1-3*

In Jeremiah, we see three of the mountains that are represented by the seven heads of the dragon. In fact, Babylon is called a destroying mountain in this word of the Lord against Babylon. As we read through this prophecy, notice how God both watches over Israel and uses them at the same time to do His work in the earth of separating the sheep from the goats. The first verse simply sets the stage by alerting us to the fact that God is dealing with Babylon here.

> ¹*The word that the* Lord *spake against Babylon and against the land of the Chaldeans by Jeremiah the prophet.*
>
> *Jeremiah 50:1, 17-18, 29-32*

302

God declares that He is going to punish Babylon, the third head of the dragon, just like He punished Assyria, the second head or mountain of the dragon.

> [17]Israel is a scattered sheep; the lions have driven him away: *first the king of Assyria hath devoured him; and last this Nebuchadnezzar king of Babylon hath broken his bones.* [18]Therefore thus saith the Lord of hosts, the God of Israel; Behold, *I will punish the king of Babylon and his land, as I have punished the king of Assyria.*

In the next four verses, God is calling for the archers of the enemy against Babylon. That enemy is revealed in 51:11 and is none other than the fourth head/mountain of the dragon, the Medo-Persian Empire. As you read, notice that the first two verses are speaking of the city as being feminine, calling it "her." In verse 31, there is a transition as God confronts the most proud one who He refers to in the masculine. In verse 18 in the previous scriptures, Nebuchadnezzar was mentioned, but if we recall from the book of Daniel how Nebuchadnezzar became humbled before God after spending seven years out in the field as a beast, and how years later Belshazzar was the one who faced the judgment of God after using the golden vessels from the temple as party cups and saucers, we have to wonder if God isn't speaking a double prophecy aimed at both earthly Babylon and Mystery Babylon in heaven. Nebuchadnezzar was humbled, but Satan who controls Babylon in the spirit world has no humility. This is an end-times prophecy stuck in the middle of the prophecies against ancient Babylon which is a very common thing. When we read the prophecies against earthly kings, we often see a parallel prophecy against Satan and the corrupt kingdom that he rules over. At times God weaves His judgments against Satan through the seams of His judgments against men, and at other times He deals with one first and then the other as we saw in Ezekiel 28 where He spoke first to the human king and then the spirit king. When God speaks to Babylon in the feminine in the next two verses, He is speaking to the great whore that accommodates Satan in heaven as well.

> [29]Call together the archers against Babylon: all ye that bend the bow, camp against it round about; let none

thereof escape: recompense *her* according to *her* work; according to all that *she* hath done, do unto *her*: for *she* hath been proud against the Lord against the Holy One of Israel. ³⁰Therefore shall *her* young men fall in the streets, and all *her* men of war shall be cut off in that day, saith the Lord. ³¹Behold, I am against thee, O thou most proud, saith the Lord God of hosts: for thy day is come, the time that I will visit thee. ³²And the most proud shall stumble and fall, and none shall raise *him* up: and I will kindle a fire in *his* cities, and it shall devour all round about *him*.

As we move into Jeremiah 51, the word against Babylon continues. In verse 11, we see that God uses another warring heathen nation to defeat Babylon. Satan controls this emerging empire also, and the captivity and mistreatment of the Jews will continue under their rule. However, God will raise up men in this kingdom who assist many of the Jews in returning to their land and in rebuilding the temple of God. This is the kingdom of the Medes after they become confederate with the Persians. The empire has become known as the Persian Empire. It is the fourth head of the dragon.

> ¹¹Make bright the arrows; gather the shields: *the* Lord hath
> raised up the spirit of the kings of the Medes: for his
> device is against Babylon, to destroy it; because it is the
> vengeance of the Lord, the vengeance of His temple.
>
> *Jeremiah 51:11, 19-21, 24-29, 43-45*

Verse 11 declares that God is going to take revenge for the destruction of His temple. Then in these next three verses He declares to all that He uses Israel like a sword in His hand to bring judgment against all the rebellious nations that hate Him and refuse to serve Him. The rebellion of a nation against God always translates into a rebellion against Israel as God's most visible and seemingly most vulnerable possession on the earth. In the end-times, Israel will be located right in the heart of the beast kingdom, and nations will be forced to choose between supporting Israel and resisting the beast, or just the opposite.

¹⁹The portion of Jacob is not like them; for he is the former of all things: and Israel is the rod of his inheritance: the Lord of hosts is His name. ²⁰*Thou art my battle axe and weapons of war: for with thee will I break in pieces the nations, and with thee will I destroy kingdoms*; ²¹And with thee will I break in pieces the horse and his rider; and with thee will I break in pieces the chariot and his rider;

In verse 25 we finally arrive at the place where God declares the empire of Babylon to be a destroying mountain. In verse 28 we see again that the nations of the Medes make up the mountainlike empire that will put an end to the destroying mountain of Babylon.

²⁴And I will render unto Babylon and to all the inhabitants of Chaldea all their evil that they have done in Zion in your sight, saith the Lord. ²⁵Behold, I am against thee, O *destroying mountain*, saith the Lord, *which destroyest all the earth*: and I will stretch out mine hand upon thee, and roll thee down from the rocks, *and will make thee a burnt mountain*. ²⁶And they shall not take of thee a stone for a corner, nor a stone for foundations; but thou shalt be desolate for ever, saith the Lord. ²⁷Set ye up a standard in the land, blow the trumpet among the nations, prepare the nations against her, call together against her the kingdoms of Ararat, Minni, and Ashchenaz; appoint a captain against her; cause the horses to come up as the rough caterpillers. ²⁸Prepare against her the nations with the kings of the *Medes*, the captains thereof, and all the rulers thereof, and all the land of his dominion. ²⁹And the land shall tremble and sorrow: for every purpose of the Lord shall be performed against Babylon, *to make the land of Babylon a desolation without an inhabitant*.

In the last three verses, we again have masculine and feminine references. In verse 43, the ancient city of Babylon is laid waste at the onslaught of the Medes. In the end-times, Michael and his angels will fight against Satan and his angels in heaven, and the wall of Mystery Babylon will fall. In verse 44 Bel, who was a god in Babylon, was punished for the destruction of the cities he was able to capture. In the end-times, Satan will be cast out of heaven and to the earth for a short time to rule from earthly Babylon. After Satan has had a short time to terrorize the earth, the prophecy will be fulfilled again as the earthly Babylon is laid low and Satan is cast into the Lake of Fire.

> [43]*Her cities are a desolation, a dry land, and a wilderness,* a land wherein no man dwelleth, neither doth any son of man pass thereby. [44]And I will punish Bel in Babylon, and I will bring forth out of *his* mouth that which *he* hath swallowed up: and the nations shall not flow together any more unto *him*: yea, the wall of Babylon shall fall. [45]*My people, go ye out of the midst of her, and deliver ye every man his soul from the fierce anger of the* Lord.

Verse 45 is a warning from God to all the ages not to partake of the prostituted world system, particularly in those nations that bow to another god. We are *in* the world but not *of* it. John repeats this very same thought in Revelation 18:4 as he dictates the words that he hears from a voice in heaven.

As we study the end-times, we have to be able to distinguish between the activities of the Antichrist during the time of the Great Tribulation and during the Wrath of God. During the Tribulation, the Antichrist will work his deception on many as he and the false prophet introduce the Mark of the Beast and convince many that he is God. He then leads those same deceived followers into wars and destruction that will reduce the overall world population by 25 percent before God intervenes by rescuing His Church and bringing wrath on all those who remain. When God's wrath begins, the Antichrist will be more of a spectator as he watches his kingdom being destroyed by the Wrath of God. The first real activity we see demonstrated by the Antichrist during God's wrath is when he makes war against the two prophets of doom that are a part of God's wrath, and he overcomes them. That occurred under the sixth trumpet of judgment in Revelation 11. At the same time, the sixth vial shows that the Antichrist is gaining a new confidence after defeating the two prophets and begins gathering armies from all corners of a world that is void of spiritual understanding. When Jesus removed the Church from the earth, God began pounding it with His retribution. When Christ comes back the second time to remain, the mountain/empire of His kingdom will crush the end-time mountain/empire of Babylon that is controlled by the Antichrist.

Verse 10 informed us that of the seven kings, five are fallen, one is, and the other is not yet come. The five fallen kings ruled over five former world empires that controlled Israel and had already fallen at the time John was writing his vision. Those kingdoms and their approximate timeframes were Egyptian, 1570 –1150 b.c.; Assyrian, 745–609 b.c.; Babylonian, 605–539 b.c.; Medo-Persian, 559–330 b.c.; and Greek, 330–160 b.c. The one that "is" was the Roman Empire that existed at the time John was writing Revelation. The western Roman Empire lasted from 241 b.c.– a.d. 476 when Romulus Augustus, the last Roman emperor, abdicated his throne and the Germanic people of Europe began to rule in Italy and Rome. The eastern or Byzantine Roman Empire that separated from the west at about a.d. 364 lasted on a declining basis until a.d. 1453 when the Ottoman Turks finally overthrew the city of Constantinople, which had been the capital of all of Rome for a short time and the capital of eastern Rome for its entirety.

Rome was the only empire not judged by God. The forgiveness Jesus granted to all mankind on the cross extended even to the Roman Empire itself. Salt and light entered into the Roman Empire through the thousands of newborn Christians who were receiving God's Word in their hearts and becoming a witness to others. The empire did eventually die a slow miserable death under the weight of its own sin and through various conquests. The Ottoman Empire, which is closely related to the Beast Empire, eventually fizzled out also and was divided into smaller regional powers. The Ottomans and the division of its territories doesn't even earn a position as one of the heads of the dragon because Israel had already been scattered among the nations when the Ottomans controlled Palestine. Things have changed with the recent reunion of the Jewish people with their promised land in 1948. The last empire or mountain that will arise to confront Israel is the empire over which the Antichrist will reign. It will form under the guidance of the seventh spirit king until the Antichrist takes over as both the spirit and fleshly or human king. It will be the last empire to conquer and enslave Israel.

The first six empires relate to the beast in more of a historical sense. Although there are seven different kings, their purpose is always the same: the destruction of the offspring of faith or those who hold to the covenants of God. That will be the purpose of the Antichrist as the eighth head of the beast. In verses 8 and 11, we are told that the beast was in the past but is being restrained in the bottomless pit until his time in the future. It's almost like he's getting a second chance. There are several ways that we can look at this.

In Daniel 8, we saw that the Greek Empire led by Alexander the Great overthrew the Medo-Persian empire. After Alexander died, the empire was split into four parts between his four generals. Years later in 167 b.c. Antiochus Epiphanies, as ruler of the Syrian division of the Greek kingdom, conquered Israel and dedicated the Jewish temple to Zeus Olympus. For two days short of three full years, the temple was used in pagan worship. Antiochus was a forerunner of the Antichrist, he was a type of the Antichrist and may have actually been the Antichrist, or he may have been possessed by the same spirit that will eventually come out of the bottomless pit and again defile the temple during the Great Tribulation. Daniel 8:23 told us that "in the latter time of *their* kingdom when the transgressors are come to the full, a king of fierce countenance and understanding dark sentences shall stand up." This is speaking of the entire geographical area of the Greek Empire and not just the Syrian portion where Antiochus reigned. This is made apparent by the use of the words "their kingdom," which signifies the reuniting of the divided Greek Empire in the end-times. The spirit king that controlled either the whole or the part of the Greek Empire may be the "he" of Revelation 17:11 that was in the past and will be again in the future—only to go into perdition, which means damnation and destruction.

The whole concept of Mystery Babylon and the seven empires that spring up on the earth is as close as we get to the theory of parallel universes. However, it's more like an invisible hand inside a visible glove. If Satan is the hand, we cannot see what he is doing until he puts the glove on and starts to move it. The Antichrist becomes the glove in the end-times, and everything we see him doing originates and is empowered by Satan as he makes his moves inside the glove. You'll recall that Revelation 13:2 said that "the dragon gave him his power, and his seat, and great authority." Just as we are able to see

God the Father through the acts of compassion that Jesus Christ did—and still does, likewise, we will see Satan through the acts of hatred and destruction of the Antichrist. The way Jesus and His followers are able to bind things on earth and have them bound in heaven is very similar to the way the Antichrist will loose the rage of Satan on the earth which is first loosed in the spirit realm. The Antichrist and his kingdom, just like the others that came before, are empowered by Satan and the demon spirits that obey him. The earthly Babylon is just a mirror image of the same city of sin and abomination that exists somewhere just beyond our five natural senses, in a spiritual world that we will freely traverse one day after shedding this fleshly body.

Verse 14 points out what we have already said: The purpose of the beast and the ten nations that give their power over to him is to take on the children of God. It starts with Gog, as the ten nations form an alliance that is unwavering in its commitment to eliminating Israel from the map. It continues as they regroup under the strong leadership of the beast. He makes a false covenant of peace with Israel and then breaks it three-and-one-half years later to begin the three-and-one-half-year Great Tribulation. Immediately after the Tribulation the skies turn black at the onset of the Wrath of God, but before it begins, Jesus collects His elect and takes them to heaven with Him. During the Wrath of God there is not much purpose in the lives of those who truly hate God until the two witnesses show up to torment them. After they show up, the beast and those who follow him try to destroy the two prophets, but the prophets are able to destroy their enemies with their fiery breath and the plagues they are enabled to dish out until the time when their prophecy is completed. Then the beast makes war against them and kills them. After they are gone, the world prepares for the return of Jesus Christ from heaven. They've defeated the two prophets so what's to say they can't repeat that success and defeat the One who sent them. They gather and wait at Armageddon, ready to defeat the One who is the cause of all of their problems—Jesus Christ. But the saints who accompany Him will prevail.

> [12]And the ten horns which thou sawest are ten kings,
> which have received no kingdom as yet; but receive power

as kings one hour with the beast. [13]These have one mind, and shall give their power and strength unto the beast. [14]*These shall make war with the Lamb, and the Lamb shall overcome them*: for he is Lord of lords, and King of kings: and they that are with him are called, and chosen, and faithful.

Revelation 17:12-14

The empire of the beast has been the main target of the Wrath of God, with many of the plagues of wrath beginning either in Iraq where Babylon will be located or Jerusalem where the beast occupies the temple until the two witnesses arrive to throw him out. The original armies of the Antichrist's league of ten nations will be pretty much depleted by the time the Battle of Armageddon rolls around. There will no doubt be many new soldiers added to this army from the population of the Beast Empire as young men mature with the same hatred for the God of the Jews that their parents possessed before them. Many others will come from the general population who before were doctors, lawyers, teachers, store clerks, farmhands, businessmen and so on. For this decisive battle, the rest of the nations of the world are going to join the beast as the three unclean spirits of Revelation 16:13 and 14 "go forth unto the kings of the earth and of the whole world, to gather them to the battle of that great day of God Almighty." The saints of God have been gone from the earth for several years now, and there is no one around to bring grace and understanding to the people, so they slowly begin to see things from the perspective of the beast. There has been resistance and an arms-length approach to the beast as the world witnesses the full fury of God being poured on the kingdom of the beast, with a ripple effect going out into the rest of the world—that is, until the three spirits spread their deception across the face of the globe.

Verse 15 simply explains that the word "waters" in verse 1 represents a diversity of people. In Revelation 7:9, after the Church had been raptured and shown in heaven all at one time, we saw all nations, kindreds, peoples and tongues that had inherited salvation. Here we see the same thing—nations, kindreds, peoples and tongues—but these are the ones who have rejected God. Just like the kingdom of God that we enjoy right now comes without observation through righteousness, peace and joy in the Holy Spirit, the kingdom of Satan also comes without observation through anger, deception and lust in the great whore. Satan has been working to establish his kingdom on the earth from the beginning of time. The Antichrist, both during the Tribulation and during the Wrath of God, is an observable picture of what the kingdom of Satan looks like at its finest. The peoples, tongues, nations and multitudes or "waters" that the great whore sits upon are the people of the earth who give themselves over to serve Satan in his kingdom by fulfilling his will on the earth.

> 15And he saith unto me, The waters which thou sawest, where the whore sitteth, are peoples, and multitudes, and nations, and tongues. 16And the ten horns which thou sawest upon the beast, these shall hate the whore, and shall make her desolate and naked, and shall eat her flesh, *and burn her with fire.* 17For God hath put in their hearts to fulfill his will, and to agree, and give their kingdom unto the beast, until the words of God shall be fulfilled.
>
> *Revelation 17:15-17*

God puts it in the hearts of the leaders of the ten confederate nations who submit to the beast to burn the great whore called Babylon. Satan is cast out of heaven, and his place there is destroyed before the Tribulation and the Wrath of God even get started. During the intervening years, he has been overseeing the build-up of the city of Babylon into a monument unto himself. The earthly Babylon is the only remnant of Mystery Babylon the Great, and now, at the end of God's wrath, God is going to have those who serve the Antichrist turn against the city itself to destroy it. Even though God puts it in their hearts to destroy the city, it is not just a mindless reaction. There will be some kind of justification for destroying the city that will motivate the followers of the beast into action. One reason they may want to destroy Babylon is that after the beast makes war with the two witnesses and destroys them, he may remain in Jerusalem seated in the temple of God once more, and he has no desire for any other city to outshine his self-aggrandizing glory. The kings, merchants and people of the earth are enthralled with the decadent beauty and wealth of Babylon, which causes much attention to be diverted away from the Antichrist as he attempts to regroup and prepare for the return of the saints. It could also be a skirmish between the Antichrist and Satan. Perhaps the destruction of Babylon is the Antichrist rebelling against Satan who resides in the city because he thinks that he would make a better god than Satan. Maybe the kings and multitudes who follow the Antichrist need no other justification for their actions than a simple command from the Antichrist to destroy. Regardless of how they justify their actions, Revelation 18 is the fulfillment of Revelation 17:16 as people watch from afar while the smoke of the burning city rises to the heavens.

> And the woman which thou sawest is that great city, which reigneth over the kings of the earth.
>
> *Revelation 17:18*

When reading that final verse, we have to recall that John is seeing an overarching view of Mystery Babylon and not just the end-times city of Babylon on earth. Satan has ruled the earth from that city in heaven for ages even though he does not exercise total control of the earth. After Mystery Babylon is cast down in heaven, Satan is thrown to the earth and takes up residence in the city of Babylon in Iraq. He will not exercise total control of the earth at that time either, nor will the Antichrist. But, through both the troubles that he causes during the Great Tribulation and the perceived need to do business with the Iraqi city of Babylon which many around the world will feel, Satan will engage the whole earth to a point in which he is very much in control over the major events taking place on the earth. Babylon in Iraq will not only replace, but will become the great whore, and will reign over the kings of the earth in the end-times for a short while.

THINK ABOUT IT!

— Is it possible that the beast that was, and yet is not, but shall ascend out of the bottomless pit, is a real being that is restrained in a real pit?

— Although the second half of Revelation 17 narrows the influence of the beast, do you think the first half of the chapter can be considered more broadly to encompass all of mankind throughout history?

Selah

The secret things belong unto the Lord our God: but those things which are revealed belong unto us and to our children for ever, that we may do all the words of this law.

Deuteronomy 29:29

A Map Laid Out in Scripture

The more things came into focus concerning the beast—the Antichrist of the latter days—the more Islam kept troubling my mind. Could it be that there was a direct tie? The birth place and the stronghold of Islam, the Middle East, daily news reports of terrorism, ten nations and the destruction of Israel. Muslim leaders, in affirming their patience, have declared that even if Israel wins the next hundred, or even thousand wars, all the Muslims need do is win one war, and then it's all over for Israel. So much hatred there. Needing to find out what Muslims believe, I purchased a Koran and started reading for myself. Much of the Koran directs Muslims into good works and so forth, but the things that pertained to me as a nonMuslim scared me. If I were Jewish, I'd be even more scared. Thank God for His promises. Pray for the peace of Jerusalem. Pray for revival in Israel and the Middle East.

The idea of a revised Roman Empire began during the time of the early Roman Empire and has been plaguing the Church ever since. Many still believe that the beast will rule from Rome as a pope or some other high Catholic official, from Brussels, Belgium, as the leader of NATO or as the leader of the European Union. As of the summer of 2004, the European Union had twenty-five member nations with three additional candidate nations and two applicants that could be added in the future, disqualifying it as the ten-nation empire of the beast. The current membership of the E.U. includes Austria, Belgium, Denmark, England, Finland, France, Germany, Greece, Ireland, Italy, Luxembourg, Netherlands, Portugal, Spain and Sweden. Added to that list on May 1, 2004, were Cyprus, the Czech Republic, Estonia, Hungary, Latvia, Lithuania, Malta, Poland, Slovakia and Slovenia. Bulgaria, Romania and Turkey are candidates under consideration, while Croatia and Macedonia are making application. Several of these nations never were a part of the original Roman Empire.

The list of twenty-six NATO members looks much like that of the E.U., but includes the U.S. and Iceland which makes it an unlikely candidate to be a revised Roman Empire from a geographic sense. What is missing from the Roman Catholic Church, NATO and the European Union is any control at all over the countries of the Middle East and North Africa that are mentioned in the prophecies. They were a part of the Roman Empire, but a revised Roman Empire, Europe and the nations of Europe are not a part of the end-times prophecies. Turkey is a member of NATO and is a candidate for the E.U., and it is the only country out of all of those mentioned that receives any prophetic mention when it comes to the ten-nation kingdom of the latter-days beast. Turkey is a part of the European continent and the Middle East at the same time, and as such, they are pulled in two different directions when it comes to the type of country they desire to be—a free nation that embraces the rest of the world or one controlled by Islam.

The theories about a revised Roman Empire are just that. There are no scriptures that come right out and name Rome in regards to the end-times the way other kingdoms and nations are named. Jesus, after spending His life in Israel as a part of the Roman Empire, never once gave any indication that Rome would be a part of the end-times kingdom of the beast. After Jesus' resurrection, the saints became salt and light in the Roman Empire and, despite some persecution from Rome, the empire actually provided the order and cohesiveness needed to spread the gospel quickly and effectively. In a.d. 330 Constantine moved the capital of Rome to Constantinople in Turkey (modern-day Istanbul). One of the primary reasons for moving the capital was because he saw Turkey and the Middle East as a more fertile territory for Christianity to flourish, as opposed to Rome and most of Europe, which were more atheistic and pagan even though Constantine had declared

Christianity to be the official religion of Rome. Eventually things changed and Italy is now over ninety percent Catholic, with other Christian denominations claiming small percentages. Constantinople, on the other hand, was overthrown by the Ottoman Turks in a.d. 1453 who then renamed it Istanbul, and it replaced Baghdad as the center of the Islamic world at the time. The lands and people whom Constantinople saw as primary candidates for Christian conversion are now predominately Muslim.

John, who wrote the Revelation, along with Matthew, Mark, Luke, Peter and Paul, who all contributed significantly to our knowledge of the end-times, never gave any indication that Rome would be revived as an end-times empire. Many of the ideas of a revived Rome come to us from the times of the Roman Empire itself. Church leaders of that time felt that the seven mountains mentioned in Revelation 17 had to do with the seven hills Rome is built upon. (Coincidentally, Constantinople also happens to be built upon seven hills just like Rome, which by itself should cast some doubt on that theory.) After the demise of the Roman Empire, church leaders continued to hold to that idea by creating a revised Rome for the end-times. There will always be things happening in and around the European continent that will lend themselves over to the appearance of some type of Roman revision. However, even if the European Union renamed itself "Revised Roman Empire," it is still not going to be the ten-nation kingdom of the beast. In fact, the only real possible mention of the Roman Empire in relation to the Antichrist is found in Daniel 11:30 where it informs us that "the ships of Chittim shall come against him." The ships of Chittim appear to be a naval force that originates to the northwest sector of the Mediterranean Sea. That would possibly make it a latter-day version of the European portion of the old Roman Empire, possibly NATO. Rather than hosting or even supporting the Antichrist, the ships of Chittim resist him.

There are other people who believe that the Antichrist will rule the world as the Secretary General of the U.N. The U.N. has most of the nations of the world as members, approximately 191 at this writing, which—contrary to traditional thinking—makes it too large an organization to be consistent with prophecy. The Antichrist will not rule the world but will terrorize it through wars and other destructive activities from his base of ten nations in the Middle East. There are no scriptures that say he will rule the world, but plenty that say he will tread down and destroy much of the world and deceive those who are unsaved.

We just read in Revelation 17:10 about the seven kings who control the seven mountains. Five had already fallen; one was currently in existence, which was the Roman Empire, and the final empire of the beast has "not yet come." The separation between the one that "is" and the one that has "not yet come" makes them as distinctly different as the five that came before them. They were all related to each other, but yet they were all different. In Revelation 17:8, John informs us that the beast "was" in the past, but "is not" at the time when he was writing, but "he...shall ascend out of the bottomless pit" in the future. The end-times beast never was a part of the Roman Empire, but yet the Roman Empire was a part of the seven-headed beast. The beast of the final empire had some sort of connection to one of the previous empires. However, it was not the Roman Empire; it was one of the five that preceded it.

The prophecies always draw us back to the Middle East where the five former kingdoms existed and where the Roman Empire overlapped the entire area of all of the previous kingdoms. We already mentioned that the prophecy of Daniel 8:23 has not been fulfilled yet. It is an end-times prophecy that foretells the breakup of the Greek Empire into four smaller nations, and then jumps all the way to the end of time when the Antichrist rules over "the latter time of *their* kingdom when transgressors are come to the full." The use of the word "their" suggests that it is the full extent of the divided Greek Empire being discussed.

The Greek Empire of Alexander controlled only a small portion of the Greek Isles. On the other hand, it fanned out from the midst of the Greek Isles and controlled a major portion of Turkey, most of the Middle East including Afghanistan and Pakistan and a part of Egypt. This is almost exactly the same geography we see in the makeup of Gog. If you exclude Greece itself and add Ethiopia and Libya, you end up with a pretty good idea of what the beast kingdom will look like. The countries most likely to be included in the beast kingdom are Iraq, Iran, Syria, Jordan, Lebanon, Kuwait and parts of Saudi Arabia, Turkey, Pakistan, Afghanistan, Turkmenistan and Uzbekistan, Ethiopia, Libya and possibly Egypt. That adds up to fifteen countries, but out of those fifteen, we will see the empire of the beast arise. Turkmenistan and Uzbekistan may be too insignificant to include in this group, Kuwait has a different heart from the rest of these nations and Egypt appears from Scripture to be a nation that the Antichrist will simply overrun. That leaves only eleven countries, and we can't eliminate Iraq because that is where the city of Babylon will be located on the Euphrates River.

Several things come to mind when we read this list of nations. The first is the unwavering hatred they share for the nation of Israel. From early biblical times, many of these nations were the ones who fought against Israel, trying to destroy her. That has been the intent of the seven heads of the dragon all along—to destroy Israel. But yet, with all of that history of hatred and war behind them, Israel still remains a nation to this day. A simple hatred of the Jews is not enough to be included in the list of nations, nor is an energetic war against the Jews enough to gain inclusion. And Hitler with his Nazi death camps that wiped out millions of Jews does not gain Germany inclusion into this list of nations. There's more to it than that.

Another thing we see is the close proximity to Israel, but that is not a real factor since Libya and Ethiopia are somewhat removed to the west and south, respectively, on the African continent. They are named specifically as participants in the attack launched by Gog of Magog, so they cannot be eliminated as members of the Antichrist kingdom. Afghanistan and Pakistan are well to the eastern edge of the Middle East, putting some distance between them and Israel. So what other similarities would draw these nations together?

For one thing, the political and social climate of the nations. Many of these nations are terrorist nations. They support, train, harbor and finance terrorists. This is not yet true of all of these nations in a political sense, but the social underpinnings that will bring a change in the political outlook and behavior of those other countries will continue to gurgle just under the surface until they fissure to the top and force change. The social structure that defines each of these nations can be summed up in one word—Islam.

Some would say "radical Islam," but all of Islam is radical if you look to the Koran and the history of Islam to gain an in-depth understanding of it. To be sure, many, if not most, Muslims are peace-loving individuals who look to the Koran as a source of understanding of who God is and for guidance in how they should live their lives. However, if the God of the Jews is or ever was the one true God, and if the God of the New Testament is for real, then the god of Islam cannot be the same God. There is such a wide gulf, such a divergent theology and such a different worldview between the Bible and the Koran that they cannot be from the same God. The Bible and the Koran are so diametrically opposed to each other that there is no way to truly and honestly believe they come from the same source, or to believe that Islam is a part of a continuum that started with the Old Covenant and dramatically improved with the New Covenant. The Koran is written as though it is a replacement for the Torah and a correction to the New Testament. It supports the authenticity of the Torah as the Word of God and then contradicts it. To believe the Koran is to believe that God suddenly changed His mind about all that He had planned and prophesied for thousands of years, and then did more than a one-hundred-and-eighty degree about-face by going back to something that is lacking in substance, even compared to the Old Covenant.

Islam is a totally Antichrist religion, even from the pages of the Koran. The Koran singles out Christians and Jews as infidels, and it perverts the Scriptures whenever it makes mention of them. It denies the deity of Christ and the existence of the Trinity, which it identifies as God the Father, Jesus the Son and Mary. Muslims believe that Jesus lived but never died. They believe that God took Him and allowed an impostor to die in His place. They believe that Jesus (they refer to him as Isa) is going to come back as a leader of Islam who will lead them in war against Christians and Jews to fulfill the mandate of the Koran of bringing the whole world under the control of Islam; however, it won't be Jesus they are following. Muslims are prepared right now to follow the Antichrist under the banner of Islam to destroy God's people as they usher in the golden age of Islam—the perfect religion.

One of the most important things to note about the makeup of the beast kingdom is that it is limited in size. That limitation eliminates other Islamic nations as being a part of the kingdom. Other Islamic nations surround the Middle East that God never mentions, even indirectly, in regards to the end-times or the empire of the beast. If He had mentioned them, we would know who they are and that their fate as nations is already sealed. The very lack of mention could suggest that these nations could see revival to such a magnitude as to change the religious and political nature of the entire nations. Or, it may be that they reject the more radical Islam of nonstop jihad permeating the nations that are a part of the beast kingdom. The danger is that these nations may face the wrath of the Antichrist. There is a death sentence on Muslims who turn away from Islam. Turning to Jesus will really infuriate the beast and those who are charged with the duty of killing them.

Most Muslims hate the Jews with an extreme passion. They believe the Jews have been rejected by God and feel it is their responsibility to eliminate them as a race of people. Indeed, Allah makes these things clear in the Koran. They often hide their hatred behind the struggle for a Palestinian state, but if the Palestinians were given all but one square foot of Israeli land, the hatred would remain, along with the determination to finish off the Jews. Beyond the resentment many Arabs and Muslims feel towards the Jews is the issue of who controls Jerusalem. Muslims believe that Gabriel escorted Mohammed into heaven from the temple mount—or more precisely from the spot on the temple mount where the Muslim's Dome of the Rock now stands—to meet with Jesus, Abraham and Noah and lead them in prayer. The Palestinian Liberation Organization has laid claim to this site as a part of their homeland and religious heritage and is sworn to the destruction of the nation of Israel. Nothing on this earth is going to stop the Arab Muslims from pursuing their dream of a Middle East without Israel. When the end comes and the Antichrist arrives to lead them, the ten-nation kingdom he presides over will not stop with just the ravaging of Israel but will resume the expansionist activities of the Ottoman Empire, which had made significant inroads into southern Europe and North Africa. And that is how world wars begin. It just might be that today's terrorism coming out of the Middle East is the very thing that galvanizes the rest of the world against the beast kingdom, thus limiting its core size to only ten nations.

Many peace-loving Muslims interpret the Koran in a way that is more acceptable to them and those around them. They have a desire for peace and tranquility and that seasons their interpretations. To them, a jihad is first and foremost an inner struggle to follow Allah and to keep the dictates of the Koran. There are other jihads, however. The struggle to bring others over to the Muslim way of thinking is also considered a jihad. As far as armed conflict is concerned, it is considered a lesser jihad and is meant to be a self-defense rather than a means of conquering. However, Islam started out under the leadership of a warrior named Mohammed, proceeded with a history of wars and conquest, currently practices persecution and ethnic cleansing, and will end with a world war and the judgment of God. Islam is not a religion of peace, and many peace-loving Muslims will one day wake up to a choice between taking the same mark of the beast that their bloodthirsty neighbors are displaying or die at their hands. A relative calmness exists on the earth right now that allows the more peaceful Muslims to hold to their beliefs, but when the seals of the book are broken and peace is taken from the earth and the slaughter of one quarter of mankind begins, there will be only two choices—Jesus Christ and eternity in heaven, or the beast with the Wrath of God.

If the Lord should not come again for another thousand years and the entire political and religious makeup of the Middle East should change entirely, the one thing that will not change is the fact that this is the region and these are the people who will make up the final end-time ten-nation empire. Until the Rapture occurs, it is never too late to introduce them to Christ. That is, of course, as long as they are not displaying the mark of the beast on their foreheads or right hands.

THINK ABOUT IT!

— How much do you know about Islam?

— Did you realize that those whom we consider to be radical Muslims are only following the dictates of Allah?

— Do you think that a literal mark of the beast could be the final device that galvanizes the followers of the beast into submissive action?

Selah

Why do the heathen rage, and the people imagine a vain thing? The kings of the earth set themselves, and the rulers take counsel together, against the Lord, and against his anointed, saying, Let us break their bands asunder, and cast away their cords from us. He that sitteth in the heavens shall laugh: the Lord shall have them in derision. Then shall He speak unto them in his wrath, and vex them in his sore displeasure. Yet have I set my king upon my holy hill of Zion.

Psalms 2:1-6

ISAIAH 13–14

Satan, King of Babylon

I spent a lot of time trying to reconcile the differences between the prophecies that seemed to bring a complete end to Babylon in the past and those that speak of it in future terms. How could it be? Was one literal and the other figurative? Could I just ignore the statements declaring that Babylon would not be inhabited? Babylon of the future seemed so real. How could it be just an analogy? I can't wait for the day when Satan is finally put where he belongs. I wish I could see the faces of those who have rejected God for the ways of Satan as their hero and their god is cast into the pit along with them. But I guess I will just have to pass on that one.

Isaiah 13–14 and Revelation 18 are all speaking of Babylon's destruction in the latter days during the time of God's wrath. Isaiah 13, by itself, is a double or extended prophecy speaking of the eminent destruction of Babylon by the Medes thousands of years ago, and then the latter-day destruction of the end-times city of Babylon. Isaiah 13:1-13 speaks to the end-times Babylon. The end-times ten-nation empire of the beast may not be called Babylon, but the city of Babylon will be at the center of it. The city could actually be called by a different name, but more than likely it will be called Babylon and be built right alongside the ancient city of Babylon. Regardless of what it is called, it will be the manifestation of the direct rule of Satan on the earth after his beloved city in heaven is cast down. Verses 14-16 speak to both old and new Babylon as though they were one. In a very real sense, they are one as we have seen by the historical and spiritual threads that bind them together. And finally, verse 17 through the end of the chapter speak only to ancient Babylon.

Isaiah 13 makes several references to the Day of the Lord and the heavens withholding their light, etc., which refers to the coming judgment of wrath. Verse 13:17 refers to the Medes who, in league with the Persians, are one of the seven world powers represented by the seven mountains, the seven heads of the dragon and the seven kings that enabled those empires to exist and dominate Israel at various times. The Medo-Persians are one of the kingdoms that has already fallen, but it will also be a part of the league of ten nations the Antichrist will control during the end-times. The league of ten nations, or final empire, will destroy the literal end-times city of Babylon with fire, and that will be followed by a great earthquake and the third coming of Christ to put down all earthly authority and rule as He defeats the armies of the world at Armageddon.

Notice that Isaiah 13 starts with the words "The burden of Babylon," and then continues with God calling upon His holy army in heaven to the battle. This is the final battle at Armageddon, but why is it called the burden of Babylon? Again, this is speaking of Mystery Babylon. When we look at Isaiah 14, we see that Satan himself is the king of Babylon. Satan rules from his place in heaven until he is cast out, and then, according to this prophecy, his forces will be defeated on the earth and everything that even smells of Babylon will be destroyed. Verse 10 describes the same heavenly events as in Matthew 24:29, which Jesus assured us would take place immediately after the Tribulation when He comes for His New Testament elect. In fact, it declares that the sun shall be darkened "in his going forth." Verse 11 shows the Wrath of God beginning immediately after the skies are darkened. The Rapture is not mentioned here because the focus is on the punishment of Babylon and not the victory of the Church, however, these verses are further confirmation that the Rapture separates between the Tribulation and the Wrath of God because Jesus said He would come for His

New Testament elect at that time after the Tribulation when the skies turn black. That time immediately precedes God's wrath in these verses.

The army He is calling upon is made up of His righteous servants who have just finished participating in and enjoying the Marriage Supper of the Lamb in heaven while God's wrath is being poured out upon sinners below, and now those warring saints will help bring a conclusion to the Day of the Lord at Armageddon. Remember, this is an Old Testament prophecy showing a faded glimpse of what was to come. Only through the New Testament are we able to bring it into a much sharper focus, giving us a clearer understanding of what is happening here.

(Verses 1-13 are directed at the end-times Babylon.)

> ¹*The burden of Babylon*, which Isaiah the son of Amoz did see. ²Lift ye up a banner upon the high mountain, exalt the voice unto them, shake the hand, that they may go into the gates of the nobles. ³I have commanded my sanctified ones, I have also called my mighty ones for mine anger, even them that rejoice in my highness. ⁴The noise of a multitude in the mountains, like as of a great people; a tumultuous noise of the kingdoms of nations gathered together: the Lord of hosts mustereth the host of the battle. ⁵They come from a far country, *from the end of heaven, even the* Lord, and the weapons of his indignation, to destroy the whole land. ⁶Howl ye; *for the day of the* Lord is at hand; *it shall come as a destruction from the Almighty.* ⁷Therefore shall all hands be faint, and every man's heart shall melt: ⁸And they shall be afraid: pangs and sorrows shall take hold of them; they shall be in pain as a woman that travaileth: they shall be amazed one at another; their faces shall be as flames. ⁹*Behold, the day of the* Lord cometh, cruel both with wrath and fierce anger, to lay the land desolate: and he shall destroy the sinners thereof out of it. ¹⁰*For the stars of heaven and the constellations thereof shall not give their light: the sun shall be darkened in his going forth, and the moon shall not cause her light to shine.* ¹¹*And I will punish the world for their evil, and the wicked*

for their iniquity; and I will cause the arrogancy of the proud to cease, and will lay low the haughtiness of the terrible. [12]I will make a man more precious than fine gold; even a man than the golden wedge of Ophir. [13]*Therefore I will shake the heavens, and the earth shall remove out of her place, in the wrath of the Lord of hosts,* and in the day of his fierce anger.

(Verses 14-16 are directed at both old and new Babylon.)

[14]And it shall be as the chased roe, and as a sheep that no man taketh up: they shall every man turn to his own people, and flee every one into his own land. [15]Every one that is found shall be thrust through; and every one that is joined unto them shall fall by the sword. [16]Their children also shall be dashed to pieces before their eyes; their houses shall be spoiled, and their wives ravished.

(Verses 17-22 are directed at ancient Babylon.)

[17]Behold, I will stir up the Medes against them, which shall not regard silver; and as for gold, they shall not delight in it. [18]Their bows also shall dash the young men to pieces; and they shall have no pity on the fruit of the womb; their eye shall not spare children. [19]And Babylon, the glory of kingdoms, the beauty of the Chaldees' excellency, shall be as when God overthrew Sodom and Gomorrah. [20]It shall never be inhabited, neither shall it be dwelt in from generation to generation: neither shall the Arabian pitch tent there; neither shall the shepherds make their fold there. [21]But wild beasts of the desert shall lie there; and their houses shall be full of doleful creatures; and owls shall dwell there, and satyrs shall dance there. [22]And the wild beasts of the islands shall cry in their desolate houses, and dragons in their pleasant palaces: and her time is near to come, and her days shall not be prolonged.

Isaiah 13:1-22

The first half of Isaiah 13 repeatedly makes mention of the fierce anger and wrath of God. Verse 6 declares that the Day of the Lord will come as destruction from the Almighty after the sun and moon are darkened. We are told that His wrath comes to punish the world and to destroy sinners from the land. This is speaking of God's stored-up anger He withholds from mankind while His compassion is being extended to them until the work of salvation is done. This anger and wrath is being directed at the whole world and not just the inhabitants of the empire of Babylon, even though He was about to judge the ancient empire for its sins at the time the prophecy was written.

God's wrath is not an unholy thing. It is focused towards and against the wrath and anger of Satan and those who follow after his pattern of rebellion. In verse 6 below, we see that Satan's wrath and anger is ongoing and unending. It continues all day and into the night, which is just the opposite of *the mercies of the Lord* which are new every morning. Satan's wrath will continue until God brings an end to it. We also see that Satan's wrath and anger is directed towards all people, including those who willingly obey him. Satan's wrath has been against mankind from the very beginning in the Garden of Eden, and will only intensify after his heavenly Babylon is cast down and he is thrown out into the earth. Revelation 12:12 tells us that Satan's wrath will be elevated to "great wrath" in the final days after he is cast out of heaven and he sees that his days are running out. Satan's wrath causes tribulation throughout the earth on an ongoing basis until the very end when his "great wrath" will cause great tribulation to all that dwell on the earth. Once again, the Great Tribulation is not the Wrath of God and it does not coincide with the Wrath of God. It is the wrath of Satan, and the Church will not be raptured until it has been buffeted by the wrath of Satan and his Antichrist. The Church will be in its greatest glory at the time of its greatest persecution during the Tribulation. Because the gospel has already been preached to all the world before the Tribulation begins, the Tribulation will provide the clearest contrast between good and evil that the world has ever seen. The Church will be tasked at that time with bringing in a tremendous harvest of souls as multitudes of people make their final decisions.

Isaiah 14 speaks primarily of Satan as the ruler of Babylon. The prophecy was leveled against Babylon in general, but the whole prophecy probably did not make a lot of sense to anyone unless they possessed great spiritual insight. The kings of Babylon were not known for their spiritual acumen. However, as the prophecy unfolded, Satan no doubt was trembling in his little red jumpsuit because he knew that parts of it were against him and his home place. God's mention of the golden city in verse 4 is probably a literal description of Mystery Babylon in heaven—a city made of gold. Nothing but the best for Satan. Until he is able to take the throne of God and rule over the city with gates of pearl and streets of pure gold, he pampers himself with his own city made out of the gold of heaven. Ancient Babylon was a fabulous city with much gold in it, and the end-times Babylon will be a city full of gold. However, they are no match for the ancient city in heaven where Satan rules the earth as a surrogate god. In verses 13 and 14, God lays bare the secrets of Satan's heart. His desire to be like God is published for all creation to see. In verse 12, God calls him by name and declares his fate thousands of years before it befalls him. Mystery Babylon is going to fall and Satan will be cast out of heaven. Many of the other verses either give further description of him as the one who ruled the nations in wrath and wasted the cities thereof, or they speak of his final destination in the pits of hell with all the kings of the earth looking down upon him and wondering with amazement how he could have been brought to such a lowly state.

> ¹For the Lord will have mercy on Jacob, and will yet choose Israel, and set them in their own land: and the strangers shall be joined with them, and they shall cleave to the house of Jacob. ²And the people shall take them, and bring them to their place: and the house of Israel shall possess them in the land of the Lord for servants and handmaids: and they shall take them captives, whose captives they were; and they shall rule over their oppressors. ³And it shall come to pass in the day that the Lord shall give thee rest from thy sorrow, and from thy fear, and from the hard bondage wherein thou wast made to serve, ⁴That thou shalt take up this proverb *against the king of Babylon*, and say, How hath the oppressor ceased! *the golden city ceased*! ⁵The Lord hath broken the staff of the wicked, and the

sceptre of the rulers. [6]He who smote the people in wrath with a continual stroke, he that ruled the nations in anger, is persecuted, and none hindereth. [7]The whole earth is at rest, and is quiet: they break forth into singing. [8]Yea, the fir trees rejoice at thee, and the cedars of Lebanon, saying, Since thou art laid down, no feller is come up against us. [9]Hell from beneath is moved for thee to meet thee at thy coming: it stirreth up the dead for thee, even all the chief ones of the earth; it hath raised up from their thrones all the kings of the nations. [10]All they shall speak and say unto thee, Art thou also become weak as we? art thou become like unto us? [11]Thy pomp is brought down to the grave, and the noise of thy viols: the worm is spread under thee, and the worms cover thee. [12]*How art thou fallen from heaven, O Lucifer, son of the morning! how art thou cut down to the ground, which didst weaken the nations!* [13]*For thou hast said in thine heart, I will ascend into heaven, I will exalt my throne above the stars of God: I will sit also upon the mount of the congregation, in the sides of the north:* [14]*I will ascend above the heights of the clouds; I will be like the most High.* [15]Yet thou shalt be brought down to hell, to the sides of the pit. [16]They that see thee shall narrowly look upon thee, and consider thee, saying, Is this the man that made the earth to tremble, that did shake kingdoms; [17]That made the world as a wilderness, *and destroyed the cities thereof;* that opened not the house of his prisoners? [18]All the kings of the nations, even all of them, lie in glory, every one in his own house. [19]But thou art cast out of thy grave like an abominable branch, and as the raiment of those that are slain, thrust through with a sword, that go down to the stones of the pit; as a carcass trodden under feet. [20]Thou shalt not be joined with them in burial, because thou hast destroyed thy land, and slain thy people: the seed of evildoers shall never be renowned. [21]Prepare slaughter for his children for the iniquity of their fathers; that they do not rise, nor possess the land, nor fill the face of the world with cities. [22]For I will rise up against them, saith the Lord of hosts, and cut off from Babylon the name, and remnant, and son, and nephew, saith the Lord. [23]I will also make it a possession for the bittern, and pools of water: and I will sweep it with the besom [dust broom] of destruction, saith the Lord of hosts.

Isaiah 14:1-22

Isaiah 14 is a double prophecy that declares the fall of ancient Babylon just like Isaiah 13, but more than that, it is a declaration of the fall of Satan and his heavenly city in the end-times. As of yet, he has not been brought down to hell to the sides of the pit. That doesn't occur until Revelation 20:1-3 where he is cast into the bottomless pit for a thousand years, and in verse 10 of the same chapter, Satan is cast into the Lake of Fire which is the final place of unrest for all those who bring corruption and devastation upon the creation of God.

THINK ABOUT IT!

— Considering that Lucifer, or Satan, and the end of the world are tied repeatedly to Babylon, do you think that the prophecies concerning Babylon were fulfilled when ancient Babylon fell?

Selah

For we wrestle not against flesh and blood, but against principalities, against powers, against the rulers of the darkness of this world, against spiritual wickedness in high places. Wherefore take unto you the whole armour of God, that ye may be able to withstand in the evil day...

Ephesians 6:12-13

Revelation 18

Sailing to Babylon

B abylon. Past. Present. Future. Literal. Figurative. Power. Influence. Decadence. Love of money. Rebellion. Godlessness. Bondage. It's all here. A city and an empire of the past, destroyed by God. A city of the future that will rise along the banks of the Euphrates River. The kingdom of the beast. The seat of his power. Come out from her My people after she rises again. Come out of her now and do not partake of her sins.

Revelation 17 ended with the ten kings that are joined with the Antichrist showing disdain for the great whore and the city that bears her name. Their last recorded act before they meet Jesus at Armageddon is to burn the city of Babylon with fire. This chapter paints a vivid picture of the latter-day city and her consumption by flames at the hands of the ten kings.

Verse 2 takes us back to Isaiah 13:19-22, the double prophecy concerning ancient Babylon, and Satan as the ultimate spiritual being who controlled earthly Babylon from a place called Mystery Babylon in heaven. It was declared that Babylon, the glory of kingdoms, would be laid waste forever just like the cities of Sodom and Gomorrah. God proclaimed that Babylon would not be inhabited again by humans, but by wild beasts, doleful creatures and dragons. The city of Babylon in Iraq has not been inhabited again, but there will be a new Babylon in the end-times that will fall, yet, once again. That makes Isaiah a triple prophecy because it not only speaks to ancient Babylon and Mystery Babylon but the Babylon of the future. Verse 2 is a paraphrase of the last four verses of Isaiah 13, just as verse 4 is a rewording of Jeremiah 51:45 where God warns His people to go out of Babylon. In verse 4, we are told to depart from and do not partake of her sins lest we partake of her plagues also. In Jeremiah 51:45, her plagues are revealed to be the "fierce anger of the Lord."

> ¹And after these things I saw another angel come down from heaven, having great power; and the earth was lightened with his glory. ²And he cried mightily with a strong voice, saying, Babylon the great is fallen, is fallen, and is become the habitation of devils, and the hold of every foul spirit, and a cage of every unclean and hateful bird. ³For all nations have drunk of the wine of the wrath of her fornication, and the kings of the earth have committed fornication with her, and the merchants of the earth are waxed rich through the abundance of her delicacies. ⁴And I heard another voice from heaven, saying, Come out of her, my people, that ye be not partakers of her sins, and that ye receive not of her plagues. ⁵For her sins have reached unto heaven, and God hath remembered her iniquities. ⁶Reward her even as she rewarded you, and double unto her double according to her works: in the cup which she hath filled fill to her double.
>
> *Revelation 18:1-6*

The odd thing about the directive to "come out" in verse 4 is its placement near the end of the time of God's wrath—years after the Rapture has taken place. The events of Revelation 18 are not a part of the Tribulation; they are a part of the Wrath of God. Therefore, if anyone does get saved during this time, they would be saved out of God's wrath and not the Tribulation. As we have seen in various places in this study, the people who remain on the earth after the Tribulation who experience God's wrath are characterized by their anger towards God and the hardness of their hearts. Very little in the prophecies of God's wrath would indicate that anyone gets saved at all, but maybe there is hope of a lesser sort. We do have to remember that there will be a whole new generation growing up at this time, and they may be a little brighter than their parents in figuring out that you don't rebel against God and get away with it. The multitudes left on the earth at the conclusion of God's wrath, who will be ruled by Christ in His Millenial Kingdom, will experience God's wrath, but they don't experience death during His wrath. The message from verse 4 and Jeremiah 51 could be to late bloomers during God's wrath, but, more than likely, it is nothing more than a warning to every generation that we must be constantly on our toes with regards to a world system that rewards those who practice evil.

It is clear from Scripture that the concept of Mystery Babylon goes way beyond ancient Babylon and the Babylon of the future, and even the little harlot cities who are forced into a prostituted world system by corrupt leaders. Through cable, broadcast and satellite TV, the internet and radio, billions of people all over the globe are able to wallow in the corruption and filthiness of the great whore in the privacy of their own homes. There may even be a future channel called something like B-SPAN or BABEL-SPAN that will pump live shots from the heart of Babylon 24 hours a day. But you don't have to own a TV, and you don't even have to live in a city to partake of her sins. The farmer who chemically enhances his crops for a bigger yield and higher profits, with no regard to the adverse affects on humans or nature, is partaking in a corrupt world system. There may be times a farmer must consider the trade-off between using insecticides or harvesting worm-eaten fruits but that doesn't constitute a surrender to the whore or the world system that she controls. There are times people must live in cities, but that isn't a sellout to sin either. We are not being instructed to quit life and go hide in a cave. God wants us here to season and preserve life on this earth. When we partake in commerce, we should do so with God's moral codes directing our actions. If we conduct ourselves with truth, honesty and faith in God, we may be lighting the way for someone else to break free from a lifestyle that is going to be condemned. With that said, there may be times when a city, a business, an organization and even a church may become so corrupted by the ways of the great whore that there is nothing left to do but to leave.

In Verse 7, Babylon declares herself to be a queen without cares or worries, and she lavishes great wealth upon herself. There may actually be female spirits who look after the domestic part of every city and kingdom. Israel is referred to by God in the feminine gender, even though Jacob, the namesake of Israel, and Michael, the guardian angel of Israel, are both males. The male spirits are always shown ruling over nations and cities while a female counterpart—if one exists—always represents the residence or home place that the male rules over.

Verse 8 declares that the city will be burned with fire. This is talking about a very real city and the commerce that flows through her. There are very real kings of the earth and sea merchants who look on as the smoke of the city rises towards heaven. Verses 12-14 list some of the types of costly goods that will flow through this great city of trade, and then we see the merchants mourning her destruction.

> 7How much she hath glorified herself, and lived deliciously, so much torment and sorrow give her: for she saith in her heart, I sit a queen, and am no widow, and shall see no sorrow. 8Therefore shall her plagues come in one day, death, and mourning, and famine; and *she shall be utterly burned with fire*: for strong is the Lord God who judgeth her. 9And the kings of the earth, who have committed fornication and lived deliciously with her, shall bewail her, and lament for her, when *they shall see the smoke of her burning*, 10Standing afar off for the fear of her torment, saying, Alas, alas, that great city Babylon, that mighty city! for in one hour is thy judgment come. 11And the merchants of the earth shall weep and mourn over her; for no man buyeth their merchandise any more: 12The merchandise of gold, and silver, and precious stones, and of pearls, and fine linen, and purple, and silk, and scarlet, and all thyine wood, and all manner vessels of ivory, and all manner vessels of most precious wood, and of brass, and iron, and marble, 13And cinnamon, and odours, and ointments, and frankincense, and wine, and oil, and fine flour, and wheat, and beasts, and sheep, and horses, and chariots, and slaves, and souls of men. 14And the fruits that thy soul lusted after are departed from thee, and all things which were dainty and goodly are departed from thee, and thou shalt find them no more at all. 15The merchants of these things, which were made rich by her, shall stand afar off for the fear of her torment, weeping and wailing, 16And saying, Alas, alas, that great city, that was clothed in fine linen, and

purple, and scarlet, and decked with gold, and precious
stones, and pearls! [17]For in one hour so great riches is come
to nought. And every shipmaster, and all the company in
ships, and sailors, and as many as trade by sea, stood afar off,
[18]And cried when *they saw the smoke of her burning*, saying,
What city is like unto this great city! [19]And they cast dust on
their heads, and cried, weeping and wailing, saying, Alas,
alas, that great city, wherein were made rich all that had ships
in the sea by reason of her costliness! for in one hour is she
made desolate.

Revelation 18:7-19

The description of the woman brings to mind many scriptures, two
of which are shown below.

And the cares of this world, and the deceitfulness of riches,
and the lusts of other things entering in, choke the word,
and it becometh unfruitful.

Mark 4:19

Choosing rather to suffer affliction with the people of God,
than to enjoy the pleasures of sin for a season.

Hebrews 11:25

The list of merchandise that will pass through Babylon is pretty
complete. It includes food stuff, building materials, precious metals,
stones and gems, perfumes, textiles, vehicles, livestock and slaves, and
you can even sell your soul there. New Babylon will truly be one of
the greatest port cities of all time. Verse 17 mentions shipmasters,
sailors and all that trade by sea standing afar off watching Babylon
burn. Alexander the Great had intentions of dredging the Euphrates
and making ancient Babylon the capital of the Greek empire and a
great center of trade. Had he not died such a premature death, he
could very well have accomplished that goal. During the reign of the
Antichrist, New Babylon will be such a city. The verses above repeatedly state that all those involved with the city will stand afar off
watching it burn. This suggests that New Babylon will be close to the
site of the ancient Babylonian remains, as that is about 300 miles
inland and would provide plenty of standing room to watch the

show. The city could, however, be built closer to the Persian Gulf to reduce travel time up the Euphrates River.

As the trumpets and vials were being released in earlier chapters, we saw how New Babylon and the Euphrates River were inextricably linked to the events of the end-times and the activities of the Antichrist. The burning of the city seems to be one of the final events of the seventh vial, taking place just before the return of the saints to rule. The Euphrates runs right down the middle of Iraq, and the Tower of Babel and ancient Babylon are about dead center of the country. New Babylon will more than likely be near the old Babylon. Things seem to be shaping up right at this moment for New Babylon to be built. Before the U.S.-led coalition entered into battle with the brutal regime of Saddam Hussein, there was much opposition to the war from another coalition led by France. France, along with its major allies, Russia and Germany, attempted to avert war in Iraq in order to protect their financial dealings with Saddam. Now that the war is over, all the world is looking for ways to get back into Iraq for one reason alone—to make money. It doesn't matter if it is actual cash or oil for goods or if the trade involves food for survival or technology for mass destruction. As long as a payday is involved, the nations of the world are anxious to do business.

Right now the U.S. is on the moral highroad, and President Bush's intentions are just and good. He wants a Middle East free trade zone centered in Iraq for the purpose of creating a vibrant economy that will support a free Iraq. Although the idea and concept are highly commendable and is similar to what was done in Germany and Japan after World War II, the heart of Iraq may not be as repentant as that of the aforementioned. There are millions of Iraqis who will use their new freedoms for nothing but good, but if we are anywhere close to the end-times, we know there are more people in Iraq and environs who are ready to cast truth to the ground and follow after the Antichrist. If the Army Core of Engineers devises a plan to dredge the Euphrates River to facilitate the trade of a Middle East free trade port—which not only accommodates Iraq but all the nations of the Middle East—then they may be taking the first step towards building New Babylon. A port near ancient Babylon would place it near Baghdad, which is located along the Tigris River. If Baghdad sprawls over to this new port, it could be transformed into the New Babylon. Regardless of how it happens, the world is again bickering over the opportunity to get back into the morals free trading zone of Babylon and turn a profit any way they can.

Even after the devastating fire that the ten kings ignite on Babylon, there is still more peril in store for the city. God is going to take a whack at her also. Verse 21 alerts the world that Babylon will be thrown down with violence. The seventh vial indicates that the earthly city of Babylon will be divided into three parts and fall as a consequence of the great earthquake which takes place about the end of the Wrath of God. Babylon's fall will predate the Battle of Armageddon by just a small amount of time, perhaps just days, weeks or months. In verse 20, the heavens are encouraged to rejoice over the fall of Babylon. All of God's redeemed will be in heaven at this time enjoying the Marriage Supper of the Lamb, but we will be aware of what is taking place on the earth as it happens. The final downfall of Babylon will be a true Kodak moment because of its symbolism. Satan's last stronghold is being destroyed, and soon heaven will empty of all its warring saints who will take back the earth from his deceived multitudes.

> [20]Rejoice over her, thou heaven, and ye holy apostles and prophets; for God hath avenged you on her. [21]And a mighty angel took up a stone like a great millstone, and cast it into the sea, saying, Thus with violence shall that great city Babylon be thrown down, and shall be found no more at all. [22]And the voice of harpers, and musicians, and of pipers, and trumpeters, shall be heard no more at all in thee; and no craftsman, of whatsoever craft he be, shall be found any more in thee; and the sound of a millstone shall be heard no more at all in thee; [23]And the light of a candle shall shine no more at all in thee; and the voice of the bridegroom and of the bride shall be heard no more at all in thee: for thy merchants were the great men of the earth; for by thy sorceries were all nations deceived. [24]And in her was found the blood of prophets, and of saints, and of all that were slain upon the earth.
>
> *Revelation 18:20-24*

One last thought before we move on. In verse 23, we see that the nations are deceived by the sorceries of this great city of trade in particular and Mystery Babylon in general. The Greek word for sorceries is *pharmakeia* from which we derive the word pharmacy. The definition involves a combination of medication, magic, and witchcraft. It seems that drug and alcohol abuse, along with demonic powers, are working together to make this city and the whole system work for Satan's glory. Babylon may end up having a 24/7/365 Mardi Gras or carnival atmosphere. Although the new and old Babylon and some of the other ancient cities of Iraq may be on the tour maps of cruise ships and airliners, this is not a place for Christian sightseeing tours, pleasure cruises and shopping sprees.

THINK ABOUT IT!

— In this chapter, is Babylon a symbolic city or a real city that carries a lot of symbolism?

— If it is only symbolic, why would God go to such lengths to describe the destruction of the city, the merchandise of the city and the main means of transporting the merchandise, especially since sea trade is not a hallmark of Babylon?

— Do you think there will be another Babylon in the future?

Selah

Be ye not unequally yoked together with unbelievers: for what fellowship hath righteousness with unrighteousness? and what communion hath light with darkness? And what concord hath Christ with Belial? or what part hath he that believeth with an infidel? And what agreement hath the temple of God with idols? for ye are the temple of the living God; as God hath said, I will dwell in them, and walk in them; and I will be their God, and they shall be my people. Wherefore come out from among them, and be ye separate, saith the Lord, and touch not the unclean thing; and I will receive you, And will be a Father unto you, and ye shall be my sons and daughters, saith the Lord Almighty.

2 Corinthians 6:14-18

Wedding Feasts and War Plans

Though I was in a free fall myself, I am still amazed at how far people can actually fall from the goodness of God. I am also amazed at the depth of deception that people come under. I have looked some people straight in the eye and told them a simple Bible truth, and instead of receiving it, they dig around in their minds for some way to counter it. You can tell that they do not want the truth, but you have to give it to them anyway. One day it may save their lives.

The first half of chapter 19 is about the Marriage Supper of the Lamb. Verses 1, 4, 5 and 6 show all of God's redeemed gathered in heaven, giving praise unto God along with the four beasts, who apparently spend all of their time before the Throne of God worshipping Him. The reason the marriage supper doesn't show up until chapter 19 is because we are catching the tail end of it. You'll recall that at the end of Revelation 18 the city of Babylon was being burned, and we pointed out that the great earthquake of the seventh trumpet/vial combination was about to tear the city into three parts and leave it in ruins. All who are in heaven are told to rejoice over the final destruction of Babylon because she has shed the blood of the prophets. That's where we enter into this scene of the marriage supper. In the first three verses everyone in heaven begins to praise God over His judgment of the great whore that concludes with the destruction of the end-times city. The great whore has been judged, but the final battle of this age has not yet taken place. The destruction and removal of Satan's place in heaven, before the Tribulation ever began, set in motion the process of final salvation for the saints, which includes a cleansing of God's creation of all those things that oppose God and His redeemed. With the fall of the earthly city, the process is nearly completed. All that is left is the Battle of Armageddon.

God's wrath did not begin to pour forth until the last saint stepped off the white cloud shuttle that transports the raptured saints from earth to heaven. The marriage celebration of the Lamb begins as soon as we are raptured, and takes place during the same time that God's wrath is being poured out. We saw earlier that the two witnesses would not complete their prophecy until six years, two months, and five days have elapsed on the Wrath of God. We then assumed that God's wrath would more than likely be a full seven years. Jewish wedding celebrations involve a full week of activities, being modeled after heavenly things. A week of years is seven years, so we should be looking forward to a full seven years of festivities when we arrive in heaven, while the earth gets hammered with wrath.

> [1]And after these things I heard a great voice of much people in heaven, saying, Alleluia; salvation, and glory, and honor, and power, unto the Lord our God: [2]For true and righteous are his judgments: for he hath judged the great whore, which did corrupt the earth with her fornication, and hath avenged the blood of his servants at her hand. [3]And again they said, Alleluia. And her smoke rose up for ever and ever. [4]And the four and twenty elders and the four beasts fell down and worshipped God that sat on the throne, saying, Amen; Alleluia. [5]And a voice came out of the throne, saying, Praise our God, all ye his servants, and ye that fear him, both small and great. [6]And I heard as it were the voice of a great multitude, and as the voice of many waters, and as the voice of mighty thunderings, saying, Alleluia: for the Lord God omnipotent reigneth.
>
> *Revelation 19:1-6*

In verse 8 of the following scriptures, we discover that the Bride of the Lamb is arrayed in fine linen, which is the righteousness of the saints. It does not say that the saints are the bride but that the righteousness Jesus bestowed upon us will clothe her. Not until chapter 21 do we discover the bride is New Jerusalem. In 1 Peter 2:4-5, we are called "living stones" that are part of a spiritual house with Jesus being the chief cornerstone, but that does not make us New Jerusalem. If that were so, Jesus would be a part of the bride Himself as the chief cornerstone. In 2 Corinthians 11:2, Paul tells us that he has "espoused you to one husband, that I may present you as a chaste virgin to Christ." However, that is just one of many figurative statements make throughout the Scriptures about the Church and its relationship to the Lord. Jesus referred to us as virgins in a wedding party and bridesmaids in the bride's chamber waiting for the bridegroom, and not all of those were allowed into the wedding. He also described us as friends of the groom, laborers, stewards, children, sheep, kings, priests, branches on the vine and so on. More literally we are the body of Christ—masculine, not the bride, feminine. When we are introduced to the bride, we are given a literal physical description of New Jerusalem coming down out of heaven after the Millennial Reign. As soon as this wedding feast ends, we are going to be real warriors on real white horses fighting a real battle. That's a heck of a way to treat your new bride—to lead her into battle—but we are not the bride; we are going to prepare a safe dwelling place for the bride before she descends from heaven. Verse 9 says that we are blessed just to be called to the marriage supper, which reduces us from the bride status to that of guests.

> 7Let us be glad and rejoice, and give honor to him: for the marriage of the Lamb is come, and his wife hath made herself ready. 8And to her was granted that she should be arrayed in fine linen, clean and white: for the fine linen is the righteousness of saints. 9And he saith unto me, Write, Blessed are they which are called unto the marriage supper of the Lamb. And he saith unto me, These are the true sayings of God. 10And I fell at his feet to worship him. And he said unto me, See thou do it not: I am thy fellowservant, and of thy brethren that have the testimony of

Jesus: worship God: for the testimony of Jesus is the spirit of prophecy.

Revelation 19:7-10

As the Marriage Supper of the Lamb finishes up, the saints will have to prep themselves for a little after-dinner activity. Jesus will soon depart for heaven en route to Armageddon with His army, comprised of both His saints and the angels of God. The saints are clothed in the same fine white linen worn at the wedding and are now returning to the earth with Jesus in verse 14: First, to fight the great battle, and then to reign with Him a thousand years. There clearly is no hope for the armies fighting at Armageddon. Even after all the judgments poured forth by God, the only thing they want to do is go to war again, this time against Jesus and His armies.

In verse 15, the scripture says that He shall rule the nations with a rod of iron. Nowhere does it say that all mankind will be destroyed during God's wrath or the Battle of Armageddon. There will be people left living, perhaps billions, who will be ruled by Jesus and His saints.

> [11]And I saw heaven opened, and behold a white horse; and he that sat upon him was called Faithful and True, and in righteousness he doth judge and make war. [12]His eyes were as a flame of fire, and on his head were many crowns; and he had a name written, that no man knew, but he himself. [13]And he was clothed with a vesture dipped in blood: and his name is called The Word of God. [14]And the armies which were in heaven followed him upon white horses, clothed in fine linen, white and clean. [15]And out of his mouth goeth a sharp sword, that with it he should smite the nations: and he shall rule them with a rod of iron: and he treadeth the winepress of the fierceness and wrath of Almighty God.
>
> *Revelation 19:11-15*

How can Jesus rule the nations with a rod of iron if they are all destroyed in the battle? The answer is—they're not. The soldiers will be completely decimated, but the world will still be populated by the nations that sent these soldiers to fight for them. The statement in verse 15 about treading the winepress of the Wrath of God takes us back to the end of Revelation 14 where we saw two reapings taking place. The first was a reaping of believers as Jesus came upon a cloud to reap His elect. The second was to reap sinners and cast them into the great winepress of the Wrath of God. We were told there that the blood flow would be as high as a horse's bridle and two hundred miles long.

> [16]And he hath on his vesture and on his thigh a name written, KING OF KINGS, AND LORD OF LORDS. [17]And I saw an angel standing in the sun; and he cried with a loud voice, saying to all the fowls that fly in the midst of heaven, Come and gather yourselves together unto the supper of the great God; [18]That ye may eat the flesh of kings, and the flesh of captains, and the flesh of mighty men, and the flesh of horses, and of them that sit on them, and the flesh of all men, both free and bond, both small and great. [19]And I saw the beast, and the kings of the earth, and their armies, *gathered together to make war against him that sat on the horse, and against his army.*
>
> *Revelation 19:16-19*

Verse 19 clearly defines the reason that the armies of the earth are gathered at Armageddon in the first place: to meet Jesus and the armies of heaven when they return to the earth to reign. In Revelation 16:13, we saw the three foul spirits from the mouths of the dragon, beast and false prophet go to gather the armies of the earth to Armageddon, but ultimately, it is God who draws them there. He is the one who designates the place, and He uses the anger of sinners and the deception of Satan to draw them into the place of their destruction. In the book of Joel, God issues a decree to the sinners of the end-times to beat their plows into swords and to gather together to meet the saints who will come down to engage them in war. Joel calls the heathen to the valley of Jehoshaphat, which means "Jehovah judged." This is speaking of the same general location in Israel as Megiddo, which means "rendezvous," and Armageddon, which means "mountain range of rendezvous." Because the blood flow from the battle will be two hundred miles long, that would stretch nearly the entire length of Israel from north to south. Jesus is going to drench the soil of Israel with the blood of His enemies.

The word "thither" in the second half of verse 11 means "there" or "that very place." This verse announces that after sinners have gathered themselves for the battle, God is going to cause His mighty warriors to come down to that very same place where they have gathered. Joel is proclaiming that all people will have made their decision before the Day of the Lord ever arrives. That day begins when the sun and moon are darkened and the Church is raptured at the first appearing of Jesus Christ. It continues throughout the entire time of God's wrath until Jesus' second appearing at the final Battle of Armageddon.

> [9]Proclaim ye this among the Gentiles; Prepare war, wake up the mighty men, let all the men of war draw near; let them come up: [10]Beat your plowshares into swords, and your pruning hooks into spears: let the weak say, I am strong. [11]*Assemble yourselves, and come, all ye heathen, and gather yourselves* together round about: *thither* cause thy mighty ones to come down, O Lord. [12]Let the heathen be wakened, and come up to the valley of Jehoshaphat: for there will I sit to judge all the heathen round about. [13]Put ye in the sickle, for the harvest is ripe: come, get you down; for the press is full, the fats overflow; for their wickedness is great. [14]Multitudes, multitudes in the valley of decision: for the day of the Lord is near in the valley of decision. [15]The sun and the moon shall be darkened, and the stars shall withdraw their shining. [16]The Lord also shall roar out of Zion, and utter his voice from Jerusalem; and the heavens and the earth shall shake: but the Lord will be the hope of his people, and the strength of the children of Israel. [17]So shall ye know that I am the Lord your God dwelling in Zion, my holy mountain: then shall Jerusalem be holy, and there shall no strangers pass through her any more.
>
> *Joel 3:9-17*

It's interesting to note in verses 9-12 in the Scriptures above that God is calling the heathen to convert their farm tools into weapons of war as He calls them to the final great Battle of Armageddon. How often do we hear those who are not living for the Lord quote the passages from Isaiah 2:4 and Micah 4:3, which speak of converting weapons of war into farm implements. The heathen quote Micah and Isaiah thinking that they are the ones who will bring in this golden age of peace in their own power and wisdom. In free societies, they love to ridicule strong governments that stand up for peace and civil authorities who keep the peace. They call for unilateral disarmament while totally ignoring the dangers presented by those who are more evil and deceived than themselves, not to mention the wicked spirits who thrive on chaos and destruction. Before the day that weapons can be converted into farm tools, the farm tools must be fashioned into weapons, as the heathen prepare for the great battle to come when Jesus returns with His armies to bind Satan and rule according to the dictates of God so there can finally be real peace on the earth.

> ³And He shall judge among many people, and rebuke
> strong nations afar off; and they shall beat their swords
> into plowshares, and their spears into pruning hooks:
> nation shall not lift up a sword against nation, neither shall
> they learn war any more. ⁴But they shall sit every man
> under his vine and under his fig tree; and none shall make
> them afraid: for the mouth of the Lord of hosts hath spo-
> ken it. ⁵For all people will walk every one in the name of
> his god, and we will walk in the name of the Lord our God
> for ever and ever.
>
> *Micah 4:3-5*

Joel 2:1-11 describes the same battle scene as Revelation 19. He is describing the army of saints coming together to fight the Battle of Armageddon at the end of the time of wrath. Verses 1 and 2 are not describing the shaking of the heavens that begin the Day of the Lord, but rather a dark and gloomy day for the armies of the earth, both literally and figuratively, as Jesus returns to reign on the earth. The literal darkness includes thick clouds and skies darkened by the approaching armies of heaven. It could also include a catastrophic result from the angel casting a huge millstone into the ocean, which is recorded in Revelation 18:21 and takes place before the Battle of

Armageddon. The figurative is expounded upon in verse 6 where the faces of the soldiers on earth are filled with pain and darkness. Verse 11 declares that the Lord shall utter His voice before His army, and verse 2 tells us that nothing shall escape from before them. Verses 4 and 5 describe the same army of saints from Revelation 19 who mount up on white horses and ride out of heaven with their Lord. Verse 10 describes the heavenly lights that cease to shine at the first appearing of the Lord for the Rapture. This is one of those places in Scripture where the full spectrum of the events of the Wrath of God is condensed to include just the beginning and the end, without all of the other details we learn from the Book of Revelation.

> [15]Alas for the day! for *the Day of the Lord* is at hand, and as a destruction from the Almighty shall it come.
>
> *Joel 1:15*

> [1]Blow ye the trumpet in Zion, and sound an alarm in my holy mountain: let all the inhabitants of the land tremble: for the Day of the Lord cometh, for it is nigh at hand; [2]A day of darkness and of gloominess, a day of clouds and of thick darkness, as the morning spread upon the mountains: a great people and a strong; there hath not been ever the like, neither shall be any more after it, even to the years of many generations. [3]A fire devoureth before them; and behind them a flame burneth: the land is as the garden of Eden before them, and behind them a desolate wilderness; yea, and *nothing shall escape them.* [4]The appearance of them is as the appearance of horses; and as horsemen, so shall they run. [5]Like the noise of chariots on the tops of mountains shall they leap, like the noise of a flame of fire that devoureth the stubble, as a strong people set in battle array. [6]Before their face the people shall be much pained: all faces shall gather blackness. [7]They shall run like mighty men; they shall climb the wall like men of war; and they shall march every one on his ways, and they shall not break their ranks: [8]Neither shall one thrust another; they shall walk every one in his path: and when they fall upon the sword, they shall not be wounded. [9]They shall run to

and fro in the city; they shall run upon the wall, they shall climb up upon the houses; they shall enter in at the windows like a thief. [10]The earth shall quake before them; the heavens shall tremble: the sun and the moon shall be dark, and the stars shall withdraw their shining: [11]And *the* Lord shall utter his voice before his army: for his camp is very great: for he is strong that executeth his word: for the Day of the Lord is great and very terrible; and who can abide it?

Joel 2:1-11

The following portion of Scripture from Thessalonians has caused confusion for many. Before it can make sense, you have to believe that Jesus will be revealed from heaven twice. The first time He appears in His full glory for all to see as He approaches the earth to rescue His elect. This first appearance brings an abrupt halt to the Tribulation and makes ready for the Wrath of God. Jesus never sets foot on the earth during His first appearing. His second appearing is on His white horse to wage a righteous war against sinners. The passage from Thessalonians also reveals to us that He will appear in flames of fire as He comes to take vengeance on those who refuse to obey the gospel. So His first appearance ushers in the Wrath of God as He removes the saints out of the earth, and the second appearing brings an end to the Wrath of God as He leads the saints back into the earth to rule with Him. Verse 10 of 2 Thessalonians 1 tells us that He is revealed with His mighty angels when He comes for vengeance. In the Gospels, we learn that these same angels that accompany Jesus when He comes for vengeance also accompany Him when He comes the first time to gather His elect. In verse 14 of Revelation 19, we see that the saints of God mount up and follow the Lord when He returns for war. When Jesus leaves the Marriage Supper of the Lamb, both the angels and the saints will accompany Him to the battle. The angels will be fighting a war against the spirit world, even to the point of taking Satan and throwing him into the bottomless pit while the saints fight against the people who reject His lordship.

One of the reasons the following scriptures have caused confusion is because of the use of the word "tribulation" when it says, "it is a righteous thing with God to recompense tribulation to them that trouble you." Many believe that means God is going to give them the Great Tribulation as a punishment. However, the words "tribulation" and "trouble" are the exact same words. The troubles, persecutions and tribulations that the saints endure at the end of this age at the hands of the ungodly are the Great Tribulation. The recompense, or payback, that God gives to sinners is the Wrath of God. God's wrath doesn't just wipe out sinners in an instant, but it lasts for years. It is a long-term troubling that is a punishment against sinners. Many will die, but many will live through the whole time of wrath and must endure the troubling of God right up to the end. God is not giving them "The Great Tribulation" but paying them back for the Great Tribulation and all the other tribulation that sinners have caused throughout the ages. Romans 12:19 says, " 'Dearly beloved, avenge not yourselves, but rather give place unto wrath: for it is written, Vengeance is mine; I will repay,' saith the Lord."

> [4]So that we ourselves glory in you in the churches of God for your patience and faith in all your persecutions and tribulations that ye endure: [5]Which is a manifest token of the righteous judgment of God, that ye may be counted worthy of the kingdom of God, for which ye also suffer: [6]Seeing it is a righteous thing with God to recompense tribulation to them that trouble you; [7]And to you who are troubled rest with us, when the Lord Jesus shall be revealed from heaven with his mighty angels, [8]In flaming fire taking vengeance on them that know not God, and that obey not the gospel of our Lord Jesus Christ: [9]Who shall be punished with everlasting destruction from the presence of the Lord, and from the glory of his power; [10]When he shall come to be glorified in his saints, and to be admired in all them that believe because our testimony among you was believed in that day.
>
> *2 Thessalonians 1:4-10*

The book of Jude is one more place that tells us Jesus will return with His saints for war as part of His vengeance against the ungodly. Again, this is at the end of years of punishment that sinners must endure.

¹⁴And Enoch also, the seventh from Adam, prophesied of these, saying, Behold, the Lord cometh with ten thousands of his saints, ¹⁵To execute judgment upon all, and to convince all that are ungodly among them of all their ungodly deeds which they have ungodly committed, and of all their hard speeches which ungodly sinners have spoken against Him.

Jude 1:14

As we finish up Revelation 19, we see the beast and the false prophet cast alive into the Lake of Fire. The fact that they are cast directly into the lake suggests that they are spiritual beings rather than human beings, although they will appear and move about as men. The rest of lost humanity is resurrected unto the White Throne Judgment of Jesus Christ and then cast into the Lake of Fire. Satan is the only other creature cast directly into the Lake of Fire without facing the White Throne Judgment. The beast and false prophet seem to be in the same class of beings as Satan rather than mankind. They could actually be Antiochus and some other despot resurrected from the bottomless pit, which makes them fully equipped with their eternal bodies and ready for the bottomless pit, if they are in fact men.

The Battle of Armageddon and the removal of the beast and false prophet bring an end to approximately fourteen years of time that the Antichrist has ruled on the earth to varying degrees—the seven years leading up to the Rapture, which includes the seven-year peace treaty and the Tribulation that begins in the middle of it, and then the seven years of wrath afterwards. All of the armies that gather together under the leadership of the Antichrist are destroyed in the battle. The remnant mentioned in verse 21 is talking only of the soldiers that have come to wage war against Christ. They are the ones destroyed at this time. The fact that they are all destroyed clearly illustrates that this is a different battle from the battle of Gog and Magog where a sixth of the army survives to retreat in shame. In Joel 1:3, the difference between Armageddon and the battle of Gog is evident when it states that "nothing shall escape them" during that final war at Megiddo. The rest of mankind that have survived the Wrath of God will be a ragtag, bruised and battered bunch. They will be the subjects of the everlasting kingdom that Jesus and his saints have come to establish.

²⁰And the beast was taken, and with him the false prophet that wrought miracles before him, with which he deceived them that had received the mark of the beast, and them that worshipped his image. These both were cast alive into a lake of fire burning with brimstone. ²¹And the remnant were slain with the sword of him that sat upon the horse, which sword proceeded out of his mouth: and all the fowls were filled with their flesh.

Revelation 19:20-21

Zechariah provides us with another view of the second return of Jesus as He conquers the heathen that have congregated at Jerusalem with the sword of His mouth. This passage begins with the Great Tribulation and ends with Jesus setting up His millennial kingdom and reigning with a rod of iron in verses 16-21. The first verse simply states that the Day of the Lord is approaching. The second verse describes the fall of Jerusalem during the Great Tribulation. The same destruction of Jerusalem is described in Luke 21:20-24 where Jesus warns His people to flee to the mountains when they see the armies of the Antichrist surround the city. He declares that those who remain will fall by the sword or be led captive into other nations. He further declares that the city will be trodden by the Gentiles until their time is complete. That is partially a reference to the 2300 days of no sacrifices that end when the two witnesses show up during the Wrath of God to cleanse the temple. However, the two witnesses do not cleanse the city. It remains under the firm control of the Antichrist until the end of the Wrath of God when Jesus returns. Any Jews that escape death in the city will remain under the power of the Antichrist until Jesus returns.

¹Behold, the day of the Lord cometh, and thy spoil shall be divided in the midst of thee. ²For I will gather all nations against Jerusalem to battle; and the city shall be taken, and the houses rifled, and the women ravished; and half of the city shall go forth into captivity, and the residue of the people shall not be cut off from the city.

Zechariah 14:1-21

Next, we fast forward to the Battle of Armageddon where the Lord and His saints descend out of heaven to wage war. As the saints are fighting the battle against the armies of the earth and the angels are fighting against the demon world—throwing the beast and false prophet into the Lake of Fire and Satan into the bottomless pit—Jesus will descend and set foot upon the mount of Olives to remain on earth and reign forever.

> [3]Then shall the Lord go forth, and fight against those nations, as when he fought in the day of battle. [4]And His feet shall stand in that day upon the mount of Olives, which is before Jerusalem on the east, and the mount of Olives shall cleave in the midst thereof toward the east and toward the west, and there shall be a very great valley; and half of the mountain shall remove toward the north, and half of it toward the south. [5]And ye shall flee to the valley of the mountains; for the valley of the mountains shall reach unto Azal: yea, ye shall flee, like as ye fled from before the earthquake in the days of Uzziah king of Judah: and the Lord my God shall come, and all the saints with thee. [6]And it shall come to pass in that day, that the light shall not be clear, nor dark: [7]But it shall be one day which shall be known to the Lord, not day, nor night: but it shall come to pass, that at evening time it shall be light.

The next four verses declare that Jesus will rule forever from Jerusalem. The description of how things will be must be literal for the Millennial Reign because afterwards there will be no seas on the new earth that God will create.

> [8]And it shall be in that day, that living waters shall go out from Jerusalem; half of them toward the former sea, and half of them toward the hinder sea: in summer and in winter shall it be. [9]And the Lord shall be king over all the earth: in that day shall there be one Lord, and his name one. [10]All the land shall be turned as a plain from Geba to Rimmon south of Jerusalem: and it shall be lifted up, and

inhabited in her place, from Benjamin's gate unto the place
of the first gate, unto the corner gate, and from the tower
of Hananeel unto the king's winepresses. ¹¹And men shall
dwell in it, and there shall be no more utter destruction;
but Jerusalem shall be safely inhabited.

Verses 12-15 backtrack a little to give a casualty report from the
war. Joel 1:3 declares of the saints in the battle that "a fire devoureth
before them; and behind them a flame burneth." In the next verse, we
see that the enemy will just consume away at the onslaught of the
saints. Verse 14 tells us that the wealth of the heathen will be gathered
as booty to rebuild the new residence of Jesus Christ and His saints.
That would include the salvageable wealth from Babylon.

> ¹²And this shall be the plague wherewith the Lord will
> smite all the people that have fought against Jerusalem;
> Their flesh shall consume away while they stand upon
> their feet, and their eyes shall consume away in their holes,
> and their tongue shall consume away in their mouth.
> ¹³And it shall come to pass in that day, that a great tumult
> from the Lord shall be among them; and they shall lay
> hold every one on the hand of his neighbor, and his hand
> shall rise up against the hand of his neighbor. ¹⁴And Judah
> also shall fight at Jerusalem; and the wealth of all the hea-
> then round about shall be gathered together, gold, and sil-
> ver, and apparel, in great abundance. ¹⁵And so shall be the
> plague of the horse, of the mule, of the camel, and of the
> ass, and of all the beasts that shall be in these tents, as this
> plague.

Once again we see that there will be nations left after the Battle of
Armageddon. People—not land—are what make a nation, both dur-
ing the Millennial Reign and perhaps forever after. Even after New
Jerusalem descends to the earth, and the nations of the earth come to
Jerusalem to worship the Lord.

> ¹⁶And it shall come to pass, that *every one that is left of all
> the nations which came against Jerusalem* shall even go up

from year to year to worship the King, the Lord of hosts, and to keep the feast of tabernacles. [17]And it shall be, that whoso will not come up of all the families of the earth unto Jerusalem to worship the King, the Lord of hosts, even upon them shall be no rain. [18]And if the family of Egypt go not up, and come not, that have no rain; there shall be the plague, wherewith the Lord will smite the heathen that come not up to keep the feast of tabernacles. [19]This shall be the punishment of Egypt, and the punishment of all nations that come not up to keep the feast of tabernacles. [20]In that day shall there be upon the bells of the horses, HOLINESS UNTO THE LORD; and the pots in the Lord's house shall be like the bowls before the altar. [21]Yea, every pot in Jerusalem and in Judah shall be holiness unto the Lord of hosts: and all they that sacrifice shall come and take of them, and seethe therein: and in that day there shall be no more the Canaanite in the house of the Lord of hosts.

THINK ABOUT IT!

— How long does a Jewish wedding last?

— Does this wedding begin or end in Revelation 19?

— Is it possible that it began earlier when all of the wedding guests had arrived together?

— Is this the first time Jesus leaves heaven to return to the earth?

— If so, how did all of the wedding guests arrive?

— Is Jesus going to rapture anyone on this trip to the earth?

— If so, does that mean that they were left out of the wedding?

— What is the stated purpose for Jesus and His saints returning to the earth?

— Does this begin or end the Wrath of God, or is this all there is to it?

Selah

The Lord shall go forth as a mighty man, he shall stir up jealousy like a man of war: he shall cry, yea, roar; he shall prevail against his enemies.

Isaiah 42:13

REVELATION 20

———•——•——

Victory and Judgment

S ome people feel that I am very critical, but I am not trying to judge, I am just a very analytical thinker. I want to understand things and know how they work. I want to understand God, I want to understand faith, I want to understand the spirit world, I want to understand prophecy and I want to understand how they all work and interact. While many people often jump to conclusions, or are satisfied with simply being taught and trained, I'm looking more in-depth and asking why? I want to know that I know the truth. When reading the Bible there should be an interaction between the heart and soul. You can analyze and ask questions with your mind, but you cannot determine the truth and figure out the Scriptures with your mind. You can absorb the Word of God into your heart, but if you don't think about it and inquire of God, you may never understand it. Understanding the Scriptures comes from one source—the Spirit of God. Jesus said the Holy Spirit would lead us into truth, guide us and show us things to come. Without the involvement of the Holy Spirit, there can be no understanding of the Scriptures. The carnal mind is enmity against God and it cannot understand the things of God. Through the interaction between our spirits, the Holy Spirit, the Word of God and our thought process, we can be renewed in the spirit of our minds. The Bible says we can know the love of God that passes understanding. I am satisfied with just knowing His love in my heart without understanding it with my head, but I am learning how love works.

After the Battle of Armageddon, Satan—that old serpent, which is the devil—is bound in a chain and cast into the bottomless pit where he is unable to cause any more trouble for the next 1000 years. Although it does not specifically say that the demons and fallen angels that follow Satan are cast into the bottomless pit, it should be assumed that his lying little helpers must be with him and equally restrained if the deception of Satan stops while he is locked away in the pit.

> ¹And I saw an angel come down from heaven, having the key of the bottomless pit and a great chain in his hand.
> ²And he laid hold on the dragon, that old serpent, which is the Devil, and Satan, and bound him a thousand years,
> ³And cast him into the bottomless pit, and shut him up, and set a seal upon him, that he should deceive the nations no more, till the thousand years should be fulfilled: and after that he must be loosed a little season.
>
> *Revelation 20:1-3*

The next few verses inform us that the saints will reign with Christ for 1000 years. The thrones set up are those from which the saints will rule, alongside their Lord, for the thousand-year period between the Battle of Armageddon and the White Throne Judgment. The thrones have nothing to do with the White Throne Judgment. When that final judgment takes place, the righteous will stand before the Lord on the opposite side of the Throne Room from the wicked. Romans 14:10 says that we shall all stand before the judgment seat of Christ. Even though verse 4 describes the saints that reign with Christ—as though only those who successfully go through the Great Tribulation will be included in the Millennial Reign—verse 6 lets us know that all saints, from every age, are part of this ruling class of nobility. It declares that those who take part in the first resurrection are a part of the thousand-year reign and that they are exempt from the second death. As we saw earlier, those who are a part of the first resurrection includes those who have already died before Christ returns to rapture His Church and all of those who are alive and remain at His coming. That's everyone who is saved!

Not until after the thousand-year reign are the dead without Christ (sinners) resurrected to the final judgment. We learned in the last chapter that not everyone who is on the earth when Jesus returns a second time with his saints will be destroyed. Jesus will defeat the spiritual armies of Satan and the human armies of the Antichrist and then take the kingdom to Himself, or in other words, take charge of the earth and rule forever.

> ⁴And I saw thrones, and they sat upon them, and judgment was given unto them: and I saw the souls of them that were beheaded for the witness of Jesus, and for the word of God, and which had not worshipped the beast, neither his image, neither had received his mark upon their foreheads, or in their hands; and *they lived and reigned with Christ a thousand years.* ⁵But the rest of the dead lived not again until the thousand years were finished. This is the first resurrection. ⁶*Blessed and holy is he that hath part in the first resurrection: on such the second death hath no power, but they shall be priests of God and of Christ, and shall reign with Him a thousand years.*
>
> *Revelation 20:4-6*

In verses 7-9, Satan is given one last chance to deceive the nations. It's important to remember that the people he is deceiving are those that have had 1000 years of the peace of God on earth, living with Jesus and the glorified saints. If they are not the very ones who survived the Wrath of God (1 Corinthians 15:25-26 and 54 all maintain that Jesus completely defeats death at the Resurrection of the just, and these people will not die unless He wants them to), then they are the descendants of those who survived the wrath. They've heard the stories, they've interacted with the saints, they've seen Jesus with their own eyes and they know the truth. Now they are being deceived for the first time in 1000 years with all advance warning, and yet so many of them choose to follow the lies of Satan and are destroyed by fire. The people that live on the earth, whom Christ and His saints will reign over during the Millennial Reign, start out as heathens just as the saints once were. It is not clear whether the people who survive the wrath are given the same opportunity for salvation as we are given before the Rapture takes place, but it is clear by the response of many at the end of the 1000 years that, even with evil being held in check by the government that God will establish with His Son at the helm, many will still despise the rule of God in their hearts.

We know firsthand how difficult it is to live as new creations in a fallen world with the temptations that come at us everyday, but what will it be like for sinners of the new millennium when there is no temptation, where they will be able to see Jesus with their eyes and yet the old sin nature will continue to be a part of their lives? If God is still offering salvation through the everlasting gospel, it must be a lot easier for them to believe and be saved, but will it be permanent? For all of us during this present age until the day we die, we can always reject God after being saved and go back to our old nature of sin—not just backsliding, but telling God we do not want Him in our lives anymore. Our salvation is assured to us as long as we continue to hold to it, but it is not completely sealed until after we die and become the glorified saints of God. Will this be true for the people of the Millennium? What will the Millennium be like? After the dragon, the beast and prophet are removed from the earth, there will be no tempter for 1000 years; therefore, righteousness will be able to flourish for generations. However, the unregenerate nature of mankind will remain a part of the Millennium, and that in itself will spell trouble at the end.

> ⁷And when the thousand years are expired, Satan shall be loosed out of his prison, ⁸And shall go out to deceive the nations which are in the four quarters of the earth, Gog and Magog, to gather them together to battle: the number of whom is as the sand of the sea. ⁹And they went up on the breadth of the earth, and compassed the camp of the saints about, and the beloved city: and fire came down from God out of heaven, and devoured them. ¹⁰And the devil that deceived them was cast into the lake of fire and brimstone, where the beast and the false prophet are, and shall be tormented day and night for ever and ever.
>
> *Revelation 20:7-10*

Satan will finally be discarded forever. Praise God! And the great White Throne Judgment follows. The saints are gathered on the right hand of the Lord and invited to enter into the joy of their Lord, while all the dead are gathered to His left side and then cast into the Lake of Fire. We are all judged for our works, but only those who are found in the Book of Life will live forever. Those not found in the Book of Life will experience the second death of eternal damnation in a resurrected body that will experience the pains of death—the fire is not quenched, and their worm dieth not—forever.

First Corinthians 6:2-3 tells us that the saints will judge the world, but it is speaking more to the time of the Millennium when they are seated on their thrones to rule and judge the people of the Millennium and perhaps beyond the Millennium. The righteousness of the saints, which they receive through faith in Jesus Christ, will be the standard by which sinners are judged.

> [11]And I saw a great white throne, and him that sat on it, from whose face the earth and the heaven fled away; and there was found no place for them. [12]And I saw the dead, small and great, stand before God; and the books were opened: and another book was opened, which is the book of life: and the dead were judged out of those things which were written in the books, according to their works. [13]And the sea gave up the dead which were in it; and death and hell delivered up the dead which were in them: and they were judged every man according to their works. [14]And death and hell were cast into the lake of fire. This is the second death. [15]And whosoever was not found written in the book of life was cast into the lake of fire.
>
> *Revelation 20:11-15*

No second chances. Death and hell are cast into the Lake of Fire, along with all those who reject God and His plan of salvation. First Corinthians 3:11-15 tells us that Jesus Christ is the foundation upon which our lives will be judged. Our acceptance of Him as Lord and Saviour is what gets our name written in the Lamb's Book of Life. All the works we do in this life that survive the judgment of God are built upon the foundation of the gospel and our submission and servitude to Jesus Christ. Everything else will be destroyed by fire, which leads us into the next chapter.

> [11]For other foundation can no man lay than that is laid, which is Jesus Christ. [12]Now if any man build upon this foundation gold, silver, precious stones, wood, hay, stubble; [13]Every man's work shall be made manifest: for the day shall declare it, because it shall be revealed by fire; and the fire shall try every man's work of what sort it is. [14]If any man's work abide which he hath built thereupon, he shall receive a reward. [15]If any man's work shall be burned, he shall suffer loss: but he himself shall be saved; yet so as by fire.
>
> *1 Corinthians 3:11-15*

THINK ABOUT IT!

— Is Satan literally bound in the bottomless pit for a thousand years?

— If so, is it the same pit where the beast is bound right now?

— Does the final judgment of all mankind take place at the end of the thousand years?

— In 2 Peter 3 where Peter said that a day is as a thousand years with the Lord, he also also seems to suggest that the heavens and the earth would be dissolved in the Day of the Lord when Christ returns. In this chapter and the next we see that there is a thousand years between the return of Christ and the judgment, at which time the old earth is replaced by the new. Which is literal and which figurative?

Selah

Because he hath appointed a day, in the which he will judge the world in righteousness by that man whom he hath ordained; whereof he hath given assurance unto all men, in that he hath raised him from the dead.

Acts 17:31

The Lamb's Wife, a Home for God

I sometimes think about what life will be like on the new earth. If we are to reign with Christ forever and ever, who and what do we reign over? Will God preserve the fallen lineage of Adam after the White Throne Judgment? Do we reign over them? If we have mansions in the city of God, do we spend the night there and return to our work in the morning? Will we be able to choose or even create the environment we work in? For many millions of people on this earth, the thought of paradise is lying in the tropical sun on a tropical beach with tropical breezes blowing as tropical waves pound against tropical sand. Will I be able to reign in a place where the ski slope descends down through a tropical forest to the beach below? I love getting in the waves and body surfing and occasionally being turned upside down by that big wave I didn't see coming, and living to talk about it. What will it be like without oceans? What will surfers do? Will God provide other sources of enjoyment? Will He give us rivers that make waves. I love staring out at the grandeur of the ocean with the mighty roar of crashing waves and thinking about the One who created it all. Will I miss the ocean if it is no longer there?

The great White Throne Judgment has now been completed. While this judgment is in progress, the old heavens and old earth are being dissolved by fire, along with all of the unrighteous works of the saints, just as Peter said they would be.

> [10]But the Day of the Lord will come as a thief in the night;
> in the which the heavens shall pass away with a great noise,
> and the elements shall melt with fervent heat, the earth
> also and the works that are therein shall be burned up.
> [11]Seeing then that all these things shall be dissolved, what
> manner of persons ought ye to be in all holy conversation
> and godliness, [12]Looking for and hasting unto the coming
> of the day of God, wherein the heavens being on fire shall
> be dissolved, and the elements shall melt with fervent heat?
> [13]Nevertheless we, according to his promise, look for new
> heavens and a new earth, wherein dwelleth righteousness.
>
> *2 Peter 3:10-13*

When Peter speaks of the Day of the Lord, he is speaking of the entire time from the Rapture of the Church and the wrath that follows, all the way to the end of the Millennial Reign, including the White Throne Judgment. That is over a thousand years of time as opposed to about a seven-year period that many scripture refer to when they mention the Day of the Lord. The explanation for that is contained in the preceding verses where Peter makes his famous statement about a thousand years being like a single day to the Lord.

> [7]But the heavens and the earth, which are now, by the same
> word are kept in store, reserved unto fire against the day of
> judgment and perdition of ungodly men. [8]But, beloved, be
> not ignorant of this one thing, that one day is with the
> Lord as a thousand years, and a thousand years as one day.
> [9]The Lord is not slack concerning His promise, as some
> men count slackness; but is longsuffering to us-ward, not
> willing that any should perish, but that all should come to
> repentance.
>
> *2 Peter 3:7-9*

Notice that there is no more sea after the earth has been renewed. God used the seas to divide the nations at the time He confused their language at Babel as stated in Genesis 10:25, "And unto Eber were born two sons: the name of one was Peleg; for in his days was the earth divided." After the earth is renewed, the bride, which is the holy city of New Jerusalem, will come down from heaven to the new earth.

> ¹And I saw a new heaven and a new earth: for the first heaven and the first earth were passed away; and there was no more sea. ²And I John saw the holy city, New Jerusalem, coming down from God out of heaven, prepared as a bride adorned for her husband. ³And I heard a great voice out of heaven saying, *Behold, the tabernacle of God is with men, and he will dwell with them,* and they shall be his people, and *God himself shall be with them,* and be their God. ⁴And God shall wipe away all tears from their eyes; and there shall be no more death, neither sorrow, nor crying, neither shall there be any more pain: for the former things are passed away. ⁵And he that sat upon the throne said, Behold, I make all things new. And he said unto me, Write: for these words are true and faithful. ⁶And he said unto me, It is done. I am Alpha and Omega, the beginning and the end. I will give unto him that is athirst of the fountain of the water of life freely. ⁷He that overcometh shall inherit all things; and I will be his God, and he shall be my son. ⁸But the fearful, and unbelieving, and the abominable, and murderers, and whoremongers, and sorcerers, and idolaters, and all liars, shall have their part in the lake which burneth with fire and brimstone: which is the second death.
>
> *Revelation 21:1-8*

The following is a description of the bride of the Lamb. Notice that a literal heavenly city is being described and not the Church or Body of Christ. The most amazing things about this city are 1) it is the dwelling place of God, and 2) He is now bringing it down to the earth so that He may dwell in the city with the Lamb and the redeemed of the Lord on the earth as they all live and reign happily ever after. Also, despite the overwhelming beauty and comeliness of the city, Revelation 19:8 points out that it is "clothed with a white garment which is the righteousness of the saints." Once again, that shows how important God's redeemed children are to Him and how highly He esteems them. It is also interesting to note that the city is lighted entirely by the glory of God. If you contrast this to Babylon, which God calls a whore and the mother of other harlot cities, it should be clear that He is definitely speaking of real cities.

> 9And there came unto me one of the seven angels which had the seven vials full of the seven last plagues, and talked with me, saying, Come hither, I will shew thee the bride, the Lamb's wife. 10And he carried me away in the spirit to a great and high mountain, and shewed me that great city, the holy Jerusalem, descending out of heaven from God, 11Having the glory of God: and her light was like unto a stone most precious, even like a jasper stone, clear as crystal; 12And had a wall great and high, and had twelve gates, and at the gates twelve angels, and names written thereon, which are the names of the twelve tribes of the children of Israel: 13On the east three gates; on the north three gates; on the south three gates; and on the west three gates. 14And the wall of the city had twelve foundations, and in them the names of the twelve apostles of the Lamb. 15And he that talked with me had a golden reed to measure the city, and the gates thereof, and the wall thereof.
>
> *Revelation 21:9-15*

There are a few things about the New Jerusalem that deserve mentioning. First is the sheer size of it. A furlong is one eighth of a mile so the measurement of 12,000 furlongs would equal 1500 miles square and 1500 miles high. The outer wall that surrounds the city is measured in cubits, which are about 18 inches long. That would make the wall about 216 feet high. The city of God could be a perfect cube shape, but it has been suggested that it may be a pyramid. The measurements would accommodate either shape. If it is a pyramid, that would explain why so many ancient structures that dealt with worship and the afterlife were pyramid shaped. The blueprints were simply downloaded from heaven. We'll have to wait and see, but it seems logical to build such a huge structure as a pyramid; otherwise, we'll be looking at walls that go straight up for 1500 miles. If the city of God is a pyramid, God will no doubt be seated at the very pinnacle with Jesus, the chief cornerstone, seated at His side, with the light of their glory flowing down and bathing the city and the world around it. With transparent streets of gold, the light of their glory will be able to filter down to every level of the city.

Second, and more important, we want to notice that everything is done in twelves. Twelve gates, twelve foundations, twelve thousand furlongs and even the walls are twelve times twelve cubits. It seems that even though the city is lit by the glory of God, He wants to share His glory with His redeemed, which is what all these twelves represent as seen in verse 14 by the names of the twelve apostles written in the twelve foundations. The number twelve is repeatedly used in regards to the redeemed—twelve tribes, twelve apostles, 12x12,000=144,000 sealed Israelites, and so on. What a God! He does it all for us, and then He shares the glory. Incidentally, this may provide a clue to the number of the beast, which is made up of three sixes—half of twelve and the number of an unredeemed man.

> 16And the city lieth foursquare, and the length is as large as the breadth: and he measured the city with the reed, twelve thousand furlongs. The length and the breadth and the height of it are equal. 17And he measured the wall thereof, an hundred and forty and four cubits, according to the measure of a man, that is, of the angel. 18And the building of the wall of it was of jasper: and the city was pure gold, like unto clear glass. 19And the foundations of the wall of the city were garnished with all manner of precious stones. The first foundation was jasper; the second, sapphire; the third, a chalcedony; the fourth, an emerald; 20The fifth, sardonyx; the sixth, sardius; the seventh, chrysolite; the eighth, beryl; the ninth, a topaz; the tenth, a chrysoprasus; the eleventh, a jacinth; the twelfth, an amethyst. 21And the twelve gates were twelve pearls; every several gate was of one pearl: and the street of the city was pure gold, as it were transparent glass. 22And I saw no temple therein: for the Lord God Almighty and the Lamb are the temple of it. 23And the city had no need of the sun, neither of the moon, to shine in it: for the glory of

God did lighten it, and the Lamb is the light thereof. [24]And the
nations of them which are saved shall walk in the light of it:
and the kings of the earth do bring their glory and honor
into it. [25]And the gates of it shall not be shut at all by day:
for there shall be no night there. [26]And they shall bring the
glory and honor of the nations into it. [27]And there shall in
no wise enter into it any thing that defileth, neither whatsoever worketh abomination, or maketh a lie: but they which
are written in the Lamb's book of life.

Revelation 21:16-27

We looked at Isaiah 13 and 14 earlier without mentioning the first
two verses from Isaiah 14. At first glance, it may appear these verses are
speaking only of the time after the rebirth of Israel and before the end-
times begin, but from the rest of Scripture, we know that only part of
the following verses are related to this present time. In verses 1 and 2,
we are told that strangers will bring the Jews back to their place. God
has already begun bringing the Israelites back into their land, and He
is using everybody and every means at His disposal to accomplish that
task. In verse 3, God declares that He will give them rest from their sorrows and fears. That will be partially fulfilled as many of the Jews take
a second look at Jesus and discover that He is indeed their Messiah.
However, verse 3 is also speaking of the Millennium, and perhaps
beyond, when Israel becomes the capital of the world and the twenty-
four elders and 144,000 chosen saints of Israel serve as governing ministers of Jesus Christ. Israel will at least begin to see the fulfillment of
these prophecies as the Millennium begins with Satan being cast into
the bottomless pit. But the complete fulfillment will not come until
after the Millennium when he is discarded in the Lake of Fire. That
brings us to verse 4 where the downfall of Satan begins with the fall of
his golden city—Mystery Babylon.

[1]For the Lord will have mercy on Jacob, and will yet choose
Israel, and set them in their own land: and the strangers
shall be joined with them, and they shall cleave to the house
of Jacob. [2]And the people shall take them, and bring them to
their place: and the house of Israel shall possess them in the
land of the Lord for servants and handmaids: and they shall

take them captives, whose captives they were; and they shall rule over their oppressors. ³And it shall come to pass in the day that the Lord shall give thee rest from thy sorrow, and from thy fear, and from the hard bondage wherein thou wast made to serve, ⁴That thou shalt take up this proverb against the king of Babylon, and say, How hath the oppressor ceased! the golden city ceased!

Isaiah 14:1-4

In previous chapters of Revelation, we saw Satan's place in heaven eliminated as he, himself, was being cast out. Then we saw the City of Babylon on earth fall. After that, Jesus descended from heaven with His elect to take over the earth to reign from the land of Israel. In this chapter, we see New Jerusalem descend to the land of Israel to be the everlasting home of God and His elect. All of these things must take place before the remainder of Isaiah 14 can be completely fulfilled.

Isaiah 60 has been thought by many to be a premillennial prophecy from God promising a golden age to Israel during this age of grace. In other words, if we all pray real hard for the peace of Jerusalem, then all the heathen nations are going to favor Israel and bless her with all of their abundance, and Israel will be the pearl of everyone's eye. There may be a little bit of truth to that concerning some of the peoples and nations of the earth, but Israel is never going to experience the fullness of what God is promising here until after Jesus returns at Armageddon to take the kingdom. Isaiah 60 is simply stating the same thing Isaiah 14 was saying, but in a greatly expanded manner. Revelation 21:23-27, which we just read, actually draws from and paraphrases the earlier prophecy of Isaiah 60. After reading Isaiah 60, reread those five verses from Revelation to see just how strikingly similar they are.

¹Arise, shine; for thy light is come, and the glory of the Lord is risen upon thee. ²For, behold, the darkness shall cover the earth, and gross darkness the people: but the Lord shall arise upon thee, and his glory shall be seen upon thee. ³And the Gentiles shall come to thy light, and kings to the brightness of thy rising. ⁴Lift up thine eyes round about, and see: all they gather themselves together, they come to thee: thy sons shall come from far, and thy daughters shall be nursed at thy

side. ⁵Then thou shalt see, and flow together, and thine heart shall fear, and be enlarged; because the abundance of the sea shall be converted unto thee, the forces of the Gentiles shall come unto thee. ⁶The multitude of camels shall cover thee, the dromedaries of Midian and Ephah; all they from Sheba shall come: they shall bring gold and incense; and they shall shew forth the praises of the Lord. ⁷All the flocks of Kedar shall be gathered together unto thee, the rams of Nebaioth shall minister unto thee: they shall come up with acceptance on mine altar, and I will glorify the house of My glory. ⁸Who are these that fly as a cloud, and as the doves to their windows? ⁹Surely the isles shall wait for me, and the ships of Tarshish first, to bring thy sons from far, their silver and their gold with them, unto the name of the Lord thy God, and to the Holy One of Israel, because he hath glorified thee. ¹⁰And the sons of strangers shall build up thy walls, and their kings shall minister unto thee: for in my wrath I smote thee, but in my favor have I had mercy on thee. ¹¹*Therefore thy gates shall be open continually; they shall not be shut day nor night; that men may bring unto thee the forces of the Gentiles, and that their kings may be brought.* ¹²*For the nation and kingdom that will not serve thee shall perish; yea, those nations shall be utterly wasted.* ¹³The glory of Lebanon shall come unto thee, the fir tree, the pine tree, and the box together, to beautify the place of my sanctuary; and I will make the place of my feet glorious. ¹⁴The sons also of them that afflicted thee shall come bending unto thee; and all they that despised thee shall bow themselves down at the soles of thy feet; and they shall call thee, The city of the Lord, The Zion of the Holy One of Israel. ¹⁵Whereas thou hast been forsaken and hated, so that no man went through thee, I will make thee an eternal excellency, a joy of many generations. ¹⁶Thou shalt also suck the milk of the Gentiles, and shalt suck the breast of kings: and thou shalt know that I the Lord am thy Saviour and thy Redeemer, the mighty One of Jacob. ¹⁷For brass I will bring gold, and for iron I will bring silver, and for wood brass, and for stones iron: I will also make thy officers peace, and thine exactors righteousness.

18Violence shall no more be heard in thy land, wasting nor destruction within thy borders; but thou shalt call thy walls Salvation, and thy gates Praise. 19The sun shall be no more thy light by day; neither for brightness shall the moon give light unto thee: but the Lord *shall be unto thee an everlasting light, and thy God thy glory. 20Thy sun shall no more go down; neither shall thy moon withdraw itself: for the* Lord *shall be thine everlasting light, and the days of thy mourning shall be ended. 21Thy people also shall be all righteous: they shall inherit the land for ever*, the branch of my planting, the work of my hands, that I may be glorified. *22A little one shall become a thousand, and a small one a strong nation: I the* Lord *will hasten it in his time.*

Isaiah 60:1-22

THINK ABOUT IT!

— Who is the Lamb's wife?

— Describe her features.

— Do the saints descend to earth at this time, or did they return on white horses a thousand years earlier?

— Will there still be unsaved people or nations outside of New Jerusalem?

— Is the city of God the same as the temple of God?

Selah

Him that overcometh will I make a pillar in the temple of my God, and he shall go no more out: and I will write upon him the name of my God, and the name of the city of my God, which is new Jerusalem, which cometh down out of heaven from my God: and I will write upon him my new name.

Revelation 3:12

REVELATION 22

"I'll Be Back"

I hope that you have enjoyed this journey of enlightenment as much as I did. Fortunately we both don't have to spend 25-plus years learning these truths. Perhaps the words written in this book will give you a little more intensity in your relationship with God and in sharing the gospel or your testimony with others. Maybe this book is an introduction for you to the God of the Bible, or maybe it will help inspire you to reach out to others in leading them to a saving knowledge of Jesus Christ. Despite how frightening the prophecies may seem, they are still the gospel of the end of a world that is plagued by sin, corruption and the curse. It is the story of a happy ending *if* you are not one of those who refuses and despises the ways of God and the savior who died to rescue us from our own sinful ways. My prayer is that I will see everyone who reads this book in heaven. That's why I am asking you to share it with a friend that I might see them too. Oh, and by the way, the last time I went to that old Baptist church it was overflowing with life!

This chapter continues to describe aspects of the city of God and it contains some final admonitions from Jesus, but it also has some interesting statements that are hard to ignore. For starters, let's just notice some of the description of the city and what it implies. In the first five verses, we see a River of Life issuing forth from the very throne of God. In verse 2, we see the Tree of Life that brings healing to the nations. Verse 3 reiterates that the throne of God will be present. Verse 4 makes it known that the saints who serve their God will be able to look upon His face. Verse 5 again tells us that the sun and the moon and even the night are absent from the city because there is no need for them. All of this in total paints a picture of an existence that is superior even to the Garden of Eden. In Eden, Adam and Eve had access to the Tree of Life, but they never partook of it. There were four pure and unpolluted rivers, but they were not rivers of life. Even though they communed and conversed with God, they still depended on the sun and moon for light, and we are never told that they actually saw God face to face. We might say that the city of God is more advanced than the garden of God. Verse 4 also tells us that God's name will be in the forehead of all of His servants. Unlike Adam and Eve, there is no chance that we will ever fall to sin, deception or the curse.

> ¹And he shewed me a pure river of water of life, clear as crystal, proceeding out of the throne of God and of the Lamb. ²In the midst of the street of it, and on either side of the river, was there the tree of life, which bare twelve manner of fruits, and yielded her fruit every month: and the leaves of the tree were for the healing of the nations. ³And there shall be no more curse: but the throne of God and of the Lamb shall be in it; and His servants shall serve him: ⁴And they shall see his face; and his name shall be in their foreheads. ⁵And there shall be no night there; and they need no candle, neither light of the sun; for the Lord God giveth them light: and they shall reign for ever and ever.
>
> *Revelation 22:1-5*

Verse 3 contains one of those very curious statements that we really need to consider. It declares that there will be no more curse, but then it continues with the phrase "but the throne of God and of the Lamb shall be *in it*." Those words seem to limit the area in which the curse has been totally removed to only that area within the perimeter of the city. In other words, it is saying that there is no curse in "it," and the throne of God is in "it," but no mention is made about the world outside of the city. If this were the only place that suggested a difference between inside the city and outside the city, we could perhaps ignore it or explain it away. However, it is not alone in suggesting that the city of God is more of a refuge on earth than an example of what the entire earth will be like. At the end of Revelation 21, we read about the nations that are saved walking in the light of it and bringing their glory into it. That by itself suggests that there could be nations that are unsaved that are not allowed to enter the city, but not necessarily. The final verse of chapter 21 declares that "there shall in no wise enter into it any thing that defileth, neither whatsoever worketh abomination, or maketh a lie: but they which are written in the Lamb's book of life." This could all be talking about the fact that sin has been judged and Satan has been cast into the Lake of Fire, along with all of those who are not written in the Lamb's Book of Life. But the way that verse is written gives the clear impression that there is still something going on on the outside of the walls that is not totally in line with the way God created things. During the Millennial Reign, the things we are reading will be true to some extent because those who survive the Wrath of God will be unsaved peoples ruled by the saints of God, but the city of God does not descend down to the earth until after the Millennium. So, are there still going to be sinners outside the city after the Millennium? Were all sinners destroyed by the fire that falls from heaven in Revelation 20:9 or just those who surrounded the city? Does the resurrection of the dead include those that are alive at the Millennium? Will the work of salvation continue for eternity as the saints minister life to the descendants of Adam who are outside New Jerusalem? It at least appears that God has big plans for His people in the ages to come.

The next eight verses contain admonitions and instructions from Jesus to all of mankind. After reading them, we will get back to the questions presented in the last paragraph. In verse 10, John is told not to seal up the prophecy of this book. That is just the opposite of what Daniel was told in Daniel 12:4 when he was told to "shut up the words, and seal the book, even to the time of the end." This prophecy has never been sealed from our understanding; we just didn't always understand it too well. In fact, it is through this prophecy that we are finally able to understand Daniel's prophecies, and Daniel's prophecies help us to understand the Revelation. In verse 7, Jesus instructs us to keep the prophecies of this book. Not only should we live by the words of the four Gospels and the Epistles, but we should have a clear understanding of The Revelation and live by it. He is coming soon, and we should be proclaiming the coming Day of the Lord, along with the grace, promises and love of God, and His sacrificial lamb—Jesus Christ.

> ⁶And he said unto me, These sayings are faithful and true: and the Lord God of the holy prophets sent his angel to shew unto his servants the things which must shortly be done. ⁷Behold, I come quickly: blessed is he that keepeth the sayings of the prophecy of this book. ⁸And I John saw these things, and heard them. And when I had heard and seen, I fell down to worship before the feet of the angel which shewed me these things. ⁹Then saith he unto me, See thou do it not: for I am thy fellowservant, and of thy brethren the prophets, and of them which keep the sayings of this book: worship God. ¹⁰And he saith unto me, *Seal not the sayings of the prophecy of this book: for the time is at hand.* ¹¹He that is unjust, let him be unjust still: and he which is filthy, let him be filthy still: and he that is righteous, let him be righteous still: and he that is holy, let him be holy still. ¹²And, behold, I come quickly; and my reward is with me, to give every man according as his work shall be. ¹³I am Alpha and Omega, the beginning and the end, the first and the last.
>
> *Revelation 22:6-13*

The next few verses are hard to reconcile to the idea of a universe of bliss in the sweet by and by. The last fifty verses of Revelation have been talking about Satan being cast into the Lake of Fire, the White Throne Judgment, the temple of God coming to earth and God wiping away the tears of His people. Now verse 15 informs us that on the outside of the city walls are evildoers. Could this be? There were evildoers at the end of the Millennial Reign that came up against the city of the saints. That city was not New Jerusalem but rather the old Jerusalem where Jesus steps out of heaven and onto the mount of Olives to begin the 1000-year reign. After 1000 years of glory, the only thing needed to motivate the multitudes who despise the reign of the saints is the leadership of Satan. Those who rebel are destroyed by a rain of fire that falls upon them from heaven to devour them. Those who remain at the end of the Millennium, who refuse to take part in the rebellion, will likely number in the billions. After all this takes place, the White Throne Judgment occurs, but if we read with understanding about that judgment, it is the judgment of the two resurrections. Not everyone who takes part in the first resurrection has to die. Those who are still alive and serving Christ will be changed into immortal bodies at the same instant that the dead are changed and then raptured. The second resurrection is different.

We are never told that the people at the end of the Millennium who refuse to follow Satan are resurrected or changed at the same time as the dead, as in the resurrection of the just. And why would they be? They are the ones who are still living obediently under the reign of the Lord Jesus Christ. But, we are never told that they are saved either. Their names will be included in the Lamb's Book of Life if they are saved, and they will experience the better part of the White Throne Judgment. But, what about all those who are alive at the end of the Millennial Reign who don't quite find it in their hearts to accept Jesus as Saviour, if that is an option for them; yet, they don't feel compelled to rebel against Him either? They're willing enough to go along with the program as far as obeying the saints is concerned, but deep down they prefer to do their own thing and hold on to their secret sins. They are the descendants of Adam just like we are. Because there is no more tempter does not mean that they are suddenly "new creatures" or "born again" or free from the fallen nature. They are sinners at heart, even in the absence of the father of lies, but they are smart enough, and perhaps "good enough," to avoid the fate of those who surround the city of the saints.

They are not a part of the resurrection of the living at the final trump. Are they included in the resurrection of the dead? Does God find a way to preserve them during the White Throne Judgment? Verse 14 seems to suggest that there will still be unregenerate human beings on the earth after the New Jerusalem is lowered down to the new earth during the judgment. The very fact that there are walls around the city, and that access through the gates is limited to those who have logged into the Book of Life, strongly suggest that there will be an eternity of people who have to make the same decision that is before us today—receive the gospel, reject it or just ignore it. Verse 15 comes right out and tells us that there will besinners of every variety on the outside of the city. There is a heavenly Jerusalem where God abides right now, but it is just heavenly Jerusalem. The New Jerusalem is not created until Revelation 21:1-2 when the new heavens and new earth are created, while the judgment is in progress and right before it is lowered down to the earth. That makes it very hard to simply make verse 15 figurative concerning dogs, whoremongers and lovers of lies being outside the city with no access. If they were all judged, they would be in the Lake of Fire with no possible way of escape and no possible way to gain access to the city. Jesus said that He would prepare each of us a place in His Father's house. If we all live inside the city, what is on the outside that we need to rule and reign over?

> [14]Blessed are they that do His commandments, that they may have right to the tree of life, and may enter in through the gates into the city. [15]For without are dogs, and sorcerers, and whoremongers, and murderers, and idolaters, and whosoever loveth and maketh a lie.
>
> *Revelation 22:14-21*

Verse 17 is just one more place where the theory of the Church being the bride of the Lamb is seriously challenged. The first line declares that the Holy Spirit and the bride of Christ say, "Come." That is the drawing we all feel as the Spirit of God draws our hearts to God. It is the beckoning of heaven itself that we all feel deep down inside of us as the very city of heaven and the hope of a better future tug at our heartstrings in a supernatural way. The next line is the one that speaks of the Church—let him that heareth say, "Come." All of those who have heard the gospel and responded to it are now ambassadors of God on this earth. We have been instructed to preach the gospel to all nations and to give an answer to every man of the hope that lies within us. The bride is calling the Church, and they will be joined together one day as though they were one. Christ is the head of the Church which is His body, and the Church will be joined to the bride with Jesus as one body.

Verses 18 and 19 warn us not to add to or delete from the things that are written. Many have confused and misinterpreted the prophecies of the book, but that does not rise to the level of changing the prophecies outright. Some translators, in ignorance, have rewritten the prophecies to reflect their own personal beliefs. That comes closer to the accusations made by Jesus below and may even cross the line. But what Jesus is really addressing are those who change things to the point of wholesale deception, those who change the nature of Christ and diminish His deity, those who deny His coming and those who restate the purpose of the return of Christ as being for the destruction of His elect and His chosen. His prophecies are for the purpose of preparing the Church for that which is coming and giving us the assurance that when those things do come, we will know that God is still in control. The prophecies are also a warning to the world in general that they might repent and receive the only Savior and sacrifice that can cleanse their souls.

> [16]I Jesus have sent mine angel to testify unto you these things in the churches. I am the root and the offspring of David, and the bright and morning star. [17]And the Spirit and the bride say, Come. And let him that heareth say, Come. And let him that is athirst come. And whosoever will, let him take the water of life freely. [18]For I testify unto every man that heareth the words of the prophecy of this book, If any man shall add unto these things, God shall add unto him the plagues that are written in this book: [19]And if any man shall take away from the words of the book of this prophecy, God shall take away his part out of the book of life, and out of the holy city, and from the things which are written in this book. [20]He which testifieth these things saith, Surely I come quickly. Amen. Even so, come, Lord Jesus. [21]The grace of our Lord Jesus Christ be with you all. Amen.
>
> *Revelation 22:16-21*

And *when these things begin to come to pass, then look up, and lift up your heads; for your redemption draweth nigh.*
Luke 21:28

[30]When thou art in tribulation, and all these things are come upon thee, *even in the latter days*, if thou turn to the Lord thy God, and shalt be obedient unto His voice; [31]For the Lord thy God is a merciful God; he will not forsake thee, neither destroy thee, nor forget the covenant of thy fathers which he sware unto them.

Deuteronomy 4:30-31

Think about it!

— In the fulfilment of these chapters, does God still live in heaven?

Selah

And if I go and prepare a place for you, I will come again, and receive you unto myself; that where I am, there ye may be also.

John 14:3

THE END

A New Beginning

The end of this world is actually just the end of doing things the wrong way. It is the end of sin, corruption and the rule of Satan as the god of this earth. Even the heavens and the earth, which we are a part of, will be dissolved. But, even as we see the end of all these things approaching, we also see the beginning of something transcendently better coming our way—the beginning of a new life in a new body on a new earth where the fruits of righteousness reign supreme. It will be an eternity of bliss where all of our tears are wiped away by God and where we no longer have to consider what kind of troubles and tribulations might be coming our way. There will no longer be anyone to cause us trouble. Our salvation will be complete, and our peace will be eternal.

How can we end this book about the end-times Revelation without giving an invitation to all to be a part of the family of God and the eternity He has planned? As we have seen, being one of God's children does not mean that we never see bad times in our life. In fact, being one of God's beloved often makes us targets of persecution—if not from unbelievers, then definitely from the demons of hell. Yet, through it all, God gives us victory through Christ Jesus, in all the troubles we endure, and no amount of suffering in this life is worth giving up heaven and God's eternal kingdom over—not ever. The disciples of Jesus counted it an honor to be thought worthy of the persecution they endured for the work of the Lord, and so should we.

The first thing you need to realize is there is no other way into heaven except through Jesus Christ our redeemer, and we must do it God's way because there is no other way. All it takes to be saved is a little faith in your heart and a prayer on your lips.

> 9That if thou shalt *confess with thy mouth the Lord Jesus,* and shalt *believe in thine heart that God hath raised* him from the dead, *thou shalt be saved.* 10For with the heart man believeth unto righteousness; and with the mouth confession is made unto salvation.
>
> *Romans 10:9-10*

It's a true and recognizable miracle. Something happens on the inside of you, and that something is a brand new spirit created in the likeness of God down in the very core of your being. This does not mean your personality or who you are is changed, but something deeper is taking place in that part of you that either has hope or despair, love or hate, faith or doubt, joy or anguish, peace or fear, righteousness or separation, meekness or arrogance. God wants you to have the better of these spiritual attitudes, and they are attainable with the new spirit that He births inside of you.

> 23*Being born again,* not of corruptible seed, but of incorruptible, *by the word of God,* which liveth and abideth for ever.
>
> *1 Peter 1:23*

All the mess that is inside you—the heaviness of sin, the feelings of unworthiness and hopelessness—are all taken away so that God can start filling your heart with His life and His joy.

> 17Therefore *if any man be in Christ, he is a new creature: old things are passed away; behold, all things are become new.* 18*And all things are of God,* who hath reconciled us to himself by Jesus Christ, and hath given to us the ministry of reconciliation;
>
> *2 Corinthians 5:17-18*

The life of God is a collection of desirable spiritual attributes that make you more like Jesus and enable you to serve God as you put away the destructive works of the flesh and submit to His Holy Spirit. This all becomes a reality after you are born again, and the Word of God and the Spirit of God begin to work on the inside of you.

> [19]Now the works of the flesh are manifest, which are these; adultery, fornication, uncleanness, lasciviousness, [20]Idolatry, witchcraft, hatred, variance, emulations, wrath, strife, seditions, heresies, [21]Envyings, murders, drunkenness, revellings, and such like: of which I tell you before, as I have also told you in time past, that they which do such things shall not inherit the kingdom of God. [22]But *the fruit of the Spirit is love, joy, peace, longsuffering, gentleness, goodness, faith,* [23]*Meekness, temperance*: against such there is no law. [24]And they that are Christ's have crucified the flesh with the affections and lusts.
>
> *Galatians 5:19-24*

The word "gospel" means "good news," and the good news is this: We don't have to make ourselves good enough to go to heaven because He did it all for us. When we are born again in our spirit, our new spirit is created in the likeness of God. His goodness is placed inside of us, and we are made righteous in His eyes. Jesus has taken the guilt and punishment for our sins, and He makes us righteous when we receive Him as our Savior.

> For He hath *made Him to be sin for us,* who knew no sin; *that we might be made the righteousness of God in him.*
>
> *2 Corinthians 5:21*

As I said earlier, all it takes is a little faith and a simple prayer. Do you believe what God is saying to you in these verses? That's called faith when you believe God's Word before you ever see the promise fulfilled. So, now that you have faith, all you have to do is pray.

> For whosoever shall call upon the name of the Lord shall be saved.
>
> *Romans 10:13*

Now pray this prayer:

Father God, I thank You for sending Your Son Jesus to die for me on the cross to pay the penalty for my sins. Jesus, I receive You into my heart and my life right now as my Lord and Savior. Take away from the inside of me the things that are not what You want for me and create in me a new heart that is just like Yours. Fill me with Your Holy Spirit. Teach me to live for You all the rest of my days and lead me into the destiny that You have for me. In Jesus name I pray. Amen!

Now that you have received Jesus as your Lord and Savior, your life will begin again with a new direction and with new desires. All you have to do is follow after those new heartfelt desires as you put aside the desires of the flesh. Congratulations, and God bless you in the rest of your life because this is just…**THE BEGINNING!**

Kingdom of the Beast
Order Form

For volume discount orders please contact:
orders@RevelationStation.com

All others order below.

Please send *Kingdom of the Beast* to:

Name: _____

Address: _____

City: _____ State: _____

Zip: _____ Telephone: (_____) _____

Book Price: $18.95

Shipping: $3.00 for the first book and $1.00 for each additional book to cover shipping and handling within US, Canada, and Mexico. International orders add $6.00 for the first book and $2.00 for each additional book.

Order from:
ACW Press
1200 HWY 231 South #273
Ozark, AL 36360

(800) 931-BOOK

or contact your local bookstore

Ask for the topical version of this book called *The End Times Simplified* (ISBN 1591609224 perfect bond; ISBN 1591609232 hardcover) wherever you buy books.

The End Times Simplified breaks things down into simple-to-understand topics like:

- The difference between tribulation and wrath and then the difference between the Tribulation of the Antichrist and the Wrath of God.
- What Mystery Babylon really is.
- The extent of the rule of the beast. And, believe it or not, what Islam has to do with the end-times.

You won't regret reading this book.

——•+•——

Also be watching for future books by J.C. Alexander.